An essential dictionary

An essential dictionary

compiled by
E.W. Hobson

Schofield & Sims
HELPING CHILDREN TO LEARN

First published 1980
This edition revised by Jo Phillips for SMALL PRINT
This edition first printed 2002

Cover design and illustration
by Curve Creative, Bradford

Printed in Great Britain
at Fulcrum Colour Printers Ltd, Ripponden

Contents

Preface

An Essential Dictionary contains over 11 000 words and has been compiled to meet the needs of children at Key Stage 2.

To say that the dictionary is for use by one particular age group would be wrong, as abilities and needs vary from child to child within any age group.

The dictionary includes words that are in common use in both spoken and written English and also a great number of words which children hear in the media, especially those relating to scientific, political, cultural and recreational activities, which so many young people wish to discuss and communicate in speech and writing.

The clear layout is designed to encourage quick and easy reference. The definitions have been written to give accurate and easily understood meanings and to extend the child's vocabulary and knowledge.

Essential Dictionary Exercises   0 7217 0940 0

A companion book of exercises, **Essential Dictionary Exercises**, has been designed to encourage all students to make fuller and more effective use of *An Essential Dictionary* and any other dictionaries they may have access to.

PRONUNCIATION

The meanings of many words can be made known in speech only by pronouncing one syllable with a stronger emphasis or stress than another.

In *An Essential Dictionary* such a word has its stressed syllable printed in small capitals, and it is separated from its unstressed syllable by a hyphen (-). Also, where necessary, the word is respelt in letters combined to convey the familiar sounds.

Examples

object *n.* (pron. OB-ject) 1 a thing that can be seen or touched. 2 an aim or purpose. OBJECT *v.* (pron. ob-JECT) to protest; to disapprove.

record *v.* (pron. re-KORD) 1 to write (something) down. 2 to make a reproduction of. RECORD *n.* (pron. RE-kord) 1 a written account. 2 a disc on which music or sound has been recorded. 3 an unbeaten performance. RECORDED *adj.*

ABBREVIATIONS USED IN *AN ESSENTIAL DICTIONARY*

abbrev.	abbreviation	*L.*	Latin
adj.	adjective	*masc.*	masculine
adv.	adverb	*n.*	noun
conj.	conjunction	*pl.*	plural
e.g.	for example	*prep.*	preposition
esp.	especially	pron.	pronunciation
fem.	feminine	*pron.*	pronoun
Fr.	French	*R.*	Russian
Gk.	Greek	*sing.*	singular
inter.	interjection	*v.*	verb
Ital.	Italian		

A

abandon *v.* to give up; to forsake.
ABANDON *n.* lack of restraint.

abate *v.* to lessen; to diminish.

abattoir *n.* a public slaughterhouse for cattle.

abbess *n.* the female head of an abbey or a convent.

abbey *n.* a church, once part of a monastery.

abbot *n.* the head (male) of an abbey.

abbreviate *v.* to shorten. ABBREVIATION *n.*

abdicate *v.* to give up (a throne or high position). ABDICATION *n.*

abdomen *n.* the belly; the part of the body below the chest.

abduct *v.* to carry off by force; to kidnap.

abide *v.* to remain; to dwell.

ability *n.* skill or power to do things. *pl.* ABILITIES.

ablaze *adj.* on fire, burning strongly.

able *adj.* clever; talented; having the power or skill to do something.

abnormal *adj.* unusual; strange.

abolish *v.* to do away with; to end;

abound *v.* to be plentiful; exist in great quantity.

abrasion *n.* a graze, an injury made by rubbing or scraping.

abreast *adv.* 1 side by side. 2 up-to-date.

abroad *adv.* in another country.

abrupt *adj.* 1 very sudden; unexpected. 2 rude and hasty in speech or manner. ABRUPTLY *adv.*

abscess *n.* an inflamed boil or ulcer.

absence *n.* non-attendance; a lack.

absent *adj.* (pron. AB-sent) not present; away. ABSENT *v.* (pron. ab-SENT) to keep (oneself) away; to stay away.

absorb *v.* to soak up. 2 to be interested in. ABSORBENT *adj.* able to soak up.

abstain *v.* to avoid doing; to keep away from.

absurd *adj.* ridiculous, unreasonable. ABSURDITY *n.*

abundance *n.* a large quantity; an excess.

abundant *adj.* plentiful.

abuse *n.* (pron. ab-USE) 1 a wrong use. 2 insulting language. ABUSE *v.* (pron. ab-UZE) to misuse; to harm.

academy *n.* a college; school.

accelerate *v.* to increase speed. ACCELERATION *n.*

accent *n.* 1 stress; emphasis. 2 a manner of pronunciation. 3 a tone of voice.

accept *v.* to take something offered; to agree to. ACCEPTABLE *adj.* ACCEPTANCE *n.*

access *n.* the way in. ACCESS *v.* to reach; to contact.

accident *n.* a mishap; an unexpected happening.

accidental *adj.* unintended; happening by chance.

accommodate *v.* 1 to fit in with. 2 to find room for.

accommodation *n.* 1 a lodging place. 2 a service.

accompany *v.* 1 to go with. 2 to play an instrument while someone sings or plays.

accomplish *v.* to complete; to achieve.

accord *v.* to be in agreement or harmony. ACCORD *n.* agreement; friendship.

account *n.* 1 a statement of money received and spent. 2 a bill. 3 a story or description. ACCOUNT (FOR) *v.* to explain; to be a reason for.

accumulate *v.* to gather more and more; to pile up.

accurate *adj.* exact; correct in detail. ACCURACY *n.* ACCURATELY *adv.*

accuse *v.* to blame. ACCUSER *n.*

accustom *v.* to become used to something.

ace *n.* 1 the one-spot on playing cards and dominoes. 2 person who excels at some activity.

ache *n.* 1 a continuous pain. 2 a longing; yearning. ACHE *v.* 1 to give continuous pain. 2 to yearn.

achieve *v.* to succeed in doing; to attain.

acid *adj.* sour; bitter. ACID *n.* a sour or corrosive substance.

acknowledge *v.* to admit the truth or the receipt of something.

acorn *n.* the fruit of the oak tree.

acquaint (with) *v.* 1 to inform (somebody) of. 2 to make (oneself) familiar with.

acquire *v.* to obtain; to gain.

acquit *v.* 1 to declare a person innocent. 2 to do one's work.

acre *n.* an imperial measure of land; an area of 4840 yd^2 (about 4000 m^2).

acrobat *n.* a gymnast; trapeze artist. ACROBATIC *adj.*

acrostic *n.* a type of poem based on a word or phrase.

act *v.* 1 to do. 2 to play a part in. 3 to pretend. ACT *n.* 1 a deed. 2 a law made by Parliament. 3 a section of a stage play.

action *n.* 1 a style of movement. 2 a law case. 3 a battle. 4 a thing done.

active *adj.* 1 lively; busy; energetic. 2 still working.

activity *n.* 1 an occupation. 2 alertness; quickness. *pl.* ACTIVITIES.

actor *n.* a player on stage, radio, television or in films. *fem.* ACTRESS.

actual *adj.* real; existing. ACTUALLY *adv.*

acute *adj.* sharp; quick at understanding. ACUTENESS *n.* ACUTELY *adv.*

adamant *adj.* hard; stubborn.

adapt *v.* to fit in; to use in the best way.

add *v.* 1 to count up. 2 to join one thing to another. 3 to increase.

adder *n.* a small, poisonous snake.

addition *n.* 1 the process of adding. 2 a thing joined on to another. ADDITIONAL *adj.*

address *v.* 1 to speak or write to. 2 to make a speech. ADDRESS *n.* 1 a speech. 2 a residence or place of business. 3 manner or behaviour.

adenoids *n. pl.* growth at the back of the nose which affects speech and breathing.

adequate *adj.* enough; sufficient. ADEQUACY *n.*

adhesive *adj.* sticky. ADHESIVE *n.* a glue or a gum.

adjacent *adj.* next to; near by.

adjective *n.* a word which describes or qualifies a noun. ADJECTIVAL *adj.*

adjourn *v.* to put off; to postpone. ADJOURNMENT *n.*

adjust *v.* to put in order; to make right; to adapt. ADJUSTMENT *n.*

admiral *n.* a naval officer commanding a fleet or squadron.

admire *v.* to be pleased with; to look up to. ADMIRATION *n.*

admission *n.* 1 being allowed to enter. 2 entrance. 3 a confession.

admit *v.* 1 to allow to enter. 2 to acknowledge. 3 to confess.

adolescent *n.* a person approaching maturity. ADOLESCENT *adj.* youthful; near-adult. ADOLESCENCE *n.*

adopt *v.* 1 to be allowed to take another's child as one's own. 2 to choose. ADOPTION *n.* ADOPTIVE *adj.*

adorable *adj.* worthy of being loved.

adore *v.* to worship; to love very much. ADORATION *n.*

adrift *adj.* 1 floating without control. 2 unsettled

adult *adj.* grown-up; responsible. ADULT *n.* a grown-up person; a man or woman.

advance *v.* 1 to go forward. 2 to increase the price. ADVANCE *n.* 1 progress. 2 a loan.

advantage *n.* 1 ability or knowledge that places one above or before others. 2 a profit; benefit. TO TAKE ADVANTAGE to act unfairly.

advent *n.* a coming; an arrival.

adventure *n.* an exciting experience. ADVENTURE *v.* to dare; to do something risky.

adventurous *adj.* ready to dare; venturesome.

adverb *n.* a word which tells more about a verb, adjective or other adverb. ADVERBIAL *adj.*

adversary *n.* an opponent; an enemy.

advertise *v.* to make public or well known.

advertisement *n.* a public notice, as in a newspaper or on television. ADVERTISER *n.*

advice *n.* an opinion about what to do.

advise *v.* to give advice. ADVISER *n.*

aerial *n.* metal rods or wires which transmit or receive television or radio messages. AERIAL *adj.* seen from the air, from a bird's-eye 'view', as in an aerial photograph or plan.

aerodrome *n.* an airfield.

aeronautics *n.* the science of navigation in the air

aeroplane *n.* a powered heavier-than-air flying machine.

aerosol *n.* a container capable of expelling liquid in a fine spray.

affect *v.* 1 to act upon. 2 to pretend.

affection *n.* love; great liking. AFFECTIONATE *adj.*

affix *v.* (a-FIX) to stick; to attach; to join. AFFIX *n.* (AF-fix) a part added to a word to change or add to its meaning (see PREFIX, SUFFIX).

afford *v*. 1 to be able to buy or act without loss or injury. 2 to spare. 3 to supply or furnish.

afloat *adv*. at sea; floating; on board ship.

afraid *adj*. frightened.

afternoon *n*. the time of day between noon and evening.

afterwards *adv*. later.

again *adv*. once more; another time.

against *prep*. opposite to; facing.

age *n*. 1 the length of time a person or an animal has lived. 2 a particular period in history, e.g. the Stone Age. AGE *v*. to grow old.

agent *n*. one who acts for another; a representative.

aggravate *v*. to make worse; to annoy. AGGRAVATION *n*. AGGRAVATOR *n*.

agile *adj*. nimble; active. AGILITY *n*. AGILELY *adv*.

agitate *v*. to shake; to stir up. AGITATION *n*. AGITATOR *n*.

agony *n*. great pain; anguish. AGONISING *adj*.

agree *v*. to be alike; to give consent; to accept. AGREEMENT *n*.

agreeable *adj*. 1 pleasing; delightful. 2 willing.

agriculture *n*. the cultivation of the land; farming. AGRICULTURAL *adj*.

aground *adv*. stuck fast in the ground in shallow water; stranded; beached.

ahead *adv*. on in front; in advance.

aid *v*. to help. AID *n*. help; assistance.

aim *v*. to point at. AIM *n*. an intention; a purpose.

air *n*. 1 the atmosphere. 2 a tune. AIR *v*. to dry; to warm.

airborne *adj*. carried by the wind; in flight.

aircraft *n*. any flying machine.

airfield *n*. a place where aircraft take off and land.

airman *n*. a man who flies, or helps to fly, an aircraft.

airport *n*. an airfield for passenger and freight aircraft.

airtight *adj*. not allowing air to enter or escape.

aisle *n*. a passage between rows of seats.

alarm *v*. 1 to warn of danger. 2 to startle. ALARM *n*. 1 a sudden warning. 2 fear.

album *n*. 1 a book containing a collection of pictures, stamps, etc. 2 a collection of songs on a recording.

alcohol *n*. spirit formed in wine, beer, etc. ALCOHOLIC *adj*.

alcove *n*. an arched recess in a wall; a small room.

alert *adj*. watchful; wide awake. ALERT *n*. a warning.

algebra *n*. a branch of mathematics in which letters are used as numbers.

alien *n*. a foreigner. ALIEN *adj*. foreign.

alight *v*. to dismount; to get down; to come to earth from the air. ALIGHT *adj*. lit up; on fire.

alike *adj*. resembling; similar. ALIKE *adv*. in the same way, manner or form.

alive *adj*. 1 living. 2 aware, alert. 3 filled with living beings.

all *adj*. the whole quantity, time, extent, etc. ALL *adv*. wholly; completely. ALL *n*. everyone; everything.

Allah *n*. the God of the Muslim people in the religion of Islam.

allege *v*. to state; to declare without proof.

alligator *n*. a large reptile in the crocodile family.

alliteration *n*. where several words in a sentence or phrase begin with the same sound. ALLITERATE *v*.

allocate *v*. to share out; to distribute.

allow *v*. 1 to let; to permit. 2 to grant a payment. 3 to take into account.

allure *v*. to tempt; to attract. ALLURE *n*. charm.

ally *n*. (AL-lie) a friend; partner. *pl*. ALLIES. ALLY *v*. (a-LIE) to unite with.

almighty *adj*. all-powerful. ALMIGHTY *n*. God.

almond *n*. a nut from the almond tree.

almost *adv*. very nearly.

alms *n*. *sing*. money or gifts to help the poor.

aloft *adv*. above; overhead.

alone *adj*. single; solitary. ALONE *adv*. by itself; separately.

aloud *adv*. in a voice loud enough to be heard.

alp *n*. a high mountain or pasture (esp. in Switzerland) ALPINE *adj*.

alphabet *n*. the letters of a language arranged in order; the *"ABC"*. ALPHABETICAL *adj*.

also *adv*. in addition; as well.

altar *n*. the communion table in a Christian church; a raised table where sacrifices are offered.

alter *v*. to change. ALTERATION *n*. ALTERABLE *adj*.

alternative *n*. offering the choice between two things.

although *conj.* though; otherwise; supposing.

altitude *n.* height, esp. above sea-level.

altogether *adv.* entirely; wholly.

always *adv.* at all times.

amateur *n.* a person who does things for pleasure as a hobby, and not professionally or for profit.

amaze *v.* to astonish; to astound. AMAZEMENT *n.*

ambiguity *n.* having more than one possible meaning. AMBIGUOUS *adj.*

ambition *n.* a determination to win success or distinction. AMBITIOUS *adj.*

ambulance *n.* a vehicle for conveying the sick or injured.

ambush *v.* to lie in wait and then attack. AMBUSH *n.* a surprise attack from a hiding place.

amen *n. & inter.* so be it *(Gk.)*.

amend *v.* to improve; to set right. AMENDMENT *n.*

amenity *n.* something that gives pleasure or makes life easier. *pl.* AMENITIES.

American *adj.* belonging to America. AMERICAN *n.* a citizen of the USA.

amiable *adj.* friendly. AMIABILITY *n.* AMIABLY *adv.*

amid, amidst *prep.* in the middle of; among, in the course of.

ammunition *n.* bombs, shells, cartridges for firearms, etc.

among, amongst *prep.* mixed with; making part of, amidst.

amount *n.* the quantity, value or sum. AMOUNT (TO) *v.* to come to (a total); to add up to.

amphibian *n.* an animal able to live both on land and in water; a vehicle for use on both land and water. AMPHIBIOUS *adj.*

ample *adj.* quite enough, sufficient. AMPLY *adv.*

amputate *v.* to cut off. AMPUTATION *n.*

amuse *v.* to please; to cause laughter. AMUSEMENT *n.* AMUSING *adj.*

anaesthetic *n.* a drug which causes loss of feeling.

anagram *n.* a word formed from the letters of another word.

analyse *v.* to break up something into its separate parts.

ancestor *n.* a forefather, forbear. ANCESTRAL *adj.*

ancestry *n.* line of descent, series of ancestors.

anchor *n.* a heavy metal hook which grips the sea-bed and holds a ship at its moorings. ANCHOR *v.* to secure a ship with an anchor; to cast anchor. TO WEIGH ANCHOR to haul up the anchor.

ancient *adj.* very old; of times long past.

and *conj.* also; together with. A word used to join words, phrases, clauses or sentences.

anecdote *n.* a short account of an amusing story. ANECDOTAL *adj.*

angel *n.* a heavenly messenger; a good and helpful person. ANGELIC *adj.*

anger *n.* displeasure; rage. ANGER *v.* to vex; to make angry.

angle *n.* a corner; the space between two lines meeting at a point. ANGLE *v.* to fish with a rod and line.

angler *n.* a fisherman/woman.

angry *adj.* vexed; annoyed. ANGRILY *adv.*

animal *n.* 1 a beast; a creature. 2 any living organism, including man, that is not a plant.

ankle *n.* the joint connecting foot and leg.

anniversary *n.* the date of an annual event or celebration. *pl.* ANNIVERSARIES.

announce *v.* to make known. ANNOUNCEMENT *n.*

annoy *v.* to vex; to tease. ANNOYANCE *n.*

annual *adj.* happening yearly. ANNUAL *n.* a plant that lives for only one year; a book published yearly. ANNUALLY *adv.*

anonymous *adj.* nameless; not known. ANONYMITY *n.*

anorak *n.* a hooded, waterproof jacket.

another *adj.* not the same; different. ANOTHER *pron.* anyone else; one more. *pl.* OTHERS.

answer *v.* to reply. ANSWER *n.* a reply to a question.

ant *n.* a small, busy insect.

antarctic *n.* the south polar region. ANTARCTIC *adj.* concerning the south polar region.

antelope *n.* animal resembling a deer.

antenna *n.* 1 one of the feelers on the head of an insect. 2 a kind of aerial. *pl.* ANTENNAE.

anthem *n.* a song of praise.

anticipate *v.* to use in advance; to foresee; to look forward to.

antics *n. pl.* amusing or silly actions.

anticyclone *n.* widespread air conditions which often bring dry weather.

antique *adj.* old and rare. ANTIQUE *n.* something old and rare.

antler *n.* a branch of a stag's horn.

antonym *n.* a word which means the opposite of another, e.g. hot → cold; large → small.

anvil *n.* a blacksmith's iron block.

anxiety *n.* worry; disquiet.

anxious *adj.* troubled; worried.

any *pron., adj. & adv.* one out of many; some; whichever you like.

anybody *pron.* any person, no matter who.

apart *adv.* aside; separately; independently.

apartheid *n.* the policy of keeping people of separate races apart.

ape *n.* a tailless monkey. APE *v.* to mimic.

apex *n.* tip; top; peak; vertex (of a triangle).

apologise *v.* to express regret. APOLOGY *n.* APOLOGETIC *adj.*

apostle *n.* a messenger; a missionary.

apostrophe *n.* the sign (') used to show 1 the omission of a letter or letters ("don't," for "do not") or 2 possession (the boy's cap).

apparatus *n.* equipment needed for a particular purpose.

apparent *adj.* easily seen or understood; plain, clear.

appeal *v.* to ask for help or sympathy. APPEAL *n.* 1 an earnest request. 2 a request for a case to be reconsidered.

appear *v.* to come into sight. 2 to seem. APPEARANCE *n.*

appendix *n.* a section at the end of a book or text which gives extra information. *pl.* APPENDICES or APPENDIXES. APPEND *v.*

appetite *n.* a desire, especially for food.

applaud *v.* to show approval by clapping; to praise loudly. APPLAUSE *n.*

apple *n.* the fruit of the apple tree.

appliance *n.* a piece of apparatus or an instrument applied for a particular purpose.

application *n.* 1 a request. 2 attention to work; perseverance.

apply *v.* 1 APPLY FOR to ask for. 2 APPLY ONESELF TO to attend to.

appoint *v.* 1 to choose a person for a post or job. 2 to arrange a meeting. APPOINTMENT *n.*

appreciate *v.* 1 to value highly. 2 to understand. 3 to grow in value.

apprentice *n.* one learning a trade.

approach *v.* to come nearer; to be nearly equal to. APPROACH *n.* the way leading to a place.

approve *v.* to be pleased with; to give permission. APPROVAL *n.*

approximate *adj.* very near; nearly correct.

April *n.* the fourth month of the year.

apron *n.* 1 a garment worn to protect the clothes. 2 area used for loading and unloading aircraft.

aqualung *n.* a diver's breathing apparatus carried on the back.

aquarium *n.* a tank for live fish.

aqueduct *n.* a bridge built to carry water or a canal across a valley; a conduit or pipe.

arable *adj.* (land) fit for ploughing and growing crops.

arbitration *n.* settlement of a dispute by an independent person or committee.

arc *n.* 1 a curve; part of a circle. 2 a powerful electric lamp.

arch *n.* a curved structure upholding weight. *pl.* ARCHES.

archaeology *n.* the study of objects and remains from ancient times. ARCHAEOLOGIST *n.* a person who studies historical objects and remains. ARCHAEOLOGICAL *adj.*

archbishop *n.* a chief bishop.

archer *n.* one who shoots with a bow and arrow.

architect *n.* one who plans and designs buildings. ARCHITECTURAL *adj.* ARCHITECTURE *n.*

arctic *n.* the north polar region. ARCTIC *adj.* north polar.

ardent *adj.* eager; keen; passionate.

area *n.* 1 the size or extent of a surface. 2 a region.

argue *v.* to discuss; to debate; to dispute. ARGUMENT *n.* ARGUMENTATIVE *adj.*

ark *n.* a box or chest. THE ARK *n.* Noah's Ark, or boat.

arm *n.* 1 an upper limb. 2 part of a chair that supports the sitter's arm. 3 a weapon. ARM *v.* to equip with weapons.

armada *n.* a fleet of warships. THE ARMADA the strong fleet sent by Philip II of Spain to attack England, 1588.

armistice *n.* an agreement to stop fighting for a time; a truce.

armour *n.* a protective covering for cars, tanks, etc., also for the body in olden days.

arms *n. pl.* WEAPONS; firearms.

army *n.* a large number of trained soldiers. *pl.* ARMIES.

around *adv. & prep.* on all sides of; in every direction.

arouse *v.* to rouse; to awaken.

arrange *v.* 1 to put in proper order. 2 to make plans. ARRANGEMENT *n.*

arrears *n. pl.* anything overdue or behindhand.

arrest *v.* 1 to stop. 2 to take prisoner. ARREST *n.*

arrive (at) *v.* to reach a destination; to come to (a conclusion). ARRIVAL *n.*

arrow *n.* a straight, barbed shaft shot from a bow; the sign →.

arson *n.* the crime of deliberately setting property on fire.

art *n.* skill, especially in painting, music, etc.

artefact *n.* an object made by a person, usually of historical interest.

artery *n.* a blood-vessel carrying blood away from the heart. *pl.* ARTERIES.

article *n.* 1 a single thing. 2 an account in a newspaper or magazine.

artificial *adj.* not natural; manufactured.

artillery *n.* guns; cannon.

artist *n.* one skilled in any art. ARTISTIC *adj.*

ascend *v.* to climb up; to rise. ASCENSION *n.*

ascender *n.* in writing, the tall part of a letter like b or d (see DESCENDER).

ascent *n.* 1 an upward movement. 2 a gradient.

ash *n.* 1 a common tree. 2 the powdery remains left after burning wood, coal, etc.

ashamed *adj.* feeling disgraced.

ashore *adv.* 1 on shore. 2 aground; stranded.

aside *adv.* to or at one side; away. ASIDE *n.* words spoken to someone (esp. the audience at a play) which others are supposed not to hear.

ask *v.* to inquire; to request; to invite.

asleep *adv.* sleeping, not awake.

aspect *n.* a view; an outlook; a facet.

asphalt *n.* a kind of pitch used in road-making and for roofing.

assault *n.* a sudden attack. ASSAULT *v.* to attack.

assemble *v.* 1 to gather or meet together. 2 to put (something) together. ASSEMBLY *n.*

assess *v.* to estimate the value or quality of.

asset *n.* a possession worth something.

assist *v.* to help. ASSISTANCE *n.* ASSISTANT *n.*

associate *v.* to join in with. ASSOCIATE *n.* a companion.

association *n.* a society; a company.

assonance *n.* repeated vowel sounds, e.g. dr<u>ea</u>m-t<u>ea</u>m.

assortment *n.* a mixture of different kinds; a variety.

assume *v.* to suppose, to pretend.

assurance *n.* 1 a feeling of sureness; confidence. 2 a guarantee.

assured *adj.* certain; sure.

asterisk *n.* a small, star-shaped mark * used to draw attention to parts of text or to replace letters in rude words.

astern *adv.* towards the stern; behind.

asthma *n.* a disease that makes breathing difficult.

astonish *v.* to surprise; to amaze. ASTONISHMENT *n.*

astound *v.* to amaze; to shock with surprise. ASTOUNDING *adj.*

astray *adv.* lost; wandering.

astrology *n.* fortune-telling by the position of the stars. ASTROLOGER *n.*

astronaut *n.* a person who travels in space; a cosmonaut *(R)*.

astronomy *n.* the study of the stars and their movements. ASTRONOMER *n.*

asylum *n.* 1 a place of refuge or safety. 2 a home for the care of the mentally ill.

ate *v.* past tense of verb *to eat*.

athlete *n.* a person active in sports.

atlas *n.* a book of maps. *pl.* ATLASES.

atmosphere *n.* 1 the air surrounding the Earth. 2 feeling; mood. ATMOSPHERIC *adj.*

atoll *n.* a coral reef enclosing a lagoon.

atom *n.* smallest part of an element; anything very small. ATOMIC *adj.*

attach *v.* 1 to fasten. 2 to make fond of.
ATTACHMENT *n.*

attack *v.* to begin to fight; to assault.
ATTACK *n.* a battle; an onslaught. ATTACKER *n.*

attain *v.* to reach or gain after an effort.
ATTAINMENT *n.*

attempt *v.* to try; to make an effort.
ATTEMPT *n.* an effort; an endeavour.

attend *v.* 1 to be present at (a meeting etc).
2 ATTEND TO to consider. ATTENDANCE *n.*
presence.

attendant *n.* a servant or helper.

attention *n.* consideration; care.

attic *n.* a room in the roof of a house.

attitude *n.* 1 a position of the body. 2 a way of
thinking or behaving.

attract *v.* to draw towards. ATTRACTION *n.* being
drawn together (as in magnetism).

attractive *adj.* pleasing; charming.

auction *n.* a sale in which goods are sold to one
who bids or offers the highest price. AUCTION *v.*

audible *adj.* loud enough to hear. AUDIBLY *adv.*

audience *n.* 1 a group of listeners or readers; the
people a text is written for. 2 an interview.

audition *n.* a hearing given to a singer, speaker
or actor as a test.

August *n.* the eighth month of the year.
AUGUST *adj.* (pron. aug-UST) noble; stately.

aunt *n.* 1 father's or mother's sister. 2 uncle's
wife.

authentic *adj.* genuine; true. AUTHENTICITY *n.*

author *n.* 1 a writer of books or plays. 2 the
creator of anything. *fem.* AUTHORESS.

authority *n.* 1 legal power; right. 2 a person or
group having official power. 3 a reliable source
of knowledge.

autobiography *n.* the life story of a person,
written by himself or herself.

autograph *n.* a person's own signature.

automatic *adj.* self-acting; acting mechanically
and without thought.

automation *n.* the automatic control of machines
by computers or other machines.

autumn *n.* third season of the year, between
summer and winter.

available *adj.* within reach; able to be made use
of.

avalanche *n.* a mass of ice, snow, and rock
sliding down from a mountain.

avenge *v.* to take revenge for.

avenue *n.* a tree-bordered road or driveway.

average *adj.* ordinary; everyday. AVERAGE *n.* the
result obtained by adding several amounts and
dividing by the number of amounts.

aviary *n.* a bird-house.

aviation *n.* the art of flying aircraft.

avoid *v.* to keep away from (something); to shun.
AVOIDANCE *n.* AVOIDABLE *adj.*

await *v.* to wait for; to expect.

awake *v.* to arouse; to wake up. AWAKE *adj.* not
asleep; alert. AWAKENING *n.*

award *v.* to give a prize or penalty.
AWARD *n.* a prize or an honour.

aware *adj.* conscious; watchful. AWARENESS *n.*

awe *n.* a feeling of reverence, fear or wonder.
AWE *v.* to fill with reverence, fear or wonder.
AWESOME *adj.* causing awe.

awful *adj.* terrible; dreadful.

awhile *adv.* for a short time.

awkward *adj.* 1 clumsy. 2 inconvenient.
3 embarrassing.

axe *v.* to chop down. AXE *n.* a sharp-edged
chopping tool.

axle *n.* a bar or rod on which a wheel rotates.

B

baby *n.* a very young child. *pl.* BABIES.

bachelor *n.* an unmarried man.

back *n.* the rear part of anything. BACK *v.* 1 to go
backwards. 2 to bet on. 3 to support.
BACK *adv.* BACKWARDS *adv.*

backbone *n.* 1 the spine. 2 courage.

backward *adj.* 1 towards the back. 2 not very
clever.

bacon *n.* cured back and sides of a pig.

bacteria *n. pl.* disease germs or microbes.
sing. BACTERIUM.

bad *adj.* 1 wicked. 2 decayed. BADNESS *n.*

badge *n.* a special button worn by members of a
society; a symbol; an emblem.

badger *n.* a burrowing, nocturnal, grey-coated
wild animal. BADGER *v.* to bother; to tease.

baffle *v.* to puzzle; to bewilder. BAFFLING *adj.*

bag *n*. a pouch or container made of paper, fabric, etc., and having an opening top.
BAG *v*. 1 to put in a bag. 2 to swell; to bulge. 3 to droop; to hang in folds.

bail *v*. 1 to secure the release of an accused person by promising to pay a certain sum of money if he fails to appear for his trial. 1 to ladle water out of a boat (see BALE).
BAIL *n*. 1 the sum forfeited if a prisoner breaks his bail. 2 a small bar placed on top of the stumps in cricket.

bailiff *n*. 1 a law-officer. 2 a manager of a farm or an estate; a steward.

bait *v*. to torment; to lure. BAIT *n*. a temptation; a lure; food put on a hook to catch fish or in a trap to catch animals.

bake *v*. to cook hard by heat; to cook in an oven.

baker *n*. a person who bakes and sells bread.

balance *v*. 1 to keep steady; to keep upright. 2 to make things equal. BALANCE *n*. 1 scales. 2 steadiness; stability. BALANCED *adj*.
BALANCED DIET *n*. a diet that gives the right amount of all types of food.
BALANCED FORCES *n. pl.* in science, two equal forces acting in opposite directions to cancel each other out.

balcony *n*. a platform projecting from a window or wall.

bald *adj*. 1 hairless. 2 bare. BALDNESS *n*.

bale *n*. a large bundle. BALE *v*. to throw water out (of a boat).

ball *n*. 1 a sphere; a spherical object. 2 an assembly for dancing.

ballad *n*. a simple song or poem telling a story.

ballast *n*. a steadying weight.

ballerina *n*. a female ballet-dancer.

ballet *n*. a performance which is set to music but which is wholly dancing and mime, and without songs or speech.

balloon *n*. 1 a large airtight envelope which, when filled with gas lighter than air, rises skywards. 2 a small coloured rubber bag filled with air and used as a toy or decoration.
BALLOON *v*. 1 to ascent in a balloon. 2 to swell out like a balloon.

ballot *n*. a system of secret voting.
BALLOT *v*. to vote; to hold a ballot.

ball-point *n*. a pen using a small ball instead of a nib.

balsa *n*. a South American tree with very light wood used for making models.

bamboo *n*. giant, woody grasses.

ban *v*. to forbid; to prohibit. BAN *n*. an order forbidding something.

banana *n*. a tropical tree; its fruit.

band *v*. to join together in a group.
BAND *n*. 1 a strip of cloth or other material. 2 a group of persons; a group of musicians.

bandit *n*. an outlaw who robs people.
BANDITRY *n*.

bang *v*. to strike noisily; to beat. BANG *n*. a loud thump; a violent blow.

banish *v*. to drive away; to exile. BANISHMENT *n*.

bank *n*. 1 a place where money is kept and paid out. 2 the sides of a river or lake. 3 a shallow place in a river or sea. 4 an earth mound, ridge or barrier. BANK *v*. 1 to place money in a bank. 2 to raise an earth mound or barrier. 3 to fly an aircraft at an angle in turning.

bankrupt *n*. a person who, by legal declaration, is unable to pay his debts.

banner *n*. a flag; an ensign.

banquet *n*. a feast; a dinner with speeches.
BANQUET *v*. to feast.

baptise *v*. to christen and name. BAPTISMAL *adj*.

baptism *n*. a christening; a naming.

bar *n*. 1 a rigid rod. 2 any obstruction. 3 a counter where drinks are sold. BAR *v*. 1 to hold back with bars. 2 to stop; to obstruct.

barbecue *n*. 1 a framework for roasting meat over a fire. 2 an open-air party where meat is roasted.

bare *adj*. 1 naked; uncovered. 2 empty.
BARENESS *n*.

bargain *v*. to argue about price or terms.
BARGAIN *n*. something bought or sold cheaply.
BARGAINER *n*.

barge *n*. a flat-bottomed boat used on rivers and canals. BARGEE *n*. a barge worker.

baritone *n*. 1 a male singer. 2 a deep-toned voice between tenor (high) and bass (low).

bark *n*. 1 the cry of a dog, fox, etc. 2 the outer covering of trees. BARK *v*. 1 to utter a bark. 2 to speak sharply. 3 to knock the shin, elbow, etc.

barley *n.* a grain; a cereal.

barn *n.* a farm building used for storage.

barometer *n.* an instrument which measures air pressure. BAROMETRIC *adj.*

baron *n.* a nobleman's title. *fem.* BARONESS.

barrack *n.* a building in which soldiers live. BARRACK *v.* to jeer (at); to protest.

barrel *n.* 1 a metal or wooden cask. 2 the tube of a gun.

barren *adj.* 1 fruitless. 2 bare.

barricade *n.* a barrier put up to block a street. BARRICADE *v.* to build a barrier.

barrier *n.* something standing in the way.

barrister *n.* a lawyer who defends or prosecutes people in court.

barter *n.* the exchange of goods for other goods. BARTER *v.* to exchange goods.

base *n.* the bottom; foundation; starting point. BASE *adj.* low; vile.

basement *n.* the floor below ground level in a building.

basilica *n.* 1 a large Roman building used for public administration. 2 a type of church.

basin *n.* 1 a bowl. 2 a harbour. 3 the land drained by a river.

basis *n.* 1 a foundation. 2 the chief ingredient. *pl.* BASES (pron. BAY-sees). BASIC *adj.*

bask *v.* to lie in the warmth; to sun oneself.

basket *n.* a container with handle, made of cane, rushes or grasses.

bass *n.* 1 a fish. 2 (pron. BASE) a deep-toned voice.

bat *n.* 1 a club for striking a ball. 2 a night-flying mouse-like animal. BAT *v.* to strike with a bat. BATSMAN *n.*

batch *n.* a number of persons or things. *pl.* BATCHES.

bath *n.* 1 a large container in which to bath. 2 a large indoor or open-air pool for public bathing, swimming or sports. BATH *v.*

bathe *v.* 1 to bath. 2 to go swimming. BATHING *n.*

battalion *n.* a part of a regiment of soldiers.

batter *v.* to strike again and again. BATTER *n.* cooking ingredients beaten up with liquid.

battery *n.* 1 a device for making or storing electricity. 2 a beating; an attack. 3 a group of big guns. *pl.* BATTERIES.

battle *v.* to struggle with; to fight. BATTLE *n.* a mass fight between two armies.

battlefield *n.* the place where a battle is fought.

battlement *n.* the top of a castle wall with openings through which shots can be fired.

battleship *n.* a heavily armed warship.

bawl *v.* to shout or cry out loudly. BAWL *n.* a loud cry; a continued yelling.

bay *n.* 1 an inlet of the sea. 2 a wall recess. 3 the long, low bark of a hound. BAY *v.* to make a hound's cry.
BAY *adj.* reddish-brown.

bazooka *n.* a weapon for firing armour-piercing rockets.

be *v.* 1 to live or exist. 2 to become.

beach *n.* the sea-shore; sands. BEACH *v.* to run a ship ashore.

beacon *n.* a warning signal light or fire; a lighthouse.

bead *n.* a small pierced ball of glass, wood or other material.

beak *n.* 1 a bird's bill. 2 a bill-like projection.

beaker *n.* a large cup, usually without a handle.

beam *n.* 1 a ray of light. 2 a long piece of timber. 3 a bright, smiling look. 4 a radio signal. BEAM *v.* 1 to give light; to shine. 2 to send radio signals.

beaming *adj.* bright; smiling.

bean *n.* plant with long pods containing edible seeds.

bear *n.* a large, flat-footed, furry animal. BEAR *v.* 1 to carry; to support. 2 to endure.

beard *n.* the hair grown on the cheeks and chin of a man. BEARD *v.* to defy.

bearing *n.* 1 behaviour; manner. 2 a direction; an aim. BEARINGS *pl.* the supports of a moving piece of machinery.

beast *n.* 1 a four-footed animal. 2 a brutal person. BEASTLY *adj.*

beat *v.* 1 to strike. 2 to bang. 3 to defeat. 4 to throb. 5 to mark time in music. BEAT *n.* 1 a stroke; bang; throb. 2 a policeman's round.

beaten *adj.* 1 defeated. 2 hammered into shape.

beautiful *adj.* lovely; pleasing to the eye or ear.

beauty *n.* a person or thing pleasing to the sight or hearing.

beckon *v.* to summon with a nod or wave.

become *v.* 1 to change into or begin to be. 2 to suit; to grace.

becoming *adj.* 1 suitable. 2 attractive.

bee *n.* a winged, honey-making insect.

beech *n.* a large tree with smooth, grey-green bark.

beef *n.* meat from cattle.

beehive *n.* bees' home and store.

beer *n.* an alcoholic drink brewed from hops and malt; ale.

beet *n.* a vegetable with a sweet, fleshy root. SUGAR-BEET a kind of beet from which sugar is extracted.

beetle *n.* an insect with horny wing-covers.

beetroot *n.* the edible root of the red beet.

befall *v.* to happen to; to occur.

before *prep.* in front of; earlier or sooner. BEFORE *adv.* ahead of. BEFORE *conj.* sooner than.

beforehand *adv.* in advance; earlier; before the time.

beg *v.* 1 to implore. 2 to ask for help, food or money.

beggar *n.* one who begs.

begin *v.* to start; to commence.

beginning *n.* a start; origin.

behave *v.* to act properly or in some other way.

behaviour *n.* conduct, good or bad; a way of behaving.

behold *v.* to look at; to see.

belfry *n.* a bell-tower. *pl.* BELFRIES.

belief *n.* faith; confidence.

believe *v.* to trust; to accept something as true.

bell *n.* 1 a hollow metal object which will ring when tapped. 2 any object designed to make a bell-like sound for calling attention.

bellow *v.* to roar; to shout loudly. BELLOW *n.* a bull-like roar.

bellows *n. pl.* a device with a bag for blowing air into a fire or an organ.

belly *n.* abdomen; the underside of an animal's body.

belong *v.* to be the property of; to be part of.

belongings *n. pl.* a person's possessions.

beloved *adj.* much loved; very dear. BELOVED *n.* a loved one.

below *prep.* under, beneath; underneath. BELOW *adv.* beneath, in a lower place.

belt *n.* 1 a band of leather or cloth, usually worn round the waist. 2 a strip of land. BELTED *adj.*

bench *n.* 1 a seat. 2 a work-table. 3 a group, as bench of magistrates.

bend *v.* 1 to curve. 2 to bow or stoop. 3 to subdue. BEND *n.* a curve, an angle or a turning.

benefit *n.* a gain; an advantage. BENEFIT *v.* 1 to do good to (someone). 2 BENEFIT FROM to gain an advantage from.

benevolent *adj.* kind; generous.

bent *adj.* curved; twisted. BENT *n.* a liking for; an inclination.

bequeath *v.* to leave one's estate (to someone) by will; to hand down.

beret *n.* a flat, brimless woollen cap.

berry *n.* a small, juicy fruit enclosing seeds.

berth *n.* 1 the place where a ship is tied up in port. 2 a sleeping-bunk in a ship or train.

beside *prep.* by the side of; next to; close to; adjacent to.

besides *adv.* moreover; furthermore; also; in addition. BESIDES *prep.* over and above; in addition to.

betray *v.* to reveal information to the enemy. BETRAYER *n.*

between *prep.* 1 in the space separating two persons or things. 2 shared by two or more; among. BETWEEN *adv.*

bevel *n.* a slanting edge; an incline.

beverage *n.* a refreshing drink.

beware *v.* to be careful; to be cautious.

bewilder *v.* to puzzle; to confuse. BEWILDERED *adj.*

beyond *prep.* on the farther side of; out of reach BEYOND *adv.* yonder; at a distance. BEYOND *n.* a distant place; the unknown.

bias *n.* a leaning towards, an influence. BIAS *v.* to influence.

Bible *n.* the Christian and Jewish scriptures.

bibliography *n.* a list of books.

bicker *v.* to quarrel. BICKERING *n.*

bicycle *n.* a two-wheeled vehicle driven by pedals.

bid *v.* to invite; to make an offer. BID *n.* price offered.

big *adj.* large; great; important. BIGNESS *n.*

bile *n.* a brown fluid made by the liver to help digestion.

bill *n.* 1 a proposed law. 2 an account of money owing; an invoice. 3 a bird's beak. BILL *v.* 1 to announce; to advertise. 2 to send note of charge to.

billion *n.* a thousand million.

bin *n.* 1 a container for rubbish. 2 a storage can, box or tub.

binary *adj.* with 2 (not 10) as the base of a number system.

bind *v.* 1 to fasten or tie together. 2 to promise faithfully.

binding *n.* an outside cover. BINDING *adj.* firm.

bingo *n.* a game of chance played on numbered squares.

binoculars *n. pl.* field-glasses; opera-glasses.

biography *n.* the written life story of a person. *pl.* BIOGRAPHIES.

biology *n.* the study of living things. BIOLOGICAL *adj.*

biped *n.* a two-footed animal.

biplane *n.* an aircraft having two sets of wings, one above the other.

birch *n.* 1 a tree with smooth, silvery bark. 2 a rod; a cane. BIRCH *v.* to flog with a cane.

bird *n.* a creature with feathers and wings.

birth *n.* being born.

biscuit *n.* a thin, crisp, hard-baked cake.

bisect *v.* to cut into two equal parts. BISECTION *n.*

bishop *n.* 1 a clergyman or woman of high rank. 2 a chess-piece.

bison *n.* a wild ox or buffalo of North America and Europe.

bit *n.* 1 a small piece. 2 a boring tool. 3 the part of the bridle that goes into the horse's mouth.

bitch *n.* a female dog, fox or wolf.

bite *v.* 1 to cut or nip with the teeth. 2 to sting. 3 to take bait. BITE *n.* 1 the piece bitten off. 2 a wound made by biting.

bitter *adj.* 1 opposite of sweet; one of the four tastes – sweet, salt, sour and bitter. 2 unpleasant.

black *n.* the colour of soot; the opposite of white. BLACK *adj.* 1 dark. 2 gloomy; mournful. 3 wicked.

blackberry *n.* the fruit of the bramble. *pl.* BLACKBERRIES.

blackbird *n.* a black song-bird.

blackmail *n.* money, goods or services obtained from a person by threats of exposure. BLACKMAIL *v.* to obtain anything from another by threats.

bladder *n.* 1 a bag-like organ, containing urine, in the body of a human or an animal. 2 a thin bag which can be inflated with air, as that in a football.

blade *n.* 1 the flat cutting part of a knife, sword, etc. 2 the broad part of a bat, an oar, etc. 3 the flat pat of a leaf or a shoulder-bone.

blame *v.* to find fault with; to hold responsible. BLAME *n.* responsibility for a mistake.

blank *adj.* without any writing or marks; without expression. BLANK *n.* an empty space. BLANKNESS *n.*

blanket *n.* a warm covering for a bed.

blast *n.* a sudden rush of air; an explosion. BLAST *v.* 1 to blow up. 2 to break by explosion.

blaze *n.* 1 a bright flame. 2 a storm of anger. BLAZE *v.* to burn brightly. BLAZING *adj.*

bleach *v.* to make white. BLEACH *n.* substance used to make something white.

bleak *adj.* cold and unsheltered; dull, cheerless.

bleat *v.* to cry as a sheep, goat or calf. BLEAT *n.*

bleed *v.* to lose blood.

blend *v.* to mix; to mingle. BLEND *n.* a mixture.

bless *v.* 1 to make holy. 2 to wish success and happiness to.

blind *adj.* 1 unable to see. 2 unable to look ahead. BLIND *n.* 1 a window-screen. 2 a pretence intended to deceive. BLIND *v.* 1 to make sightless. 2 to dazzle. 3 to deceive; to mislead.

bliss *n.* very great happiness. BLISSFUL *adj.*

blister *n.* 1 a painful, bubble-like swelling filled with fluid, on the skin. 2 a similar swelling on a plant leaf, paintwork, etc. BLISTER *v.* to cause a blister.

blizzard *n.* a violent storm of snow and wind.

block *n.* 1 a solid mass of material. 2 a row or connected buildings. 3 an obstruction. BLOCK *v.* to obstruct.

blond *n.* a fair-haired man or boy. *fem.* BLONDE.

blood *n.* a red liquid flowing in the arteries and veins of animals, such as birds and mammals.

bloom *n*. 1 a flower; blossom. 2 freshness; vigour. BLOOM *v*. 1 to flower. 2 to flourish; to glow.

blossom *v*. to flower; to bloom. BLOSSOM *n*. a flower; a bloom.

blot *v*. 1 to spot or stain. 2 to disgrace. BLOT *n*. 1 a spot or stain. 2 a blemish.

blow *v*. 1 to force air out of the mouth. 2 to cause air to move. BLOW *n*. 1 a puff of air from the mouth. 2 a gust of wind. 3 a knock; a rap. 4 a shock; a disaster.

blubber *n*. whale fat. BLUBBER *v*. to weep noisily.

blue *n*. the colour of a cloudless sky. BLUE *adj*. 1 of the colour blue; sky-coloured. 2 dismal; down-hearted.

bluff *n*. 1 a pretence. 2 a steep high bank or cliff. BLUFF *v*. to deceive; to pretend. BLUFF *adj*. 1 rough and hearty. 2 steep.

blunder *v*. to make a bad mistake. BLUNDER *n*. a bad mistake; an oversight. BLUNDERER *n*. BLUNDERING *adj*.

blunt *adj*. 1 without a sharp edge or point. 2 outspoken; candid; frank. BLUNT *v*. to dull the edge or point; to deaden.

blur *v*. to dim; to make indistinct; to smudge. BLUR *n*. a smudge.

blurb *n*. information about a book printed on the back or inside flap.

blurt *v*. to speak hastily; to burst out with.

blush *v*. to flush; to become red-faced. BLUSH *n*. a rosy glow.

bluster *v*. 1 to blow gustily. 2 to boast; to bully. 3 to fume. BLUSTER *n*. boasting.

boar *n*. a male pig.

board *n*. 1 a plank. 2 daily meals. 3 a committee. BOARD *v*. 1 to cover with boards. 2 to supply with meals. 3 to enter a ship, train, bus, aircraft, etc.

boast *v*. to brag; to praise oneself. BOAST *n*. bragging; self-praise. BOASTFUL *adj*.

boat *n*. a small vessel or ship.

bobbin *n*. a reel; spool holding thread or yarn.

body *n*. 1 the main part of a person or animal. 2 a group; a crowd. *pl*. BODIES.

bog *n*. a swamp; a marsh. BOGGY *adj*.

bogus *adj*. false; fake.

boil *v*. 1 to turn a liquid into a vapour; to cook by boiling. 2 to be angry. BOIL *n*. a hard, painful swelling.

boiler *n*. a strong metal container in which steam is made or liquids are heated.

boisterous *adj*. rough; noisy; stormy.

bold *adj*. 1 brave; daring. 2 clear; well-marked.

bollard *n*. a post for securing a ship's mooring ropes; an indicator post on a traffic island.

bolt *n*. a metal fastening for a door. BOLT *v*. 1 to fasten. 2 to run away. 3 to eat quickly.

bomb *n*. a metal case filled with explosives. BOMB *v*. to attack with bombs.

bombard *v*. 1 to attack with bombs and shells. 2 to question again and again. BOMBARDMENT *n*.

bomber *n*. 1 a bomb-carrying aircraft. 2 a person who plants a bomb.

bond *n*. 1 a contract; an agreement. 2 a link; a tie. BOND *v*. to join (together).

bone *n*. a hard substance forming the skeleton of an animal's body. BONY *adj*.

bonfire *n*. a large, open-air fire.

bonny *adj*. healthy; chubby; pretty.

bonus *n*. an extra goodwill payment.

book *n*. written or printed sheets bound together. BOOKSELLER *n*. BOOK *v*. to reserve a place beforehand.

boom *n*. 1 a long spar. 2 a barrier across a harbour mouth. 3 a deep, hollow sound. 4 a sudden increase in trade, prosperity. BOOM *v*. to make a deep, hollow sound.

boomerang *n*. Australian weapon, a curved stick which, when thrown, returns to its thrower if the target is missed.

boot *n*. 1 footwear reaching above the ankles. 2 a place for luggage in a car or coach.

booty *n*. plunder; loot; stolen objects.

border *n*. an edge; a boundary; a margin. BORDERING *adj*.

bore *v*. 1 to pierce. 2 to weary. BORE *n*. 1 a hole. 2 the width of a hole. 3 anything wearisome. 4 a tidal wave.

boredom *n*. dullness; weariness.

borrow *v*. to obtain on loan. BORROWER *n*.

boss *v*. to give orders to. BOSS *n*. the master; the manager.

botanist *n*. a person who studies plants.

botany *n*. the study of plants. BOTANICAL *adj*.

bother *v*. to be troublesome to; to annoy. BOTHER *n*. trouble; worry.

bottle *n.* a hollow, narrow-necked container for liquids, usually made of glass or plastic. BOTTLE *v.* to store or preserve in a bottle.

bottom *n.* the lowest part; base.

bough *n.* a branch of a tree.

boulder *n.* a large stone or rock.

bounce *v.* to spring suddenly; to rebound; to cause to rebound. BOUNCE *n.* a rebound. BOUNCY *adj.*

bound *v.* to leap; to spring. BOUND *n.* 1 a leap. 2 a boundary.

boundary *n.* a line dividing one area from another.

bouquet *n.* 1 a bunch of flowers. 2 the perfume of wine.

bout *n.* a contest; a period.

bow *v.* (pron. like "NOW") 1 to bend the head or body forward in respect or greeting. 2 to give in; to submit. BOW *n.* 1 a forward bending of the head or body. 2 the curved front part of a ship; its prow.

bow *n.* (pron. like "LOW") 1 a weapon for shooting arrows. 2 a looped knot in a tie or ribbon. 3 a stringed rod used to play various stringed instruments. 4 anything curved.

bowl *n.* a round dish to hold food or liquids.

bowls *n.* an outdoor game played on a smooth lawn, using heavy wooden balls. BOWLER *n.* BOWLING *n. & adj.*

box *n.* 1 a container made of wood, cardboard, metal, etc. 2 a smack, esp. on the ear. *pl.* BOXES. BOX *v.* 1 to encase. 2 to fight with gloved fists.

boxer *n.* 1 a fighter with gloved fists. 2 a type of dog.

boy *n.* a male child.

brace *v.* to tighten or strengthen. BRACE *n.* 1 a support. 2 a pair; a couple. 3 a tool for holding a bit for drilling holes.

bracken *n.* 1 a coarse variety of wild fern, common on hillsides and heath land.

bracket *n.* 1 a small shelf or support. 2 a mark used in pairs ( ) to enclose words, etc., and separate them from the rest of the sentence.

brag *n.* boastful talk. BRAG *v.* to boast. BRAGGING *n.*

braid *v.* to weave or plait together. BRAID *n.* a cord or tape made by weaving different strands together. BRAIDED *adj.*

Braille *n.* a system of writing and printing using raised marks which blind people can read by feeling.

brain *n.* the centre of the nervous system.

brake *n.* an apparatus for stopping or slowing a moving vehicle. BRAKE *v.* to check; to slow down.

bramble *n.* a rough, prickly bush bearing blackberries.

bran *n.* husks of grain, separated from flour after grinding.

branch *n.* 1 the bough of a tree. 2 an offshoot of a business, bank, library etc. *pl.* BRANCHES. BRANCH *v.* to divide into or spread out.

brand *n.* 1 a mark made with a hot iron. 2 a burning or charred piece of wood; a fiery torch. 3 a trade mark. BRAND *v.* to mark with a hot iron.

brass *n.* 1 a yellow alloy of copper and zinc. 2 brass wind instruments.

brave *adj.* daring; courageous. BRAVE *n.* a North American Indian warrior.

bravery *n.* courage; valour. BRAVELY *adv.*

brawl *v.* to quarrel. BRAWL *n.* a noisy quarrel; a row. BRAWLER. *n.*

breach *n.* 1 a break; a gap. 2 a quarrel. BREACH *v.* to make a gap in; to break.

bread *n.* a food made from flour and water.

breadth *n.* broadness; the distance from side to side.

break *v.* to damage or spoil; to fracture. BREAK *n.* a pause; an interruption. BREAKAGE *n.* BREAKABLE *adj.*

breaker *n.* a foam-topped wave breaking on to rocks or a beach.

breakfast *n.* the first meal of the day. BREAKFAST *v.*

bream *n.* a river fish.

breast *n.* 1 the chest; bosom. 2 the front of anything. BREAST *v.* to face; to withstand.

breath *n.* 1 air drawn in and expelled by the lungs. 2 a breath of wind; a light wind or gentle breeze.

breathe *v.* 1 to draw breath into the lungs and expel it. 2 to whisper or utter. 3 to be alive.

breed *v.* to produce young; to rear. BREED *n.* the race; the family.

breeding *n*. the result of rearing or training.

breeze *n*. a light wind. BREEZY *adj*.

brew *v*. to make beer, tea, etc. BREW *n*. a single brewing. BREWER *n*. BREWERY *n*.

briar, brier *n*. 1 the prickly wild rose. 2 the tree heath plant and the tobacco pipes made from its root.

bribe *n*. money or a gift offered to gain a favour. BRIBE *v*. to tempt with a bribe.

brick *n*. a fire-hardened and moulded block of clay used as a building material.

bride *n*. a newly-married woman.

bridegroom *n*. a newly-married man.

bridge *n*. 1 a structure to carry traffic over a river, railway or road. 2 the raised structure of a ship from which the captain operates. 3 a card game. BRIDGE *v*. to span a gap.

bridle *n*. the headgear of a horse's harness; a check; a restraint. BRIDLE *v*.

brief *adj*. short, concise. BRIEFLY *adv*.

brigade *n*. several regiments or battalions; an organised band of people.

bright *adj*. 1 shining. 2 clever. 3 cheerful. BRIGHTNESS *n*.

brighten *v*. to make or become bright.

brilliance *n*. great brightness or cleverness.

brilliant *adj*. 1 bright; sparkling. 2 very clever.

brim *n*. the edge of a bowl or drinking vessel.

brine *n*. salt water; pickle. BRINY *adj*.

bring *v*. to fetch; to carry.

brink *n*. the edge of a cliff or steep place.

brisk *adj*. active; lively; quick. BRISKLY *adv*.

bristle *n*. a stiff, coarse hair. BRISTLE *v*. 1 to stand up straight like an angry animal's hair. 2 to show anger. BRISTLY *adj*.

brittle *adj*. easy to break; fragile.

broad *adj*. wide; large; full. BROAD *n*. a flooded fen.

broadcast *n*. a radio or television transmission. BROADCAST *v*. 1 to transmit by radio or television. 2 to scatter.

broaden *v*. to make wide or wider.

brochure *n*. a small booklet.

brogue *n*. 1 an Irish accent. 2 a strong shoe.

bronchitis *n*. inflammation of the tubes of the lungs.

bronze *n*. a red-brown alloy of copper and tin. BRONZE *v*. to tan. BRONZE *adj*. made of bronze; bronze-coloured.

brooch *n*. an ornament clasp or pin. *pl*. BROOCHES.

brood *n*. 1 a number of young birds hatched at the same time. 2 a swarm. BROOD *v*. to worry for some time; to think anxiously.

brook *n*. a small stream.

broom *n*. 1 a sweeping brush with stiff bristles. 2 a yellow-flowered shrub.

brother *n*. 1 a son of the same parents as another person. 2 a friend; a comrade. *pl*. BROTHERS or BRETHREN. BROTHERLY *adj*.

brow *n*. 1 the forehead. 2 the top of a hill.

brown *n*. red, blue and yellow mixed. BROWN *v*. 1 to make brown; to toast. 2 to tan; to sunburn. BROWN *adj*. brown in colour; tanned.

bruise *n*. a skin injury caused by pressure or a blow. BRUISE *v*. to press; to crush.

brush *n*. 1 an implement for painting, sweeping or scrubbing. 2 a short encounter. 3 a fox's tail. BRUSH *v*. 1 to sweep. 2 to touch in passing.

brutal *adj*. cruel; like a brute.

brute *n*. 1 a beast. 2 a cruel or savage person.

bubble *n*. a thin, ball-shaped film of liquid full of air. BUBBLE *v*. 1 to rise in bubbles. 2 to flow with a gurgling noise.

buck *n*. the male of many animals – deer, goat, rabbit, etc. BUCK *v*. to jump with an arched back.

bucket *n*. a container for carrying water, coal, etc.; a pail.

buckle *n*. a metal clasp. BUCKLE *v*. 1 to bend. 2 to fasten with a buckle.

bud *n*. a leaf or flower not fully open. BUD *v*. to begin growing.

Buddhism *n*. a religious teaching based on the life of the Buddha. BUDDHIST *n*. a person who believes in and practises Buddhism.

budget *n*. a plan to show how money will be spent. THE BUDGET *n*. the annual financial statement of the Chancellor of the Exchequer.

buff *n*. a pale yellow colour. BUFF *v*. to polish.

buffalo *n*. a wild ox (see BISON). *pl*. BUFFALOES.

buffer *n*. anything that softens a blow; a fender.

buffet *v.* to strike; to knock about. BUFFET *n.* 1 a blow. 2 (pron. BU-fay) a refreshment bar.

bug *n.* 1 a small insect. 2 a hidden listening device. 3 a problem or mistake in a computer program. BUG *v.* to annoy (someone).

bugle *n.* a small trumpet. BUGLER *n.*

bulb *n.* 1 a large ball-shaped base of a plant stem, e.g. onion. 2 an electric lamp shaped like a bulb.

bulge *v.* to swell outwards. BULGE *n.* a swelling. BULGING *adj.*

bulk *n.* the size; the volume; the greater part.

bull *n.* the male of cattle, elephants, whales, etc.

bulldozer *n.* a powerful caterpillar vehicle used for levelling or clearing land.

bullet *n.* a missile shot from a rifle or pistol.

bullet points *n.* small, circular marks (•) used to draw attention to parts of text, e.g. in a leaflet or report.

bulletin *n.* a short, official news report.

bullion *n.* gold or silver in the form of bars.

bullock *n.* a young bull.

bully *n.* one who frightens or ill-treats someone weaker. BULLY *v.* to frighten; to ill-treat.

bump *n.* 1 a knock; a collision. 2 a swelling. BUMP *v.* to knock into.

bun *n.* a small round cake.

bunch *n.* a cluster or group of things tied or growing together. BUNCH *v.* to cluster; to gather together.

bundle *n.* a package; a parcel. BUNDLE *v.* to bind together.

bungalow *n.* a one-storey house.

bungle *v.* to blunder; to do clumsily.

bunk *n.* a box-like bed; a sleeping berth in a ship or train.

bunker *n.* 1 a large bin for storing coal, etc. 2 a sandy hollow on a gold-course.

buoy *n.* a large, anchored float to guide ships. BUOY *v.* 1 to keep afloat. 2 to cheer; to comfort.

burden *n.* a load; a weight. BURDEN *v.* to lay weight upon; to load.

burglar *n.* someone who breaks into a house or building to steal.

burial *n.* a funeral; the burying of anything.

burn *n.* 1 an injury or a mark caused by burning. 2 a small stream. BURN *v.* to blaze; to set fire to; to destroy by fire.

burrow *n.* a hole in the earth dug by an animal as a home and shelter. BURROW *v.* to make holes underground. BURROWING *adj.*

burst *v.* to fly into pieces; to explode. BURST *n.* a splitting apart; a sudden spurt; an explosion.

bury *v.* to cover over; to hide in the earth. TO BURY THE HATCHET to forgive and forget. BURIAL *n.*

bus *n.* a public passenger-carrying motor vehicle.

bush *n.* 1 a shrub. 2 wild, uncultivated country.

bushy *adj.* thick and overgrown.

business *n.* occupation; work; trade; profession. BUSINESS *adj.* concerning business.

bust *n.* 1 a sculpture of the upper part of the body. 2 the upper part of the body, esp. female.

bustle *n.* fuss; noisy stir. BUSTLE *v.* to hurry about fussily. BUSTLING *adj.*

busy *adj.* fully occupied; active; working hard. BUSILY *adv.*

butcher *n.* a person who kills animals for meat; a shopkeeper who sells meat. BUTCHER *v.* to kill, to slaughter.

butt *n.* 1 the thicker end of anything. 2 a large cask. BUTT *v.* to push or strike with the head.

butter *n.* a yellow fatty food made from milk. BUTTER *v.* 1 to spread (bread etc.) with butter. 2 BUTTER UP to flatter (someone).

button *n.* a round, flat disc or knob for fastening clothing. BUTTON *v.* to fasten with buttons.

buxom *adj.* plump and attractive.

buy *v.* to purchase. BUYER *n.*

buzz *n.* 1 the humming sound made by a flying bee. 2 the hum of many people in conversation. BUZZ *v.* to hum.

bypass *v.* to go round, not through. BYPASS *n.* a road round a town centre.

C

cabaret *n.* entertainment provided in a restaurant, night club, etc.

cabbage *n.* a large, green vegetable.

cabin *n.* 1 a hut. 2 a room in a ship or aeroplane.

cabinet *n.* a cupboard having drawers and shelves.

cable *n*. 1 a strong rope, wire or chain. 2 covered electric or telegraph wires.

cache *n*. (pron. KASH) a hidden store of provisions, treasure, ammunition, etc.

cackle *n*. 1 the noise of a hen or goose. 2 a giggle. CACKLE *v*. 1 to cluck. 2 to giggle.

cactus *n*. a prickly desert plant with thick stems.

cadet *n*. a young man training in the armed forces (usually as an officer) or the police.

café *n*. a coffee-house, or tea-shop; a restaurant.

cage *n*. a barred enclosure for birds or animals. CAGE *v*. to imprison.

cairn *n*. 1 a heap of stones built as a landmark or monument. 2 a terrier dog.

calamity *n*. a disaster; a great misfortune. *pl*. CALAMITIES.

calculate *v*. to count or reckon with figures; to work out. CALCULATION *n*. CALCULATOR *n*. a machine that does calculations.

calendar *n*. a table showing the days, weeks and months of a particular year; a list of events.

calf *n*. 1 the young of certain animals, such as the cow, elephant, etc. 2 the back bulging part of the leg below the knee. *pl*. CALVES.

call *v*. 1 to shout or cry out. 2 to name or summon. 3 to visit. CALL *n*. 1 a shout. 2 an invitation. 3 a visit. CALLER *n*.

calligram *n*. a shape poem.

calligraphy *n*. handwriting; the art of beautiful handwriting.

callous *adj*. unfeeling; hard-hearted.

calm *adj*. 1 still; windless. 2 not easily upset. CALM *v*. to make peaceful; to quieten.

calorie *n*. 1 the energy value of food. 2 a unit measure of heat.

calypso *n*. a West Indian folk song.

camber *n*. the slope of a road from the middle.

camel *n*. a large, humped, domesticated Asian or African animal.

camera *n*. a device for taking photographs or making films.

camouflage *v*. to disguise an object by making it merge into its background. CAMOUFLAGE *n*.

camp *v*. to live in tents. CAMP *n*. a group of inhabited tents. CAMPER *n*.

campaign *n*. 1 a series of military operations in one area. 2 a series of efforts for a definite purpose. CAMPAIGN *v*. to carry on a campaign.

can *n*. a small metal container. CAN *v*. 1 to be able. 2 to preserve in airtight tins.

canal *n*. an artificial waterway for ships, boats, barges and drainage.

canary *n*. a yellow song-bird. *pl*. CANARIES. CANARY *adj*. bright yellow.

cancel *v*. to cross out; to withdraw; to call off.

cancer *n*. a harmful growth in the body.

candid *adj*. frank, honest and straightforward.

candle *n*. a cylinder of wax surrounding a wick, for giving light by burning.

cane *n*. a thin, flexible stick. CANE *v*. to beat with a cane.

canine *adj*. to do with dogs. CANINE *n*. long, sharp tooth in animals and humans; fang.

canister *n*. a small box or container.

canned *adj*. preserved in tins.

cannibal *n*. a person who eats human flesh; an animal which eats others of its own kind.

cannon *n*. a large gun. CANNON *v*. to collide.

canoe *n*. a light, open boat propelled by using a paddle. CANOE *v*. to sail or paddle a canoe. CANOEIST *n*.

canopy *n*. a light, overhead covering. *pl*. CANOPIES.

canteen *n*. 1 a dining-room in an office or factory. 2 a case of cutlery.

canter *n*. an easy gallop. CANTER *v*. to ride at an easy gallop.

canvas *n*. strong, coarse cloth for sails, tents, oil-paintings, etc.

canvass *v*. to seek votes, orders, subscriptions and opinions. CANVASSER *n*.

canyon *n*. a deep, narrow gorge or valley.

cap *n*. 1 a soft, peaked head-covering. 2 a cover or top. CAP *v*. 1 to cover. 2 to outdo.

capable *adj*. able to do; efficient.

capacity *n*. the amount that a container holds. 2 ability. *pl*. CAPACITIES.

cape *n*. 1 a headland. 2 a short cloak.

capital *n*. 1 a chief city. 2 money or goods used for business. 3 a large letter used to begin a sentence or name. CAPITAL *adj*. excellent.

capsize *v*. to overturn.

capsule *n.* 1 a pill. 2 a seed-pod. 3 part of a spacecraft.

captain *n.* 1 an officer qualified to command a ship or aircraft. 2 an army officer commanding a company. 3 the leader of a sports team or club. CAPTAIN *v.* to lead; to command.

caption *n.* a short title for a chapter, story, article or illustration.

captive *n.* a prisoner. CAPTIVE *adj.* kept as a prisoner; not free.

capture *v.* 1 to catch. 2 to imprison. 3 to attract or hold. CAPTOR *n.*

car *n.* a box-like vehicle on wheels.

caravan *n.* 1 a home on wheels. 2 a desert convoy.

carbohydrate *n.* the food group which gives humans and animals energy, found in bread, pasta and cereals.

carcass (-ase) *n.* the body of an animal, esp. a dead body.

card *n.* a piece or sheet of very stiff paper.

cardigan *n.* a knitted woollen jacket.

cardinal *n.* a member of the Pope's Council. CARDINAL *adj.* most important; chief.

cardinal (number) *n.* a number which represents amount, such as 1,2,3,4, not order (see ORDINAL (NUMBER)).

care *n.* 1 attention. 2 worry. 3 caution. CARE (FOR or ABOUT) *v.* 1 to be interested. 2 to be concerned. 3 to watch over.

career *n.* a person's profession or course in life. CAREER *v.* to move quickly and wildly.

careful *adj.* painstaking; watchful; cautious. CAREFULLY *adv.*

careless *adj.* thoughtless; unconcerned; inaccurate. CARELESSNESS *n.*

cargo *n.* the load carried by a ship or aircraft; freight. *pl.* CARGOES.

carmine *adj. & n.* a purplish-red colour.

carnation *n.* 1 a garden flower of the pink family. 2 a pink colour.

carnival *n.* a merrymaking; festivity.

carnivore *n.* a meat-eater.

carol *n.* a joyous song; a Christmas hymn. CAROL *v.* to sing gaily. CAROLLING *adj.*

carp *n.* a freshwater fish. CARP (AT) *v.* to find fault with. CARPING *adj.*

carpel *n.* the female reproductive part of a flower, including the ovary, style and stigma.

carpenter *n.* a joiner; a tradesman who works with wood.

carpet *n.* a woven floor-covering. CARPET *v.* to cover with carpet.

carriage *n.* 1 a wheeled vehicle. 2 a person's bearing. 3 the cost of transport.

carrion *n.* dead rotting flesh.

carrot *n.* an orange-coloured root vegetable.

carry *v.* 1 to convey. 2 to transport.

cart *n.* a waggon. CART *v.* to convey by cart or waggon. CARTER *n.*

carton *n.* a cardboard or plastic container.

cartoon *n.* a comic drawing or film. CARTOONIST *n.* one who draws cartoons for a living.

carve *v.* to shape by cutting; to sculpt. 2 to slice meat. CARVER *n.*

case *n.* 1 a container. 2 a lawsuit. 3 an example. CASE *v.* to enclose.

cash *n.* coins or banknotes. CASH *v.* to turn into money.

cash crop *n.* a crop grown to make money rather than to be eaten by the grower.

cast *v.* 1 to throw. 2 to shape in a mould. 3 to drop; to shed. CAST *n.* 1 a throw. 2 anything moulded. 3 the actors in a play.

castaway *n.* a shipwrecked sailor.

castle *n.* 1 a stronghold; a fortress. 2 a chess-piece.

casual *adj.* due to chance; informal; offhand.

casualty *n.* 1 an accident. 2 the victim of an accident. *pl.* CASUALTIES.

cat *n.* a common domestic animal; a feline.

catalogue *n.* a complete list, usually in alphabetical or other order. CATALOGUE *v.* to make a list.

catamaran *n.* a boat with twin hulls.

catastrophe *n.* a sudden disaster. CATASTROPHIC *adj.*

catch *v.* 1 to capture; to seize and hold. 2 to be in time for. CATCH *n.* 1 a capture. 2 a fastening-clasp or hook.

cater *v.* to supply what is needed. CATERER *n.*

caterpillar *n.* 1 the larva of a moth or butterfly. 2 an endless belt with treads that is used to drive some vehicles.

cathedral *n.* the principal church of a diocese.

catholic *adj.* world-wide; universal; general.
CATHOLIC *n.* a member of the Roman Catholic Church.

catkins *n. pl.* hanging flowers of the willow, birch, hazel, etc.

cattle *n. pl.* cows, bulls, calves, etc.

cauliflower *n.* a kind of cabbage with a large white flower head.

cause *n.* 1 a beginning. 2 a reason. 3 a purpose.
CAUSE *v.* to make happen.

caution *n.* 1 watchfulness; care. 2 a warning.
CAUTION *v.* to warn.

cavalry *n.* mounted soldiers.

cave *n.* a hole in a cliff or hillside.

cavern *n.* a large underground cave.

cavity *n.* a hollow place; a hole. *pl.* CAVITIES.

cease *v.* to stop; to come to an end.

cedar *n.* an evergreen cone-bearing tree.

ceiling *n.* 1 the top of a room. 2 the maximum altitude an aircraft can reach. 3 the upper limit.

celebrate *v.* to honour; to praise.

celebration *n.* a special festivity; merry-making.

celebrity *n.* a celebrated person. *pl.* CELEBRITIES.

cell *n.* 1 a small room in a prison or monastery. 2 a small unit of living matter from which all living things are made. 3 a unit in an electric battery.

cellar *n.* an underground room where coal, wine, etc., is stored.

cello *n.* (pron. CHEL-oh) a musical instrument like a violin but which is large and rests on the floor.

Celsius *adj.* the common temperature scale, on which water freezes at 0° and boils at 100°.

Celt *n.* a member of an ancient race, the ancestors of the Bretons, Welsh, Cornish, Manx, Scots and Irish. CELTIC *adj.*

cement *n.* a mixture of quicklime and clay used with sand and water to make mortar. CEMENT *v.* to join securely.

cemetery *n.* a burial-ground.

censor *n.* an official who examines and prohibits offensive books, plays or films. CENSOR *v.* to prohibit; to ban. CENSORSHIP *n.*

censure *v.* to blame; to express disapproval of. CENSURE *n.* blame, reproach.

census *n.* an official counting of the population.

cent *n.* 1 100, as in 10 per cent, or 10 in each hundred (10%). 2 a coin which is one-hundredth part of a larger amount.

centenary *n.* the hundredth anniversary.

centigram *n.* one hundredth part of a gram; a measure of mass.

centilitre *n.* one hundredth part of a litre; a measure of volume or capacity.

centimetre *n.* one hundredth part of a metre.

central *adj.* 1 in the middle. 2 chief; leading.
CENTRALLY *adv.*

centre *n.* the middle point or part. CENTRE *v.* to place in the middle.

centurion *n.* the officer commanding a century in the Roman army.

century *n.* 1 100 years. 2 a cricket score of 100 runs. 3 in ancient Rome, a unit of 100 foot soldiers. *pl.* CENTURIES.

ceramic *n.* a decorative article made of clay or porcelain. CERAMIC *adj.*

cereal *n.* any grass grain used as food.

ceremony *n.* a solemn or stately celebration. *pl.* CEREMONIES.

certain *adj.* sure; without any doubt.

certainly *adv.* willingly; surely.

certainty *n.* a fact; something that is certain to happen.

certificate *n.* a written proof.

certify *v.* to inform truthfully and accurately; to guarantee.

chaff *v.* to tease. CHAFF *n.* 1 husks of grain. 2 teasing. CHAFFING *adj.*

chaffinch *n.* a small grain-eating bird.

chain *n.* 1 a length of joined links or rings. 2 an imperial measure of length (22 yards). 3 a series of events. CHAIN *v.* to bind; to secure with a chain.

chair *n.* a backed, four-legged seat for one.
CHAIR *v.* 1 to preside over a meeting. 2 to raise and carry in a chair as an honour.

chalet *n.* (pron. SHAL-ay) 1 a wooden house built in the Swiss style. 2 a small dwelling in a holiday camp.

chalk *n.* soft, white limestone. CHALK *v.* to mark with chalk.
CHALKY *adj.*

hallenge *v.* to question or doubt something; to dare (someone to do something). CHALLENGE *n.* 1 a summons to a contest. 2 a query or an objection. CHALLENGER *n.*

hampagne *n.* a sparkling white wine from the district of Champagne, in France.

hampion *n.* 1 one who defends others. 2 a victor over all competitors. CHAMPION *v.* to uphold; to defend. CHAMPIONSHIP *n.*

hance *n.* 1 an unexpected or unplanned event. 2 an opportunity; a risk. CHANCE *v.* to risk. CHANCY *adj.*

hancel *n.* the part of a church where the altar stands.

hange *n.* 1 an alteration; a variation. 2 money received back from a sum offered. CHANGE *v.* to alter; to substitute or exchange.

hannel *n.* 1 a waterway. 2 a groove. THE CHANNEL the English Channel. CHANNEL *v.* 1 to groove. 2 to cut a canal.

hant *v.* to sing. CHANT *n.* a sacred song.

haos *n.* (pron KAY-oss) disorder.

hap *v.* to crack or to split open in cracks. CHAP *n.* a crack in the skin caused by frost, wind, etc. 2 a boy; a man. CHAPPED *adj.*

hapel *n.* a house of worship.

hapter *n.* 1 a division of a book. 2 the clergy of a cathedral.

har *v.* to burn partially; to scorch.

haracter *n.* 1 a person's own nature. 2 a reputation. 3 a person in a story or play.

haracteristic *n.* a feature; a quality.

harge *v.* 1 to rush at. 2 to fill up. 3 to ask a price. 4 to accuse. CHARGE *n.* 1 an onslaught. 2 a filling. 3 a price. 4 an accusation.

hariot *n.* a horse-drawn cart used in ancient warfare and racing.

harity *n.* 1 kindness or goodwill felt towards other people. 2 an institution that gives help to those in need.

harm *n.* 1 attractiveness. 2 a magic spell. 3 a good-luck object. CHARM *v.* 1 to attract. 2 to delight.

hart *n.* 1 a map showing coasts, shoals, rocks, etc. 2 a diagram giving information (such as a weather-chart). CHART *v.* to plan; to show on a chart.

charter *n.* a document granting certain rights. CHARTER *v.* to hire for a period.

chase *v.* to pursue; to hunt; to drive away. CHASE *n.* a pursuit; the hunt.

chat *v.* to talk in an easy familiar way. CHAT *n.* a friendly talk.

cheap *adj.* costing little; of poor value. CHEAPNESS *n.*

cheapen *v.* to make or to become cheap.

cheat *v.* to be dishonest; to deceive. CHEAT *n.* a person who cheats.

check *v.* 1 to hinder or stop. 2 to look for faults in. 3 to make sure. CHECK *n.* 1 a hindrance. 2 a control. 3 a pattern of squares.

cheek *n.* 1 each side of the face. 2 impudence.

cheer *v.* 1 to applaud by shouting. 2 to gladden. CHEER *n.* 1 a cry of applause or welcome. 2 happiness.

cheerful *adj.* happy and lively. CHEERFULNESS *n.*

cheese *n.* a food made from milk curd, pressed and dried.

chef *n.* (pron. SHEF) a cook in a hotel or restaurant.

chemical *n.* a substance made by chemistry. CHEMICAL *adj.* CHEMICALLY *adv.*

chemist *n.* 1 a person skilled in chemistry. 2 a person who is qualified to dispense drugs and medicines.

cheque *n.* a written order to a banker to pay money.

cherry *n.* a small sweet stone-fruit. *pl.* CHERRIES. CHERRY *adj.* reddish; ruddy.

chess *n.* a game for two played on a squared board. CHESS-BOARD *n.*

chest *n.* 1 the upper front part of the body; the thorax. 2 a large box.

chew *v.* to crush or grind with the teeth; masticate.

chick *n.* a newly-hatched bird.

chicken *n.* a young fowl.

chief *n.* a leader; a head. CHIEF *adj.* most important.

chiffon *n.* (pron. SHIF-on) a thin material.

child *n.* a young boy or girl. *pl.* CHILDREN.

chill *n.* 1 a coolness; a feeling of coldness. 2 a shivery cold. CHILL *v.* to make cold.

chime *n.* the music of bells. CHIME *v.* to ring tunefully.

chimney *n.* a tube-like passage to carry smoke away; a flue.

chimpanzee *n.* an African ape.

chin *n.* the part of the face below the mouth.

china *n.* fine, thin porcelain.

chink *n.* a narrow opening. CHINK *v.* to jingle.

chip *n.* 1 a tiny piece. 2 a piece of fried potato. 3 an abbreviation for MICROCHIP. CHIP *v.* to break off a fragment. CHIPPED *adj.*

chirp *n.* a shrill bird-call. CHIRP *v.* to call like a young bird. CHIRPING *n.*

chisel *n.* a wood or stone-cutting tool. CHISEL *v.* to cut or carve with a chisel.

chlorophyll *n.* the green pigment in plants that traps the energy of sunlight for photosynthesis.

chocolate *n.* a sweet or drink made from cocoa. CHOCOLATE *adj.* deep brown.

choice *n.* 1 anything chosen or selected. 2 a variety to choose from. CHOICE *adj.* rare; excellent.

choir *n.* 1 a group of people trained to sing together. 2 that part of a church occupied by the choir; the chancel.

choke *v.* 1 to smother. 2 to block up. 3 to catch the breath.

choose *v.* to select; to decide between.

chop *v.* to cut with short down-strokes; to cut into small pieces.

choral *adj.* sung by a chorus or choir.

chord *n.* 1 two or more musical notes in harmony. 2 a string of a musical instrument. 3 the straight line joining the ends of an arc of a circle.

chorister *n.* a member of a choir.

chorus *n.* music which all join in singing.

chosen *adj.* picked; selected.

chrysalis *n.* (pron. KRIS-a-lis) an insect covered by a hard case just before it develops wings; pupa; cocoon. *pl.* CHRYSALISES.

christen *v.* to baptise and name. CHRISTENING *n.*

Christian *adj.* of or belonging to Christ and His teaching, or to His followers. CHRISTIAN *n.* a believer in Christ's teaching. CHRISTIANITY *n.* the Christian religion.

Christmas *n.* the festival celebrating Christ's birth (25th December).

chronicle *n.* a written record of historical events.

chronological *adj.* (particularly of events) arranged in time order. CHRONOLOGY *n.*

chub *n.* a freshwater fish in the carp family.

chuckle *v.* to laugh quietly. CHUCKLE *n.* an amused laugh held back or suppressed.

church *n.* a building set apart for worship.

Church *n.* the whole body of Christians.

churchyard *n.* a burial-ground next to or surrounding a church.

churn *n.* 1 a butter-making machine. 2 a large milk can. CHURN *v.* to make butter.

chute *n.* 1 a sloping trough or slide. 2 an abbreviation for PARACHUTE.

cider *n.* a fermented drink made from apple juice.

cigarette *n.* tobacco rolled in paper for smoking.

cinder *n.* a substance burnt, but not to ashes. CINDERY *adj.*

cinema *n.* a moving-picture theatre.

cinquain *n.* a 5-line poem (similar to a HAIKU) with a total of 22 syllables (in the pattern 2,4,5,8,2).

cipher *n.* 1 a zero or nought (0). 2 a code. CIPHER *v.* 1 to count; to calculate. 2 to write in code.

circle *n.* 1 a perfect ring. 2 a group of people who have a common interest. CIRCLE *v.* to revolve.

circuit *n.* 1 a complete (circular) path that electricity can flow through. 2 in sport, a circular track; a number of activities arranged in a circle.

circular *adj.* round; ring-like; moving in a circle. CIRCULAR *n.* a notice or letter, many copies of which are distributed.

circulate *v.* to distribute; to go or spread around.

circulation *n.* 1 distribution. 2 the movement of blood around the body.

circumference *n.* the line enclosing a circle; the distance round anything circular in form.

circumstance *n.* a particular incident; a fact.

circus *n.* a travelling show of horse riders, acrobats, clowns, etc. *pl.* CIRCUSES.

cistern *n.* a water-storage tank.

citizen *n.* 1 an inhabitant of a town or city. 2 a member of a country or nation.

ity *n.* an important town. *pl.* CITIES.
THE CITY = London's business centre.

ivic *adj.* concerned with a citizen or city.

ivil *adj.* 1 concerned with a nation or community. 2 courteous.

ivilian *n.* one not serving in the armed forces.

ivilisation *n.* socially and culturally developed communities and nations.

ivilise *v.* to educate, enlighten and develop socially.

laim *v.* to demand as a right. CLAIM *n.* a demand for something regarded as a right.

lamber *v.* to climb by clinging; to scramble.

lamp *v.* to grip together. CLAMP *n.* 1 a device for holding things together firmly. 2 a pile of potatoes, turnips, etc. stored under earth and straw.

lan *n.* a tribe united under a chieftain. CLANNISH *adj.*

lang *n.* the loud, ringing sound of a heavy bell or cymbal. CLANG *v.*

lap *v.* to strike the hands together in applause. CLAP *n.* 1 the sound of clapping. 2 a peal of thunder. CLAPPING *adj.*

larinet *n.* a musical wind instrument.

lasp *v.* 1 to grasp. 2 to embrace. 3 to buckle. CLASP *n.* 1 a grasp. 2 an embrace. 3 a buckle.

class *n.* a group of persons or things of the same kind. CLASS *v.* to place in a class.

classic *n.* a model example; the best kind. CLASSIC *adj.*

classify *v.* to sort into kinds or groups.

clatter *v.* to rattle noisily. CLATTER *n.* a repeated rattling noise.

clause *n.* 1 a part of a sentence containing a verb. 2 a complete paragraph in an agreement.

claw *n.* an animal's hooked nail; a talon. CLAW *v.* to tear or scratch with claws.

clay *n.* moist, sticky earth.

clean *v.* to free from dirt or smoke. CLEAN *adj.* fresh; pure. CLEAN *adv.* altogether; completely.

clear *v.* 1 to make or become clear. 2 to prove innocent. 3 to pass over or by without touching, esp. by jumping. CLEAR *adj.* 1 distinct. 2 open. 3 transparent.

clench *v.* to close teeth or fingers tightly. CLENCHED *adj.*

clergy *n. pl.* ministers of the Church. CLERGYMAN, CLERGYWOMAN *n.*

clerihew *n.* a 4-line comic poem with two rhyming couplets (named after its inventor).

clerk *n.* (pron. KLARK) a person employed in an office, bank, etc., to make entries, keep accounts, etc.

clever *adj.* quick to learn and understand; talented.

cliché *n.* a phrase which has been used too many times, so that it has lost meaning, e.g. her eyes shone like stars.

client *n.* someone who employs the services of a professional person.

cliff *n.* a steep rock-face.

climate *n.* the normal weather over a region or zone.

climax *n.* 1 the highest point; turning point. 2 the most exciting part of a book or film.

climb *v.* to ascend; to go up or down; to grow upwards. CLIMBER *n.*

cling (to) *v.* to hold firmly (to). CLINGING *adj.*

clip *v.* to cut; to trim. CLIP *n.* a fastener.

cloak *v.* to screen; to hide. CLOAK *n.* 1 a sleeveless outer garment. 2 a pretence.

clock *n.* an instrument for measuring time.

close *v.* (pron. KLOZE) 1 to shut. 2 to bring or come to an end. 3 to draw nearer. CLOSE *n.* the end; conclusion. CLOSED *adj.*

close *adj.* (pron. KLOSE) 1 near. 2 hot and stuffy. 3 secret. CLOSENESS *n.* CLOSELY *adv.*

cloth *n.* a woven material.

clothe *v.* to dress; to provide with clothes.

clothes *n. pl.* garments.

clothing *n.* garments.

cloud *v.* to darken; to obscure. CLOUD *n.* a mass of watery vapour, dust or smoke floating in the air.

club *n.* 1 a heavy stick or cudgel. 2 a stick used in golf, etc. 3 a society or its meeting-place. CLUB *v.* to beat with a club. TO CLUB TOGETHER to unite.

clue *n.* a hint or idea that helps to solve a puzzle or mystery.

clump *n*. a group of trees or plants. CLUMP *v*. to walk heavily.

clumsy *adj*. awkward; tactless. CLUMSILY *adj*.

cluster *v*. to form a group. CLUSTER *n*. a bunch; a group.

clutch *v*. to grasp at; to hold tightly. CLUTCH *n*. 1 a grip. 2 a set of eggs. 3 a device for connecting two moving parts of a machine.

clutter *v*. to make untidy. CLUTTER *n*. untidiness.

coach *n*. a large, covered road or rail carriage. COACHMAN *n*.

coach *v*. to teach. COACH *n*. a teacher. COACHING *n*.

coal *n*. a hard, black mineral used as fuel.

coarse *adj*. 1 rough. 2 rude. COARSELY *adv*.

coast *n*. the land bordering the sea. COASTAL *adj*.

coaster *n*. a vessel trading between home ports.

coat *v*. to cover; to spread over. COAT *n*. 1 an outer garment. 2 an animal's fur or hair. 3 a layer of paint, etc.

coax *v*. to persuade gently. COAXING *n*. & *adj*.

cobble *v*. 1 to mend or patch (esp. shoes). 2 to pave with cobble-stones. COBBLE *n*. a worn, round stone used for paving.

cobra *n*. a poisonous, hooded snake.

cocaine *n*. a drug used to deaden pain.

cock *n*. 1 a male bird. 2 a tap or valve controlling the flow of a liquid or gas.

cocoa *n*. 1 a drink made from the powdered seeds of the cacao tree. 2 a powder used to make chocolate.

coconut *n*. a large nut, fruit of the coco-palm, containing a white liquid and edible tissue.

cocoon *n*. a silky case spun by many insects to protect themselves in the pupal stage.

cod *n*. a large, edible sea-fish.

code *n*. 1 a set of laws or rules. 2 words or signs having a secret meaning. 3 an agreed set of symbols. CODE *v*. to give words a secret meaning.

coffee *n*. 1 the roasted and ground beans of the coffee tree. 2 a hot drink made from roasted and ground coffee beans.

cog *n*. a tooth on the rim of a wheel.

coherent *adj*. logical, makes sense. COHERE *v*. to hold together; to be logical.

coil *v*. to wind in loops. COIL *n*. a length wound in loops.

coin *n*. a metal piece of money. COIN *v*. 1 to mak into money; to mint. 2 to invent a new word or phrase.

coinage *n*. the money in general use in a country

coincide *v*. 1 to agree or fit exactly. 2 to happen at the same time. COINCIDENCE *n*.

cold *adj*. 1 low in temperature. 2 unfriendly. COLD *n*. a chill.

collaborate *v*. to work with someone else on a project or task. COLLABORATION *n*. COLLABORATIVE *adj*.

collage *n*. an artistic arrangement of pieces of paper, cloth, photographs, etc. stuck onto a surface.

collapse *n*. a sudden failure. COLLAPSE *v*. to fall down; to give way.

collar *n*. a neckband. COLLAR *v*. to seize; to grasp.

collect *v*. to gather together, to accumulate.

collection *n*. money collected; set of things collected.

collide *v*. to come into collision.

colliery *n*. a coal-mine. *pl*. COLLIERIES.

colon *n*. a punctuation mark (:) used to introduce a list, a quotation or extra information.

colonel *n*. (pron. KER-nel) a senior army officer who usually commands a regiment.

colony *n*. 1 a settlement formed in a new land by emigrants, or a group of people forming a community in a town. 2 a settled swarm of insects, birds, etc.

colossal *adj*. vast; very large.

colour *v*. 1 to dye; to paint. 2 to exaggerate. COLOUR *n*. 1 any particular hue. 2 paint.

colt *n*. a young horse. *fem*. FILLY.

column *n*. 1 an upright pillar. 2 a vertical row of figures or printing. 3 troops in marching order.

coma *n*. a prolonged unconscious state.

comb *v*. 1 to draw a comb through. 2 to search very carefully. COMB *n*. 1 a toothed implement for dressing the hair. 2 a cock's crest. 3 bees' storage place for honey.

combat *v*. to fight against; to oppose. COMBAT *n*. a fight; a struggle.

combination *n*. a union of things or people.

combine *v*. (pron. kom-BINE) to unite; to join together.

come *v.* to move towards; to arrive.

comedian *n.* an actor who takes comic parts. *fem.* COMEDIENNE.

comedy *n.* an amusing play, film or incident.

comet *n.* a spherical body, smaller than a planet, moving through space with a shining "tail" that always points away from the sun.

comfort *v.* to console; to cheer; to soothe. COMFORT *n.* ease, contentment; consolation.

comfortable *adj.* cosy; happy; easy.

comic *adj.* funny; laughable. COMIC *n.* a comic actor or person.

coming *adj.* approaching; future.

comma *n.* a punctuation mark indicating a short pause (,).

command *v.* to order; to be in command. COMMAND *n.* an order.

commander *n.* someone who commands.

commando *n.* 1 a soldier trained for a special mission. 2 a small body of hand-picked troops.

commence *v.* to begin.

comment *v.* to make remarks; to say.

commentary *n.* a series of comments. *pl.* COMMENTARIES.

commentator *n.* someone who comments in written or spoken words.

commercial *adj.* concerning trade.

commit *v.* 1 to do; to perform (a crime). 2 to entrust (something to someone's care). 3 COMMIT TO to imprison.

committee *n.* a body of people chosen to deal with some special business.

common *adj.* 1 ordinary. 2 shared by many. 3 vulgar. COMMON *n.* an area of public land.

Commons *n. pl.* 1 Members of the House of Commons as a body. 2 the House of Commons.

commonwealth *n.* a self-governing state or states. THE COMMONWEALTH the British Commonwealth of Britain and its member nations; Canada, Australia, New Zealand, etc.

commotion *n.* a noisy confusion; disturbance.

communicate *v.* to make known; to correspond with.

community *n.* a group of people living in one place. *pl.* COMMUNITIES.

compact *adj.* (pron. kom-PACT) 1 closely packed. 2 concise.

compact disc *n.* (pron. KOM-pact) a disc on which music or other information can be digitally recorded.

companion *n.* a person who accompanies another; a friend; an associate. COMPANIONSHIP *n.*

company *n.* a group of people; an assembly; a business. *pl.* COMPANIES.

compare *v.* to liken.

comparison *n.* likeness; similarity.

compartment *n.* a separate section.

compass *n.* an instrument for showing magnetic north. COMPASS *v.* to go round; to encircle.

compasses *n. pl.* an instrument for drawing circles and arcs.

compel *v.* to force; to make. COMPELLING *adj.*

compete *v.* to strive against others.

competition *n.* a contest; rivalry. COMPETITOR *n.*

compile *v.* to collect; to make a book by collecting information. COMPILATION *n.*

complain *v.* to express dissatisfaction or discontent.

complaint *n.* 1 a grievance. 2 an ailment.

complete *adj.* whole; finished; thorough. COMPLETE *v.* to finish.

complicate *v.* to entangle; to make difficult.

compliment *v.* to praise; to congratulate. COMPLIMENT *n.* a tribute.

component *v.* one of the parts that forms a whole.

compose *v.* 1 to form by putting parts together. 2 to arrange.

composition *n.* 1 the act of composing. 2 a mixture. 3 a painting, a photograph, or a piece of writing or music.

compost *n.* a mixture of decaying natural waste (plants, food, etc.) used to improve soil and to help other plants grown.

compound *v.* (pron. kom-POUND) to mix; to combine. COMPOUND *n.* (pron. KOM-pound) a mixture.

COMPOUND WORD *n.* a word made up of two other words, e.g. football, broomstick.

comprehension *n.* understanding.

comprehensive *adj.* wide; complete; all-embracing.

compress *v.* to press or squeeze tightly together; to reduce in length or size. COMPRESSION *n.*

comprise *v.* to consist of; to include.

compulsion *n.* a strong impulse.

compulsory *adj.* requiring to be done; enforced.

compute *v.* to reckon; to calculate.

computer *n.* an electrical machine which can calculate and store and retrieve information.

concave *adj.* hollow, saucer-like in shape; opposite to CONVEX.

conceal *v.* to hide; to keep secret.

concede *v.* to allow; to grant; to admit.

conceit *n.* vanity. CONCEITED *adj.*

conceive *v.* 1 to imagine; to think. 2 to become pregnant. CONCEIVABLE *adj.*

concentrate *v.* 1 to bring to one point. 2 to focus on. 3 to make stronger.

concern *v.* 1 to affect; to interest.
2 BE CONCERNED ABOUT to be anxious about. CONCERN *n.* 1 interest. 2 anxiety. 3 a business.

concert *n.* a musical entertainment.

concise *adj.* brief; in a few words.

conclude *v.* 1 to finish; to bring to an end. 2 to decide.

conclusion *n.* 1 an end. 2 a decision.

conclusive *adj.* 1 convincing. 2 definite.

concord *n.* agreement; harmony.

concrete *adj.* real; definite. CONCRETE *n.* a mixture of cement, gravel and water that is used in building.

concussion *n.* 1 a violent shock.
2 unconsciousness caused by a heavy blow.

condemn *v.* 1 to blame. 2 to sentence to punishment.

condensation *n.* 1 the changing of a vapour gas into a liquid. 2 reduction in volume or size.

condense *v.* 1 to reduce in size. 2 to change a vapour gas into a liquid.

condenser *n.* 1 apparatus for cooling vapour gas so that it changes into a liquid. 2 a device for collecting electricity.

condition *n.* state.

condone *v.* 1 to overlook an offence. 2 to forgive.

conduct *n.* (pron. KON-duct) 1 management. 2 behaviour. CONDUCT *v.* (pron. kon-DUCT) 1 to lead; to guide. 2 to convey; to transmit. 3 to behave.

conductor *n.* 1 a guide; a leader. 2 a carrier; a transmitter. 3 a material that allows heat or electricity to pass through it.
fem. CONDUCTRESS.

conduit *n.* a channel or pipe; a tube protecting electric cables.

cone *n.* 1 a solid body tapering from a circular base to a point. 2 the fruit of a coniferous tree. CONICAL *adj.* cone-shaped.

conference *n.* a meeting for discussion.

confess *v.* to make a confession; to admit. CONFESSOR *n.*

confession *n.* an admission.

confetti *n.* small pieces of coloured paper thrown by guests at a wedding.

confidence *n.* trust; belief in; self-reliance.

confidential *adj.* secret; private; not to be told to others.

confinement *n.* 1 being confined; imprisonment. 2 being in bed for the birth of a child.

confirm *v.* 1 to strengthen. 2 to prove (something) to be true.

confirmation *n.* 1 proof; certainty. 2 admission to Church membership. CONFIRMATIVE *adj.*

confiscate *v.* 1 to take for public use. 2 to take forcibly.

conflict *n.* (pron. KON-flict) 1 a struggle. 2 a contest. CONFLICT *v.* (pron. kon-FLICT) to disagree; to oppose.

conform *v.* to behave according to rule, custom or law; to comply.

confound *v.* to confuse; to defeat.

confront *v.* to face; to oppose. CONFRONTING *adj.* CONFRONTATION *n.*

confuse *v.* 1 to mix up. 2 to bewilder.

confusion *n.* 1 a mixture; disorder. 2 embarrassment. 3 tumult; ruin.

congeal *v.* to become solid by cooling; to stiffen.

congratulate *v.* to offer good wishes to.

congregate *v.* to gather together; to assemble.

congregation *n.* a gathering of people for religious worship.

congress *n.* 1 an assembly of delegates. 2 Congress – the parliament of the United States of America.

congruent *adj.* in maths, having the same size and shape as another.

conifer *n.* a cone-bearing tree. CONIFEROUS *adj.*

conjunction *n.* 1 a connection. 2 a word used to join sentences, e.g. and, but, so.

conjure *v.* to work magic; to perform tricks.

connect *v.* to join; to fasten; to link. CONNECTION *n.*

connective *n.* a word which connects different parts of a text.

conquer *v.* to defeat; to overcome. CONQUEROR *n.* a person who conquers a town, country or people.

conquest *n.* the act of conquering; capture.

conscience *n.* the sense of right and wrong.

conscientious *adj.* careful; thorough; honest.

conscious *adj.* awake; knowing; aware.

conscript *n.* (pron. KON-script) a person compelled to serve in the armed forces. CONSCRIPT *v.* (pron. kon-SCRIPT).

consecutive *adj.* following one after the other and in order.

consent *v.* to agree. CONSENT *n.* permission; agreement.

conservation *n.* preservation; prevention of waste.

conservative *adj.* disliking change; moderate. CONSERVATIVE *n.* a person or party opposed to rapid political and social change.

conserve *v.* to preserve; to keep from damage or loss. CONSERVE *n.* a preserve; jam.

consider *v.* to think about; to reflect; to allow for.

considerate *adj.* thoughtful for others. CONSIDERATION *n.*

consign *v.* to send goods or a person to a destination.

consignment *n.* a load; a shipment.

consist *v.* to be composed of.

console *v.* to give comfort to. CONSOLATION *n.* comfort, relief.

consonant *n.* a letter denoting a speech sound other than a vowel.

conspiracy *n.* a plot. *pl.* CONSPIRACIES. CONSPIRATOR *n.*

constable *n.* a policeman or policewoman.

constant *adj.* unchanging; unceasing; faithful.

constantly *adv.* always; often.

constellation *n.* a group of stars forming a system and having a name, e.g. Andromeda.

consternation *n.* surprise and dismay.

constituency *n.* the area, or the voters in the area, represented by a Member of Parliament.

constrict *v.* to press together tightly; to squeeze.

construct *v.* to make. to build; to fit together.

construction *n.* something constructed.

consul *n.* a country's agent in a foreign country. CONSULATE *n.* the office of a consul. CONSULAR *adj.*

consult *v.* to seek information or advice.

consume *v.* 1 to use up. 2 to eat. 3 to destroy.

consumer *n.* 1 a user; a buyer. 2 in a food chain, any animal that consumes (eats) food.

consumption *n.* 1 the amount used. 2 a lung disease.

contact *v.* to touch; to meet. CONTACT *n.* an electrical connection.

contagious *adj.* catching; spread by touching.

contain *v.* to hold within; to enclose; to include. CONTAINER *n.*

contaminate *v.* 1 to infect. 2 to make dirty or impure.

contemplate *v.* 1 to think about; to study. 2 to intend.

contempt *n.* scorn; disregard.

contend *v.* 1 to fight. 2 to argue. 3 to compete. CONTENDER *n.*

content *n.* (pron. KON-tent) the amount contained. CONTENT *v.* (pron. kon-TENT) to satisfy. CONTENT(ED) *adj.* satisfied; pleased.

contents *n. pl.* 1 that which is contained. 2 a list of matters written about in a book.

contest *v.* (pron. kon-TEST) to dispute; to compete; to argue against. CONTEST *n.* (pron. KON-test) 1 a fight or struggle. 2 a competition.

continent *n.* one of the large land masses of the Earth's surface. CONTINENTAL *adj.*

continual *adj.* always happening; very frequent.

continuation *n.* an extension; an addition.

continue *v.* to go on; to prolong.

continuous *adj.* unbroken; non-stop.

contour *n.* an outline; a shape.

contract *n.* (pron. KON-tract) a written agreement. CONTRACT *v.* (pron. kon-TRACT) to become smaller or shorter.

contraction *n.* a shortened word or two words shortened to make one, e.g. do not → don't, cannot → can't (see APOSTROPHE).

contractor n. a person who undertakes to do certain work or to supply goods.

contradict v. to deny (something); to speak against (someone). CONTRADICTION n.

contralto n. the lowest singing voice for women.

contrary adj. opposite; against. CONTRARY n. the opposite or different opinion, intention or action.

contrast n. opposite; a difference; an unlikeness. CONTRAST v. to compare so as to find or show differences.

contribute v. to give something; to help; to pay a share.

control v. to regulate; to guide. CONTROL n. authority; power.

conundrum n. a riddle; a puzzle.

conurbation n. a group of towns which have expanded to make one large urban area.

convenience n. handiness; suitability.

convenient adj. handy; suitable.

convent n. religious community, esp. of nuns.

converge v. to approach a point from different directions, and as if to meet or join together.

conversation n. talk between two or more people.

conversion n. a change from one belief, side, etc., to another.

convert v. (pron. kon-VERT) to change. CONVERT n. (pron. KON-vert) one who has changed.

convex adj. curved outwards; the opposite of CONCAVE.

convey v. 1 to carry; to transport. 2 to transfer property.

convict v. (pron. kon-VICT) to prove guilty. CONVICT n. (pron KON-vict) an imprisoned criminal.

conviction n. 1 a proving of guilt. 2 a firm belief.

convince v. to make someone feel sure; to satisfy.

convoy n. 1 a protected fleet of ships. 2 a column of vehicles. CONVOY v. to guard on a journey.

cook v. to prepare food by heating. COOK n. a person who cooks food.

cool adj. 1 slightly cold. 2 calm. COOL v. 1 to make colder. 2 to become calmer.

coolly adv. calmly; without excitement.

co-operate (with) v. to work together; to help one another.

co-operation n. working together to help one another; mutual aid.

co-operative adj. ready to help.

cope v. to handle successfully.

copper n. a hard, reddish-brown metal. COPPERY adj.

coppice n. a small wood of young trees; a copse.

copse n. See COPPICE.

copy v. to imitate. COPY n. an imitation. pl. COPIES.

cord n. strong, thick string, or rope.

cordon n. a line or ring of guards or police. CORDON v. to close off an area.

core n. the inner part of anything.

cork n. the bark of the cork-oak and the bottle stopper made from it. CORK v. to stop or plug with a cork.

cormorant n. a diving sea-bird.

corn n. 1 the seeds of wheat, barley, oats, etc; cereals. 1 a painful hard growth on a toe.

corner n. the place where two lines, walls, streets, etc., meet. CORNER v. to drive into a trap.

cornet n. a brass or silver trumpet; formerly a junior cavalry officer.

coronation n. the ceremony of crowning a king or queen.

corporal n. a non-commissioned officer of the army or air force. CORPORAL adj. bodily.

corporation n. 1 a large trading concern. 2 the body of persons governing a city or town.

corpse n. a dead body.

correct adj. right; true; accurate. CORRECT v. 1 to put right. 2 to mark for errors. 3 to punish.

correction n. 1 the correcting of something. 2 punishment.

correspond v. 1 to be similar (to). 2 CORRESPOND WITH to exchange letters.

correspondence n. 1 similarity. 2 letters.

corridor n. a passageway.

corrode v. to wear away; to destroy gradually. CORROSION n. CORROSIVE adj.

corrupt v. 1 to decay. 2 to make another person dishonest. CORRUPT adj. 1 rotten. 2 dishonest.

cosily adv. snugly; comfortably.

cosmic rays *n. pl.* radioactive particles which reach the Earth from outer space.

cosmonaut *n.* a person who travels in space *(R);* an astronaut.

cost *v.* to have a price or value. COST *n.* the price.

costly *adj.* highly-priced; expensive.

costume *n.* style of dress.

cosy *adj.* snug; comfortable. COSY *n.* a padded covering for a teapot.

cot *n.* a child's bed; a crib.

cottage *n.* a small house, esp. in the country.

cotton *n.* 1 a plant bearing soft, white down, 2 thread or cloth made from this.

cough *n.* a sudden, noisy outburst of air from the lungs. COUGH *v.*

council *n.* a group of people appointed or elected to advise and make decisions.

councillor *n.* a member of a council.

counsel *v.* to advise. COUNSEL *n.* 1 a lawyer; a barrister. 2 advice.

counsellor *n.* an adviser; someone who counsels.

count *v.* to number; to reckon; to matter. COUNT *n.* the act of counting.

counter *v.* to oppose. COUNTER *n.* 1 a serving-point in a shop or bank. 2 a small disc or token used in scoring.

countless *adj.* too many to count; very many.

country *n.* 1 any separate land or nation. 2 rural areas. *pl.* COUNTRIES. COUNTRY *adj.* belonging to the country; rural.

county *n.* a division of the country.

couple *v.* to link two things together. COUPLE *n.* a pair; two of a kind.

couplet *n.* two lines of poetry sharing length or rhyme.

coupon *n.* a ticket exchangeable for something.

courage *n.* bravery; lack of fear.

courageous *adj.* brave; fearless. COURAGEOUSLY *adv.*

courier *n.* a messenger; a guide on holiday tours.

course *n.* 1 the path or direction in which anything moves. 2 a ground used for a sport. 3 a line of bricks or stones in a wall. 4 a part of a meal.

court *v.* to try to please. COURT *n.* 1 a place of justice. 2 a ruler's palace. 3 a yard. 4 a quadrangle for games such as tennis.

courteous *adj.* respectful; polite; considerate.

courtesy *n.* polite and considerate behaviour.

cousin *n.* the son or daughter of an uncle or aunt.

cover *v.* 1 to spread over. 2 to hide. 3 to include. COVER *n.* 1 something that covers. 2 a shelter or hiding-place.

covet *v.* to desire greatly; to envy.

cow *n.* female of the ox, elephant, whale, etc. COW *v.* to make afraid; to intimidate.

coward *n.* a person without courage.

coxswain *n.* (pron. KOKS-n) a boat's steersman.

crab *n.* an edible shellfish with five pairs of legs.

crack *v.* 1 to split or break apart. 2 to make a sharp, snapping noise. CRACK *n.* 1 a small opening or split. 2 a snapping noise. CRACKED *adj.*

crackle *n.* a crisp noise.

cradle *n.* 1 a rocking bed for a baby. 2 a frame used as a support. CRADLE *v.* to lay or rock in a cradle or in the arms.

craft *n.* 1 a skill. 2 a ship or an aircraft. 3 a trade. 4 cunning.

craftily *adv.* cunningly.

craftsman *n.* a person skilled in a craft or trade.

crafty *adj.* sly; cunning.

crag *n.* a steep, rugged rock.

cram *v.* to pack tightly; to overfill.

cramp *v.* to restrict; to tighten. CRAMP *n.* 1 a sudden, severe pain in a muscle; a spasm. 2 a clamp.

crane *n.* 1 a machine for raising and lowering heavy weights. 2 a long-necked wading bird. CRANE *v.* to thrust the chest and neck forward.

crank *v.* to wind; to turn a handle. CRANK *n.* 1 a bend; turn. 2 a person with odd ideas.

crash *n.* 1 the loud noise of things breaking. 2 a sudden failure or ruin, esp. in business. CRASH *v.* 1 to break noisily. 2 to fail; to become bankrupt. 3 to collide.

crate *n.* a large packing-case.

crater *n.* 1 the mouth of a volcano. 2 a hollow in the ground caused by an explosion.

crave *v.* to beg for; to long for.

crawl *v.* to creep on hands and knees. CRAWL *n.* a swimming stroke.

crayon *n*. 1 a pencil or stick of coloured chalk. 2 a drawing made with crayons. CRAYON *v*. to sketch with crayons.

craze *n*. a popular fashion; a fad.

crazy *adj*. 1 mad; foolish. 2 made of odd pieces, as crazy paving.

creak *n*. a sharp, grating sound. CREAK *v*. to make such a noise.

cream *n*. 1 the rich, fatty substance which rises to the surface on milk. 2 the best part of anything. CREAM OFF *v*. to remove the best of anything. CREAMY *adj*.

crease *n*. 1 a line or mark made by folding. 2 a line marked on a cricket pitch to define the position of batsman and bowler.

create *v*. 1 to make; to invent. 2 to make a fuss. CREATION *n*.

creature *n*. a living person or animal.

credit *n*. 1 a good reputation. 2 allowing a deferred payment. CREDIT *v*. to believe; to trust.

creditor *n*. a person to whom a debt is owed.

credulous *adj*. willing to believe.

creed *n*. a summary of beliefs.

creek *n*. a narrow coastal inlet; a small stream.

creep *v*. 1 to move close to the ground. 2 to move silently on tiptoe. 3 to grow along the ground or up a wall.

creeper *n*. 1 one who creeps. 2 a climbing plant.

cremate *v*. to burn (a body) to ashes.

crescent *adj*. shaped like a new moon.

crest *n*. 1 a tuft or comb on a bird's head. 2 a design on a coat of arms. 3 the top of a hill or wave.

crevice *n*. a crack or narrow opening, esp. in rock.

crew *n*. 1 the people manning a ship, aircraft or train. 2 a gang; a mob.

crib *n*. a child's cot; a manger. CRIB *v*. to cheat; to copy unfairly.

cricket *n*. 1 an outdoor game for two teams, eleven a side, played with ball, bats and wickets. 2 a small jumping, chirping insect.

crime *n*. an offence or offences against the law; sin.

criminal *adj*. concerned with crime. CRIMINAL *n*. someone who has committed a crime.

crimson *n*. a deep red colour. CRIMSON *adj*.

cringe *v*. to crouch; to shrink from in fear.

cripple *v*. to disable; to ruin. CRIPPLE *n*. a lame or disabled person.

crisis *n*. a turning-point; a time of emergency. *pl* CRISES (pron CRY-sees).

crisp, *adj*. brittle; hard but fragile.

criteria *n. pl*. the standards or reasons used to reach a decision. *sing*. CRITERION.

critic *n*. a person who examines and judges; a faultfinder.

criticise *v*. to examine and judge; to find fault with.

criticism *n*. an opinion; a judgement; disapproval.

crocodile *n*. a large four-footed aquatic reptile with a scaly skin (see ALLIGATOR).

croft *n*. a small farm or enclosed piece of land.

crook *n*. 1 a hook; a hooked staff. 2 a criminal.

crooked *adj*. 1 bent. 2 dishonest.

crop *v*. 1 to harvest. 2 to cut short. CROP *n*. 1 the produce of field or farm. 2 a riding-whip. 3 the first stomach of many birds.

cross *n*. 1 anything X-shaped. 2 a monument. CROSS *v*. 1 to pass from one side to the other. 2 to oppose. 3 to make angry. CROSS *adj*. annoyed. CROSSLY *adv*.

crotchet *n*. a black-headed music note with a stem, equal to half a minim. (♩)

crouch *v*. to stoop with the knees bent; to bend down. CROUCH *n*. stooping; bending.

crow *v*. 1 to boast. 2 to make a sound like a cock. CROW *n*. 1 a large black bird. 2 a cock's cry.

crowd *n*. a large number of persons or things. CROWD *v*. 1 to pack closely together; to cram. 2 to gather in a large number.

crown *n*. 1 the head-dress worn by a king or queen on special occasions. 2 the top of many objects. CROWN *v*. 1 to place a crown on. 2 to reward.

crucify *v*. to put to death on a cross.

crude *adj*. raw; rough; coarse. CRUDELY *adv*.

cruel *adj*. liking to cause pain. CRUELLY *adv*.

cruelty *n*. cruel action or behaviour.

cruise *v*. to sail about; to travel at random. CRUISE *n*. a sea voyage for pleasure.

cruiser *n*. a fast warship; a small boat for pleasure cruising.

crumb *n.* a small fragment, esp. of bread. CRUMB *v.* to cover with crumbs.

crumble *v.* to break into crumbs.

crumpet *n.* a soft cake eaten toasted with butter.

crumple *v.* to crush out of shape. CRUMPLE *n.* a wrinkle; a crease.

crunch *v.* 1 to crush with the teeth. 2 to grind underfoot. CRUNCH *n.* the noise of chewing or grinding.

crusade *v.* to fight or campaign for a cause. CRUSADE *n.* 1 a war between Christians and Muslims in the Middle Ages. 2 activity in support of a cause.

crush *v.* 1 to squeeze together or squash. 2 to overcome; to ruin. CRUSH *n.* a closely-packed crowd.

crust *n.* a hard coating, rind or shell.

cry *v.* 1 to shed tears. 2 to shout; to yell. CRY *n.* a sob; a shout. *pl.* CRIES.

crying *adj.* 1 shedding tears. 2 calling for notice. CRYING *n.* the act or sound of crying.

crystal *n.* 1 a glass-like stone having all its faces flat. 2 a gem. CRYSTAL *adj.* clear; transparent.

cub *n.* 1 the young of such animals as the bear, fox, lion, etc. 2 a junior Scout.

cube *n.* a solid body with six equal square sides or faces.

cubic *adj.* 1 having the shape of a cube. 2 having volume, capacity.

cubicle *n.* a small partitioned compartment.

cuckoo *n.* a bird that lays its eggs in the nests of other birds.

cucumber *n.* a long, green vegetable eaten as salad.

cue *n.* 1 a sign; a hint. 2 a tapering stick used in playing billiards and snooker.

cuff *n.* 1 a slap. 2 the end of a sleeve. CUFF *v.* to strike with the open hand.

cull *v.* 1 to pick here and there. 2 to select and kill (surplus deer, seals, etc.). 3 to gather.

culprit *n.* an offender; a guilty person.

cultivate *v.* 1 to prepare the ground and grow crops. 2 to develop or improve. 3 to give attention to.

cultivation *n.* the practice of cultivating.

cumulus *n.* white, woolly clouds heaped one above the other. *pl.* CUMULI.

cunning *adj.* skilful; crafty in a sly way. CUNNING *n.* skill; deceit.

cup *n.* 1 a small drinking-vessel, usually with a handle. 2 ornamental cup used as a prize or trophy. CUP *v.* to place the hands in the form of a cup.

curable *adj.* that can be cured or healed.

curate *n.* a clergyman who assists a rector, vicar or parish priest.

curator *n.* a person in charge of a museum, an art gallery, etc.

curb *v.* to check; to restrain. CURB *n.* a check; a bridle. CURBING *adj.*

curd *n.* thick sour milk, used in making cheese.

cure *v.* 1 to heal; to restore. 2 to preserve foodstuffs by salting and drying. CURE *n.* 1 a remedy. 2 a recovery.

curfew *n.* an order to remain indoors after a stated time.

curio *n.* a rare and curious article.

curiosity *n.* 1 eagerness to find out. 2 inquisitiveness. 3 a strange or rare thing. *pl.* CURIOSITIES.

curious *adj.* 1 inquisitive. 2 eager to know. 3 strange or odd. CURIOUSLY *adv.*

curl *v.* to twist into ringlets; to bend into a curve. CURL *n.* 1 a ringlet. 2 a curving line or movement.

curlew *n.* a wading bird with a long, slender bill.

currant *n.* 1 a small dried grape. 2 a shrub bearing clusters of edible berries.

currency *n.* 1 money in use in a country. 2 time during which a thing is current.

current *n.* the flowing of a liquid (stream) or air (wind) or of electricity. CURRENT *adj.* 1 popular; in circulation. 2 of the present time; now.

curriculum *n.* a set course of study at a school or college.

curry *n.* a seasoning of mixed spices; a dish spiced with curry.

curse *v.* 1 to wish evil upon; to swear. 2 to harm. CURSE *n.* 1 an utterance wishing evil. 2 a great evil (e.g. warfare, epidemic, etc.) causing suffering.

curtain *n.* 1 a cloth hung to screen a window. 2 the cloth concealing the stage in a theatre. CURTAIN *v.* to enclose or provide with a curtain.

curve *n.* a line that bends without angles.
CURVE *v.* to bend or shape to form a curve.

cushion *n.* a bag stuffed with soft material, a pillow. CUSHION *v.* to lessen a shock or blow.

custard *n.* a mixture of milk, eggs and sugar, baked or boiled.

custody *n.* 1 care; safe keeping. 2 imprisonment before trial.

custom *n.* 1 a habit; usual practice. 2 support given to a business by its customers.
CUSTOMS *n. pl.* 1 a tax on imports. 2 the government department responsible for collecting this tax.

customer *n.* a regular buyer or user of a service.

cut *v.* to open, divide or slit with anything sharp. CUT *n.* 1 a wound from a sharp edge. 2 a piece of meat.

cuticle *n.* the outer layer of skin; skin at base of finger-nail or toe-nail.

cutlery *n.* knives, forks and spoons.

cycle *n.* 1 a series of events that is repeated constantly. 2 a bicycle, tricycle or motor cycle. CYCLE *v.* to ride a bicycle. CYCLIST *n.*

cyclone *n.* a violent storm in which the wind moves round a centre of low atmospheric pressure.

cygnet *n.* a young swan.

cylinder *n.* 1 a roll-shaped object. 2 part of a petrol or diesel engine.

cymbals *n. pl.* a pair of round brass plates used as a musical instrument.

D

dab *v.* to pat or touch gently and quickly.
DAB *n.* 1 a gentle pat. 2 a small blob or smear. 3 a flat-fish.

dad, daddy *n.* father.

daffodil *n.* a yellow spring flower, grown from a bulb.

daft *adj.* silly; foolish.

dagger *n.* a weapon with a short, pointed blade.

daily *adj.* every day. DAILY *n.* a newspaper published every weekday. *pl.* DAILIES.

dainty *adj.* small and delicate; pretty. DAINTY *n.* a delicacy.

dairy *n.* a building for keeping, processing or selling milk. *pl.* DAIRIES.
DAIRY PRODUCTS *n. pl.* butter, milk, yoghurts.

daisy *n.* a common wild flower with small white petals and a yellow centre.

dale *n.* a valley; a glen.

dam *v.* to hold back by means of a dam. DAM *n.* 1 a bank or wall to hold back water. 2 a mother, esp. of animals.

damage *v.* to cause injury; to hurt. DAMAGE *n.* injury, breakage or loss.

damp *n.* **dampness** *n.* moisture; slight wetness. DAMP *v.* 1 to moisten. 2 to discourage.

dance *v.* 1 to move rhythmically to music 2 to leap or jump about in a lively manner. DANCE *n.* 1 the act of dancing. 2 a social gathering at which people dance. DANCER *n.*

dandelion *n.* a yellow-flowered wild plant.

danger *n.* a risk or peril.

dangerous *adj.* unsafe; very risky.
DANGEROUSLY *adv.*

dangle *v.* to hold or hang loosely.

Danish *adj.* of or belonging to Denmark.
DANISH *n.* language of Denmark; the Danes.

dare *v.* to attempt; to challenge. DARE *n.* a challenge.

daring *adj.* bold; fearless. DARING *n.* boldness.

dark *adj.* without light; gloomy.

darkness *n.* 1 absence of light. 2 night.

dart *v.* to move quickly and suddenly.
DART *n.* 1 a quick, sudden movement. 2 a small arrow thrown by hand.

dash *v.* 1 to rush suddenly. 2 to throw violently. DASH *n.* 1 a rush. 2 a small amount. 3 a stroke in punctuation (–), used to add extra information (instead of a comma or semi-colon) or instead of brackets.

data *n. pl.* facts; information.

database *n.* a collection of information stored in such a way that it can easily be looked at or changed (usually on a computer).

date *n.* 1 the day, month and year. 2 the time of an event. 3 the fruit of the date-palm. DATE *v.* to give a date to.

daub *v.* 1 to smear. 2 to paint badly. DAUB *n.* a smear.

daughter *n.* a person's female child.

dawdle *v.* to loiter; to move slowly. DAWDLING *adj.*

dawn *v.* 1 to begin to grow light. 2 to grow clear. DAWN *n.* 1 the first light of day; daybreak. 2 a beginning.

day *n.* 1 the time between sunrise and sunset. 2 the twenty-four hours from one midnight to the next.

daze *v.* to confuse; to bewilder. DAZE *n.* a dazed state. DAZED *adj.*

dazzle *v.* 1 to blind with light. 2 to confuse. DAZZLE *n.* a confusing or blinding light.

dead *adj.* no longer alive; lifeless. DEAD *n. pl.* persons no longer alive.

deaf *adj.* unable or unwilling to hear. DEAFNESS *n.* inability to hear.

deal *v.* 1 to trade or do business with. 2 to hand out. 3 to deliver. DEAL *n.* 1 a business arrangement. 2 a large amount.

dear *adj.* 1 much loved; lovable. 2 costly; expensive. DEAR *n.* beloved; favourite.

death *n.* the end of life.

debate *v.* 1 to discuss. 2 to consider alternatives. DEBATE *n.* a discussion; a public argument.

debris *n.* (pron. DAY-bree) remains of something broken to pieces; wreckage; rubbish.

debt *n.* 1 money owing. 2 a duty or obligation. DEBTOR *n.*

decade *n.* a period of ten years.

decapitate *v.* to cut off the head of.

decay *v.* to rot; to wither. DECAY *n.* a wasting away; a ruined state. DECAYED *adj.*

decease *n.* death. DECEASE *v.* to die.

deceit *n.* misrepresentation; trick.

December *n.* the twelfth month of the year.

decent *adj.* 1 proper; respectable. 2 satisfactory; passable. DECENTLY *adv.*

deception *n.* 1 a trick; a fraud. 2 the act of deceiving.

deciduous *adj.* 1 shedding periodically. 2 losing leaves annually.

decimal *adj.* numbered by tens or tenths. DECIMAL *n.* a fraction in terms of tenths.

decimetre *n.* the tenth part of a metre.

decipher *v.* 1 to translate (a secret message). 2 to find the meaning of.

decision *n.* 1 the act of deciding. 2 conclusion reached. 3 firmness.

deck *n.* the floor of a ship or bus. DECK *v.* to decorate; to adorn.

declare *v.* 1 to announce or make known publicly. 2 to state at Customs the goods carried. 3 to end an innings in cricket before all the wickets have fallen. DECLARATION *n.*

decline *v.* 1 to refuse. 2 to slope down. 3 to weaken or worsen. DECLINE *n.* 1 a downward slope. 2 a weakening.

decode *v.* to change or translate a message so that it can be easily understood.

decorate *v.* 1 to make beautiful. 2 to paint or paper. 3 to give a medal or title. DECORATOR *n.*

decrease *v.* (pron. de-KREASE) to make or become less. DECREASE *n.* (pron. DEE-krease) a reduction; a lessening.

dedicate *v.* to devote to a particular purpose; to make sacred.

deduce *v.* to work out an answer by reasoning (thinking logically).

deduct *v.* to subtract; to take away.

deduction *n.* 1 the amount taken away. 2 the conclusion reached by reasoning.

deed *n.* 1 an action; something done. 2 a legal document.

deep *adj.* 1 reaching far down or far back. 2 intense or strong. 3 secretive; hard to understand. THE DEEP *n.* the sea.

deer *n.* a swift-running, cud-chewing, cloven-hoofed, four-footed mammal (the males usually have horns). DEER *pl.*

deface *v.* to spoil the appearance or beauty of. DEFACEMENT *n.*

defeat *v.* to beat in battle or contest; to conquer. DEFEAT *n.* the loss of a battle or contest.

defect *n.* (pron. DEE-fect) a fault; a flaw. DEFECT *v.* (pron. de-FECT) to desert.

defence *n.* 1 a means of protection. 2 fortifications. 3 argument against an accusation.

defend *v.* 1 to guard or protect against attack. 2 to argue in favour of.

defiant *adj.* openly disobedient; challenging. DEFIANTLY *adv.*

definite *adj*. exact, distinct; not doubtful. DEFINITELY *adv*.

definition *n*. 1 an explanation of the exact meaning of a word. 2 clearness; sharpness.

deflect *v*. to turn (something) aside or to change its course.

deform *v*. to spoil the shape of; to disfigure. DEFORMED *adj*.

defraud *v*. to take something by fraud; to cheat.

deft *adj*. quick and skilful. DEFTLY *adv*.

defy *v*. to challenge; to resist openly.

degree *n*. 1 a unit of measurement of temperature, angles, etc. 2 a step or stage. 3 a qualification given by a university or polytechnic.

delay *v*. to postpone; to hinder. DELAY *n*. a postponement; a hindrance.

delegate *v*. 1 to appoint and send as a representative. 2 to entrust (duties or responsibilities) to others. DELEGATE *n*. a person appointed to represent.

delegation *n*. 1 a group of delegates. 2 the act of delegating.

delete *v*. to erase or cross out. DELETION *n*.

deliberate *adj*. 1 intentional; done on purpose. DELIBERATE *v*. to discuss or think over carefully.

delicate *adj*. 1 fine; dainty; not strong. 2 sensitive. DELICATELY *adv*.

delicious *adj*. very pleasing to taste and eat.

delight *v*. 1 to give pleasure to (someone) or to receive pleasure from. 2 DELIGHT IN to take pleasure in. DELIGHT *n*. great pleasure; joy.

delightful *adj*. giving delight.

deliver *v*. 1 to hand over. 2 to rescue; to set free. 3 to help in the birth of.

delivery *n*. the act of delivering.

delta *n*. a triangle of land formed by the mouths of a large river.

deluge *n*. 1 a great flood or downpour. 2 a great quantity. DELUGE *v*. to overwhelm with a great quantity.

delve *v*. 1 to search carefully. 2 to dig.

demand *v*. to claim (something from someone) as a right; to ask firmly (for). DEMAND *n*. an urgent request or claim.

democracy *n*. government by representatives freely elected by the people.

DEMOCRATIC *adj*. elected by the people; fair.

demolish *v*. to destroy; to pull down.

demonstrate *v*. 1 to show clearly; to prove. 2 to take part in a demonstration.

demonstration *n*. 1 a practical display or explanation. 2 an organised expression of opinion or feeling by a procession or meeting.

den *n*. 1 a wild beast's lair. 2 a small private room or study.

denial *n*. 1 the refusal of a request. 2 a contradiction.

denominator *n*. the number below the line in a vulgar fraction.

denote *v*. 1 to stand for or to mean. 2 to indicate.

dense *adj*. 1 closely-packed. 2 stupid.

density *n*. 1 proportion of mass to volume. 2 crowded state.

dent *n*. a hollow in a surface caused by a blow or pressure. DENT *v*. to make a dent.

dental *adj*. concerned with the teeth or with dentists.

dentist *n*. a person qualified and skilled in the care of the teeth.

deny *v*. 1 to say something is untrue. 2 to refuse a request.

depart *v*. to go away; to leave; to set out.

department *n*. a separate division or section.

departure *n*. going away; leaving; setting out.

depend on or **upon** *v*. to rely on; to trust.

deport *v*. to expel from a country. DEPORTATION *n*.

deposit *v*. 1 to put or set something down. 2 to place money in a bank. 3 to give in part payment. DEPOSIT *n*. 1 a layer of solid matter. 2 money placed in a bank. 3 money given as part payment.

depot *n*. 1 a storehouse. 2 a garage for buses or lorries. 3 a military headquarters.

depress *v*. 1 to make sad or lower (a person's spirit). 2 to press down or in.

depression *n*. 1 mood of sadness or low spirits. 2 a hollow place on a surface. 3 an area of low atmospheric pressure. 4 a low level of trade, economy and employment.

deprive *v*. to take away (something) from (someone); to prevent (someone) from having. DEPRIVATION *n*.

depth *n.* distance downwards or inwards.

deputation *n.* a group of persons chosen to speak for others.

deputy *n.* a person acting in place of another.

derail *v.* to cause (a train or truck) to run off the rails.

derelict *adj.* forsaken; abandoned. DERELICT *n.* abandoned property, esp. a ship.

descant *n.* a part sung above a melody in harmony.

descend *v.* 1 to come or go down; to climb down. 2 to pass from one generation to another.

descendant *n.* a person or thing descended from another.

descender *n.* in writing, the part of a letter like g or p which goes below the line (see ASCENDER).

descent *n.* 1 a slope or way down. 2 ancestry.

describe *v.* 1 to give a description of. 2 to mark out.

description *n.* a written or spoken account or report.

desert *v.* (pron. di-ZERT) to abandon; to run away from. DESERT *n.* (pron. DEZ-ert) an area of dry, barren wasteland.

deserted *adj.* abandoned; forsaken.

deserts *n. pl.* what a person deserves; a reward or punishment.

deserve *v.* to earn; to be worthy of.

design *v.* to make a plan or pattern of something. DESIGN *n.* 1 a plan; a pattern. 2 an intention.

desirable *adj.* worth having; sought after; pleasing.

desire *v.* to long or wish for. DESIRE *n.* a longing; a wish.

desolate *adj.* 1 alone; solitary. 2 uninhabited; deserted. 3 neglected; dreary. 4 forlorn; wretched.

despair *v.* to give up hope. DESPAIR *n.* loss of hope.

despatch *v.* 1 to send. 2 to kill quickly. DESPATCH *n.* 1 a sending away. 2 a quick killing. 3 an official message. See DISPATCH.

desperate *adj.* 1 almost without hope. 2 reckless.

despise *v.* to feel contempt for.

despite *prep.* in spite of.

dessert *n.* fruit or sweet dish served at the end of a meal.

destination *n.* the place to which a person or thing is going.

destitute *adj.* living in poverty without any means of support. DESTITUTION *n.* poverty, need.

destroy *v.* 1 to break up; to spoil. 2 to kill.

detach *v.* to unfasten, to disconnect.

detail *n.* a small part; an item. DETAIL *v.* to give all the facts.

detain *v.* 1 to keep back; to keep waiting. 2 to keep in custody.

detect *v.* to discover; to find out.

detective *n.* a police or private investigator.

deter *v.* to discourage; to prevent; to hinder.

detergent *n.* a chemical preparation used for washing and cleaning.

deteriorate *v.* to become worse.

determine *v.* to decide; to settle. DETERMINED *adj.*

detest *v.* to hate or dislike deeply.

detonate *v.* to explode or cause to explode. DETONATION *n.*

detour *n.* a roundabout way; a deviation.

detract *v.* to take away from (value, reputation etc.); to lessen.

devastate *v.* 1 to lay waste. 2 to destroy completely. DEVASTATING *adj.*

develop *v.* to grow or improve gradually.

development *n.* 1 gradual growth. 2 new facts affecting a situation. 3 a planned area of housing or buildings.

device *n.* 1 an invention; a contrivance. 2 a plan; a trick. 3 an emblem.

devil *n.* 1 an evil spirit. 2 a wicked person.

devise *v.* to plan; to invent; to work out.

devote (to) *v.* 1 to give (one's) full attention to. 2 to dedicate (oneself) to.

devour *v.* to eat greedily; to consume.

dew *n.* drops of moisture which form on the ground, leaves and grass during the night when water vapour in cold air condenses.

diagnose *v.* 1 to discover the nature of an illness from a study of the symptoms. 2 to trace the cause of any trouble.

diagonal *n.* a straight line drawn between opposite corners.

diagram *n*. a plan or sketch drawn to explain something.

dial *n*. the face of a watch, clock or instrument. DIAL *v*. to call a number on a telephone.

dialect *n*. a way of speech used in a particular district or part of a country.

dialogue *n*. a conversation between two people or characters.

diameter *n*. 1 a straight line passing from side to side through the centre of a circle. 2 the length of such a line.

diamond *n*. an extremely hard and precious stone.

diary *n*. a daily record of events.

dice *n*. *pl*. small cubes marked with spots (1 to 6) on each of the sides, used in games of chance. *sing*. DICE.

dictate *v*. 1 to say or read aloud for another person to write down or record. 2 to command or give orders firmly. DICTATION *n*. DICTATOR *n*.

dictionary *n*. a book listing words in alphabetical order with their meanings.

die *v*. 1 to cease living. 2 to wither. DIE *n*. a block for making coins or patterns.

diesel *n*. 1 an engine using diesel oil. 2 a locomotive driven by a diesel engine.

diet *n*. 1 the kind of food normally eaten by a particular person, community or animal. 2 a set course of food, usually arranged for medical reasons. DIET *v*. to eat certain kinds of food only.

differ *v*. 1 to be different. 2 to disagree.

difference *n*. 1 anything which makes one thing unlike another. 2 a quarrel or disagreement. 3 in maths, the number by which one amount is bigger or smaller than another. FIND THE DIFFERENCE *v*. to take away; to subtract.

different *adj*. unlike; not the same.

difficult *adj*. 1 not easy; hard to do. 2 hard to get along with.

difficulty *n*. 1 anything hard to do or understand. 2 a problem or an obstacle. *pl*. DIFFICULTIES.

dig *v*. 1 to turn soil with a spade or machine. 2 to prod or to poke. DIG *n*. an archaeological excavation.

digest *v*. (pron. die-JEST) 1 to dissolve (food in the stomach). 2 to think over carefully. DIGEST *n*. (pron. DIE-jest) a short version.

digit *n*. 1 any of the numbers from 0 to 9. 2 a finger, thumb or toe.

digital *adj*. concerning or using digits, as in a computer.

dignified *adj*. noble; stately; showing dignity.

dignity *n*. worthiness; excellence; high rank and position

digraph *n*. two letters representing one sound, e.g. shop, rain.

dike, dyke *n*. 1 a wall or embankment built to prevent flooding. 2 a ditch or channel to lead water away.

dilapidated *adj*. neglected and needing repair.

diligent *adj*. hard-working; persevering.

dilute *v*. to weaken the strength of (esp. a liquid by adding another liquid).

dilution *n*. the weakening of a liquid.

dim *adj*. not bright or clear; faint, indistinct. DIM *v*. to make or become dim. DIMLY *adv*. faintly; indistinctly.

dimension *n*. the measurement of length, breadth (width) or depth.

diminish *v*. to make, or become, less. DIMINISHED *adj*.

diminutive *adj*. very small. DIMINUTIVE *n*. the form of a word referring to something small or young, e.g. starlet, piglet.

dimple *n*. a small hollow in the cheek or chin. DIMPLE *v*. to mark with dimples.

din *n*. a loud and continuous noise.

dinghy *n*. a small boat; an inflatable rubber boat.

dingy *adj*. shabby; faded.

dinner *n*. the main meal of the day.

dinosaur *n*. any of various huge prehistoric reptiles.

dint *n*. 1 a dent. 2 a mark made by a blow. DINT *v*. to dent.

diocese *n*. the district under a bishop's authority and care.

dip *v*. 1 to put in and out of a liquid; to immerse. 2 to slope downwards. DIP *n*. 1 a quick immersion. 2 a downward slope.

diphthong *n*. two vowel sounds blended into one sound (for example, out).

diploma *n*. a certificate confirming that a person has gained success in an examination or has gained an honour or a privilege.

diplomacy *n.* skill in negotiating or managing.

diplomat *n.* a skilled negotiator, esp. for a government.

diplomatic *adj.* tactful; skilled in diplomacy.

direct *adj.* 1 straight, straightforward. 2 outspoken. DIRECT *v.* 1 to aim. 2 to give directions.

direction *n.* 1 the way anything goes or moves. 2 an order or a command. 3 instructions.

directly *adv.* 1 in a direct manner. 2 at once; immediately.

director *n.* 1 a person who directs. 2 a manager or controller.

directory *n.* a book in which names are listed, in alphabetical order, with addresses, e.g. a telephone directory. *pl.* DIRECTORIES.

dirt *n.* mud, earth, filth; anything unclean. DIRTY *adj.*

disability *n.* a thing that disables or disqualifies. *pl.* DISABILITIES.

disable *v.* to make powerless; to cripple.

disadvantage *n.* an unfavourable circumstance; a drawback.

disagree *v.* to fail to agree; to differ; to quarrel.

disagreeable *adj.* unpleasant; bad-tempered.

disagreement *n.* a failure to agree; a difference; a quarrel.

disappear *v.* to go out of sight, to become obsolete; to cease to exist.

disappearance *n.* vanishing; going out of existence.

disappoint *v.* to fail to fulfil hopes and desires of (someone).

disappointing *adj.* causing disappointment; failing to please.

disapprove *n.* to show dislike; to have a poor opinion of.

disarm *v.* to take someone's weapons away; to win over.

disaster *n.* a great misfortune; a sudden calamity.

disband *v.* to break up; to disperse.

disbelief *n.* 1 doubt; distrust. 2 lack of belief.

disbelieve *v.* 1 to refuse to believe. 2 to have no faith (in).

disc, disk *n.* 1 a flat circular object. 2 a plastic disc, with a recording of sound and/or pictures on it (see RECORD).

discard *v.* to throw away; to reject.

discharge *v.* 1 to dismiss; to release. 2 to unload cargo. 3 to fire a gun. DISCHARGE *n.* 1 dismissal. 2 unloading. 3 gunfire.

disciple *n.* a follower; someone who believes in a person's teaching.

discipline *n.* obedience to orders; training and self-control. DISCIPLINE *v.* to bring under control; to train; to teach.

disclose *v.* to show; to uncover; to reveal.

discolour *v.* to spoil or change the colour of; to stain. DISCOLOURED *adj.*

discomfort *n.* lack of comfort; uneasiness.

disconnect *v.* to remove a connection; to detach. DISCONNECTED *adj.*

discontinue *v.* to stop; to bring to an end. DISCONTINUED *adj.* DISCONTINUANCE *n.*

discord *n.* 1 disagreement or quarrelling. 2 lack of harmony.

discount *n.* (pron. DIS-count) an amount deducted from an account. DISCOUNT *v.* (pron. dis-COUNT) to reduce; to disregard.

discourage *v.* to try to prevent; to dishearten. DISCOURAGEMENT *n.*

discourteous *adj.* not polite; rude; lacking in manners.

discover *v.* to find out; to find by chance.

discovery *n.* 1 anything discovered. 2 the act of discovering.

discredit *v.* 1 to disbelieve. 2 to dishonour. DISCREDIT *n.*

discreet *adj.* careful in speech and action. DISCREETLY *adv.*

discretion *n.* 1 sound judgement. 2 freedom to act as one thinks fit.

discriminate (**between**) *v.* to make or see differences (between); to show unfair preference for.

discrimination *n.* 1 good judgement. 2 a difference in the way two persons are treated.

discuss *v.* to talk about; to debate.

discussion *n.* a conversation or debate on a subject.

disease *n.* 1 an illness. 2 an unhealthy condition of the body or mind, or of plants, etc.

disembark *v.* to put or go ashore from a ship. DISEMBARKATION *n.*

disengage *v.* 1 to release. 2 to free or detach something.

disfigure *v.* to spoil the appearance or beauty of.

disgrace *v.* to bring shame upon; to dishonour. DISGRACE *n.* loss of favour, dishonour.

disgraceful *adj.* shameful; causing disgrace.

disguise *v.* to alter the appearance of (someone or something) in order to deceive; to hide the truth of.

disgust *v.* to cause a strong feeling of dislike. DISGUST *n.* a strong feeling of dislike.

dish *n.* 1 a plate for holding food. 2 a particular kind of food. DISH *v.* to serve out.

dishearten *v.* to take away courage or hope from (someone); to sadden.

dishonest *adj.* not honest.

disinfect *v.* to free from infection.

disinfectant *n.* anything that disinfects.

disintegrate *v.* to fall to pieces; to break up; to crumble.

dislike *v.* to have no liking for; to disapprove of. DISLIKE *n.* displeasure; disapproval.

dislocate *v.* to put out of joint; to put out of order.

disloyal *adj.* not loyal; unfaithful. DISLOYALTY *n.*

dismal *adj.* gloomy; cheerless; sad.

dismantle *v.* to take to pieces; to remove fittings etc. DISMANTLED *adj.*

dismay *v.* to fill with alarm. DISMAY *n.* a feeling of alarm and consternation.

dismiss *v.* to send away; to discharge. DISMISSED *adj.*

disobedient *adj.* refusing or failing to obey.

disobey *v.* to refuse or ignore an instruction or order.

disorder *v.* to upset or confuse. DISORDER *n.* 1 lack of order; confusion. 2 illness.

dispatch *v.* see DESPATCH.

dispense *v.* 1 to deal out. 2 to prepare medicines.

disperse *v.* to scatter; to go in different directions. DISPERSED *adj.*

display *v.* to show; to exhibit. DISPLAY *n.* a show or an exhibition.

displease *v.* to offend. DISPLEASURE *n.*

dispute *n.* an argument; a quarrel. DISPUTE *v.* to argue; to quarrel.

disqualify *v.* to take away permission or qualification. DISQUALIFIED *adj.*

disquiet *v.* to make uneasy; to make anxious. DISQUIET *n.* uneasiness; anxiety.

disregard *v.* to ignore. DISREGARD *n.* lack of attention.

disrepair *n.* bad condition due to lack of repairs.

disrupt *v.* to break up; to cause confusion.

dissatisfaction *n.* discontent. DISSATISFIED *adj.*

dissect *v.* to cut up for examination. DISSECTION *n.*

dissolve *v.* 1 to break up or melt in a liquid. 2 to bring to an end.

dissuade *v.* to advise or persuade (someone) against doing (something).

distance *n.* 1 the space between two points. 2 a far-off place or point.

distant *adj.* 1 far away; remote. 2 shy; reserved in manner.

distaste *n.* dislike; disgust. DISTASTEFUL *adj.*

distil *v.* to condense the vapour from a heated liquid.

distinct *adj.* 1 clearly seen or heard; plain. 2 separate; different.

distinction *n.* 1 a difference between things. 2 a mark of honour or outstanding merit.

distinguish *v.* 1 to make or notice a difference (between one thing and another). 2 DISTINGUISH ONESELF to gain distinction (for oneself).

distinguished *adj.* famous; important.

distort *v.* 1 to turn or twist out of shape. 2 to misrepresent. DISTORTED *adj.*

distract *v.* to draw a person's attention from one thing to another. DISTRACTED *adj.*

distress *v.* to cause pain or sorrow to. DISTRESS *n.* 1 a great pain, sorrow or worry. 2 danger or difficulty.

distribute *v.* to give out to or share (something) among a number of people.

distribution *n.* distributing; sharing.

distributor *n.* a person who distributes or shares.

district *n.* an area or a region; part of a country or town.

distrust *v.* to have no trust in; to doubt. DISTRUST *n.* lack of trust; doubt.

disturb *v.* 1 to upset the quiet or calm of. 2 to worry; to bother.

disturbance *n.* the act of disturbing; disorder.

disuse *v.* (pron. dis-UZE) to stop using. DISUSE *n.* (pron. dis-USE) neglect; discontinuance. DISUSED *adj.* (pron. dis-UZD) no longer used.

ditch *n.* a narrow trench. DITCH *v.* to make or repair ditches.

ditto *n.* the same; as before; also.

ditty *n.* a short and simple song. *pl.* DITTIES.

Divali, Diwali *n.* a Hindu festival of light.

divan *n.* a low seat or bed.

dive *v.* 1 to plunge head first into (water). 2 to descend under water. 3 to descend steeply and fast (bird or aircraft).

diver *n.* a person who dives.

diversion *n.* 1 an alternative route. 2 an amusement or a relaxation.

divert *v.* 1 to turn (something) in another direction. 2 to amuse or entertain.

divide *v.* 1 to separate or cut into parts. 2 to find out how many times one number contains another.

dividend *n.* 1 a share of the profit from a business. 2 a number that is to be divided.

divine *adj.* belonging to God; holy. DIVINE *v.* to predict, to discover.

division *n.* 1 the process of dividing. 2 a separate section; a barrier.

divorce *n.* 1 the legal ending of a marriage. 2 separation. DIVORCE *v.* 1 to end a marriage by law. 2 to separate.

divulge *v.* to make (something) known; to reveal a secret.

dizziness *n.* faintness; giddiness. DIZZY *adj.* DIZZILY *adv.*

do *v.* 1 to perform or carry out (any action). 2 to make or produce. 3 to be suitable.

docile *adj.* tame; easily managed; obedient.

dock *n.* 1 the place where ships berth to load and unload or to be repaired. 2 the place in a law court where the accused person stands. DOCK *v.* to bring a ship into dock; to moor one spacecraft to another when in orbit.

doctor *n.* 1 a person qualified to treat the sick and injured; a medical practitioner. 2 a person who has received the highest degree from a university.

document *n.* a paper containing written information or evidence; a written deed; a certificate.

documentary *adj.* in the form of a document. DOCUMENTARY *n.* a television programme or film which deals with facts about a subject.

dodge *v.* to avoid (something) by moving quickly. DODGE *n.* 1 a movement to avoid something. 2 a trick.

doe *n.* the female of many animals, such as deer, hare, rabbit, etc.

dog *n.* a common domestic animal, related to the fox and wolf. DOG *v.* to follow closely.

doldrums *n. pl.* 1 the equatorial ocean region where there is little wind. 2 low spirits.

doll *n.* a toy in the form of a baby or person.

dollar *n.* a unit of money ($1) equivalent to 100 cents, in the USA, Canada, Australia and other countries.

dolphin *n.* a marine, fish-like mammal similar to a porpoise.

dome *n.* the top of a tower or roof in the shape of a half-sphere.

domestic *adj.* 1 to do with the family or home. 2 tame (domestic animals).

dominate *v.* to have a very strong influence over; to rule over. DOMINATED *adj.*

dominion *n.* a country or territory under the control of a king, queen, lord or government.

domino *n.* 1 one of the 28 small oblong pieces, marked with spots, used in the game of dominoes. 2 a loose cloak with a half-mask worn to conceal identity at a masquerade.

donate *v.* to give (something) to someone; to make a donation.

donation *n.* a gift; a contribution.

donkey *n.* 1 an ass, which is a long-eared, horse-like animal. 2 an obstinate or stupid person.

doodle *v.* to draw or scribble aimlessly.

doom *v.* to pass sentence on; to condemn; to ruin. DOOM *n.* judgement; ruin; fate. DOOMED *adj.* ruined; condemned; fated.

door *n.* a hinged or sliding barrier of wood, metal or glass at the entrance to a building, room or cupboard, which can be opened and closed.

dope *n.* a drug that affects the mind or senses. DOPE *v.* to drug.

dormant *adj.* 1 sleeping. 2 not active.

dormer *n.* a projecting, upright window set in a sloping roof.

dormitory *n.* a large bedroom with many beds. *pl.* DORMITORIES.

dormouse *n.* a small hibernating rodent. *pl.* DORMICE.

dose *n.* the amount of medicine to be taken at one time. DOSE *v.* to give (medicine) in doses to (someone).

dot *n.* a small spot. DOT *v.* to mark with small spots. DOTTED *adj.*

double *v.* 1 to become, or make, twice as much. 2 to fold in two. DOUBLE *n.* 1 twice as much. 2 a person or thing very much like another.

doubt *v.* to be uncertain or undecided about; to distrust. DOUBT *n.* uncertainty; distrust.

dough *n.* flour which has been moistened and kneaded ready for baking.

dove *n.* a bird of the pigeon family.

down *n.* 1 a stretch of open, grassy upland. 2 soft, short hairs or feathers. DOWN *adv.* to, or in, a lower place, size or amount; the opposite of UP. DOWN *adj.* directed downwards. DOWN *prep.* downwards, along or through.

doze *v.* to sleep lightly; to be half asleep. DOZE *n.* a short, light sleep; a nap.

dozen *n.* a group of twelve things, twelve of anything.

drab *adj.* of dull colour; dull; dreary.

draft *v.* 1 to prepare (a letter, statement or plan). 2 to pick people for some special purpose. DRAFT *n.* 1 a rough or first copy of a letter, statement or plan. 2 a picked body of people.

drag *v.* to haul or pull along slowly.

dragon *n.* an imaginary fire-breathing monster.

drain *v.* 1 to draw off (liquid). 2 to use up or exhaust. DRAIN *n.* a pipe, ditch or sewer for carrying away water or waste.

drake *n.* a male duck.

drama *n.* 1 a play for theatre, television or radio. 2 an exciting series of events.

drape *v.* to hand or cover with cloth or other fabric. DRAPE *n.* a piece of cloth or fabric draped over something. DRAPED *adj.*

drastic *adj.* having a strong or powerful effect.

draught *n.* 1 a current of air. 2 a drink. 3 the depth of water required by a ship.

draughts *n. pl.* a game for two using 24 circular pieces (draughtsmen) on a square board.

draughtsman *n.* a person who designs and draws plans.

draw *v.* 1 to pull. 2 to attract. 3 to make a sketch, picture or design. 4 to end a game with equal scores. DRAW *n.* 1 an attraction. 2 a drawn game (of football, etc.)

drawing *n.* a sketch, picture or design.

dread *v.* to fear greatly. DREAD *n.* a great fear.

dream *n.* 1 the thoughts and images that come during sleep. 2 something that is much desired or a recalled memory. DREAM *v.* to experience dreams. DREAMER *n.* DREAMILY *adj.*

dreary *adj.* dull, boring, cheerless, gloomy.

dredge *v.* to bring up mud or sand from the bottom of a harbour, river or channel; to deepen. DREDGER *n.* a ship for dredging.

drench *v.* to make very wet; to soak through. DRENCHED *adj.*

dress *v.* 1 to put on clothes. 2 to bandage. DRESS *n.* clothing; a frock.

dribble *v.* 1 to let flow in drops; to let saliva or liquid trickle from the mouth. 2 to keep a ball moving along by giving it light taps with the feet.

drift *v.* to wander or float along; to be driven into heaps; to move off course. DRIFT *n.* a heap of sand or snow caused by the wind.

drill *n.* 1 a special tool for boring holes. 2 an exercise in marching or a routine operation. DRILL *v.* 1 to bore a hole. 2 to exercise, or follow a routine.

drink *v.* to swallow a liquid. DRINK *n.* liquid for drinking.

drip *v.* to fall in drops. DRIP *n.* a drop or the sound made by falling drops.

dripping *n.* 1 the falling of liquid in drops. 2 the fat that has dripped from meat when roasted.

drive *v.* 1 to force or urge along. 2 to guide and control. DRIVE *n.* 1 a journey by car. 2 a road. 3 a campaign. DRIVER *n.*

drizzle *n.* fine or gentle rain. DRIZZLE *v.* to rain gently.

drone *n.* 1 the male honey-bee. 2 a low humming sound. DRONE *v.* 1 to make a low humming sound. 2 to speak in a monotonous manner.

droop *v.* 1 to sag or hang limply. 2 to grow weak or faint. DROOPING *adj.*

drop *n.* 1 a tiny bead of liquid; a small quantity. 2 a fall. DROP *v.* 1 to fall in drops. 2 to fall or allow to fall. DROPPING *n.*

drought *n.* a long period of dry weather; a serious lack of rain or water.

drove *n.* a moving herd or flock; a crowd of people moving along. DROVER *n.*

drown *v.* 1 to die under water from lack of air. 2 to flood or overwhelm. DROWNING *adj.* & *n.*

drowse *v.* to doze; to sleep lightly.

drug *n.* a substance used in medicine; a substance which dulls pain or affects the senses (see DOPE). DRUG *v.* to dose with a drug. DRUGGED *adj.*

drum *n.* 1 a musical percussion instrument with skin stretched over open ends. 2 a cylinder-shaped container. DRUM *v.* to beat, or bang, on a drum; to beat or tap continuously.

dry *v.* to make or become dry. DRY *adj.* 1 waterless. 2 thirsty. 3 uninteresting.

dual *adj.* double; forming a pair.

duchess *n.* the wife or widow of a duke.

duck *n.* 1 a small web-footed water bird; a female duck (see DRAKE). 2 no-score by a batsman in cricket. DUCK *v.* to lower the head suddenly; to dip in water suddenly.

duct *n.* a tube or pipe carrying liquids, cables, etc.

due *n.* a right; that which is owing. DUE *adj.* 1 owing. 2 suitable. 3 expected.

duel *n.* a fight or contest.

duet *n.* music performed by two singers or players.

duke *n.* a nobleman of the highest rank. *fem.* DUCHESS.

dull *adj.* not bright or clear; not lively; uninteresting. DULL *v.* to make or become dull.

duly *adv.* properly; punctually.

dumb *adj.* unable to speak; silent.

dummy *n.* an imitation object; a false package. DUMMY *adj.* not real; fake.

dump *v.* to throw away; to tip out. DUMP *n.* a rubbish or storage heap.

dune *n.* a low hill of sand.

dung *n.* animal excreta; manure.

dungeon *n.* an underground cell for prisoners.

duplicate *n.* an exact copy. DUPLICATE *v.* to make an exact copy or copies of.

duplicator *n.* a machine which makes printed copies.

duration *n.* the length of time that something lasts or continues.

during *prep.* throughout; in the course of.

dusk *n.* twilight, nightfall.

dust *n.* fine dry particles of dirt carried in the air; any finely powdered particles of solid matter (e.g. coal, chalk, gold dust). DUSTY *adj.*

duty *n.* 1 anything a person has to do or ought to do. 2 a tax on goods.

dwarf *n.* an animal, plant or person much below ordinary size. DWARF *v.* to stunt in growth, to make look small by comparison.

dwell *v.* 1 to live in; to reside. 2 to speak for some time about.

dwindle *v.* to become gradually smaller in size.

dye *v.* to change the colour of a material etc., by using a dye. DYE *n.* a colouring substance.

dynamite *n.* a powerful explosive. DYNAMITE *v.* to blow up with dynamite.

dynamo *n.* a machine for producing electricity.

E

each *adj.* & *pron.* every one of a number taken singly or separately.

eager *adj.* keen; enthusiastic. EAGERLY *adv.*

eagle *n.* a large and powerful bird of prey.

ear *n.* 1 the organ of hearing. 2 a spike, or head, of corn.

earl *n.* a nobleman ranking between a marquis and a viscount. *fem.* COUNTESS. EARLDOM *n.*

early *adj.* long ago; in bygone days; in the first part of the day. EARLY *adv.* before the usual time; beforehand.

earn *v.* to gain (money) by work; to deserve.

earnest *adj.* serious, conscientious; keen; determined.

earnings *n. pl.* money earned; wages; salary.

Earth *n.* the world; the planet we live on.

earth *n.* 1 soil. 2 ground. 3 a fox's den.

earthquake *n.* underground shock waves which make the earth tremble.

earwig *n.* a small, dark-coloured insect with a pincer-like tail.

ease *n.* rest, comfort; freedom from pain.

easel *n.* a frame to support a picture, blackboard, etc.

easily *adv.* without difficulty.

east *n.* the point on the horizon where the sun rises. EAST *adj.* in or to the east. EASTWARD *adv.* towards the east.

Easter *n.* festival of Christ's resurrection.

easy *adj.* comfortable; not difficult.

eat *v.* to chew and swallow food.

eatable *adj.* pleasant or fit to eat, edible.

eaves *n. pl.* the overhanging edges of a roof.

ebb *v.* to go back; to recede. EBB *n.* 1 flowing away of the tide. 2 a decrease; a decline.

ebony *n.* a black, heavy hardwood.

eccentric *adj.* odd; strange; not normal.

echo *v.* to throw back or reflect a sound. ECHO *n.* a sound reflected. *pl.* ECHOES.

echoing *adj.* reflecting; resounding.

eclipse *n.* a darkening of the face of the sun or moon. ECLIPSE *v.* 1 to darken; to overshadow. 2 to surpass. ECLIPSING *adj.*

economic *adj.* concerned with economics.

economical *adj.* thrifty, careful in spending.

economics *n.* the study or science of management (mainly governmental) of the money and resources of an organisation or nation.

economy *n.* the management of resources and financial affairs; thrift.

ecstasy *n.* a feeling of great joy and delight.

eddy *v.* to whirl round and round. EDDY *n.* a whirling current of air, water, smoke, etc. a small whirlpool. *pl.* EDDIES.

edge *n.* 1 the rim or border. 2 the cutting side of a blade. EDGE *v.* 1 to sharpen. 2 to move gradually.

edging *n.* a border or fringe.

edible *adj.* fit to eat; wholesome.

edifice *n.* a large building or structure.

edit *v.* to correct or add to recorded work – either your own or another's – to make it suitable for publication or broadcasting.

edition *n.* the number of copies of a book or an article produced at one time.

editor *n.* 1 a person who chooses what is to be included in a book, newspaper, film, etc. 2 one who prepares the work of others for publication.

editorial *adj.* concerned with an editor. EDITORIAL *n.* an important article written by a newspaper editor, or giving his or her views.

educate *v.* to teach; to train; to discipline; to provide education for.

education *n.* the process of educating people; instruction; training.

eel *n.* a long, snake-like fish.

eerie *adj.* strange, weird; causing awe or fear. EERILY *adv.*

eeriness *n.* an atmosphere or impression of awe or fear.

effect *n.* the result of an action; consequence. EFFECT *v.* to bring about.

effective *adj.* 1 able to produce a desired effect. 2 impressive.

efficient *adj.* competent; skilful; satisfactory in use. EFFICIENCY *n.* competence, skill.

effigy *n.* a figure of a person in stone, wood, metal, etc; an image on a coin. *pl.* EFFIGIES.

effort *n.* an attempt; exertion.

effortless *adj.* without effort; with ease.

egg *n.* round, thin-shelled body laid by female bird, reptile, etc., from which its young hatch. EGG *v.* to urge on; to stir into action.

Eid *n.* a Muslim religious festival.

eiderdown *n.* a quilt filled with the soft down feathers of the eider duck, or similar material.

eight *n.* the number that is one more than seven, the symbol 8.

either *adj.* one or the other of two persons or things.

eject *v.* to throw out; to expel.

ejection *n.* a throwing out; an expulsion.

elaborate *adj.* very detailed; complicated; highly decorated. ELABORATE *v.* 1 to work out in detail. 2 to explain. 3 to exaggerate.

elapse *v.* to pass; to slip by, esp. time.

elastic *adj.* 1 able to stretch and spring back again. 2 not rigid. ELASTIC *n.* a material containing rubber which stretches and springs back easily.

elate *v.* to raise the spirits of; to make (someone) glad. ELATED *adj.*

elation *n.* great joy; high spirits.

elbow *n.* 1 the joint where the arm bends. 2 an angle; a sharp bend. ELBOW *v.* to push with the elbow; to jostle.

elder *n. & adj.* the older of two persons. ELDER *n.* 1 a senior member of a tribe or of certain churches. 2 a large shrub which produces clusters of purple berries.

elderly *adj.* past middle age.

eldest *adj.* the oldest of three or more persons.

elect *v.* to choose by voting; to select. ELECT *n.* specially chosen.

election *n.* the process of choosing, usually by voting.

elector *n.* a person who has a vote at an election.

electorate *n.* all the people entitled to vote.

electric *adj.* charged with electricity; capable of making electricity; operated or produced by electricity.

electrical *adj.* having to do with electricity.

electrically *adv.* by electricity.

electrician *n.* a person skilled in dealing with electricity or electrical equipment.

electricity *n.* a form of energy which produces light, heat and power; a flow of electrons.

electron *n.* a minute electric charge, a part of an atom.

electronics *n.* the science concerned with the behaviour of electrons and with devices to make use of them.

elegance *n.* grace; refinement.

elegant *adj.* graceful; refined; in good taste.

elegy *n.* a sad poem or song.

element *n.* 1 the simplest form of anything. 2 a chemical substance that cannot be split up into simple substances. 3 the heater wire or rod in an electric fire or an iron. ELEMENTARY *adj.*

elephant *n.* the largest land animal, which has a trunk and two ivory tusks.

elevate *v.* to raise; to improve.

elevation *n.* 1 the act of raising. 2 a height. 3 a promotion.

elevator *n.* 1 a machine for raising coal, grain, etc., to a higher level; a lift. 2 the part of an aircraft which makes it climb or dive.

eleven *adj. & n.* the number one more than ten, the symbol 11.

elf *n.* a mischievous fairy. *pl.* ELVES.

elicit *v.* to draw out information.

eligible *adj.* suitable; qualified.

eliminate *v.* to remove; to get rid of.

elimination *n.* removal; expulsion.

ellipse *n.* a regular oval shape.

ellipsis *n.* a series of dots (…) used in a text to show that something has been left out or that there is a pause (often used to create suspense).

elm *n.* a tall, rough-barked deciduous tree.

elocution *n.* the art or manner of speaking.

elongate *v.* to lengthen; to extend.

elope *v.* to run away, esp. with a lover. ELOPEMENT *n.*

eloquence *n.* fluent and persuasive speech.

else *adv.* otherwise; if not.

elsewhere *adv.* in another place; not here.

elude *v.* to dodge; to avoid; to escape.

elusive *adj.* hard to catch or grasp; evasive.

email *n.* electronic mail; messages sent using computers.

emancipate *v.* to set free; to liberate. EMANCIPATED *adj.*

embalm *v.* to preserve (a dead body).

embankment *n.* a wall or bank, of earth or stone, to hold back water or to carry a road or railway. EMBANK *v.*

embargo *n.* an official prohibition.

embark *v.* 1 to go on board a ship or an aircraft. 2 EMBARK ON to start on anything. EMBARKATION *n.*

embarrass *v.* 1 to make someone feel ill at ease. 2 to hinder.

embarrassing *adj.* causing discomfort.

embarrassment *n.* the state of being embarrassed; discomfort.

embassy *n.* 1 an ambassador and his staff. 2 an ambassador's residence. *pl.* EMBASSIES.

ember *n.* a glowing or smouldering cinder.

embezzle *v.* to steal money by fraud from a person who trusts you. EMBEZZLEMENT *n.* EMBEZZLER *n.*

embitter *v.* to make bitter; to cause ill-feeling.

emblem *n.* a badge; a sign; a symbol.

emboss *v.* to decorate with a raised pattern; to carve in relief.

embrace *v.* 1 to clasp in the arms; to hug. 2 to include. EMBRACE *n.* a clasp, a hug.

embroider *v.* 1 to ornament with needlework. 2 to add to a story; to elaborate.

embroidery *n.* ornamental needlework.

embryo *n.* an animal or plant at the earliest stage of development (see FOETUS).

emerald *n.* a green and precious stone. EMERALD *adj.* green.

emerge *v.* to arise or come out of; to come to light.

emergency *n.* a situation needing immediate action; an unexpected happening.

emigrant *n.* a person who emigrates.

emigrate *v.* to leave one's own country and settle in another.

emigration *n.* a departure to settle in another country.

eminent *adj.* famous; celebrated; distinguished.

emit *v.* to give, or send, out.

emotion *n.* a strong feeling – joy, pity, fear, love, hatred, etc.

emotional *adj.* excitable; sensitive; full of feeling.

emotive *adj.* causing strong feelings.

empathy *n.* the ability to see situations from the point of view of another. EMPATHISE *v.*

emperor *n.* the ruler of an empire. *fem.* EMPRESS.

emphasis *n.* 1 the stress put on particular words or syllables when speaking. 2 the importance given to something.

emphasise *v.* to lay stress on (something).

emphatic *adj.* expressed with emphasis; firm and forceful.

empire *n.* a group of countries or states under one ruler or government.

employ *v.* 1 to use or make use of. 2 to provide work for.

employee *n.* a person who works for an employer.

employer *n.* a person who employs others.

employment *n.* work; a job; an occupation.

empower *v.* to authorise; to give (someone) power to do (something).

empty *v.* to take everything out. EMPTY *adj.* containing nothing.

enable *v.* to make able; to supply with the means.

enamel *n.* a smooth, hard coating; a gloss paint; the hard coating on the teeth. ENAMEL *v.* to coat with enamel.

encase *v.* to put into a case.

enchant *v.* to put a charm or spell on; to delight.

enchanting *adj.* charming, pleasing; delightful.

encircle *v.* to surround; to enclose in a circle.

enclose *v.* 1 to surround. 2 to close or shut in; to contain inside.

encompass *v.* to surround; to encircle.

encore *v.* to ask for a performance or item to be repeated. ENCORE *n.* a repetition of a performance or item.

encounter *v.* 1 to meet by chance. 2 to meet (an enemy). ENCOUNTER *n.* 1 a chance meeting. 2 a fight.

encourage *v.* 1 to give hope, courage or confidence. 2 to urge someone to do something. ENCOURAGEMENT *n.*

encroach (**on**) *v.* to trespass; to intrude (on another person's rights or privacy); to invade. ENCROACHMENT *n.*

encyclopedia *n.* a reference book giving information of general knowledge or of one particular subject.

end *n.* 1 the last part; the finish. 2 the death. 3 the aim or purpose. END *v.* 1 to finish. 2 to destroy.

endanger *v.* to put in danger.

endangered *adj.* in danger.

endeavour *v.* to try; to attempt to do. ENDEAVOUR *n.* an attempt.

ending *n.* the result; conclusion.

endless *adj.* everlasting; unending.

endorse *v.* to approve; to confirm; to write one's signature, indicating approval or acceptance, on the back of a document. ENDORSEMENT *n.*

endow *v.* 1 to give land or money to (an institution). 2 to give a quality to (a person).

endure *v.* 1 to bear, or accept, with patience. 2 to last. ENDURING *adj.*

enemy *n.* a foe; an adversary. *pl.* ENEMIES.

energetic *adj.* very active; vigorous. ENERGETICALLY *adv.*

energy *n.* force; vigour. *pl.* ENERGIES.

enfold *v.* 1 to wrap up. 2 to embrace.

enforce *v.* to put (a law) into force; to compel someone to obey.

engage *v.* 1 to employ. 2 to promise. 3 to begin fighting. 4 to interlock (two or more parts), esp. machinery.

engagement *n.* 1 an appointment. 2 a promise to marry. 3 a fight.

engaging *adj.* attractive; pleasing; interesting.

engine *n.* a machine which produces power.

engineer *n.* a person who designs, makes or operates machinery.

English *adj.* belonging to England or its people. ENGLISH *n.* 1 the language of the British people. 2 the people of England.

engrave *v.* to cut letters or designs on (hard material).

engraving *n.* 1 the process of engraving. 2 a picture printed from an engraved plate.

engulf *v.* to swallow up; to overwhelm.

enhance *v.* to improve (something); to make (something) look better. ENHANCEMENT *n.*

enjoy *v.* 1 to like; to find pleasure in. 2 to experience.

enjoyable *adj.* able to be enjoyed.

enjoyment *n.* pleasure.

enlarge *v.* to make or become larger, to make a larger copy.

enlighten *v.* 1 to throw light on. 2 to give information or an explanation to (someone).

enlist *v.* 1 to join up for military service. 2 to obtain the help of.

enliven *v.* to make lively; to brighten (something) up.

enmity *n.* hatred; hostility.

enormous *adj.* very large; immense; huge. ENORMOUSLY *adv.*

enough *adj.* sufficient; ample. ENOUGH *n.* a sufficient quantity.

enquire *v.* see INQUIRE.

enrage *v.* to make angry; to infuriate.

enrich *v.* to make rich.

enrol, enroll *v.* to enter a name in a register or list; to enlist.

ensign *n.* 1 a flag; a banner. 2 formerly, lowest rank of army infantry officer.

enslave *v.* to make a slave of someone.

ensue *v.* to follow or come after; to result.

ensure *v.* to make sure of.

entangle *v.* to make tangled; to involve in difficulties.

enter *v.* 1 to go or come into. 2 to record in a book or list.

enterprise *n.* 1 a bold venture. 2 readiness to try a new thing.

enterprising *adj.* full of enterprise; showing courage or imagination.

entertain *v.* 1 to amuse. 2 to consider. 3 to treat as a guest. ENTERTAINER *n.*

entertaining *adj.* amusing. ENTERTAINING *n.* catering for guests.

enthral *v.* to give great delight to; to fascinate.

enthralling *adj.* interesting; fascinating.

enthrone *v.* to place on a throne.

enthusiasm *n.* eagerness; great interest.

enthusiastic *adj.* acting with enthusiasm.

entice *v.* to tempt; to lure.

enticement *n.* a temptation; an attraction; a bribe.

enticing *adj.* tempting; attractive.

entire *adj.* complete; whole.

entirely *adv.* completely; wholly.

entitle *v.* 1 to give (someone) a right to (something). 2 to give a title to a book, film, etc.

entomb *v.* to place in a tomb; to bury.

entrance *n.* (pron. EN-trance) a place of entering; a doorway; a gateway.

entrance *v.* (pron. en-TRANCE) to charm; to delight.

entrant *n.* one who enters.

entreat *v.* to beg; to implore.

entry *n.* 1 the act of entering. 2 an entrance. 3 an item entered in a book or record.

enumerate *v.* 1 to count. 2 to name one by one.

envelop *v.* to wrap up; to enclose.

envelope *n.* a folded cover or wrapper, esp. for a letter.

enviable *adj.* worth envying; desirable.

envious *adj.* showing or feeling envy.
ENVIOUSLY *adv.*

environment *n.* surroundings; conditions.

envoy *n.* a special messenger or representative.

envy *v.* to be jealous of. ENVY *n.* jealousy.

epic *n.* a long poem telling of heroic deeds.

epidemic *n.* a quickly-spreading outbreak of disease, crime, etc.

epilogue *n.* a speech or poem to end a play; the concluding, usually short, chapter of a book.

episode *n.* an interesting event; one incident in a series of incidents.

epistle *n.* a letter; a message.

epitaph *n.* words inscribed on a tomb telling about the dead person.

equal *adj.* of the same size, number, value, etc.

equalise *v.* to make equal.

equality *n.* the state of being equal.

equally *adv.* to the same extent.

equation *n.* a mathematical statement in which two things are regarded as being equal.

equator *n.* an imaginary line around the Earth, midway between the North and South Poles.

equatorial *adj.* having to do with the equator; on or near the equator.

equerry *n.* an officer in attendance on a member of the Royal Family.

equestrian *adj.* having to do with horses or horse-riding. EQUESTRIAN *n.* a person riding on horseback.

equilateral *adj.* having all sides equal.

equinox *n.* the time each year when the sun crosses the equator, making day and night equal in length (about March 20th and September 22nd).

equip *v.* to supply or fit out with everything needed for a particular purpose.

equipment *n.* what is needed for a particular task or purpose.

equivalent *adj.* equal in value, meaning, usefulness, strength, etc. EQUIVALENT *n.* a thing equal in value, or any other quality or quantity, to another.

era *n.* a period of time, dating from some particular point in history; an age.

eradicate *v.* to root out; to get rid of completely.

erase *v.* to rub or scrape out; to get rid of.

erasure *n.* a rubbing or scraping out.

erect *v.* to build; to construct. ERECT *adj.* upright.

erection *n.* a building; a structure.

ermine *n.* a stoat; a stoat's white winter fur.

Ernie *n.* popular name for an electronic device that selects prize-winning numbers of Premium Bonds (Electronic Random Number Indicator Equipment).

erode *v.* to wear away; to eat away. ERODED *adj.*

erosion *n.* a wearing down; an eating away.

err *v.* to be mistaken; to do wrong.

errand *n.* a short journey to take a message or to deliver or collect something.

erratic *adj.* wandering; uncertain; unreliable. ERRATICALLY *adv.*

error *n.* a mistake; a blunder.

erupt *v.* to break or burst out violently.

eruption *n.* 1 an outburst; a breaking out. 2 a skin rash.

escalator *n.* a moving staircase.

escapade *n.* a mischievous prank or adventure.

escape *v.* 1 to get away. 2 to avoid. 3 to leak. ESCAPE *n.* 1 the art of escaping. 2 an avoidance. 3 a leak.

escort *v.* to go with and protect. ESCORT *n.* an accompanying guard or guide.

Eskimo *n.* one of a people living on the coastlands of the Arctic regions.

especial *adj.* particular; out of the ordinary.

espionage *n.* spying or using spies.

espy *v.* to catch sight of; to see.

essay *v.* to try; to attempt. ESSAY *n.* 1 an attempt. 2 a written composition.

essential *adj.* absolutely necessary; important. ESSENTIALLY *adv.*

establish *v.* 1 to settle firmly; to set up. 2 to prove.

establishment *n.* the staff of a business or large house.

estate *n.* lands; property owned by a person or company.

esteem *v.* to value highly; to respect. ESTEEM *n.* regard; respect.

estimate *v.* to judge; to calculate. ESTIMATE *n.* a judgement; a calculation to decide size, value, etc.

estimation *n.* a judgement; a calculation.

estuary *n.* a river mouth.

etc. *abbrev. et cetera* – a Latin phrase meaning "and the others" or "and the rest" or "and so on".

etch *v.* to engrave on a metal plate, glass, etc., using acid. ETCHED *adj.*

etching *n.* a print from an etched plate.

eternal *adj.* lasting for ever; unchanging.

eternity *n.* 1 all time. 2 a very long time.

ether *n.* 1 the clear, upper air. 2 a colourless liquid used as an anaesthetic and as a solvent for fats.

etymology *n.* the study of the history of words.

eulogy *n.* a piece of writing or a speech that praises or celebrates a person or thing.

euro *n.* a unit of money used in the European Monetary Union.

Europe *n.* the smallest of the five continents. EUROPEAN *adj.* to do with Europe. EUROPEAN *n.* an inhabitant of Europe.

evacuate *v.* to leave; to empty; to withdraw from. EVACUATED *adj.*

evacuation *n.* an emptying out; a withdrawal.

evade *v.* to avoid; to dodge; to escape from.

evaluate *v.* to look at something and decide how successful or important it is.

evaluation *n.* a judgement or decision about the success or importance of something.

evaporate *v.* to turn into vapour; to vanish. EVAPORATED *adj.*

evaporation *n.* turning into vapour; disappearance.

evasion *n.* a means of avoidance; an excuse.

evasive *adj.* misleading; seeking to avoid.

eve *n.* the close of the day; evening; the time just before an important event.

even *adj.* 1 level; smooth. 2 exactly divisible by two. EVEN *v.* to make level or smooth.

evening *n.* the close of the day.

event *n.* 1 something that happens. 2 an item in a sports programme.

eventful *adj.* full of events; exciting.

eventual *adj.* happening as a result; final.

eventually *adv.* in the end; at last.

ever *adv.* always; at all times.

everlasting *adj.* lasting for ever; endless.

evermore *adv.* for ever.

every *adj.* each one of a number and without exception.

evict *v.* to turn out or expel. EVICTION *n.*

evidence *n.* 1 proof. 2 the statement of a witness; 3 clear sign or indication.

evident *adj.* plain; clearly seen and understood.

evil *n.* sin; wickedness. EVIL *adj.* wicked, unpleasant.

ewe *n.* a female sheep. *masc.* RAM.

exact *adj.* true; accurate. EXACT *v.* 1 to insist upon having (e.g. obedience from someone). 2 to enforce payment of (a debt, a fine, etc.).

exactly *adv.* just right; correctly; quite.

exaggerate *v.* to make something seem greater than it actually is; to overstate.

exalt *v.* to praise highly. EXALTED *adj.*

examination *n.* 1 a close inspection. 2 a test of knowledge or ability. 3 an investigation.

examine *v.* 1 to inspect closely. 2 to test.

example *n.* 1 a sample or specimen. 2 a model. 3 a warning.

exasperate *v.* to make very angry; to irritate. EXASPERATING *adj.*

exasperation *n.* anger, irritation.

excavate *v.* to dig or scoop out; to uncover buried ruins. EXCAVATION *n.*

excavator *n.* 1 a machine used for excavating. 2 someone who excavates.

exceed *v.* to be greater than; to go beyond.

excel *v.* to be better than; to be very good at; to do very well.

excellence *n.* high quality; great merit. EXCELLENT *adj.*

except *v.* to leave out; to omit. EXCEPT *prep.* leaving out; omitting.

exception *n.* something left out; something different from the rest.

exceptional *adj.* unusual; abnormal.

excerpt *n.* an extract from a book, play, musical work, etc.

excess *n.* 1 the extra amount; surplus. 2 going beyond what is reasonable.

excessive *adj.* too much; beyond what is right and proper.

exchange *v.* to give one thing in return for another. EXCHANGE *n.* 1 the act of exchanging. 2 a central telephone office where connections are made. 3 a building where money or goods are bought and sold.

exchequer *n.* a department that is responsible for taxation and other revenue. CHANCELLOR OF THE EXCHEQUER *n.* the government minister who is responsible for Britain's finances.

excise *n.* a tax on some goods.

excitable *adj.* easily excited.

excite *v.* to rouse; to stir up. EXCITING *adj.*

excitement *n.* the state of being excited; eager expectation.

exclaim *v.* to speak, or cry out, suddenly.

exclamation *n.* a sudden shout or cry; a punctuation mark to indicate surprise (!).

exclude *v.* to shut out; to leave out; to prevent (someone) from sharing (something); to ignore.

exclusion *n.* shutting or leaving out.

excreta *n.* waste discharged from the body; dung.

excretion *n.* the act of getting rid of waste substances.

excursion *n.* a pleasure trip; an outing.

excuse *v.* (pron. ex-KUZE) to free from blame; to overlook a fault. EXCUSE *n.* (pron. ex-KUSE) a reason given for having done something wrong.

execute *n.* 1 to do; to carry out. 2 to put to death.

execution *n.* 1 the deed; carrying out. 2 putting to death.

executive *n.* person or group responsible for a project or business.

exempt *v.* to free from; to excuse.

exemption *n.* freedom from a task or duty.

exercise *v.* to train (the body or mind) by practice or drill. EXERCISE *n.*

exert *v.* to bring into action, to make active. EXERTION *n.*

exhaust *v.* to use up completely. EXHAUST *n.* 1 the used gases or steam from an engine. 2 the pipe which lets out waste gases or steam from an engine.

exhaustion *n.* extreme tiredness; weariness.

exhibit *v.* to show; to display; to show in public.

exhibition *n.* a public show; a display.

exhilarate *v.* to enliven; to excite. EXHILARATION *n.*

exile *v.* to banish, to expel (someone) from his own country. EXILE *n.* a person who has been banished from his own country.

exist *v.* to live; to be. EXISTENCE *n.*

exit *n.* 1 a way out. 2 a departure. EXIT *v.* to go out; to leave.

exodus *n.* the departure of a large number of people.

exonerate *v.* to free from blame.

exorbitant *adj.* going beyond what is reasonable; excessive.

exotic *adj.* introduced from abroad; unusual; exceptional; rare.

expand *v.* 1 to make or grow larger. 2 to open out.

expanse *n.* a wide area.

expansion *n.* an increase in size; growing; stretching or spreading.

expect *v.* to look forward to; to wait for.

expectant *adj.* looking forward to; waiting.

expedite *v.* to hasten; to make quicker.

expedition *n.* 1 a journey with a purpose; 2 speed.

expel *v.* to drive or force out; to send away.

expend *v.* to spend (money, time or energy on some activity).

expenditure *n.* the money spent.

expense *n.* the cost.

expensive *adj.* costly; dear.

experience *n.* 1 skill and knowledge gained by doing and seeing. 2 anything that happens to a person. EXPERIENCE *v.* to undergo.

experiment *v.* to test or try out. EXPERIMENT *n.* a test; a trial.

experimental *adj.* based on experiments; used for experiments.

expert *n.* a specialist; skilled person. EXPERT *adj.* specialised; skilled.

expire *v.* 1 to die; to come to an end. 2 to breathe out.

explain *v.* to make clear or easy to understand; to give reasons for.

explanation *n.* a spoken or written statement that explains something. EXPLANATORY *adj.*

explode *v.* to blow up with a loud noise; to burst out.

exploit *v.* (pron. ex-PLOIT) to make use of selfishly; to use to advantage. EXPLOIT *n.* (pron. EX-ploit) a daring deed; an achievement.

exploration *n.* a search.

explore *v.* 1 to make a journey of exploration. 2 to examine the possibilities (of); to search. EXPLORER *n.*

explosion *n*. 1 a sudden burst or blowing-up with a loud noise. 2 a violent outburst.

explosive *n*. something that will explode. EXPLOSIVE *adj*. liable to explode.

exports *n*. pl (pron. EX-ports) goods sent abroad. EXPORT *v*. (pron. ex-PORT) to send (goods) abroad. EXPORTER *n*.

expose *v*. 1 to uncover. 2 to endanger. 3 to show up. EXPOSURE *n*.

express *v*. to state; to declare; to put into words. EXPRESS *adj*. 1 speedy. 2 definite.

expression *n*. 1 the manner in which anything is spoken, sung or written. 2 the look on a person's face.

expulsion *n*. a driving out; banishment.

exquisite *adj*. 1 delicate; of great beauty. 2 of unusual quality.

extend *v*. to stretch; to enlarge; to hold out.

extension *n*. lengthening; an addition.

extensive *adj*. wide; large; spacious.

extent *n*. the length, size or limits.

exterior *n*. the outside. EXTERIOR *adj*. outer; external.

exterminate *v*. to destroy completely; to kill off.

extermination *n*. destruction; extinction.

external *adj*. outside; lying on the outside.

extinct *adj*. dead; no longer active; no longer existing. EXTINCTION *n*. destruction.

extinguish *v*. to put an end to; to put out.

extinguisher *n*. a device for putting out fires.

extra *adj*. additional; more than is usual. EXTRA *adv*. additionally. EXTRA *n*. something additional.

extract *v*. (pron. ex-TRAKT) to draw or pull out; to squeeze out. EXTRACT *n*. (pron. EX-trakt) a part that has been taken away from the whole; a part of a story, a play, an article, etc.

extraordinarily *adv*. exceptionally; remarkably.

extraordinary *adj*. unusual; surprising; special.

extravagance *n*. lavish expenditure or waste.

extravagant *adj*. wasteful; going beyond reasonable limits.

extreme *adj*. farthest; not moderate; severe. EXTREME *n*. the opposite end; the farthest point, the limit. EXTREMELY *adv*.

eye *n*. 1 the organ of sight. 2 a small hole, as in a needle. EYE *v*. to gaze at or watch carefully.

eyrie *n*. the nesting place of eagles or any birds of prey.

F

fable *n*. a story with a lesson or moral; a legend. FABLED *adj*.

fabric *n*. 1 a woven material. 2 structure; walls, floors and roof of a building.

fabulous *adj*. legendary; astounding; marvellous.

façade *n*. 1 the face or front of a building. 2 outward appearance.

face *n*. 1 the front part of the head. 2 the front of anything. FACE *v*. 1 to turn towards. 2 to meet boldly.

facet *n*. 1 a small polished face or surface of a gem. 2 one aspect.

facial *adj*. having to do with the face.

facsimile *n*. an exact copy.

fact *n*. something known to be true.

faction *n*. 1 a disconnected party or group. 2 strife.

factor *n*. 1 a fact contributing to a result. 2 a number which divides into another number exactly. 3 an agent or merchant.

factory *n*. a building in which goods are made; a works.

factual *adj*. based on fact; true.

fad *n*. a passing interest; a fancy.

fade *v*. to grow faint; to lose colour or strength. FADED *adj*.

Fahrenheit *n*. a scale of temperature on which water freezes at 32° and boils at 212°.

fail *v*. to be unsuccessful; to disappoint; to let down.

failure *n*. 1 lack of success. 2 a person or thing that fails.

faint *adj*. 1 dim; not clear. 2 feeble, weak. FAINT *v*. to lose consciousness for a short time.

faintly *adv*. 1 dimly; not clearly. 2 feebly.

fair *adj*. 1 just; honest. 2 light-coloured. 3 free from rain. 4 pleasing. FAIR *n*. a trade exhibition; a market with amusements.

fairly *adv*. justly; moderately.

fairness *n*. rightness; justice.

fairy *n*. an imaginary small person with magical powers. *pl*. FAIRIES. FAIRY *adj*. delicate; dainty.

fairy tale *n*. a (children's) story including elements of magic, e.g. fairies, spells.

fairy-tale *adj*. magical, beautiful or romantic, e.g. a fairy-tale wedding.

faith *n*. trust; belief.

faithful *adj*. 1 loyal; true. 2 accurate.

faithless *adj*. disloyal; without belief.

fake *n*. an imitation; a sham. FAKE *v*. to cheat by making an imitation; to pretend.

falcon *n*. a bird of prey, of the hawk family.

fall *v*. to drop; to descend. to decrease. FALL *n*. a drop; a descent; a decrease.

fallow *adj*. (land) ploughed but unplanted.

false *adj*. 1 untrue; incorrect. 2 deceitful. 3 artificial.

falsehood *n*. a lie; an untruth.

falsify *v*. to alter for a dishonest purpose; to misrepresent.

falter *v*. 1 to stumble; to waver. 2 to speak hesitantly.

fame *n*. the condition of being well known; renown; reputation.

familiar *adj*. well known; intimate; impudent.

family *n*. 1 members of a household. 2 a group of plants, animals, etc., of the same kind. *pl*. FAMILIES.

famine *n*. an extreme shortage of food.

famish *v*. to starve; to be hungry. FAMISHED *adj*.

famous *adj*. very well known; celebrated.

fan *n*. 1 an appliance for creating air currents. 2 a supporter. FAN *v*. to stir the air.

fanatic *n*. a person who is very enthusiastic about something.

fancied *adj*. 1 supposed; imagined. 2 desired.

fancy *v*. to suppose; to imagine; to have a liking for. FANCY *n*. an idea; a liking. *pl*. FANCIES. FANCY *adj*. ornamental.

fanfare *n*. a flourish of trumpets.

fang *n*. a long pointed tooth.

fantastic *adj*. fanciful; unusual; odd; extraordinary.

fantasy *n*. 1 something imagined; a day-dream. 2 a story that is fantastic in content.

far *adj*. distant; remote.

farce *n*. 1 a silly but amusing play. 2 a silly or useless procedure.

fare *n*. 1 the charge made for a journey. 2 a passenger who pays. FARE *v*. to proceed well or badly.

farewell *n*. a goodbye or leave-taking.

farm *n*. the land and buildings used for growing crops or raising animals. FARM *v*. to work and cultivate the land; to raise animals. FARMER *n*.

farther *adv*. at a greater distance; in addition. FARTHER *adj*. more distant; more advanced.

farthing *n*. an old coin that was worth a quarter of an old penny.

fascinate *v*. 1 to charm. 2 to put a spell on. FASCINATING *adj*. FASCINATION *n*.

fashion *n*. the most popular style of clothes or way of doing something. FASHION *v*. to make; to shape.

fashionable *n*. following the latest fashion.

fast *adj*. 1 rapid. 2 firm; secure. FAST *v*. to go without food. FAST *n*. a period during which little or no food is eaten.

fasten *v*. to fix or tie together; to make secure. FASTENER *n*.

fastening *n*. anything that fastens things together.

fat *n*. an oily substance in animals. FAT *adj*. 1 plump. 2 rich. 3 greasy.

fatal *adj*. causing death or disaster. FATALLY *adv*.

fatality *n*. a disaster which causes death; a calamity. *pl*. FATALITIES.

fate *n*. a power which is thought to determine the future.

father *n*. 1 a male parent. 2 a priest. FATHERLY *adj*.

fathom *n*. a measure of depth (1.8 metres or six feet). FATHOM *v*. 1 to find the depth. 2 to get to the bottom of.

fatigue *n*. tiredness; exhaustion. FATIGUE *v*. to tire (someone) out.

fatten *v*. to make or become fat.

fault *n*. a defect; a flaw. FAULT *v*. to blame.

faultless *adj*. perfect; flawless.

faulty *adj*. imperfect; having faults.

fauna *n*. the animal life of a region.

favour *v*. to treat kindly; to prefer. FAVOUR *n*. a kindness; a good wish.

favourable *adj.* giving or showing approval; in favour of; promising.

favourite *n.* a well-liked person or thing; pet. FAVOURITE *adj.* preferred above others.

fawn *n.* 1 a young deer. 2 a light yellowish-brown colour. FAWN *v.* to seek favour.

fear *n.* a feeling of alarm; dread; terror. FEAR *v.* to be afraid (of). FEARED *adj.*

fearful *adj.* 1 full of fear. 2 dreadful; terrible.

fearless *adj.* courageous; bold.

fearsome *adj.* causing fear; frightening.

feast *n.* 1 a banquet; a rich meal. 2 a holiday; a religious anniversary. FEAST *v.* to eat well.

feat *n.* a difficult or brave deed.

feather *n.* a fringed quill which grows on a bird. FEATHERED *adj.*

feature *n.* 1 a part of the face. 2 a characteristic quality. 3 an important article in a newspaper etc. FEATURE *v.* to make prominent.

February *n.* the second month of the year.

federation *n.* a group of states which are united nationally but independent internally. FEDERAL *adj.*

fee *n.* a payment for services.

feeble *adj.* weak; without energy or vigour.

feed *v.* 1 to give or eat food. 2 to supply with.

feel *v.* 1 to examine by touch. 2 to be conscious of. FEEL *n.* a sense of touch.

feeler *n.* an insect's organ of touch.

feeling *n.* 1 the sense of touch. 2 an emotion such as hope, fear, sympathy, etc.

feign *v.* to pretend.

feint *n.* a pretence; a deceptive action. FEINT *v.* to take a deceptive action.

feline *adj.* cat-like; stealthy. FELINE *n.* a member of the cat family.

fell *v.* to knock down; to cut down. FELL *n.* a mountain, hill or area of moorland.

felony *n.* a serious crime.

felt *v.* past tense of feel. FELT *n.* a fabric made from shrunk and pressed wool, hair or fur.

female *n.* 1 a woman or girl. 2 an animal able to produce young. 3 a fruit-bearing plant.

feminine *adj.* womanly; having to do with women.

femur *n.* the thigh-bone.

fen *n.* a low-lying marshy area.

fence *n.* a barrier of wood, metal or wire, supported by posts, and enclosing a field or garden. FENCE *v.* 1 to enclose by means of a fence. 2 to fight with swords.

fend *v.* 1 FEND OFF to keep (something) off; to protect from (something). 2 FEND FOR to provide (food etc.) for (someone).

fender *n.* 1 an object to prevent a damaging collision, e.g. ropes or matting over the side of a ship. 2 a frame to prevent loose coals from rolling away from a fire.

ferment *v.* (pron. fer-MENT) to cause the process of fermentation; to excite. FERMENT *n.* (pron. FER-ment) 1 a substance that causes fermentation, such as yeast. 2 a state of excitement.

fern *n.* a plant with broad feathery leaves or fronds.

ferocious *adj.* savage; fierce; cruel.

ferocity *n.* fierce cruelty.

ferret *n.* a half-tamed polecat used for catching rabbits. FERRET (FOR) *v.* 1 to hunt with ferrets. 2 to search thoroughly.

ferry *v.* to convey over water. FERRY *n.* 1 a boat or aircraft which ferries passengers or freight. 2 a crossing place for a boat.

fertile *adj.* 1. fruitful; productive; full of ideas. 2 able to reproduce.

fertilisation *n.* when a sperm joins with an egg in animal reproduction, or when a pollen grain joins with an ovule in plant reproduction. FERTILISE *v.* to make fertile; to enrich. FERTILITY *n.*

fertiliser *n.* manure or chemicals put into the soil to make it more fertile.

fervent *adj.* very eager; hot; intense.

fester *v.* to become poisoned or rotten; to become bitter.

festival *n.* a feast; a day or period of rejoicing.

festive *adj.* in glad mood; joyful.

festivity *n.* a feast; joyfulness. *pl.* FESTIVITIES.

festoon *n.* a hanging chain of flowers, ribbons or paper. FESTOON *v.* to decorate with festoons.

fetch *v.* 1 to go and get. 2 to send for.

fête *n.* a festival; a gala; a carnival. FÊTE *v.* to honour and entertain (someone) by means of a fête.

fetlock *n.* the tufted part on the back of a horse's leg just above the hoof.

fetter *n.* a chain or shackle for the feet. FETTER *v.* to chain; to hinder.

feud *n.* a lasting quarrel between two persons, families, tribes, etc. FEUD *v.* to quarrel.

fever *n.* 1 an illness causing high temperature. 2 excitement.

few *adj.* not many. FEW *n.* a small number.

fez *n.* a red brimless hat with a black tassel, formerly worn by Turkish men.

fiasco *n.* a complete failure.

fibre *n.* 1. a thread of mineral or vegetable tissue from which fabrics are manufactured. 2 a substance in fruit, vegetables and brown bread/cereals which helps the body to digest food.

fiction *n.* a story which is not true; a thing invented or imagined; not factual. FICTIONAL *adj.*

fictitious *adj.* imagined; false; invented.

fidget *v.* to move restlessly. FIDGETY *adj.*

field *n.* 1 a piece of enclosed pasture or cultivated land. 2 a sports-ground. 3 an area of interest.

fiend *n.* a devil; a monster; a wicked person. FIENDISH *adj.*

fierce *adj.* violent; savage. FIERCELY *adv.*

fiery *adj.* 1 like a fire; flaming; burning. 2 quick-tempered.

fife *n.* a small flute.

fifteen *n.* a number (15).

fifty *n.* a number (50).

fight *v.* 1 to struggle with. 2 to battle with. FIGHT *n.* a combat; a battle. FIGHTER *n.*

figure *n.* 1 a human shape; image. 2 the symbol of a number. FIGURE *v.* to imagine; to write numbers; to calculate.

figurehead *n.* 1 a painted model, usually of a person or animal, fixed to the front of a ship. 2 a leader, but without power.

figurative *adj.* descriptive (language); not literal (see METAPHOR and SIMILE). FIGURATIVELY *adv.*

filament *n.* a very fine thread or wire.

file *n.* 1 a steel tool with a rough surface used for smoothing wood or metal. 2 a folder or case in which papers or documents are stored. 3 a single line of people. FILE *v.* 1 to use a file. 2 to place in a file. 3 to move one behind the other.

filings *n.* fine pieces of metal or wood rubbed off by a file.

fill *v.* to become, or make, full; to occupy all the space in. FILL *n.* a full supply.

fillet *n.* meat or fish from which the bones have been removed. FILLET *v.* to remove the bones from (meat or fish).

filly *n.* a young mare. *pl.* FILLIES.

film *n.* 1 a thin skin, layer or coating. 2 a strip of celluloid on which photographs are taken. FILM *v.* 1 to coat thinly. 2 to photograph.

filter *v.* to pass (liquid, light or air) through a filter in order to remove parts or particles. FILTER *n.* a strainer; a device for purifying.

filth *n.* 1 dirt. 2 obscenity. FILTHY *adj.*

fin *n.* 1 one of the organs which enable a fish to swim and balance itself. 2 a fin-like projection on a rocket, an aircraft, etc.

final *adj.* at the end, coming last; decisive. FINAL *n.* the last in a series of examinations, games, etc.

finale *n.* the end; the conclusion.

finally *adv.* lastly, in conclusion.

finance *n.* 1 the management of money matters. 2 money. FINANCE *v.* to provide money for.

financial *adj.* concerned with money matters.

financier *n.* a person who arranges finance.

finch *n.* one of various small song-birds.

find *v.* 1 to discover by chance. 2 to search for and discover. FIND *n.* a discovery.

fine *adj.* 1 very thin; delicate. 2 of very good quality; excellent. FINELY *adv.* FINE *n.* money paid as a penalty. FINE *v.* to impose a penalty on (someone).

finger *n.* one of the five digits at the end of the hand. FINGER *v.* to touch with the fingers.

finish *v.* to bring to an end; to complete. FINISH *n.* 1 the end; completion. 2 perfection. FINISHED *adj.*

Finn *n.* an inhabitant of Finland. FINNISH *n.* the language of Finland. FINNISH *adj.* of Finland.

fir *n.* an evergreen, cone-bearing tree.

fire *n.* 1 flame and heat from burning. 2 eagerness; excitement. FIRE *v.* 1 to cause to burn. 2 to excite. 3 to discharge from a gun.

firm *adj.* solid; fixed. FIRM *n.* a business concern; a company.

firmament *n.* the sky; the heavens.

first *adj.* coming before all others. FIRST *adv.* before anything else. FIRST *n.* a person or thing that is first.

firth *n.* a narrow inlet of the sea, especially in Scotland.

fish *n.* a water animal having backbone, fins and gills. FISH *v.* to catch fish. FISHERMAN *n.*

fissure *n.* a narrow opening; a crevice.

fist *n.* a hand with fingers tightly clenched.

fit *v.* to agree exactly (with); to be suitable (for). FIT *n.* a sudden seizure or spasm. FIT *adj.* 1 suitable. 2 in good health.

fitness *n.* 1 suitability. 2 healthiness.

fitting *adj.* suitable; appropriate. FITTING *n.* a fixture.

five *n.* the number one more than four (5).

fix *v.* 1 to make (something) firm; to secure. 2 FIX ON to decide on. FIX *n.* an awkward situation.

fixture *n.* 1 a permanent fitting. 2 the date of a future event.

flag *n.* 1 a standard or ensign. 2 a paving stone. FLAG *v.* 1 to signal with flags. 2 to pave with flags. 3 to become tired.

flagrant *adj.* openly wicked; notorious.

flair *n.* instinct; aptitude.

flake *n.* a thin layer or scale. FLAKE *v.* to come off in flakes.

flame *n.* 1 the burning gas from a fire; a blaze. 2 anger; enthusiasm. FLAME *v.* 1 to burn with a flame; to blaze. 2 to show anger or enthusiasm.

flammable *adj.* easily set on fire (see INFLAMMABLE).

flan *n.* a tart without a cover.

flange *n.* a raised rim or ridge.

flank *n.* the side of anything. FLANK *v.* to be at one side of; to attack on one side.

flannel *n.* a soft loosely-woven woollen cloth.

flap *n.* a piece of wood, metal or material that hangs down. FLAP *v.* to move up and down or from side to side; to flutter.

flare *v.* 1 to blaze; to flame. 2 to widen gradually (e.g. flared trousers). FLARE *n.* 1 a bright, unsteady flame. 2 a signal light.

flash *n.* 1 a sudden bright light. 2 a moment. FLASH *v.* to shine out suddenly.

flask *n.* a narrow-necked or flat-sided bottle.

flat *adj.* 1 level; even. 2 dull, uninteresting. FLAT *n.* 1 a home forming part of a building, with all the rooms on the same floor. 2 below the true pitch in music (sign ♭).

flatten *v.* to make or become level.

flatter *v.* to praise insincerely.

flaunt *v.* to show off.

flavour *n.* the taste. FLAVOUR *v.* to give flavour to; to season.

flavouring *n.* anything used to give a special taste to food.

flaw *n.* a fault; a crack; a defect. FLAWLESS *adj.* without fault.

flax *n.* a plant whose fibres are woven into linen.

flea *n.* a small, wingless, jumping insect.

fledgling, fledgeling *n.* a young bird just able to fly.

flee *v.* to run away from.

fleece *n.* the woolly covering of a sheep. FLEECE *v.* 1 to shear (a sheep). 2 to rob.

fleet *n.* a group of ships, aircraft, lorries, etc. FLEET *adj.* quick; swift.

flesh *n.* 1 the soft muscular tissues between the skin and bones of the body. 2 meat.

flex *n.* a flexible insulated wire which conveys electric currents. FLEX *v.* to bend.

flexible *adj.* easily bent; adaptable. FLEXIBILITY *n.*

flick *n.* a light, quick stroke. FLICK *v.* to strike lightly.

flicker *v.* to shine or burn unsteadily. FLICKER *n.* an unsteady light.

flight *n.* 1 the act of flying; the distance flown. 2 a group of birds or aircraft flying together. 3 a series of steps or stairs.

flimsy *adj.* frail, thin.

flinch *v.* to draw back; to wince.

fling *v.* to throw violently; to hurl. FLING *n.* 1 a throw. 2 a lively dance.

flint *n.* hard stone often found in chalk.

flip *v.* to flick sharply. FLIP *n.* a flick.

flit *v.* to move, or fly, lightly.

float *v.* 1 to stay on the surface of a liquid. 2 to set going or launch. FLOAT *n.* anything that floats on the surface of a liquid.

floating *adj.* 1 buoyant. 2 fluctuating.

flock *n*. 1 a group of beasts or birds. 2 a gathering of people. FLOCK *v*. to crowd together.

floe *n*. a sheet of floating ice.

flog *v*. to beat with a whip or stick.

flood *n*. 1 an overflow of water, etc. 2 an abundance of anything. 3 the flowing in of the tide. FLOOD *v*. 1 to cover, or fill, with water. 2 to overwhelm. FLOODING *n*.

floor *n*. 1 the lower surface of a room. 2 a storey of a building. FLOOR *v*. 1 to lay a floor. 2 to knock to the ground. 3 to puzzle.

floppy *adj*. limp; loose. FLOPPY DISK *n*. a small flexible disk on which information can be stored digitally.

flora *n*. the plants of a particular region.

floral *adj*. made of or concerning flowers.

florist *n*. a person who grows or sells flowers for a living.

flotilla *n*. a small fleet of ships.

flotsam *n*. cargo or wreckage found floating on the sea.

flounder *v*. to struggle helplessly. FLOUNDER *n*. a small flat-fish.

flour *n*. finely-ground wheat used for making bread, etc.

flourish *v*. 1 to grow vigorously; to prosper. 2 to wave or throw (something) about. FLOURISH *n*. 1 a waving about. 2 a fanfare. 3 an ornamental curve.

flourishing *adj*. thriving; prosperous.

flout *v*. to treat with contempt; to defy.

flow *v*. to move along easily; to glide. FLOW *n*. 1 the act of flowing. 2 a steady supply.

flow chart *n*. a diagram using boxes and arrows to show how something works (a process), or a sequence of events or actions.

flower *n*. 1 the part of a plant or tree from which the seed or fruit develops; bloom. 2 the best part of anything. FLOWER *v*. to bloom; to blossom.

fluctuate *v*. to rise and fall; to vary irregularly.

flue *n*. a pipe or duct to carry air, smoke or fumes; a ventilating shaft.

fluent *adj*. 1 speaking or writing easily and skilfully. 2 graceful and easy in movement. FLUENCY *n*.

fluid *n*. something which flows, such as a liquid or gas. FLUID *adj*. capable of flowing.

fluke *n*. 1 an unexpected and lucky success. 2 the triangular end of an arrow, harpoon or arm of an anchor.

flush *v*. 1 to clean by a flow of water. 2 to blush. FLUSH *n*. 1 a sudden flow of water. 2 a blush. FLUSH *adj*. full; level with the top.

fluster *v*. to confuse; to agitate. FLUSTER *n*. confusion; agitation. FLUSTERED *adj*.

flute *n*. 1 a musical wind instrument with finger holes. 2 a groove cut in a pillar.

flutter *v*. to flap (the wings); to move about quickly. FLUTTER *n*. 1 a quick beating (of wings etc.). 2 a state of excitement.

fly *v*. 1 to move through the air with wings or in an aircraft; to pilot an aircraft. 2 to move swiftly; to flee. FLY *n*. a two-winged insect such as the house-fly. *pl*. FLIES.

flyer, flier *n*. a person who flies; an airman.

foal *n*. a young horse. FOAL *v*. to give birth to a foal.

foam *n*. froth or bubbles on liquid. FOAM *v*. 1 to form or produce foam. 2 to be angry.

focus *n*. 1 the point at which rays of light meet. 2 a centre point. *pl*. FOCI. FOCUS *v*. 1 to adjust the eyes or a lens to get a clear image. 2 to draw attention to.

fodder *n*. dried food for cattle.

foe *n*. an enemy.

foetus, fetus *n*. (pron. FEE-tus) a young animal or human developing in its mother's body, at a later stage than the EMBRYO. *pl*. FOETUSES, FETUSES.

fog *n*. clouds of water droplets suspended in the atmosphere, either reducing visibility or causing almost complete obscurity.

foil *n*. 1 a thin sheet of metal. 2 a fencing sword. FOIL *v*. to outwit; to baffle.

fold *v*. to double something over on itself; to enclose. FOLD *n*. 1 the part folded over. 2 an enclosure for sheep.

foliage *n*. the leaves of plants or trees.

folk *n*. people; a nation or race.

folklore *n*. traditional legends, customs and beliefs.

follow *v.* 1 to go or come after. 2 to support. 3 to understand.

follower *n.* 1 a person who follows. 2 a supporter.

following *n.* all those who support. FOLLOWING *adj.* that which follows.

folly *n.* foolishness; a foolish act. *pl.* FOLLIES.

fond *adj.* affectionate; loving. FONDNESS *n.* FONDLY *adv.*

fondle *v.* to caress.

font *n.* 1 the basin holding water for baptism in a church. 2 in printing and word processing, a style or size of letters.

food *n.* 1 anything eaten. 2 nourishment for animals and plants.

food chain *n.* a series of living things which are connected because each group eats the group below it in the series (e.g. grass is eaten by cows; cows are eaten by humans).

fool *n.* a foolish person. FOOL *v.* 1 to deceive. 2 FOOL ABOUT to behave stupidly.

foolish *adj.* unwise; stupid. FOOLISHLY *adv.*

foot *n.* 1 the lower part of the leg from the ankle down. 2 an imperial measure of length; 12 inches or about 30 cm. 3 the bottom or base of anything. *pl.* FEET.

footnote *n.* a note at the bottom (the 'foot') of a page, or at the end of a text, giving extra information.

for *prep.* 1 in place of. 2 on behalf of. 3 in support of. 4 meant for. FOR *conj.* because.

forage *v.* to search for food, etc. FORAGE *n.* food for horses, cattle, etc.

forbid *v.* to order (someone) not to do (something).

force *v.* to compel (someone); to break (something) open. FORCE *n.* 1 strength; power. 2 compulsion. 3 an organised group of people. FORCEFUL *adj.* strong; determined.

forceps *n. pl.* pincers used by surgeons, dentists, etc.

forcible *adj.* done by force.

ford *n.* a shallow place where a river can be crossed on foot or in a vehicle. FORD *v.* to wade across a river.

fore *n.* the front part. FORE *adj.* in front of.

forearm *n.* (pron. FORE-arm) the arm between the wrist and the elbow. FOREARM *v.* (pron. fore-ARM) to prepare beforehand.

forebode *v.* to indicate; to suggest. FOREBODING *n.*

forecast *n.* a prediction of what may be expected. FORECAST *v.* to predict or estimate probable events.

forefather *n.* an ancestor.

forehead *n.* the part of the face above the eyebrows; the brow.

foreign *adj.* 1 belonging to or concerning another country. 2 alien; strange. FOREIGNER *n.*

foresee *v.* to know beforehand; to anticipate.

foresight *n.* 1 seeing beforehand. 2 care in preparing for future needs.

forest *n.* a large area of land covered with trees.

forester *n.* a forest worker.

foretell *v.* to tell beforehand; to predict.

forfeit *v.* to give up or lose (something) as a penalty. FORFEIT *n.* something given up as a fine, penalty or punishment.

forge *n.* a workshop where metal is heated and shaped. FORGE *v.* 1 to shape by heating and hammering. 2 to make a copy intending to deceive.

forgery *n.* a copy made with intent to deceive.

forget *v.* to fail to remember; to overlook; to neglect.

forgive *v.* to pardon; to be merciful (to someone).

forgiveness *n.* readiness to pardon.

forgotten *adj.* 1 not remembered. 2 neglected.

fork *n.* 1 a pronged implement for eating or, larger, for digging. 2 the point where a road, stream or tree divides into two or more branches. FORK *v.* 1 to use a fork on (something). 2 to branch; to divide.

form *n.* 1 the shape; appearance. 2 an official paper. 3 a school class. 4 a long seat or bench.

formal *adj.* 1 according to rule and custom. 2 dignified; exact.

format *n.* 1 the way in which a text or programme is presented or organised. 2 plan; pattern. FORMAT *v.* to prepare or organise a text or materials for presentation (especially on computer).

formation *n.* an arrangement in a particular form.

former *adj.* before in time or order. FORMER *n.* the first of two.

formerly *adv.* at an earlier time; once.

formidable *adj.* to be dreaded; hard to overcome.

formula *n.* 1 a set form of words or symbols representing a rule or statement. 2 a recipe.

formulate *v.* to set down or state clearly.

forsake *v.* to leave or desert (someone); to give up (something).

forsaken *adj.* left alone; deserted.

fort *n.* a fortified place or stronghold.

forth *adv.* onwards; forward.

forthcoming *adj.* happening soon; about to appear.

fortifications *n. pl.* defensive walls, towers, trenches, etc.

fortify *v.* 1 to defend against attack by making fortifications. 2 to strengthen (a place) against attack.

fortnight *n.* two weeks.

fortunate *adj.* lucky; prosperous.

fortune *n.* 1 good or bad luck; chance. 2 wealth; success.

forty *n.* a number (40).

forum *n.* 1 an occasion or a meeting-place for discussion. 2 a market-place in ancient Rome.

forward *adj.* 1 in front; advanced. 2 impudent. FORWARD *adv.* towards the front.

forward *v.* 1 to help on; to encourage. 2 to send on (a letter); to despatch.

fossil *n.* the preserved remains of prehistoric animal or plant life found in rocks.

foul *adj.* 1 dirty; disgusting; obscene. 2 stormy; rough (weather). 3 unfair. FOUL *n.* a breaking of the rules of a game. FOUL *v.* 1 to dirty. 2 to entangle (a rope etc.). 3 to break a rule in sport.

found *v.* to start (something); to establish.

foundation *n.* 1 the base or groundwork of a structure; basis. 2 an institution or establishment.

foundry *n.* a factory or workshop where molten metal is formed or cast in moulds.

fountain *n.* a spring of water; an artificial jet of water.

four *n.* the number one more than three (4).

fourteen *n.* a number (14).

fowl *n.* a domestic bird, cock or hen; poultry.

fox *n.* a cunning wild dog-like mammal. FOX *v.* to deceive; to puzzle (someone).

fraction *n.* 1 any part of a unit, e.g. a half, two-thirds. 2 a fragment, piece or part of anything.

fracture *n.* a break, a crack. FRACTURE *v.* to break, to crack (something).

fragile *adj.* easily broken or damaged.

fragment *n.* a part broken off; an incomplete part.

fragrance *n.* a sweet smell or perfume.

fragrant *adj.* sweet-smelling.

frail *adj.* weak; fragile.

frame *v.* 1 to put a frame round. 2 to put together; to construct. FRAME *n.* an outline, a skeleton or a basic structure.

framework *n.* 1 the frame round which something is built. 2 a system.

franc *n.* a unit of money in Switzerland and formerly in Belgium, France, etc.

franchise *n.* 1 the right to vote. 2 a right or privilege granted.

frank *adj.* outspoken; sincere; candid.

frantic *adj.* wildly excited; showing frenzy.

fraud *n.* 1 trickery; deceit. 2 someone or something that is not genuine.

fraudulent *adj.* 1 obtained by trickery. 2 deceitful.

fray *n.* a fight; a brawl. FRAY *v.* to make or become worn (esp. the edge of cloth). FRAYED *adj.* worn.

freak *n.* something very odd. FREAK *adj.* unusual (happening); eccentric (person).

free *adj.* 1 having personal rights and liberty. 2 open; frank. 3 generous. 4 costing nothing. FREE *v.* to release; to set (someone) free.

freedom *n.* liberty; independence.

freehold *n.* land and property held by legal right for life. FREEHOLDER *n.*

freeze *v.* 1 to change into ice; to change from a liquid into a solid by chilling. 2 to become suddenly still or rigid. 3 to fix (prices or wages) at a certain level.

freight *n.* goods carried by sea, air, road or rail.

freighter *n.* a cargo ship, aircraft, lorry or train.

French *adj.* belonging to France or its people. FRENCH *n.* the language or people of France.

frenzy *n.* wild excitement or fury.

frequency *n.* 1 the repeated happening of (an action, an event) 2 the rate at which something occurs.

frequent *adj.* happening often. FREQUENT *v.* to visit often.

frequently *adv.* many times; often.

fresco *n.* a picture painted on a wall.

fresh *adj.* 1 new; recent. 2 clean; refreshing. 3 vivid; lively.

fret *v.* 1 to worry oneself; to grieve. 2 to wear away.

friction *n.* 1 the resistance between things rubbing together; the force that gives us grip. 2 disagreement; bad feeling.

Friday *n.* the sixth day of the week.

friend *n.* a person attached to another by affection; a companion. FRIENDSHIP *n.*

friendliness *n.* affection; goodwill.

friendly *adj.* attached; affectionate.

frieze *n.* a decorative border.

frigate *n.* 1 a small, fast warship. 2 a fast sailing warship in earlier times.

fright *n.* sudden fear; terror.

frighten *v.* to terrify; to make afraid.

fringe *n.* 1 a border of loose threads. 2 an edge; a margin.

frisk *v.* 1 to romp and skip playfully. 2 to search a person for weapons.

frivolous *adj.* 1 trivial; not serious. 2 playful.

frock *n.* 1 a dress worn by a woman or a girl. 2 a monk's robe.

frog *n.* a small amphibious creature which grows from a tadpole.

from *prep.* starting from; out of; because of; at a distance of.

front *n.* the foremost part of anything; the face. FRONT *v.* to face; to look towards.

frontier *n.* the border or boundary between countries.

frost *n.* 1 an air temperature below freezing-point. 2 frozen dew or water vapour. FROSTY *adj.*

froth *n.* foam on liquids.

frown *v.* to wrinkle the forehead in anger or disapproval.

fruit *n.* 1 the seed-producing organ of a plant. 2 produce, e.g. apples, pears, etc.

fruiterer *n.* a person who sells fruit.

frustrate *v.* 1 to make (someone) feel annoyed or discouraged, especially because of difficulties in doing something. 2 to prevent (someone) from doing (something). FRUSTRATED *adj.* FRUSTRATION *n.*

fry *v.* to cook in hot fat or oil. FRY *n.* young fish.

fuel *n.* any substance used to provide a source of heat or other energy.

fugitive *n.* a person who runs away or flees from something.

fulcrum *n.* the point or pivot on which a lever balances.

fulfil *v.* to carry out (what is promised or expected); to complete satisfactorily.

fulfilled *adj.* carried out as promised or expected.

full *adj.* complete; filled, unable to hold any more. FULLY *adv.* completely.

fume *v.* 1 to give off steam, smoke or vapour; to send out fumes. 2 to be in a rage. FUME *n.* gas, smoke or vapour.

fun *n.* amusement; enjoyment.

function *v.* to work correctly; to operate. FUNCTION *n.* 1 a ceremony or event. 2 operation; purpose.

fund *n.* 1 money to be used for a particular purpose. 2 a supply or stock. FUND *v.* to supply money for a particular purpose.

fundamental *adj.* essential; necessary. FUNDAMENTAL *n.* an essential and necessary part.

funeral *n.* a burial or cremation ceremony.

fungus *n.* 1 a soft, spongy plant growth such as a mushroom or toadstool. 2 a disease-growth on animals and plants.

funnel *n.* 1 a tube with a cone-shaped filler for pouring liquids through a small opening. 2 a chimney on a ship or locomotive.

funny *adj.* amusing; comical; odd.

fur *n.* the soft hair of certain animals.

furious *adj.* very angry; raging.

furl *v.* to roll up.

furlong *n.* an eighth of a mile (220 yards or 201 metres).

furnace *n*. an enclosed fire which produces intense heat to melt metal, provide hot water or supply heat for an engine.

furnish *v*. to supply with furniture; to provide what is needed. FURNISHED *adj*.

furniture *n*. the larger, and often movable, articles in a room, house, office, etc., e.g. chairs, tables, bookshelves, etc.

furrow *n*. 1 a narrow trench made by a plough. 2 a wrinkle.

further *adj*. 1 in addition. 2 more distant. FURTHER *adv*. 1 at a greater distance. 2 also; besides. FURTHER *v*. 1 to help (something) forward. 2 to encourage.

furtive *adj*. sly; stealthy. FURTIVELY *adv*.

fury *n*. rage; violent anger.

fuse *v*. 1 to melt by intense heat. 2 to join together; to blend. 3 to cause an electric circuit to fail. FUSE *n*. 1 a safety device to protect electrical apparatus. 2 a device to time the detonation of an explosive.

fuselage *n*. the body of an aircraft.

fuss *n*. excitement or concern over trifling matters. FUSS (OVER) *v*. to worry over small things.

future *n*. the time still to come; events which will happen. FUTURE *adj*. about to be; still to happen.

G

gabble *v*. to talk quickly and indistinctly.

gable *n*. the triangular wall at the end of a ridged roof.

gadget *n*. a small and useful device.

gaff *n*. a spear or hook for landing large fish.

gag *n*. something placed in or over a person's mouth to keep it open or to prevent the person from speaking. GAG *v*. to silence with a gag.

gaily *adv*. happily and cheerfully.

gain *n*. an increase in wealth, profit or power. GAIN *v*. to earn; to profit; to win.

gala *n*. a festivity; a fête.

gale *n*. a strong wind; a storm.

gallant *adj*. brave; chivalrous; noble. GALLANTLY *adv*.

gallantry *n*. 1 bravery. 2 courtesy and politeness.

galleon *n*. a large Spanish sailing-ship of olden times.

gallery *n*. 1 a long narrow passage. 2 a theatre balcony. 3 a room in which paintings, etc., are exhibited.

galley *n*. 1 an ancient ship using sails and oars, usually rowed by slaves. 2 a ship's kitchen.

gallon *n*. an imperial measure of capacity, 8 pints (approx. 4.5 litres).

gallop *n*. the fastest pace of a horse. GALLOP *v*. to move rapidly in leaps.

gamble *v*. to bet; to take a chance. GAMBLE *n*. a risk.

game *n*. 1 any form of organised sport or play; amusement. 2 wild animals or birds which are hunted for sport or food.

gamekeeper *n*. a person who rears and cares for birds and animals that are bred as game.

gammon *n*. smoked or cured ham; the thigh of a pig.

gander *n*. a male goose.

gang *n*. a group of people working, playing or going about together, sometimes for criminal purposes.

gangster *n*. a member of a gang of criminals.

gangway *n*. 1 a movable bridge between a dockside and a ship. 2 a passageway between rows of seats.

gaol, jail *n*. a prison. GAOLER, JAILER *n*.

gap *n*. 1 an opening; a break. 2 an interval.

gape *v*. 1 to yawn. 2 to stare open-mouthed. 3 to be open wide.

garage *n*. a building where motor vehicles are kept; a business which sells and repairs motor vehicles.

garbage *n*. rubbish; refuse.

garden *n*. a place where flowers, shrubs, vegetables, etc., are cultivated. GARDEN *v*. to work in a garden; to cultivate a small plot.

garment *n*. an article of clothing.

garrison *n*. 1 the troops defending a town. 2 the base or depot of a particular unit, regiment, etc. GARRISON *v*. to provide with defending troops.

gas *n*. an elastic fluid that does not become solid or liquid at ordinary temperature, e.g. nitrogen, helium. *pl*. GASES. GAS *v*. to injure or poison with gas.

gash *v.* to cut deeply. GASH *n.* a deep cut.

gasp *v.* to breathe with difficulty; to struggle for breath. GASP *n.* a gulp; a sudden catching of the breath.

gate *n.* a hinged barrier to control an entrance or exit.

gateway *n.* a gated entrance.

gather *v.* 1 to assemble; to collect; to bring together. 2 to understand. 3 to draw fabric together in folds.

gathering *n.* an assembly.

gaudy *adj.* bright and showy.

gauge *n.* an instrument for measuring, testing or estimating. GAUGE *v.* to measure, test or estimate.

gaunt *adj.* thin; haggard; grim.

gauntlet *n.* a long glove that covers the wrist.

gay *adj.* lively; cheerful; full of fun.

gaze (at) *v.* to look at intently. GAZE *n.* an intent look.

gear *n.* 1 equipment; tools. 2 toothed wheels for transferring motion in machinery, as in the gearbox of a motor vehicle.

gem *n.* a precious stone; something of great value.

gender *n.* the classification of a noun or pronoun as masculine, feminine or neuter.

general *adj.* 1 concerning everybody or everything. 2 not special; widespread. GENERAL *n.* a high-ranking army officer.

generally *adv.* in most cases; commonly.

generate *v.* to produce; to set going.

generator *n.* a machine for producing electricity, steam, gases, etc.

generous *adj.* 1 liberal; giving freely. 2 kind; forgiving.

genial *adj.* good-natured; pleasant; friendly.

genius *n.* 1 exceptional power or ability. 2 a person who is highly intelligent and talented.

genre *n.* a type or style of art or of writing, e.g. adventure, science fiction, romance.

gentle *adj.* 1 mild; kind; not rough or violent. 2 soft; light.

gently *adv.* mildly; without violence.

genuine *adj.* real; sincere; authentic.

geography *n.* the study of the Earth's surface, products, climate, inhabitants, etc.

geology *n.* the study of the Earth's crust and its rocks and minerals.

geometry *n.* a branch of mathematics that is the study of lines, angles and figures.

germ *n.* 1 the beginning of a living thing. 2 a beginning. 3 a microbe which may cause disease.

German *adj.* belonging to Germany or its people. GERMAN *n.* the language or an inhabitant of Germany.

germinate *v.* to begin to grow; to sprout.

gestation *n.* the development of a young child or animal inside its mother's body.

gesture *n.* an expressive movement of the body, especially of the hands and arms.

get *v.* 1 to obtain. 2 to catch. 3 to arrive. 4 to become.

ghastly *adj.* pale; hideous; death-like.

ghost *n.* a spirit, usually supposed to be of a dead person.

giant *n.* a person, animal or plant of great height or size. GIANT *adj.* unusually large; **gigantic**; monstrous.

giddy *adj.* unsteady; dizzy.

gift *n.* 1 something given; a donation; a present. 2 a natural ability or talent.

gigantic *adj.* giant; huge; enormous.

giggle *v.* to laugh in a silly manner. GIGGLE *n.* a silly laugh.

gild *v.* to cover with gold leaf or gold paint; to make bright.

gill *n.* the breathing organ of a fish.

ginger *n.* a tropical plant with a hot spicy root.

gipsy, **gypsy** *n.* one of the Romany people; a wandering person who lives in a caravan.

giraffe *n.* an African animal with very long legs and a long neck.

girder *n.* a strong beam of concrete, metal or wood supporting a bridge, floor or roof.

girl *n.* a female child or young woman.

girth *n.* 1 the measurement round anything. 2 a band to hold a saddle in place.

give *v.* 1 to hand over; to donate. 2 to begin to break or crack; to yield.

glacial *adj.* having to do with glaciers; icy.

glacier *n.* a slow-moving mass of ice.

glad *adj.* happy; pleased; joyful.

glade *n.* an open place in a wood.

gladiator *n.* a person trained, in Roman times, to fight in an arena with other people or with wild animals. *fem.* GLADIATRIX.

glamour *n.* charm; attraction; beauty.

glance *n.* a brief look. GLANCE (AT) *v.* to look briefly at.

gland *n.* an organ of the body which stores and gives off used-up substances from the blood.

glare *v.* 1 to shine with a dazzling light. 2 to stare fiercely. GLARE *n.* 1 a dazzling light. 2 a fierce stare.

glass *n.* 1 a transparent substance made from sand and soda. 2 a mirror. 3 a vessel made of glass. GLASSY *adj.* GLASSHOUSE *n.* 1 a glass-roofed hut or room. 2 a greenhouse.

glaze *n.* a glass-like surface applied to pottery, porcelain, earthenware, etc.

gleam *n.* a brief flash of light. GLEAM *v.* to glow; to flash.

glen *n.* a long narrow valley; a dale.

glide *v.* 1 to move smoothly and slowly. 2 to fly an aircraft without an engine. GLIDE *n.* a smooth, slow motion.

glider *n.* an aircraft without an engine.

glimmer *v.* to shine faintly and unsteadily. GLIMMER *n.* a faint, unsteady light.

glimpse *n.* a quick look or glance. GLIMPSE *v.* to have a quick or incomplete view of.

glint *v.* to gleam; to sparkle. GLINT *n.* a gleam.

glitter *v.* to sparkle; to glisten.

gloat *v.* to look at or to think about greedily, evilly or selfishly.

global *adj.* world-wide; affecting everybody.

globe *n.* a ball; a sphere; the Earth.

globule *n.* a drop of liquid; a small particle.

gloom *n.* 1 dimness. 2 sadness; depression.

glorify *v.* to praise highly; to honour; to worship.

glorious *adj.* 1 splendid; magnificent. 2 famous; renowned.

glory *n.* 1 splendour; magnificence. 2 fame; renown.

gloss *n.* a smooth, shiny surface. GLOSSY *adj.*

glossary *n.* a list of words and their meanings.

glove *n.* a covering for the hand.

glow *v.* 1 to throw out light and heat without flame. 2 to feel hot and flushed.

glowing *adj.* 1 warm and bright. 2 hot and flushed. 3 enthusiastic.

glue *adj.* an adhesive.

glum *adj.* gloomy; downcast.

glut *n.* too much of something; a surfeit.

gnarled *adj.* (pron. NARLD) twisted and knotty.

gnash *v.* (pron. NASH) to grind the teeth.

gnat *n.* (pron. NAT) a small biting insect.

gnaw *v.* (pron. NAW) to bite at bit by bit; to chew.

gnome *n.* (pron. NOME) a dwarf; a goblin.

go *v.* 1 to move from one place to another; to depart from. 2 to become. GO *n.* 1 energy; activity. 2 an attempt.

goal *n.* 1 anything aimed at or wished for. 2 two upright poles with a crossbar through which a ball has to be driven in football, hockey, etc.

goat *n.* an animal of the sheep family, usually with horns and long hair.

gobble *v.* to eat and swallow quickly.

goblin *n.* a mischievous fairy.

God *n.* the Creator; the Supreme Being. GOD *n.* an idol; anything worshipped. *fem.* GODDESS.

goggles *n. pl.* spectacles to protect the eyes from dust, heat, wind, etc.

gold *n.* a yellow precious metal. GOLD, GOLDEN *adj.* like, or made of, gold.

golf *n.* an outdoor game played with clubs and a small ball. GOLFER *n.*

gong *n.* a metal plate which gives a ringing sound when struck.

good *adj.* 1 kind. 2 true. 3 well-behaved. 4 enjoyable. 5 clever; skilful. GOOD *n.* welfare; that which is right.

goodness *n.* 1 honesty. 2 kindliness. 3 nourishment.

goods *n.* possessions; things to be bought and sold.

goodwill *n.* 1 friendliness; kindly feeling. 2 the value of the success and reputation of a business.

goose *n.* a large bird with webbed feet. *pl.* GEESE. *masc.* GANDER.

gooseberry *n.* a thorny shrub bearing an edible green or red hairy fruit. *pl.* GOOSEBERRIES.

gorge *n.* a deep valley.

gorgeous *adj.* splendid; fine; magnificent.

gorilla *n.* an African ape, the largest kind of ape.

gorse *n.* a prickly shrub bearing yellow flowers.

gosling *n.* a young goose.

gospel *n.* an account of the life and teaching of Christ; one of the first four books in the New Testament.

gossip *n.* 1 idle talk, chatter or rumour. 2 a person who gossips. GOSSIP *v.* to talk and chatter idly.

Gothic *adj.* belonging to a style of architecture having high and pointed arches.

govern *v.* to rule; to control; to influence.

government *n.* 1 rule; control; authority. 2 the body of people chosen to rule a country.

grab *v.* to seize or grasp something suddenly.

grace *n.* 1 beauty, style, elegance. 2 a prayer or blessing. GRACE *v.* to give charm to; to honour.

graceful *adj.* beautiful in appearance and manner.

gracious *adj.* graceful; gentle; courteous. GRACIOUSLY *adv.*

grade *n.* step or degree in quality, rank or scale. GRADE *v.* to arrange in order.

gradient *n.* amount of slope in a road, railway, etc.

gradual *adj.* by degrees; going slowly but surely. GRADUALLY *adv.*

graduate *v.* 1 to arrange in order or mark in degrees. 2 to obtain a university degree. GRADUATE *n.* a person who has obtained a university degree.

grain *n.* 1 the seed of barley, oats, wheat, etc. 2 a small particle. 3 the lines of fibre making the pattern in wood.

gram *n.* the thousandth part of a kilogram.

grammar *n.* the study of the rules for correctly using words.

grand *adj.* fine; great; splendid.

granite *n.* a very hard rock used in building.

grant *v.* to give; to allow. GRANT *n.* an allowance; a payment.

grape *n.* the fruit of the vine.

graph *n.* a diagram which shows variations in quantity (e.g. temperature, rainfall, income, expenditure) and from which information can be extracted.

grapheme *n.* the way a particular sound is written, e.g. sh, ph.

graphite *n.* a soft, black form of carbon used in making pencil leads.

grasp *v.* 1 to grip; to seize firmly. 2 to understand. GRASP *n.* 1 a grip. 2 an understanding.

grass *n.* the common green plants which provide food for cattle and are mown to form lawns, etc.

grate *n.* a framework of iron bars for holding a fire. GRATE *v.* 1 to reduce to small pieces by scraping. 2 to make a harsh jarring sound. 3 GRATE UPON to irritate.

grateful *adj.* thankful; appreciative.

grating *n.* a grid of metal bars for covering drains, etc. GRATING *adj.* 1 harsh. 2 jarring; irritating.

gratitude *n.* thankfulness; appreciation.

gratuity *n.* money given in return for a favour or service.

grave *n.* a burial place. GRAVE *adj.* serious; solemn; important. GRAVELY *adv.* seriously; solemnly.

gravel *n.* small stones or pebbles; a mixture of sand and pebbles.

gravity *n.* 1 the force by which all bodies are drawn towards the Earth's centre. 2 seriousness; importance.

gravy *n.* the juices that come from meat that is cooking; a sauce made from these juices.

graze *v.* 1 to feed on growing grass. 2 to touch lightly. GRAZE *n.* a slight wound or scrape.

grease *n.* a thick fatty or oily substance used as a lubricant. GREASE *v.* to smear with grease; to lubricate. GREASY *adj.*

great *adj.* 1 of large amount, size, weight, etc. 2 important. 3 of remarkable ability or skill. 4 notable.

greed *n.* excessive and selfish desire for food, possessions or wealth.

Greek *adj.* belonging to Greece or its people. GREEK *n.* the language or an inhabitant of Greece.

green *n.* 1 the colour of grass and most growing plants; the colour between blue and yellow in the spectrum. 2 ground covered with grass; a lawn. GREEN *adj.* 1 grass-coloured. 2 fresh; unripe; inexperienced.

greengrocer *n.* a trader who sells fresh fruit and vegetables.

greenhouse *n.* a glasshouse where plants are grown.

greet *v.* to welcome.

greeting *n.* a welcome; a salutation;

grey *n.* a mixture of black and white; a dull colour. GREY *adj.* ash-coloured, grey-coloured; dull.

grid *n.* 1 a system of numbered squares on a map forming the basis for references. 2 a network of power lines for the distribution of electricity. 3 a grating.

gridiron *n.* a grill for cooking on.

grief *n.* 1 deep sorrow; anguish. 2 disaster.

grieve *v.* to mourn; to feel sorrow (for); to make (someone) sorrowful.

grill *v.* to cook on a grill. GRILL *n.* a gridiron.

grim *adj.* stern; dismal; sinister.

grime *n.* ingrained dirt or dust.

grimy *adj.* dirty; dusty.

grin *v.* to smile broadly; to smile scornfully. GRIN *n.* a broad or scornful smile.

grind *v.* 1 to crush to powder or small particles. 2 to sharpen or polish by grinding.

grip *v.* to grasp or hold firmly. GRIP *n.* a firm hold.

grit *n.* 1 particles of sand or stone. 2 courage; determination.

groan *v.* to make a moaning sound expressing pain, grief or disapproval. GROAN *n.* a moaning sound.

grocer *n.* a trader who sells food and provisions. GROCERIES *n. adv.*

groom *n.* 1 a bridegroom. 2 a person who is in charge of horses. GROOM *v.* 1 to feed, brush and care for horses. 2 to make oneself neat in appearance. 3 to prepare a person for a job or a position.

groove *n.* 1 a channel or hollow. 2 a fixed routine. GROOVE *v.* to cut a groove.

grope *v.* to search (for) by feeling; to see blindly.

gross *adj.* 1 fat; bulky. 2 coarse; vulgar. GROSS *n.* 1 the whole; the total including everything. 2 twelve dozen (144).

ground *n.* 1 the surface of the Earth. 2 base, foundation or surface. 3 a special area of land. 4 belief; motive; reason. GROUND *v.* 1 to run a ship ashore. 2 to keep an aircraft on the ground. GROUND *adj.* crushed or polished by grinding.

group *n.* a number of people or things gathered together; a cluster. GROUP *v.* to place in groups.

grove *n.* a small wood or cluster of trees.

grow *v.* 1 to increase in size; to develop. 2 to cultivate. GROWER *n.* GROWN *adj.* 1 enlarged. 2 fully mature.

growl *v.* to snarl; to murmur angrily. GROWL *n.* a snarling sound.

growth *n.* 1 a development; progress. 2 what has grown or is growing.

grub *n.* a newly-hatched insect.

grudge *v.* to be unwilling to give or allow (something to someone). GRUDGE *n.* a feeling of resentment or ill-will.

gruesome *adj.* horrible; repulsive; revolting.

gruff *adj.* rough and surly in manner; hoarse.

grumble *v.* to complain; to murmur. GRUMBLE *n.* a complaint; a murmur; a protest.

grunt *n.* a sound made by a pig; a low gruff sound. GRUNT *v.* to make a gruff sound.

guarantee *v.* 1 to give one's word that something has happened or will happen. 2 to agree to be responsible for. GUARANTEE *n.* an assurance; a pledge.

guard *v.* to defend against danger or attack; to protect. GUARD *n.* 1 a defender; a protector. 2 a person in charge of a train.

guardian *n.* a person who protects or guards.

guerrilla, **guerilla** *n.* a person engaged in irregular warfare.

guess *v.* 1 to estimate without exact calculation. 2 to form an opinion without sufficient evidence. 3 to imagine; to suppose. GUESS *n.* 1 a rough estimate. 2 an opinion formed without sufficient evidence.

guest *n.* 1 an invited visitor. 2 a person staying in a hotel.

guidance *n.* 1 leadership; management. 2 facts or advice which help a person to act properly.

guide *v.* to lead; to direct; to show the way.

guide *n.* a person who shows the way; a leader.

guilt *n.* the fact of having done wrong or having broken the law.

guilty *adj.* responsible for an offence or crime.

guinea *n.* a former English gold coin worth 21 shillings (£1.05).

guitar *n.* a six-stringed musical instrument.

gulf *n.* 1 a large inlet of the sea. 2 a deep place. 3 a wide gap.

gull *n.* a white, long-winged, web-footed, fish-eating sea-bird.

gully *n.* a channel worn by running water.

gulp *v.* to swallow hastily or greedily. GULP *n.* the act of gulping.

gum *n.* 1 the flesh surrounding the teeth. 2 an adhesive.

gun *n.* a firearm; a weapon firing bullets, shells, etc.

gunpowder *n.* an explosive mixture in powder form.

gust *n.* a sudden blast of wind.

gutter *n.* a channel for carrying away rain-water.

guy *n.* 1 a rope or wire used for steadying something. 2 an oddly-dressed person. 3 a dummy figure of Guy Fawkes which is burnt on 5th November.

gymkhana *n.* a sports meeting for horse-riders.

gymnasium *n.* a room or hall fitted up for gymnastics.

gymnast *n.* a person skilled in gymnastics.

gymnastics *n.* bodily exercises and activities performed in a gymnasium.

H

habit *n.* something that is done regularly or by custom.

habitable *adj.* that can be lived in.

habitat *n.* the natural home of an animal or a plant.

habitation *n.* a home; a dwelling.

habitual *adj.* 1 formed by habit. 2 usual; regular.

haddock *n.* a sea-fish of the cod family.

haft *n.* the handle of a knife or other tool or weapon.

haiku *n.* a Japanese form of poem, with three lines and a total of 17 syllables (in the pattern 5,7,5).

hail *n.* frozen drops of rain. HAIL *v.* 1 to fall as hail. 2 to greet; to welcome.

hair *n.* fine filaments growing from the skin of many mammals, including humans.

hale *adj.* healthy; robust; strong.

half *n.* one of two equal parts. HALF *adj.* forming one of two equal parts. *pl.* HALVES.

half-rhyme *n.* the use of words which almost rhyme.

hall *n.* 1 an entrance, passage or room. 2 a large room for public or private meetings and functions. 3 a large country house.

Hallowe'en *n.* 31st October, the evening before All Saints' Day.

halo *n.* a circle of light round the sun or moon or round the head of a sacred figure in a painting. *pl.* HALOES.

halt *v.* to stop; to hesitate. HALT *n.* a stopping-place.

halter *n.* a rope or strap for leading horses.

halve *v.* 1 to divide into two equal parts. 2 to reduce by half.

ham *n.* 1 the back of the thigh. 2 the salted and cured thigh of a pig; a gammon.

hamlet *n.* a small village.

hammer *n.* a tool with a heavy steel head for driving in nails, etc. HAMMER *v.* to beat or strike with a hammer; to beat as with a hammer.

hammock *n.* a bed of canvas or netting suspended by cords at each end.

hamper *v.* to hinder. HAMPER *n.* a large basket with a lid.

hand *n.* the part of the arm below the wrist. HAND *v.* to pass by hand.

handicap *n.* 1 a disadvantage; a disability. 2 an allowance given to some competitors to enable all to start on equal terms. HANDICAP *v.* to hinder.

handkerchief *n.* a square of material for wiping or blowing the nose.

handle *n.* the part by which an article is held. HANDLE *v.* 1 to touch or feel with the hand. 2 to manage.

handsome *adj.* 1 good-looking. 2 generous.

hang *v.* to suspend; to drape; to droop.

hangar *n.* a large shed for housing aircraft.

hanger *n.* a hook or device on which something is hung.

hank *n.* a coil or length of wool, yarn, etc.

haphazard *adj.* by chance or at random.

happen *v.* 1 to take place. 2 to occur by chance.

happening *n.* an event; an occurrence.

happily *adv.* 1 joyfully. 2 fortunately.

happiness *n.* joy; contentment.

happy *adj*. 1 feeling or showing joy. 2 contented; satisfied.

harbour *n*. a place of shelter for ships. HARBOUR *v*. to shelter.

hard *adj*. 1 firm; not easily broken. 2 difficult. 3 severe; harsh.

harden *v*. to make or become firm or solid.

hardly *adv*. only just; not quite.

hardship *n*. something hard to bear; severe suffering.

hardy *adj*. 1 strong; able to bear suffering. 2 (of plants) that can grow in the open in a temperate or cold climate.

hare *n*. a rodent like a large rabbit, with long ears, short tail and long hind legs.

hark (at) *v*. to listen to.

harm *v*. to injure; to damage. HARM *n*. an injury; a wrong.

harmful *adj*. causing injury or damage.

harmless *adj*. doing no harm.

harmony *n*. 1 agreeable combination of musical notes or of colours. 2 agreement; friendship.

harness *n*. the equipment of reins, bit, collar, straps, etc., for harnessing a horse. HARNESS *v*. 1 to put in harness. 2 to control and use (natural energy) for power.

harp *n*. a triangular stringed musical instrument. HARPIST *n*.

harpoon *n*. a barbed spear with rope attached for catching whales, etc.

harrow *n*. a heavy frame with iron teeth used for breaking up ploughed land. HARROW *v*. 1 to use a harrow. 2 to cause distress.

harsh *adj*. 1 rough to the touch, taste, eye or ear. 2 cruel; severe. HARSHLY *adv*.

harvest *n*. 1 the time of gathering in the ripened crops. 2 the crops gathered in. HARVEST *v*. to cut and gather the crops.

hasp *n*. a metal fastener for a door or lid.

haste *n*. speed; rapidity; urgency; hurry.

hasten *v*. to hurry; to accelerate.

hasty *adj*. 1 hurried; done without thinking. 2 quick-tempered.

hat *n*. a covering for the head.

hatch *v*. 1 to incubate (eggs); to come out of (an egg). 2 to think out a plan or scheme. HATCH *n*. 1 an opening in a deck or floor. 2 a half-door.

hate *v*. to dislike very much; to detest; to loathe. HATE *n*. a great dislike.

hateful *adj*. of hatred; causing hate.

hatred *n*. a bitter dislike of someone or something.

haul *v*. to pull or drag with effort. HAUL *n*. 1 a pull. 2 a rich find or catch.

haulage *n*. the transport of goods. HAULIER *n*.

haunt *v*. to visit a person or place often. HAUNT *n*. a place visited frequently.

have *v*. 1 to possess; to own. 2 to contain. 3 to obtain.

haven *n*. a place of refuge or shelter; a harbour.

haversack *n*. a canvas shoulder-bag for carrying food, clothing, etc.

havoc *n*. great destruction.

haw *n*. a hawthorn berry.

hawk *n*. a bird of prey in the eagle family. HAWK *v*. 1 to hunt with hawks. 2 to sell (goods) from door to door.

hawser *n*. a cable or rope used for towing or mooring ships, etc.

hawthorn *n*. a thorny bush whose fruits are red berries.

hay *n*. grass cut and dried as food for animals.

hazard *n*. 1 a risk; a danger; 2 an obstacle. HAZARD *v*. 1 to risk; to place in danger. 2 to guess. HAZARDOUS *adj*.

haze *n*. a light mist of water, smoke or dust.

hazel *n*. 1 a bush whose fruit is the hazel-nut. 2 a stick of hazel wood. 3 a reddish-brown or greenish-brown colour.

hazy *adj*. 1 misty. 2 confused; vague.

he *pron*. a male person or animal already named.

head *n*. 1 that part of the body consisting of the face, skull, brain, etc. 2 a chief part, place or person. HEAD *v*. 1 to be at the top or in front of. 2 to strike with the head.

headache *n*. a pain in the head.

heal *v*. to cure; to restore. HEALER *n*. HEALING *adj*.

health *n*. 1 the condition of a person's body and mind. 2 freedom from illness or disease.

healthy *adj*. 1 in good health. 2 wholesome.

heap *n*. a pile, mount or group of things. HEAP *v*. to pile up.

hear *v*. to perceive the sound of; to listen to.

hearing *n*. 1 the sense by which sound is perceived; the ability to hear. 2 a trial of a law case.

hearse *n*. a funeral vehicle for carrying a coffin.

heart *n*. 1 the organ that pumps blood around the body. 2 the centre; the core.

hearth *n*. the floor or base of a fireplace.

hearty *adj*. 1 strong, healthy. 2 enthusiastic; jovial.

heat *n*. 1 hotness; warmth. 2 anger. HEAT *v*. to make hot. HEATED *adj*. angry.

heater *n*. an appliance for providing warmth or heating water.

heath *n*. 1 uncultivated land covered with heather or scrub. 2 heather.

heathen *n*. a person who does not believe in God.

heather *n*. a heath plant with small purple or white flowers.

heaven *n*. 1 the dwelling-place of God. 2 the sky.

heavens *n. pl*. the sky with all the stars and planets.

heavy *adj*. having great weight, size, abundance, force, strength, etc.

Hebrew *n*. 1 an Israelite; a Jew. 2 the language of the Jewish scriptures and the modern Israelis. HEBREW *adj*. belonging to the Hebrews or their language.

hectare *n*. a metric measurement of area, 10 000 square metres (2.471 acres).

hectic *adj*. exciting; wildly active.

hedge *n*. a fence of growing shrubs, bushes or small trees. HEDGE *v*. 1 to enclose with a hedge. 2 to avoid making a decision or promise.

hedgehog *n*. a small animal covered with prickly spines.

hedgerow *n*. a hedge of bushes or small trees.

heel *n*. the back part of the foot.

hefty *adj*. sturdy; big, heavy and strong.

heifer *n*. a young cow.

height *n*. 1 distance from top to bottom. 2 altitude. 3 a high place.

heir *n*. a person who inherits; a successor. *fem*. HEIRESS.

helicopter *n*. an aircraft with rotor blades, able to take off and land vertically and to hover.

heliport *n*. a helicopter airport; a place where helicopters can take off and land.

helium *n*. a rare, light and colourless gas in the atmosphere.

hell *n*. 1 believed by some to be where the wicked go after death. 2 a place or state of misery or suffering.

helm *n*. the wheel or tiller by which a ship is steered. HELMSMAN *n*.

helmet *n*. a protective head cover worn by motor cyclists, soldiers, firemen, etc.

help *v*. to aid; to assist. HELP *n*. aid; assistance. HELPER *n*.

helpful *adj*. giving help; useful.

helpless *adj*. powerless; useless.

hem *n*. the edge of a garment, piece of material, etc., folded over and sewn down. HEM *v*. to fold over and sew down.

hemisphere *n*. 1 half a sphere. 2 half the globe or half the world.

hen *n*. a female bird.

hence *adv*. 1 from this time or place. 2 for this reason.

henceforth *adv*. from now on.

her *pron*. a female person or animal already named. HER *adj*. of, or belonging to, a female.

herald *n*. 1 an official who carries messages and makes public announcements. 2 an announcer; a messenger; a forerunner. HERALD *v*. to proclaim; to announce.

herb *n*. a plant used to provide flavour in cooking, or as a medicine.

herbivore *n*. an animal that eats only plants.

herd *n*. 1 a group of animals. 2 a crowd of people. HERD *v*. to collect together. HERDSMAN *n*. a keeper of a herd.

here *adv*. in this place or to this place.

hereabouts *adv*. near this place.

hereditary *adj*. handed down from one generation to the next.

heredity *n*. the passing on of characteristics from animals and plants to their offspring.

heritage *n*. something which is inherited or will be inherited; a right.

hermit *n*. a person who chooses to live alone.

hero *n*. a man admired for his brave deeds or courage. *fem*. HEROINE. *pl*. HEROES.

heroic *adj.* brave; courageous.

heroism *n.* great gallantry or courage.

hesitate *v.* to pause in doubt or indecision; to be reluctant.

hesitation *n.* doubt; indecision.

hessian *n.* a coarse cloth; sacking.

hexagon *n.* a six-sided plane figure with six angles. HEXAGONAL *adj.*

hibernate *v.* to pass the winter in sleep. HIBERNATION *n.*

hidden *adj.* 1 concealed. 2 kept secret.

hide *v.* 1 to put or to keep out of sight; to conceal. 2 to keep secret. HIDE *n.* 1 a place of concealment. 2 the skin of an animal.

hideous *adj.* horribly ugly; frightful.

high *adj.* 1 reaching a long way upwards; elevated. 2 chief; important. 3 strong; shrill.

highway *n.* a public road.

hijack *v.* to take over unlawfully of an aircraft, ship, train or vehicle by force.

hike *n.* a long walk.

hill *n.* a mass of high land; rising ground; a slope.

hilt *n.* the handle of a sword or dagger.

him *pron.* a male person or animal already named.

hind *n.* a female deer. HIND *adj.* situated at the back or rear.

hinder *v.* to obstruct; to delay.

Hindu *n.* a person whose religion is Hinduism. HINDU *adj.*

Hinduism *n.* a religion which originated in India and has many gods and goddesses.

hinge *n.* the joint on which a door, gate or lid hangs and swings. HINGE *v.* 1 to turn on a hinge. 2 to depend upon.

hint *n.* an indirect suggestion; a slight indication. HINT *v.* to make an indirect suggestion.

hip *n.* 1 the upper part of the thigh. 2 the fruit of the wild rose.

hippopotamus *n.* a large African animal living in or near rivers. *pl.* HIPPOPOTAMI, HIPPOPOTAMUSES.

hire *n.* 1 the payment made for the loan or use of something. 2 money paid for a service or work done. HIRE *v.* to employ (a person) and pay wages.

his *pron.* belonging to him. HIS *adj.* of or belonging to him.

history *n.* 1 the study of past events. 2 an account of what has happened in the past. *pl.* HISTORIES.

hit *v.* to strike; to collide (with). HIT *n.* 1 a stroke or blow. 2 a great success.

hitch *v.* 1 to fasten loosely. 2 to move with a jerk. HITCH *n.* 1 a fastening or tethering; a knot. 2 an unexpected difficulty or delay.

hive *n.* 1 a place where bees live. 2 a busy place.

hoard *n.* a hidden store of foods, treasure, etc. HOARD *v.* to store or to collect. HOARDER *n.*

hoarding *n.* a large board or fence on which advertisements are often displayed.

hoarse *adj.* rough and husky. HOARSELY *adv.*

hoax *n.* a practical joke. HOAX *v.* to play a practical joke on; to deceive.

hobble *v.* 1 to limp or to walk lamely. 2 to restrict the movement of an animal by tying a rope between two of its legs.

hobby *n.* a favourite pastime or recreation. *pl.* HOBBIES.

hockey *n.* an eleven-a-side team game played with curved sticks and a hard ball.

hoe *n.* a long-handled tool used for loosening soil and removing weeds.

hog *n.* 1 a pig. 2 a greedy person. HOG *v.* 1 to keep selfishly. 2 to take more than a fair share of.

hoist *v.* to lift up; to lift by means of a rope. HOIST *n.* equipment used for hoisting; an elevator.

hold *v.* 1 to grasp; to grip. 2 to stop; to restrain. 3 to have; to keep. HOLD *n.* 1 a grasp; a grip. 2 the cargo space in a ship.

holder *n.* a person or thing that holds or owns something.

hole *n.* an opening or hollow in something; a cavity.

holiday *n.* a day or period of rest or recreation.

hollow *adj.* 1 having an empty space inside; not solid; sunken. 2 insincere. HOLLOW *n.* 1 a hole. 2 a small valley. HOLLOW (OUT) *v.* to make hollow; to excavate.

holly *n.* an evergreen shrub or tree with glossy prickly leaves and red berries.

holster *n.* a pistol holder.

holy *adj.* to do with God or religion; sacred.

homograph *n.* a word with the same spelling as another, but with a different meaning or origin.

homonym *n.* a word with the same spelling or pronunciation as another, but with a different meaning or origin.

homophone *n.* a word which sounds the same as another but has a different meaning, e.g. blue/blew, pair/pear.

honest *adj.* fair; truthful; true. HONESTLY *adv.*

honey *n.* a sweet, thick fluid made by bees from the nectar of flowers.

honour *n.* 1 fame; a high reputation. 2 respect for truth, fairness and honesty. HONOUR *v.* 1 to respect. 2 to confer an honour upon.

hood *n.* 1 a covering for the head and neck. 2 anything of a hood-like shape.

hoof *n.* a horny substance protecting the feet of certain mammals. *pl.* HOOFS, HOOVES.

hook *n.* a curved piece of metal or plastic for catching or supporting something. HOOK *v.* to catch, support or hold with a hook.

hooligan *n.* a noisy, rough and violent person.

hoot *n.* 1 the cry of an owl. 2 the sound of a horn or siren. HOOT *v.* to make a hooting sound.

hop *v.* to jump on one foot. HOP *n.* 1 a short jump. 2 a climbing plant, the flowers of which are used in beer-making.

hope *v.* to expect and wish (that something will happen). HOPE *n.* expectation; belief.

horde *n.* 1 a wandering tribe. 2 a great number of people; a multitude.

horizon *n.* the distant line where the earth or sea seems to meet the sky.

horizontal *adj.* parallel to the horizon; flat.

horn *n.* 1 the hard, usually curved and pointed growths on the heads of some cattle and other mammals. 2 a musical wind instrument; a device for sounding a warning signal.

hornet *n.* a wasp-like insect with a painful sting.

horrible *adj.* causing horror; hideous; shocking.

horrid *adj.* frightful; disagreeable; unpleasant.

horrify *v.* to fill with horror; to shock.

horror *n.* intense dislike or disgust; terror.

horse *n.* a hoofed mammal used for riding and pulling loads.

horticulture *n.* the art of garden cultivation.

hospitable *adj.* friendly and welcoming.

hospital *n.* a building where sick or injured people are cared for and given medical treatment.

hospitality *n.* the friendly welcome and treatment of a guest or visitor.

host *n.* 1 a person who entertains guests. *fem.* HOSTESS. 2 a great number of people.

hostage *n.* a person held prisoner until certain demands have been met.

hostel *n.* a building where students, walkers, homeless persons, etc., are accommodated.

hostile *adj.* unfriendly; threatening; warlike.

hostilities *n. pl.* acts of warfare.

hostility *n.* warfare; enmity.

hot *adj.* 1 very warm. 2 spicy to the taste. 3 hasty; eager.

hotel *n.* a building where meals and accommodation are provided for visitors.

hound *n.* a dog used for hunting. HOUND *v.* to pursue; to persecute.

hour *n.* 1 sixty minutes; the twenty-fourth part of a day. 2 the fixed or appointed time.

hourly *adj.* occurring every hour. HOURLY *adv.* every hour.

house *n.* (pron. HOWS) a building in which people live; a building with a specified use. HOUSE *v.* (pron. HOWZ) to provide shelter or room for.

household *n.* the family or people living together in one house.

hovel *n.* a small, miserable dwelling.

hover *v.* 1 to hang in the air. 2 to hang about.

hovercraft *n.* a craft that travels over land and sea on a cushion of air.

how *adv.* 1 in what manner or way. 2 to what extent. 3 for what price. HOW *n.* the way a thing is done.

however *adv.* in whatever way; to whatever degree. HOWEVER *conj.* though; in spite of.

howl *n.* a long wailing cry. HOWL *v.* to wail.

hub *n.* 1 the central part of a wheel. 2 the central point of interest.

huddle *v.* to crowd together. HUDDLE *n.* a crowd of people or things.

hue *n.* 1 a colour; a shade of colour. 2 an outcry.

huff *n*. a fit of temper or sulking. HUFF *v*. to blow heavily.

hug *v*. 1 to clasp in the arms; to embrace. 2 to keep close to. HUG *n*. a squeeze; an embrace.

huge *adj*. very large; enormous; gigantic.

hulk *n*. 1 the hull of an old ship. 2 a big person or mass.

hull *n*. the body or frame of a ship.

human *adj*. of mankind; man-made.
HUMAN FEATURES *n. pl*. in geography, man-made parts of the landscape, e.g. buildings, roads.

humane *adj*. kind; merciful; sympathetic.

humanity *n*. 1 all human beings. 2 kindness and mercy.

humble *adj*. modest, unassuming. HUMBLE *v*. to shame; to defeat.

humid *adj*. damp; moist.

humidity *n*. 1 dampness. 2 the amount of water in the air.

humiliate *v*. to make someone feel humble; to shame.

humility *n*. humbleness; meekness.

humorous *adj*. full of humour; funny.
HUMOROUSLY *adv*.

humour *n*. 1 the ability to see the funny side of things. 2 a state of mind. HUMOUR *v*. to try to please (a person) by agreeing.

hump *n*. a rounded lump in the ground, on an animal's back, etc.

humus *n*. decayed vegetable matter.

hundred *n*. ten times ten; the number 100.

hunger *n*. the need or desire for food. HUNGER *v*. 1 to feel hunger. 2 HUNGER FOR or AFTER to desire; to crave.

hunt *v*. 1 to pursue. 2 to pursue and kill wild animals. HUNT *n*. 1 a search. 2 a group of hunters.

hunter *n*. 1 a person who hunts. 2 a horse used in hunting.

hurdle *n*. 1 a movable fence. 2 an obstacle.

hurl *v*. to throw with force.

hurricane *n*. a severe storm with high winds.

hurried *adj*. done with haste; quick.

hurry *v*. to move or to act quickly. HURRY *n*. haste; urgency.

hurt *v*. 1 to cause injury or pain to. 2 to cause offence or distress to. HURT *n*. an injury; a pain.

hurtle *v*. 1 to rush recklessly. 2 to be thrown violently through the air.

husband *n*. a married man. HUSBAND *v*. to use or manage carefully.

hush *v*. to make silent or quiet. HUSH *n*. a stillness; silence. HUSHED *adj*.

husk *n*. the dry covering of some fruits and seeds.

husky *adj*. hoarse and dry. HUSKY *n*. an Eskimo sledge-dog.

hustle *v*. 1 to push or jostle together 2. to hurry.

hut *n*. a small building, generally of wood.

hutch *n*. a coop or pen for rabbits, etc.

hydrant *n*. a pipe connection to a street water-main.

hydraulic *adj*. worked by fluid pressure.

hydrogen *n*. a gas which produces water when combined with oxygen; the lightest substance known.

hyena *n*. a wild, wolf-like animal.

hygiene *n*. the science of health.

hymn *n*. a song of praise to God.

hyphen *n*. a punctuation mark (-) which links two words or parts of words and can be used to make compound words (e.g. fairy-tale), or to join a prefix where lack of a hyphen would make it a different word (e.g. re-form).

hyphenate *v*. to join with a hyphen.

hypnosis *n*. an artificially-induced sleep.

hypnotise *v*. to put a person into a state of hypnosis. HYPNOTIST *n*.

hypocaust *n*. an under-floor heating system used by the ancient Romans.

hypocrisy *n*. a pretence of being virtuous and respectable.

hypocrite *n*. a person who pretends to be good.

hypotenuse *n*. the longest side of a right-angled triangle, the side opposite the right angle.

hypothesis *n*. a suggested explanation (see THEORY). HYPOTHESISE *v*. to form a hypothesis; to suggest an explanation.

hysterical *adj*. having hysterics; very easily excited.

hysterics *n*. an attack of uncontrollable laughing or weeping.

I

ice *n.* 1 frozen water. 2 ice cream. ICE *v.* to cover with icing.

iceberg *n.* a large floating mass of ice in the ocean.

Iceland *n.* a large island in the North Atlantic Ocean between Norway and Greenland.

icicle *n.* a hanging spike of ice formed by the freezing of dripping water.

icing *n.* a sugary layer on the top or outside of a cake, tart, etc.

icy *adj.* 1 covered in ice; very cold. 2 unfriendly, cool.

idea *n.* 1 a thought, a fancy. 2 a plan or scheme.

ideal *n.* a perfect example; the highest standard. IDEAL *adj.* perfect.

identical *adj.* exactly alike in every detail. IDENTICALLY *adv.*

identify *v.* 1 to recognise; to establish the identity of. 2 to treat as identical.

identity *n.* 1 absolute sameness. 2 who a person is.

idiocy *n.* foolishness; weakness of mind.

idiom *n.* a phrase with a meaning that cannot usually be guessed from the meanings of the separate words, e.g. over the moon, under the weather.

idiot *n.* a foolish or weak-minded person.

idle *adj.* 1 unoccupied; not working. 2 useless; lazy. IDLE *v.* to pass time idly.

idol *n.* 1 an image which is worshipped; a false god. 2 a greatly-loved person or thing; a hero.

idyll *n.* a short poem about simple and beautiful country life. IDYLLIC *adj.* simple; beautiful; perfect.

igloo *n.* a dome-shaped snow hut built by Eskimos.

igneous *adj.* 1 to do with fire. 2 produced by volcanic action.

ignite *v.* to set on fire; to catch fire.

ignition *n.* 1 a setting on fire. 2 the device for igniting the petrol-air mixture in the cylinders of a petrol engine.

ignorance *n.* lack of knowledge, information or awareness. IGNORANT *adj.* lacking knowledge; uninformed.

ignore *v.* to refuse to take notice of; to disregard.

ill *adj.* 1 sick; unwell. 2 evil; bad. 3 unfortunate; unlucky.

illegal *adj.* against the law; unlawful; not legal. ILLEGALLY *adv.*

illegible *adj.* not legible; unreadable.

illicit *adj.* unlawful; illegal; forbidden; prohibited. ILLICITLY *adv.*

illiterate *adj.* unable to read or write. ILLITERACY *n.*

illness *n.* poor health; sickness.

illogical *adj.* against the rules of reason; without logic. ILLOGICALLY *adv.*

illuminate *v.* 1 to light up; to throw light upon. 2 to decorate (a page or document) with gold, silver, colours, etc.

illumination *n.* 1 light. 2 decorated lettering.

illusion *n.* something that deceives. ILLUSORY *adj.* deceptive.

illustrate *v.* 1 to make clear; to explain. 2 to explain by examples or by drawings and pictures.

illustration *n.* 1 an example which helps to make a matter clear. 2 a drawing or picture in a book, newspaper, etc. ILLUSTRATOR *n.*

illustrious *adj.* famous; celebrated; distinguished.

image *n.* 1 a copy or close likeness; a statue. 2 a reflection seen in a mirror or camera lens.

imagery *n.* words used to describe things (see METAPHOR and SIMILE).

imaginary *adj.* imagined; existing only in the mind; unreal.

imagination *n.* the ability to form ideas and images in the mind.

imaginative *adj.* inventive; having imagination.

image *v.* to form a picture in the mind; to suppose.

imitate *v.* to copy; to mimic; to follow the example of.

imitation *n.* a copy; a sham; a counterfeit. IMITATION *adj.* false.

immaculate *adj.* pure; faultless; spotless.

immaterial *adj.* not important; trivial.

immature *adj.* not fully developed. not mature.

immediate *adj.* 1 with nothing coming between; close. 2 happening at once; prompt. IMMEDIATELY *adv.*

immense *adj.* very large; vast. IMMENSELY *adv.*

immerse *v.* 1 to dip or plunge (something) into liquid. 2 IMMERSE ONESELF IN to give (one's) total attention to. IMMERSION *n.*

immigrant *n.* a person who settles in a country that is not his or her own.

immigrate *v.* to enter a country to settle there. IMMIGRATION *n.*

imminent *adj.* about to happen.

immobile *adj.* motionless; not mobile.

immodest *adj.* shameless; impudent.

immoral *adj.* morally wrong; evil; wicked.

immortal *adj.* undying; everlasting.

immune *adj.* free or safe from; exempt from.

immunise *v.* to protect against disease.

immunity *n.* freedom from, esp. disease; exemption from.

impact *n.* 1 a blow or collision. 2 effect; influence.

impair *v.* to damage; to weaken.

impale *v.* to fix on a sharp stake or spear.

impart *v.* 1 to reveal; to tell. 2 to give.

impartial *adj.* not favouring one more than another; fair. IMPARTIALITY *n.* fairness.

impassable *adj.* that cannot be passed; blocked.

impatience *n.* restlessness; lack of patience.

impatient *adj.* restless; not patient.

impede *v.* to hinder; to obstruct. IMPEDIMENT *n.* obstruction.

impel *v.* 1 to drive forward; to urge. 2 to persuade.

impend *v.* 1 to be about to happen. 2 to threaten. IMPENDING *adj.*

imperative *adj.* very important or urgent. IMPERATIVE *n.* the form of the verb used for giving orders or instructions, e.g. shut the door.

imperfect *adj.* not perfect; faulty.

imperial *adj.* 1 concerning an empire or emperor or empress; majestic. 2 the system of weights and measures used in the United Kingdom before the introduction of the metric system.

imperil *v.* to place in peril; to put in danger.

imperishable *adj.* that cannot perish; everlasting.

impermeable *adj.* not allowing water or gas to pass through.

impersonate *v.* 1 to pretend to be someone else. 2 to act the part of.

impertinent *adj.* insolent; saucy; rude.

impervious *adj.* 1 not allowing anything to pass through; impenetrable. 2 deaf to; not responsive to.

impetuous *adj.* acting hastily and on impulse.

impetus *n.* the force moving a thing along; encouragement.

implement *n.* a tool; an instrument. IMPLEMENT *v.* 1 to complete. 2 to carry out (a plan or instructions).

implicate *v.* to involve a person in an offence, crime, etc.; to entangle in. IMPLICATION *n.* 1 suggestion, hint. 2 involvement.

implore *v.* to beg or request earnestly.

imply *v.* to suggest the meaning of; to hint.

impolite *adj.* not polite; rude.

import *v.* (pron. im-PORT) 1 to bring (goods) into a country from abroad. 2 to convey a meaning. IMPORT *n.* (pron. IM-port) the meaning; importance. IMPORTS *n. pl.* goods brought into a country from abroad. IMPORTER *n.*

important *adj.* mattering very much; of great influence, authority or consequence. IMPORTANCE *n.*

impose *v.* 1 to apply (esp. taxes, penalties). 2 to force (oneself on others). 3 IMPOSE UPON to take advantage of (someone).

imposing *adj.* grand; large, impressive.

impossible *adj.* not possible, that cannot be done. IMPOSSIBILITY *n.*

impostor *n.* a person who pretends to be somebody else in order to deceive.

impoverish *v.* to make poor.

impracticable *adj.* impossible in practice; not able to be done.

impress *v.* 1 to influence; to affect strongly. 2 to mark by pressing or stamping.

impression *n.* 1 an influence or effect on the mind or feelings; a vague feeling. 2 a pressed or stamped mark.

impressionism *n.* a (French) painting style which captures the impression of a scene or mood, using colour and light.

impressive *adj.* having a great effect on the mind or senses; dramatic; imposing.

imprison *v.* to put in prison; to confine or lock up. IMPRISONMENT *n.*

improbable *adj.* not likely to be true or to happen.

impromptu *adj.* done without previous preparation.

improper *adj.* 1 wrong; not suitable. 2 indecent.

improve *v.* to make or to become better. IMPROVEMENT *n.*

improvise *v.* to speak, play or do without preparation.

impudent *adj.* disrespectful; rude; insolent. IMPUDENCE *n.*

impulse *n.* 1 a sudden decision to do something without thinking. 2 a sudden surge.

impure *adj.* not pure; mixed with other things. IMPURITY *n.*

inability *n.* lack of ability, power or means.

inaccessible *adj.* that cannot be reached; unapproachable.

inaccurate *adj.* not accurate; not correct; not exact. INACCURACY *n.*

inactive *adj.* not active; doing nothing. INACTIVITY *n.*

inadequate *adj.* not adequate; not sufficient. INADEQUACY *n.*

inarticulate *adj.* unable to speak clearly or distinctly.

inattention *n.* lack of attention or courtesy.

inattentive *adv.* not attentive; lacking courtesy.

inaudible *adj.* not able to be heard.

inaugurate *v.* to begin; to introduce; to make a formal opening or to admit someone at a ceremony. INAUGURATION *n.*

incapable *adj.* not capable; not able to act normally.

incapacity *n.* lack of ability or power.

incendiary *n.* 1 a bomb or device for starting a fire. 2 a person who maliciously sets fire to property. 3 a person who stirs up trouble. INCENDIARY *adj.* designed for setting fire to property or to stir up strife.

incense *n.* (pron. IN-sense) a mixture of spices which gives off fragrant sweet fumes when burned. INCENSE *v.* (pron. in-SENSE) to enrage; to make angry.

incentive *n.* 1 something which encourages or incites to action. 2 an aim or urge.

inception *n.* beginning.

incessant *adj.* continual; not ceasing.

inch *n.* an imperial measure of length, one twelfth of a foot (2.54 centimetres).

incident *n.* an event; an occurrence; an episode.

incidental *adj.* happening as a result; casual.

incision *n.* a cut or gash; a cutting into something.

incisor *n.* front tooth.

incite *v.* to urge on; to stir up.

inclement *adj.* severe, esp. of weather or climate.

inclination *n.* 1 a leaning; a slope; a slant. 2 a liking or affection for.

incline *v.* 1 INCLINE TOWARDS to lean or to slope towards. 2 INCLINE TO to have a liking for. INCLINE *n.* a slope; a slant. INCLINED *adj.*

include *v.* 1 to put among others as part of a whole. 2 to contain.

inclusive *adj.* counting everything in; including everything. INCLUSION *n.*

incoherent *adj.* not making any sense.

income *n.* money that is received regularly from wages, investments, subscriptions, etc.

incomparable *adj.* not to be compared with; matchless; unequalled.

incompetent *adj.* not competent; not qualified or not able to do something; incapable.

incomplete *adj.* not complete; unfinished; imperfect.

inconsiderate *adj.* not considerate; thoughtless, lacking in regard for others; selfish.

inconsistent *adj.* not consistent; unreasonable; variable.

inconvenient *adj.* not convenient; awkward; troublesome; not suitable.

incorporate *v.* to combine into one whole.

incorrect *adj.* not correct; wrong; inaccurate; untrue.

increase *v.* (pron. in-KREASE) to become or make greater; to grow in numbers. INCREASE *n.* (pron. IN-krease) a gain; a growth. INCREASED *adj.*

incredible *adj.* hard to believe; surprising; amazing.

incredulous *adj.* unbelieving; unwilling to believe.

incubate *v.* to hatch eggs.

incur v. to bring (something) upon (oneself); to become responsible for.

incurable adj. unable to be cured.

indebted adj. owing money or gratitude.

indecent adj. offending against modesty or accepted good taste; obscene.

indecisive adj. undecided; unable to make a clear decision.

indeed adv. in fact; really.

indefinite adj. not definite; vague; uncertain; unlimited.

independence n. being independent; freedom of action and thought.

independent adj. not dependent on or controlled by other persons or things; self-governing; uncontrolled.

index n. 1 the forefinger. 2 a pointer on an instrument. 3 an alphabetical list showing the contents of a book. INDEX v. to make an index.

Indian adj. belonging to India or its people. INDIAN n. an inhabitant of India.

indicate v. to point out; to show; to make known. INDICATION n.

indifference n. lack of interest or attention.

indifferent adj. 1 not interested; not caring. 2 neither good nor bad; moderate.

indigestion n. difficulty in digesting food; pain due to poor digestion of food.

indignant adj. feeling anger, scorn or injured innocence. INDIGNATION n.

indignity n. unworthy treatment; an insult; a slight.

indirect adj. not direct; not going straight to the point. INDIRECTLY adv.

indiscreet adj. not discreet; thoughtless in speech or behaviour; lacking in caution.

indiscriminate adj. confused; making no distinctions.

indistinct adj. not distinct; not clear; dim.

individual adj. concerning only one of a group; single; special. INDIVIDUAL n. one person, animal or thing.

individually adv. one by one; separately.

induce v. to persuade; to bring about.

inducement n. something that attracts or persuades.

indulge v. 1 to satisfy (desires). 2 to spoil or pamper.

industrial adj. of industry and manufacture.

industrious adj. hard-working; diligent.

industry n. 1 the business of trade or manufacturing. 2 diligence; hard work.

inedible adj. not fit to be eaten.

ineffective adj. not producing the desired effect; having no effect; not effective.

inefficient adj. not efficient; not able or qualified to do the task or work required. INEFFICIENCY n.

inevitable adj. unavoidable; sure to happen.

inexpensive adj. not expensive; cheap.

inexperience n. lack of skill, knowledge or practice.

infallible adj. not fallible; never making mistakes; unfailing.

infant n. 1 a baby; a young child. 2 (legal) a person not yet eighteen years of age; a minor. INFANCY n.

infantry n. foot-soldiers.

infect v. 1 to pass on (a disease) to. 2 to cause somebody to share one's feelings.

infection n. 1 the means by which disease is spread. 2 anything that spreads widely and affects other people.

infer v. to reach a conclusion from the known facts or reasoning; to hint at. INFERENCE n.

inferior adj. lower in any way; not of the best quality. INFERIORITY n.

infernal adj. of hell; hellish; fiendish; abominable. INFERNO n. hell; a great fire; a scene of horror.

infest v. to overrun; to swarm over.

infiltrate v. to pass into in small numbers or to penetrate gradually.

infirm adj. feeble, weak or frail in health or mind. INFIRMITY n.

infirmary n. a hospital.

inflame v. 1 to make hot. 2 to make sore. 3 to rouse passion or anger.

inflammable adj. easily set on fire (see FLAMMABLE).

inflammation n. heat, soreness and redness in a part of the body.

inflate *v.* 1 to fill with air or gas. 2 to puff up with pride. 3 to cause a drop in the value of money. INFLATED *adj.*

inflation *n.* 1 the act of blowing up. 2 a drop in the value of money.

inflexible *adj.* 1 unbending; stubborn. 2 rigid; stiff.

inflict *v.* to impose suffering (pain, etc.) upon (someone). INFLICTION *n.*

influence *n.* the ability to affect other persons or things. INFLUENCE *v.* to have an effect on (other persons or things).

influential *adj.* having great influence.

influenza *n.* "flu", an infectious illness causing aches, shivering and fever.

inform *v.* to tell; to instruct.

informal *adj.* not according to form; free and easy; friendly.

informant *n.* a giver of information.

information *n.* knowledge; news; what is told. INFORMATION TEXT *n.* a piece of writing which informs, e.g. explanation, report.

informer *n.* a giver of information, esp. to the police.

infrequent *adj.* not frequent; not occurring often.

infringe *v.* to break laws or rules; to transgress.

infuriate *v.* to make angry; to fill with fury. INFURIATED *adj.*

ingenious *adj.* 1 clever; expert. 2 carefully planned. INGENUITY *n.*

ingot *n.* a block or bar of cast metal.

ingredient *n.* one of the materials or parts in a mixture.

inhabit *v.* to live in; to occupy. INHABITED *adj.* INHABITANT *n.*

inhabitable *adj.* fit to be lived in (see HABITABLE).

inhale *v.* to breathe in; to take into the lungs.

inherit *v.* 1 to receive property, money or title left in a will or as an heir. 2 to derive (qualities or character) from parents or ancestors.

inhuman *adj.* unlike a human; brutal; ruthless.

initial *adj.* occurring at the beginning. INITIAL *n.* the first letter of a word.

initiative *n.* 1 the first step. 2 readiness to lead.

inject *v.* to drive or force into, esp. with a syringe. INJECTION *n.*

injure *v.* to harm; to damage. INJURED *adj.*

injury *n.* 1 harm; damage. 2 wrongful action or treatment. *pl.* INJURIES.

injustice *n.* a wrong; unfairness.

ink *n.* a coloured liquid used in writing and printing.

inlet *n.* a narrow strip of water or small bay.

inmate *n.* an occupant of a house, hospital, prison, etc.

inn *n.* a public house providing food, drink and accommodation.

innings *n.* 1 a team's turn to bat during a game of cricket, rounders, etc. 2 a spell or turn.

innocent *adj.* not guilty; free from guilt or blame. INNOCENCE *n.*

inoculate *v.* to give (a person) a mild form of a disease to safeguard against more serious attacks. INOCULATION *n.*

inquest *n.* a legal inquiry into the cause of a death, accident or other matters of fact.

inquire *v.* 1 INQUIRE OF to ask; to seek information. 2 INQUIRE INTO to investigate. 3 INQUIRE AFTER to ask about someone's well-being. INQUIRY *n.*

inquisitive *adj.* inquiring; curious; prying.

insane *adj.* not sane; mad; senseless; mentally ill. INSANITY *n.*

inscribe *v.* to write or engrave words, signs, etc., on stone, metal, paper, etc. INSCRIPTION *n.*

insect *n.* a small animal, such as a bee or fly, with six legs and three parts to its body – head, chest and abdomen.

insecure *adj.* 1 unsafe; liable to give way; not feeling secure. 2 lacking confidence.

insert *v.* to put (something) in; to add (something) to. INSERTION *n.*

inside *prep.* on the inner side of; within. INSIDE *adj.* contained within; internal. INSIDE *n.* inner side or surface; the interior. INSIDE *adv.* within; internally; on or in the inside.

insight *n.* the power to understand clearly.

insignificant *adj.* unimportant, negligible; little; of no consequence.

insincere *adj.* not sincere; not to be trusted.

insist *v.* to demand or maintain firmly; to urge strongly. INSISTENCE *n.*

insolent *adj.* impudent; insulting; rude. INSOLENCE *n.*

insoluble *adj.* 1 not able to dissolve in water. 2 (problem) which cannot be solved.

inspect *v.* to examine carefully; to investigate. INSPECTION *n.*

inspector *n.* 1 an official who inspects and reports. 2 a police officer of rank above sergeant and below superintendent.

inspiration *n.* 1 taking in air (see RESPIRATION). 2 originality; a sudden good idea.

inspire *v.* to encourage with noble thoughts and ideas. INSPIRED *adj.*

install *v.* 1 to fix in position. 2 to place (a person) in rank or office, esp. at a ceremony. INSTALLATION *n.*

instance *n.* an example; a particular case.

instant *adj.* urgent; happening at once; immediate. INSTANT *n.* 1 a precise moment in time. 2 a moment.

instantly *adv.* at once; immediately.

instead *adv.* in place of; as a substitute or alternative for.

instep *n.* the upper part of the foot between the toes and the ankle.

instil, instill *v.* to put ideas into a person's mind gradually.

instinct *n.* a natural ability, or knowledge, which animals have without being taught.

institute *v.* to start; to establish. INSTITUTE *n.* 1 a society or an organisation formed for a special purpose. 2 a meeting-place for a society.

institution *n.* 1 institute; establishment. 2 a custom or practice.

instruct *v.* to teach; to order or command.

instruction *n.* 1 teaching. 2 direction; order. INSTRUCTION TEXT *n.* a piece of writing which instructs, e.g. a recipe. INSTRUCTIVE *adj.* INSTRUCTOR *n.* teacher.

instrument *n.* 1 a tool, implement or piece of apparatus. 2 apparatus for producing musical sounds.

insulate *v.* 1 to isolate; to separate. 2 to prevent loss of heat or electricity by means of a covering. INSULATION *n.* or INSULATOR *n.* a material that does not allow electricity or heat to pass through it.

insult *v.* (pron. in-SULT) to offend; to affront. INSULT *n.* (pron. IN-sult) an insulting speech or action; an affront. INSULTING *adj.*

insurance *n.* 1 the payment made to or by an insurance company. 2 a safeguard against loss, injury or damage.

insure *v.* 1 to guarantee. 2 to arrange to receive compensation in the event of loss by fire, burglary, injury, etc.

insurgent *adj.* riotous; rebellious. INSURGENT *n.* a rioter; a rebel.

intact *adj.* 1 complete; whole. 2 unbroken; undamaged.

integral *adj.* whole; complete; essentially part of a whole.

integrity *n.* wholeness; soundness; honesty.

intellect *n.* the ability to think, reason and understand. INTELLECTUAL *adj.*

intelligence *n.* 1 mental ability. 2 intellectual skill. 3 news; knowledge.

intelligent *adj.* 1 having or showing a high degree of cleverness or understanding. 2 clever; quick of mind.

intend *v.* to plan; to mean. INTENDED *adj.*

intense *adj.* very great or strong; violent. INTENSITY *n.*

intent *adj.* resolved; eager; earnest. INTENT *n.* intention; purpose.

intention *n.* an aim; a purpose. INTENTIONAL *adj.*

inter *v.* to bury. INTERMENT *n.* burial. INTERRED *adj.* buried.

intercept *v.* to stop (something or somebody) on the way from place to place; to check. INTERCEPTION *n.* an interruption or intervention.

interest *n.* 1 a sum paid for the loan of money. 2 importance; concern. 3 special attention. INTEREST *v.* to gain and hold attention (of). INTERESTING *adj.*

interested *adj.* 1 having an interest or share in. 2 displaying interest.

interfere (**with** or **in**) *v.* to meddle; to get in the way (of). INTERFERENCE *n.* INTERFERING *adj.*

interior *n.* 1 the inside. 2 the inland part of a country.

interjection *n.* an interruption; an exclamation. INTERJECT *v.*

intermediate *adj.* coming between two things in time, place or order.

intern *v.* to compel a person to live within the limits of a camp, town or country.

internal *adj.* 1 inside; situated in. 2 concerning the domestic affairs of a country.

internal rhyme *n.* the use of rhyming words within a line of poetry.

international *adj.* having to do with matters between nations. INTERNATIONAL *n.* a person who has represented his or her country at some sport; a sporting contest between nations.

internet *n.* the large system of connected computers around the world which people use to communicate and exchange information.

interpret *v.* to explain the meaning of something said or written; to translate. INTERPRETATION *n.*

interrogate *v.* to question closely; to cross-examine.

interrupt *v.* to make a break; to break in upon a person who is speaking or working.

interruption *n.* a stoppage; a sudden break into talk or work.

intersect *v.* to divide by crossing or cutting. INTERSECTION *n.* a point where lines or roads cross.

interval *n.* the time between two events; a short pause.

interview *v.* to conduct an interview with. INTERVIEW *n.* 1 a meeting for the assessment of a candidate. 2 a discussion with a person, intended for broadcasting or publication.

intimate *adj.* extremely friendly; familiar; confidential. INTIMATE *n.* a close friend.

intimate *v.* to make known; to announce. INTIMATION *n.*

intimidate *v.* to fill with fear in order to influence conduct.

intolerable *adj.* that cannot be endured.

intolerant *adj.* not tolerant of ideas or opinions of others. INTOLERANCE *n.*

intonation *n.* the way the voice is used to add expression or meaning when speaking or reading aloud.

intoxicate *v.* 1 to make drunk. 2 to excite.

intricate *adj.* complicated; difficult to understand.

intrigue *v.* to carry on an underhand plot; to make secret plans. INTRIGUE *n.* underhand plotting; a secret affair.

introduce *v.* to bring something into use; to make (one person) known (to another). INTRODUCTION *n.*

intrude (**upon**) *v.* 1 to enter uninvited. 2 to force oneself on the attention of others. INTRUDER *n.*

invade *v.* to enter a country as an enemy; to crowd into. INVADER *n.* a person who invades.

invalid *adj.* (pron. in-VAL-id) without value; having no legal force. INVALID *n.* (pron. IN-valid) a person disabled by illness or injury.

invaluable *adj.* priceless; of great value.

invariable *adj.* not variable; constant; unchangeable; always the same.

invasion *n.* an attack and entry into a country by an enemy; an encroachment.

invent *v.* 1 to make or create something new; to devise. 2 to make up in the imagination.

invention *n.* something invented.

invert *v.* to turn upside down.

invertebrate *adj.* not having a backbone. INVERTEBRATE *n.* an animal with no backbone.

invest *v.* 1 to put money into a business. 2 to buy something in the hope that its value will increase. 3 to give (a person) rank or badge of office. INVESTMENT *n.*

investigate *v.* to examine; to inquire into.

investigation *n.* an examination; an inquiry. INVESTIGATOR *n.*

invisible *adj.* not visible; that cannot be seen.

invitation *n.* a written or spoken request to do something, or to come to an event.

invite *v.* 1 to request to come; to ask for. 2 to attract. INVITING *adj.*

invoice *n.* a list of goods supplied, with their prices and total cost; a bill. INVOICE *v.* to make a detailed account (of).

involve *v.* 1 to include; to complicate. 2 to mix (someone) up in (crime etc.).

inward *adj.* situated within; directed towards the inside.

ion *n.* an atom with an excess or shortage of electrons.

iota *n. Gk.* an atom; the smallest amount; a jot.

irate *adj.* very angry; furious.

iris *n.* 1 the coloured part of the eye. 2 a plant with tuberous roots. *pl.* IRISES.

iron *n.* 1 a hard, heavy, strong, silver-grey, common metal with many uses. 2 an appliance for smoothing clothes, etc. 3 a golf-club with a metal head. IRON *v.* to smooth with an iron.

irrational *adj.* unreasonable; absurd; not logical.

irregular *adj.* 1 not regular; not according to rule. 2 uneven; variable.

irresponsible *adj.* not responsible for conduct; without sense of responsibility.

irrigate *v.* 1 to supply dry land with water. 2 to supply with a constant flow of liquid.

irrigation *n.* a system of supplying dry land with water to improve cultivation.

irritate *v.* 1 to annoy; to make angry. 2 to inflame; to cause discomfort. IRRITATION *n.*

Islam *n.* 1 the religion founded by the prophet Mohammed. 2 the Muslim world.

island *n.* 1 a piece of land surrounded by water. 2 a refuge for pedestrians in a street.

isle *n.* an island, usually small. ISLET *n.* a small island, an isolated spot.

isobar *n.* a line on a map connecting places that have the same atmospheric pressure at a given time or on average over a period of time.

isolate *v.* to keep (someone, something) apart or alone. ISOLATED *adj.*

isotherm *n.* a line on a map connecting places that have the same mean annual temperature.

isotope *n.* one of two or more forms of an element differing from each other in nuclear properties but having the same chemical properties.

Israel *n.* the Jewish people or nation.

Israeli *n.* an inhabitant of the State of Israel.

issue *v.* 1 to flow (from); to come out (of). 2 to publish; to give out; to distribute. ISSUE *n.* 1 a flowing out. 2 a publication. 3 the consequence.

Italian *adj.* belonging to Italy or its people. ITALIAN *n.* the language or an inhabitant of Italy.

italic *adj.* of type that slopes. ITALICS *n. pl.* letters in sloping type (in an Italian style).

itch *n.* 1 an irritation of the skin. 2 a restless desire; a longing for. ITCH *v.* 1 to have a skin irritation. 2 to long (for).

item *n.* 1 a single one out of a number. 2 a piece of news or an article.

itinerary *n.* the details or route of a journey.

ivory *n.* a hard, white substance from the tusks of elephants, walruses, etc.

ivy *n.* an evergreen climbing-plant that grows on trees and walls.

J

jab *v.* to poke suddenly. JAB *n.* a sharp stab.

jack *n.* 1 a screw device for lifting heavy loads. 2 a flag.

jacket *n.* 1 a short coat. 2 an outside covering.

jagged *adj.* having a sharp, rough edge.

jail, gaol *n.* a prison. JAILER, GAOLER *n.*

jam *v.* to squeeze; to block or wedge. JAM *n.* 1 a conserve of fruit boiled with sugar. 2 a blockage.

Jamaican *adj.* belonging to Jamaica or its people.

January *n.* the first month of the year.

Japanese *adj.* belonging to Japan or its people. JAPANESE *n.* the language or people of Japan.

jar *v.* 1 to jolt (nerves etc.). 2 JAR UPON or AGAINST to strike with grating sound.

jar *n.* an earthenware or glass vessel.

jargon *n.* special or technical words.

jaunt *n.* an outing or excursion for pleasure.

jaw *n.* the bones of the mouth.

jealous *adj.* 1 envious of another person's good fortune or possessions. 2 suspicious.

jealousy *n.* envy; the feeling of being jealous.

jeans *n. pl.* trousers made of strong cotton cloth.

jeer (at) *v.* to laugh or shout rudely at; to mock.

jelly *n.* a soft, transparent food made from gelatine.

jerk *n.* a short, sudden pull; a twitch. JERK *v.* to pull suddenly; to twitch.

jerkin *n.* a close-fitting jacket often made from leather.

jersey *n.* a close-fitting knitted jumper.

jest *v.* to joke or make fun. JEST *n.* a joke.

Jesus *n.* Jesus Christ, the founder of the Christian religion whose life and teachings are recorded in the New Testament.

jet *n*. 1 a stream of liquid or gas forced through a small opening under pressure. 2 an aircraft propelled by a jet engine. 3 a hard, black mineral used in making jewellery and ornaments. JET *adj*. deep, glossy black.

jetsam *n*. goods thrown overboard from a ship and washed ashore.

jettison *v*. to throw (goods or fuel) overboard from a ship, aircraft, balloon, etc., esp. to lessen load when in distress.

jetty *n*. a landing pier. *pl*. JETTIES.

Jew *n*. a person who belongs to the Jewish people or religion. *fem*. JEWESS.

jewel *n*. 1 a precious stone; an ornament containing precious stones. 2 a precious thing or person.

jewellery *n*. precious stones; personal ornaments made of precious stones or metals. JEWELLER *n*.

Jewish *adj*. belonging to the Jews or their religion.

jig *n*. 1 a lively dance. 2 the music for such a dance. 3 a device used to guide a tool. JIG *v*. to dance a jig; to move up and down jerkily and rapidly.

jingle *n*. 1 a gentle ringing sound like small bells. 2 a short, simple verse or tune, often used in advertising. JINGLE *v*. to make a gentle ringing sound.

job *n*. 1 a piece of work. 2 employment.

jockey *n*. a racehorse rider. JOCKEY (FOR) *v*. to try to gain a position of advantage.

jog *v*. 1 to push or nudge. 2 to remind. 3 to trot.

join *v*. 1 to fasten or put together. 2 to become a member of a club, team, society, etc. 3 to unite.

joiner *n*. a carpenter; a person who makes things of wood. JOINERY *n*.

joint *n*. 1 the point at which two things are joined together. 2 the place where two bones join together. 3 a large piece of meat. JOINT *adj*. shared by two or more.

joist *n*. a long beam supporting a floor or ceiling.

joke *n*. something said or done to make people laugh. JOKE *v*. to make a joke. JOKER *n*.

jolly *adj*. happy; merry.

jolt *v*. to jerk; to shake. JOLT *n*. a jerk; a shock.

jostle *v*. to knock or push against.

jot *n*. a small amount; an iota. JOT *v*. to write briefly or hastily.

jotter *n*. a notebook.

journal *n*. 1 a newspaper or magazine. 2 a diary.

journalist *n*. a person who writes for a newspaper, magazine or journal.

journey *n*. distance travelled; an expedition; a voyage. JOURNEY *v*. to travel; to make a journey.

jovial *adj*. merry; cheerful.

joy *n*. a feeling of great happiness or pleasure. JOYFUL *adj*. JOYFULLY *adv*.

jubilant *adj*. shouting or singing for joy; triumphant.

jubilee *n*. a special celebration or an anniversary of an event.

Judaism *n*. the religion of the Jewish people.

judge *n*. 1 an official appointed to try accused persons in a court of law. 2 a person who decides the result of a competition or contest. 3 a person who is qualified to decide on the merits of a matter in question. JUDGE *v*. 1 to try accused persons. 2 to be a judge or act as a judge. 3 to estimate something.

judo *n*. a Japanese form of wrestling.

jug *n*. a container, with a handle and lip, for holding liquids.

juggernaut *n*. a large, heavy goods lorry.

juggle *v*. to perform tricks using plates, balls, etc. JUGGLER *n*.

juice *n*. liquid from fruit or vegetables.

July *n*. the seventh month of the year.

jumble *v*. to mix things up, to muddle. JUMBLE *n*. a confusion; a muddle. JUMBLED *adj*.

jump *v*. 1 to leap. 2 to spring upwards or over something. 3 to give a sudden start. JUMP *n*. a leap; the act of jumping.

jumper *n*. 1 a person or thing that jumps. 2 a knitted jersey or pullover.

junction *n*. a place where roads or railway lines join.

June *n*. the sixth month of the year.

jungle *n*. land thickly overgrown with trees and tangled vegetation.

junior *adj*. 1 younger in age or less experienced. 2 lower in position. JUNICR *n*. a young or inexperienced person.

junk *n.* 1 worthless rubbish. 2 a Chinese sailing-boat.

jury *n.* a group of persons who listen to the evidence in a court of law and then give a verdict.

just *adj.* 1 fair, impartial. 2 well deserved; proper. JUST *adv.* 1 exactly. 2 recently. 3 barely, hardly. 4 only.

justice *n.* 1 fairness. 2 a magistrate.

justify *v.* to prove that something said or done is right or reasonable.

jut *v.* to stick out; to project.

juvenile *adj.* to do with young people. JUVENILE *n.* a young person.

K

kale *n.* a green vegetable similar to cabbage.

kangaroo *n.* an Australian pouched mammal that jumps along.

kayak *n.* an Eskimo canoe.

keel *n.* the beam of metal or timber on which the framework of a boat or ship is built.

keen *adj.* 1 sharp. 2 eager. 3 very cold.

keep *v.* 1 to retain possession of (something). 2 to take care of. 3 to detain. KEEP *n.* the stronghold of a castle.

keeper *n.* a person who keeps or guards something.

kennel *n.* a hut for a dog.

kenning *n.* an expression in Old English and Norse poetry which named something without using its name, e.g. a death-bringer = a sword.

kerb *n.* the edge of a pavement, path or road.

kernel *n.* 1 the soft inner part of a nut or fruit stone. 2 the important part of something.

ketch *n.* a two-masted sailing-boat.

kettle *n.* a metal vessel with a spout, lid and handle, for boiling water.

key *n.* 1 an implement for operating a lock. 2 a lever on a piano, organ or typewriter. 3 a solution to, or explanation of, a problem. 4 a set of musical notes based on a particular note.

kick *v.* to strike with the foot. KICK *n.* the act of kicking.

kid *n.* a young goat.

kidnap *v.* to carry off a person unlawfully by force. KIDNAPPER *n.* a person who kidnaps.

kidney *n.* an organ in the body that removes waste matter from the blood.

kill *v.* to put to death; to cause the death of.

kiln *n.* a type of oven or furnace for firing pottery or baking bricks.

kilogram *n.* a metric unit of mass (weight), 1000 grams.

kilometre *n.* a metric unit of length, 1000 metres.

kilowatt *n.* a unit of electrical power, 1000 watts.

kilt *n.* a pleated skirt, of tartan cloth, worn by men of the Scottish Highlands.

kimono *n.* a loose Japanese robe with wide sleeves, and tied with a sash.

kin *n.* a person's family and relations.

kind *n.* a sort; a type. KIND *adj.* gentle, friendly, considerate. KINDNESS *n.*

kindle *v.* 1 to set (something) on fire. 2 to catch fire. 3 to inspire.

kindly *adj.* acting in a kind way; sympathetic. KINDLY *adv.* gently.

king *n.* 1 a male sovereign ruler. 2 the main piece in a game of chess.

kingdom *n.* a country ruled by a king or queen.

kink *n.* a twist or bend.

kiosk *n.* 1 a small building for the sale of newspapers, refreshments, etc. 2 a telephone box.

kiss *v.* to touch with the lips as a sign of affection. KISS *n.* a touch with the lips.

kit *n.* 1 a set of tools or other equipment. 2 the equipment and clothes of a soldier or traveller.

kitchen *n.* a room used for the preparation and cooking of food.

kite *n.* 1 a lightweight frame, covered with cloth or paper, flown at the end of a long string. 2 a bird of prey of the hawk family.

kitten *n.* a young cat.

knack *n.* the ability to do something cleverly and skilfully.

knead *v.* to work by pressing and twisting with the fingers.

knee *n.* the joint between the lower and upper part of the leg.

kneel *n.* to go down on one or both knees.

knife *n.* a blade with a sharp edge for cutting, set in a handle. *pl.* KNIVES.

knight *n.* a man who has received the honour of knighthood, carrying the title of "Sir".

knit *v.* 1 to weave wool or yarn together by means of needles or a knitting machine. 2 to join closely together; to unite.

knock *v.* to strike; to hit (something). KNOCK *n.* a sharp blow; a tap.

knot *n.* 1 a tied loop or tangle in a string, rope, ribbon, etc. 2 a small group of people. 3 a dark, hard lump in wood. 4 the measure of a ship's speed, one nautical mile per hour.

know *v.* 1 to have information (about something). 2 to recognise. 3 to understand or have experience of (something).

knowing *adj.* cunning; shrewd.

knowledge *n.* understanding; information.

knuckle *n.* a joint in a finger.

Koran *n.* the Muslim scriptures.

Kremlin *n.* 1 the citadel in Moscow. 2 the government of Russia.

L

label *n.* a piece of paper, card or other material attached to something and indicating what it is, its destination or its owner. LABEL *v.* to fix a label to (something); to write a label. LABELLED *adj.*

laboratory *n.* a room or building equipped and used for scientific experiments and investigations. *pl.* LABORATORIES.

labour *n.* 1 hard work; effort. 2 the process of childbirth. LABOUR *v.* to work hard.

labyrinth *n.* a maze.

lace *n.* 1 a cord for fastening shoes and boots. 2 a fine open-work fabric. LACE *v.* to fasten with laces.

lacerate *v.* to tear; to wound. LACERATION *n.*

lack *v.* to be without; to have too little of. LACK *n.* the absence of something; a shortage.

lad *n.* a boy. *fem.* LASS.

ladder *n.* a climbing device made of wood, metal or rope, with rungs.

ladle *n.* a long-handled spoon for lifting liquids. LADLE *v.* to serve or transfer with a ladle.

lady *n.* courteous word for a woman. *pl.* LADIES. LADY *n.* the title of a noblewoman or of the wife of a knight.

lag *v.* 1 to fall behind; to dawdle. 2 to insulate against cold or to prevent loss of heat by wrapping with material.

lagoon *n.* a shallow stretch of salt water separated from the sea.

lair *n.* the den of a wild animal.

lake *n.* a large area of water enclosed by land.

lamb *n.* 1 a young sheep. 2 the meat from a young sheep.

lame *adj.* 1 crippled; unable to walk properly. 2 feeble; unconvincing.

lament *v.* to express grief or regret. LAMENT *n.* a sorrowful song or poem.

lamp *n.* a device for giving artificial light.

lance *n.* a spear with a long shaft. LANCE *v.* 1 pierce with a spear. 2 to cut open with a lancet.

lancet *n.* a sharp knife used in surgery.

land *n.* 1 the solid part of the Earth's surface. 2 a country or territory. 3 an expanse of country or an estate. LAND *v.* to alight on land from a boat or aircraft; to disembark.

landing *n.* 1 alighting on shore or ground; a disembarkation. 2 a level space at the top of a flight of stairs.

landlord *n.* 1 the owner of land, houses or property to rent. 2 the keeper of an inn or public house. *fem.* LANDLADY.

landmark *n.* a feature in a landscape which serves as a guide.

landscape *n.* a picture or view of the countryside. LANDSCAPE *v.* to lay out a garden or park to look like natural scenery.

landslide *n.* the sliding down of a mass of earth, rocks, etc.

lane *n.* 1 a narrow country road. 2 a division of a road marked out to separate streams of traffic. 3 a sea or air route.

language *n.* words spoken or written by a particular person, nation or peoples.

lank *adj.* tall and thin; straight and limp.

lanky *adj.* tall and thin.

lantern *n.* a case with transparent sides, for containing a light.

lap *n.* 1 the part from hips to knees of a sitting person. 2 one circuit of a race track. LAP *v.* 1 to lick up a liquid with the tongue. 2 to overtake by a circuit on a race track.

laptop *n.* a computer small enough to carry around and use on your lap.

lapel *n.* the front part of a coat folded back towards the shoulder.

lapse *n.* 1 a small mistake or error. 2 passing of time. LAPSE *v.* 1 to make a small mistake or error. 2 to pass gradually. 3 to come to an end; to fall into disuse.

larceny *n.* (legal term) theft or pilfering.

larch *n.* a cone-bearing tree that is not an evergreen.

lard *n.* purified pig fat used in cooking.

larder *n.* a room or cupboard used for storing food.

large *adj.* great in size; big.

largely *adv.* mainly; mostly.

lark *n.* 1 a small song-bird. 2 a prank or joke. LARK *v.* to play a prank or joke.

larva *n.* an insect in the grub or caterpillar stage.

larynx *n.* a cavity in the throat containing the vocal cords.

laser *n.* a device which strengthens an input of light, producing an extremely narrow and intense beam.

lash *n.* 1 a whip or a blow given with a whip. 2 an eyelash. LASH *v.* 1 to whip. 2 to fasten or bind tightly.

lass *n.* a young girl. *masc.* LAD.

last *adj.* 1 coming after all others. 2 most recent. LAST *v.* to continue; to remain in good condition.

last *n.* a shoemaker's tool for shaping a shoe.

lasting *adj.* continuing for a long time; permanent.

lastly *adv.* finally.

latch *n.* a fastening for a door, gate or window. LATCH *v.* to fasten with a latch.

late *adj.* 1 after the proper or usual time. 2 near the end of the day or some stated time.

lately *adv.* recently; not long ago.

lath *n.* a long, narrow strip of wood.

lathe *n.* a machine for turning wood, metal, etc., into circular and rounded shapes.

lather *n.* the froth made from soap and water. LATHER *v.* to cover with lather.

Latin *n.* the language of the ancient Romans. LATIN *adj.*

latitude *n.* 1 the distance north or south of the equator, measured in degrees. 2 a freedom from restraint.

latter *adj.* the second-mentioned of two things or people.

laugh *n.* the sound a person makes when amused, happy or scornful. LAUGH *v.* to make sounds expressing amusement, happiness or scorn.

laughter *n.* the act or sound of laughing.

launch *v.* 1 to set afloat. 2 to set in motion. LAUNCH *n.* a motor boat.

launder *v.* to wash clothes.

launderette *n.* a shop equipped with washing-machines where people can go to do their washing.

laundry *n.* 1 a place where clothes are sent to be washed. 2 clothes etc., to be washed or clothes recently washed.

laurel *n.* a shiny-leafed, evergreen shrub.

lava *n.* the molten matter that flows from a volcano and which cools and hardens into rock.

lavatory *n.* a toilet and washroom.

lavish *adj.* extremely generous; extravagant. LAVISH *v.* to give generously or extravagantly.

law *n.* the rules made by a parliament or local community according to which people are governed.

lawful *adj.* permitted by law; legal.

lawn *n.* an area of closely-mown grass.

lawsuit *n.* a claim in a court of law.

lawyer *n.* a person skilled in law or legal work; a solicitor or barrister.

lax *adj.* careless; slack.

lay *v.* 1 LAY DOWN to put something down in a particular place or way. 2 LAY OUT to arrange. 3 to produce eggs. LAY *n.* a poem or song.

layer *n.* a thickness of some material laid on another material.

lazy *adj.* not willing to work; idle. LAZILY *adv.* LAZINESS *n.*

lead *v.* (pron. LEED) 1 to guide or conduct someone. 2 to go first; to be in charge of something. LEAD *n.* the act of leading or controlling; a strap for controlling a dog.

lead *n.* (pron. LED) 1 a heavy, soft bluish-grey metal. 2 the graphite used in pencils.

leader *n.* 1 a person who leads. 2 the leading article in a newspaper.

leadership *n.* 1 command. 2 the ability to lead.

leading *adj.* 1 that which leads. 2 of most importance.

leaf *n.* 1 a part of a plant growing from a stem or branch. 2 a sheet of paper, esp. in a book and consisting of two pages. *pl.* LEAVES.

leaflet *n.* a printed sheet of paper carrying information or instructions.

league *n.* 1 an association of sports clubs which play matches against each other. 2 an old-fashioned measure of length, about 3 miles (approx. 5 kilometres).

leak *n.* 1 a crack or hole through which liquids or gases escape. 2 a disclosure of secret information. LEAK *v.* to allow liquid to enter or escape. LEAKING *adj.*

lean *v.* 1 to rest against. 2 to be in a sloping position. LEANING *adj.* in a sloping position.

lean *adj.* 1 thin. 2 without fat.

leap *v.* to jump; to bound. LEAP *n.* a jump; a bound.

learn *v.* to gain knowledge or skill by study, experience or practice. LEARNER *n.* LEARNING *n.* knowledge.

lease *n.* an agreement to let land or property for rent.

leash *n.* a dog's lead.

least *adj.* smallest. LEAST *adv.* in the smallest amount. LEAST *n.* the smallest degree.

leather *n.* the skin of an animal, prepared by tanning, used for making shoes, bags, etc.

leave *v.* 1 to go away. 2 to allow something to remain. 3 to give (something to someone) in a will. LEAVE *n.* 1 permission. 2 a holiday.

lectern *n.* a stand made to hold a book in a church or hall.

lecture *n.* 1 a talk on a particular subject given to an audience. 2 a reprimand. LECTURE *v.*

ledge *n.* a narrow shelf; a ridge.

lee *n.* the sheltered side.

leek *n.* a vegetable in the onion family.

leeward *adj. & adv.* on the sheltered side.

left *adj.* on or belonging to the same side of the body as the heart; on the side opposite to right. LEFT *n. & adv.*

leg *n.* 1 a limb used in standing, walking and running. 2 one of the supports of a table, chair, etc.

legacy *n.* property or money left to a person in a will.

legal *adj.* of the law; allowed by law.

legend *n.* 1 an ancient story handed down from generation to generation and which may or may not hold some truth. 2 an inscription on a coin or medal.

legendary *adj.* 1 existing only in legend. 2 like a legend.

legible *adj.* clearly written; easy to read.

legitimate *adj.* lawful; genuine.

leisure *n.* free time.

lemon *n.* a pale yellow acid fruit.

lend *v.* to give for temporary use.

length *n.* 1 the measurement from one end to another. 2 a space of time.

lengthen *v.* to increase the length of.

lengthwise *adv.* in the direction of the length.

lenient *adj.* not severe; merciful; tolerant. LENIENCY *n.*

lens *n.* a piece of glass with a curved surface used in spectacles, magnifying glasses and cameras to concentrate or disperse light. *pl.* LENSES.

Lent *n.* the forty days before Easter, in memory of Christ's fasting in the wilderness.

leopard *n.* a spotted wild animal in the cat family. *fem.* LEOPARDESS.

leotard *n.* a close-fitting garment worn by acrobats, dancers and gymnasts.

less *adj.* of smaller quantity; not so much of. LESS *n.* a smaller number or size.

lessen *v.* to make or become smaller.

lesson *n.* 1 something learnt or taught; a set amount of teaching given at one time. 2 a passage from the Bible read in church. 3 an example.

lest *conj.* in order to avoid or prevent.

let *v.* 1 to allow (something to happen); to permit. 2 to grant the use of land, premises, etc., for rent.

lethal *adj.* causing death.

letter *n.* 1 a symbol or character representing a sound. 2 a written message.

lettuce *n*. a green garden plant used in salads.

level *n*. 1 a flat, smooth surface. 2 an instrument for testing the flatness of a surface. LEVEL *v*. 1 to make flat. 2 to make equal.

lever *n*. 1 a bar or similar tool used to help raise a heavy load or to prise something open. 2 a handle for operating a machine. LEVER *v*. to move with a lever.

levy *v*. 1 to collect a tax. 2 to raise an army. LEVY *n*. 1 the tax collected. 2 men raised for an army. *pl*. LEVIES.

liable *adj*. 1 LIABLE FOR legally responsible for. 2 LIABLE TO likely to.

liar *n*. a person who tells lies.

libel *n*. a false written statement considered damaging to a person's reputation. LIBEL *v*. to publish a false statement about a person.

liberal *adj*. generous; open-minded.

liberate *v*. to set free; to release. LIBERATION *n*.

liberty *n*. freedom; permission.

librarian *n*. a person who looks after a library.

library *n*. 1 a building or room containing a collection of books. 2 a collection of books.

licence *n*. 1 an official permit to keep, use or do something. 2 a misuse of freedom.

license *v*. to grant a licence to. LICENSED *adj*.

lichen *n*. a moss-like plant which grows on rocks and trees.

lick *v*. to pass the tongue over (something) in order to taste, moisten or clean. LICK *n*. a stroke with the tongue.

lid *n*. the cover for the top of a container.

lie *v*. 1 to be in a flat position. 2 to make a false statement. LIE *n*. an untruth. LYING *adj*.

life *n*. 1 the state of being alive and able to respire, feed, grow and move as animals and plants do. 2 the period between birth and death. 3 activity; vitality.

lift *v*. to raise (something) to a higher position; to rise; to go higher. LIFT *n*. an apparatus for lifting goods or persons from one floor to another in a building.

ligament *n*. a fibre that holds joints together.

light *n*. 1 brightness which makes it possible to see things. 2 a source of light; a part of a window. LIGHT *v*. 1 to cause something to burn or shine. 2 to give light to.

light *adj*. 1 having little weight; not heavy. 2 pale in colour. 3 gentle.

lighten *v*. 1 to light up. 2 to make less heavy.

lightness *n*. lack of weight.

lightning *n*. a sudden flash of natural electricity usually produced during a thunderstorm.

light source *n*. something that gives out its own light, e.g. a star, a light bulb.

like *v*. to be fond of or pleased with. LIKE *prep*. resembling; similar to. LIKENESS, LIKE *n*. something which is similar or equal to another thing.

likely *adj*. probable; suitable. LIKELY *adv*. probably.

likeness *n*. a similarity; a resemblance.

liking *n*. a fondness.

lilac *n*. 1 a shrub with purple or white flowers. 2 a pale purple colour.

limb *n*. 1 an arm or leg. 2 a branch of a tree.

lime *n*. 1 a white powder prepared from limestone and used in making cement. 2 a kind of tree. 3 a fruit rather like a lemon.

limerick *n*. a five-line comic verse with the rhyme scheme AABBA.

limit *n*. 1 a boundary. 2 a point not to be passed. LIMIT *v*. to keep (something) within bounds; to restrict.

limited *adj*. narrow; restricted.

limp *adj*. soft; hanging loosely. LIMP *v*. to walk lamely.

line *n*. 1 a long, thin mark. 2 a length of thread, string or rope. 3 a row of people or things. 4 a railway track.

line *v*. to cover on the inside.

linear *adj*. developing in a line.

liner *n*. a large passenger ship.

linger *v*. to delay; to remain somewhere for a long time.

lining *n*. the covering of an inner surface.

link *n*. 1 one ring in a chain. 2 a connection. LINK *v*. to join; to connect. LINKED *adj*.

lion *n*. a large and powerful wild animal of the cat family. *fem*. LIONESS.

lip *n*. 1 one of the fleshy edges of the mouth. 2 the edge or rim of anything hollow.

liquid *n*. any substance that can flow. LIQUID *adj*. flowing.

lisp *v.* to be unable to pronounce certain sounds correctly, e.g. to say "th" for "s". LISP *n.* a lisping manner of speech.

list *n.* 1 a number of items written down one after another. 2 a catalogue. LIST *v.* to make a list. 2 to lean to one side.

listen *v.* 1 to hear or try to hear. 2 to follow the advice of.

literacy *n.* ability to read and write.

literal *adj.* giving the exact meaning of a word or phrase; factual; not figurative. LITERALLY *adv.*

literacy *adj.* having to do with authors, books and literature.

literature *n.* 1 written or printed books, plays, poetry, etc. 2 all that has been written on a subject.

litre *n.* a metric unit of capacity, 1000 millilitres.

litter *n.* 1 rubbish left lying about. 2 a number of animals born to the same mother at one time. LITTER *v.* to scatter things untidily.

little *adj.* 1 small in size or amount. 2 short in time or distance. LITTLE *n.* a small quantity. LITTLE *adv.* not much; slightly.

lively *adj.* full of life and high spirits; exciting.

liver *n.* an organ of the body which produces bile and purifies the blood.

livid *adj.* 1 black and blue in colour. 2 very angry.

living *adj.* having life. LIVING *n.* 1 the means of living. 2 all that are alive.

lizard *n.* a small four-legged reptile with a long body and tail.

load *n.* 1 a burden. 2 an amount carried; a cargo. LOAD *v.* 1 to put a load on. 2 to fill or charge. LOADED *adj.*

loaf *n.* a shaped mass of baked bread. *pl.* LOAVES. LOAF *v.* to waste time; to loiter.

loam *n.* a rich, fertile soil.

loan *n.* anything lent. LOAN *v.* to lend.

loathe *v.* to hate; to detest.

lob *n.* a slow, high ball at cricket or tennis. LOB *v.* to bowl slowly.

lobby *n.* an entrance hall.

lobe *n.* the soft lower part of the ear.

lobster *n.* a large edible shellfish with powerful claws and a long tail.

local *adj.* of a particular place or area. LOCALLY *adv.*

locality *n.* a particular place or district.

locate *v.* to find the exact position of.

location *n.* the place where something is situated.

loch *n.* in Scotland, a lake or narrow inlet of the sea.

lock *n.* 1 a device to fasten doors with a bolt turned by a key. 2 a section of canal where boats are raised or lowered to different levels. 3 a curl of hair. LOCK *v.* to fasten with a lock.

locomotive *n.* a railway engine.

locust *n.* an insect, similar to a grasshopper, that destroys crops and other plants.

lodge *n.* 1 a small house used occasionally. 2 the gate-house to a large estate. LODGE *v.* to stay somewhere as a lodger. LODGED *adj.* stuck (in something, somewhere). LODGER *n.* a paying guest.

loft *n.* a room in the roof of a house or barn; an attic.

log *n.* 1 a piece of a tree that has been felled. 2 a book for recording an aircraft's flight or a ship's voyage; a diary.

logic *n.* sound reasoning. LOGICAL *adj.*

loiter *v.* to hang about; to dawdle.

lone *adj.* alone; solitary. LONELY *adj.* LONELINESS *n.*

long *adj.* lengthy; lasting for a long time.

long *v.* to want (something) very much; to yearn for.

longboat *n.* a (Viking) ship with a large sail and oars.

longing *n.* a great desire for something.

longitude *n.* distance east or west of Greenwich (see MERIDIAN).

look *v.* 1 to turn the eyes or attention towards something. 2 to seem or appear. 3 to search. LOOK *n.* the act of looking; appearance.

loom *n.* a machine for weaving cloth. LOOM *v.* to appear in a menacing way.

loop *n.* the doubled-over part in a piece of string, rope, etc. LOOP *v.* to make a loop.

loose *adj.* 1 slack; not fixed. 2 not in captivity.

loosen *v.* to make or become loose.

loot *n.* property taken by thieves. LOOT *v.* to plunder and steal.

lop *v.* to trim or cut off a part of.

lord *n.* 1 a master; a ruler. 2 a nobleman; a peer.

lore *n.* learning and knowledge passed on by one generation to the next.

lorry *n.* a low flat road vehicle for carrying goods.

lose *v.* 1 to fail to keep. 2 to be defeated. 3 to misplace. LOSER *n.*

loss *n.* 1 the act of losing. 2 anything lost.

lost *adj.* 1 that cannot be found. 2 destroyed.

lot *n.* 1 a large number or amount. 2 the total amount. 3 an item for sale at an auction. 4 that which is drawn in a lottery (see LOTTERY).

lotion *n.* a liquid for healing or soothing the skin.

lottery *n.* a competition in which prizes are awarded by drawing lots.

loud *adj.* 1 noisy; making a great sound. 2 showy; gaudy. LOUDLY *adv.*

lounge *v.* to stand, recline or move lazily. LOUNGE *n.* a room to lounge in; sitting-room.

love *n.* fondness and affection. LOVE *v.* to feel fondness and affection for.

lovely *adj.* beautiful; pleasing; enjoyable.

loving *adj.* full of love; affectionate.

low *adj.* 1 the opposite of high; not reaching far up. 2 coarse and vulgar. LOW *n.* the sound made by cattle. LOW *v.* to make this sound.

lower *v.* 1 to let something down. 2 to reduce.

lowlands *n. pl.* low and level country.

lowly *adj.* humble; meek.

loyal *adj.* true and faithful. LOYALTY *n.*

lubricant *n.* a lubricating substance such as oil or grease.

lubricate *v.* to apply oil or grease to reduce friction.

lucid *adj.* clear, easily understood. LUCIDLY *adv.*

luck *n.* good or bad fortune; chance.

lucky *adj.* having or bringing good luck.

luggage *n.* a traveller's bags, suitcases and trunks.

lukewarm *adj.* 1 neither hot nor cold; tepid. 2 indifferent.

lull *v.* to soothe or calm. LULL *n.* 1 a pause in a storm. 2 a peaceful interval.

lullaby *n.* a soothing song to lull a child to sleep.

lumber *n.* 1 rough timber. 2 discarded goods and furniture; junk. LUMBER *v.* to move heavily.

luminous *adj.* 1 giving out light. 2 bright and shiny.

lump *n.* a shapeless mass; a swelling.

lunar *adj.* concerning the moon.

lunatic *n.* an insane person.

lunch *n.* the midday meal.

lung *n.* one of the two breathing organs in the chest.

lunge *n.* a sudden thrust or movement forward. LUNGE *v.* to thrust forward suddenly.

lurch *v.* to roll or pitch to one side. LURCH *n.* a sudden roll or stagger.

lure *v.* to tempt or entice. LURE *n.* something used to entice or bait.

lurk *v.* to lie in wait; to stay hidden.

luscious *adj.* delicious to taste or smell.

lush *adj.* fresh and juicy; growing abundantly.

lustre *n.* brilliance; splendour.

luxury *n.* something enjoyed but not really necessary.

lying *n.* the telling of a lie or lies.

lynch *v.* to put (someone) to death without a lawful trial.

lyric *n.* the words for a song.

M

macaroni *n.* a food of flour paste made into long thin tubes and dried.

mace *n.* 1 a spiked club formerly used in war. 2 a staff with an ornamental head carried before a mayor as a sign of his office.

machine *n.* a mechanism; a device for applying mechanical power.

machinery *n.* 1 machines. 2 the parts of machines.

mad *adj.* 1 mentally ill; insane. 2 very angry. MADLY *adv.*

madam *n.* a respectful title given to a woman.

madden *v.* to make mad. MADNESS *n.*

magazine *n.* 1 a periodical publication containing various articles. 2 a store for rifles, ammunition and explosives.

maggot *n.* the larva of certain types of fly.

magic *n.* 1 the supposed art of influencing events with the help of spirits or by witchcraft. 2 the art of doing conjuring tricks. MAGICIAN *n.*

magistrate *n.* a person with the authority to administer the law, a Justice of the Peace (J.P.).

magnet *n.* a piece of iron or steel which has the power to attract other pieces or iron or steel. MAGNETIC *adj.*

magnetism *n.* the power of a magnet; the ability to attract.

magnificent *adj.* splendid; grand; beautiful.

magnify *v.* 1 to make something appear larger than it is. 2 to exaggerate. MAGNIFIED *adj.*

maid *n.* 1 an unmarried girl. 2 a female servant.

mail *n.* 1 letters and parcels sent by post. 2 armour made of metal plates, chains or rings. MAIL *v.* to send by post.

main *n.* the principal pipe carrying gas or water or the principal cable carrying electricity. MAIN *adj.* most important; principal. MAINLY *adv.*

maintain *v.* to continue; to keep in good condition. MAINTENANCE *n.*

majesty *n.* 1 greatness of manner; dignity. 2 a title of a king or queen.

major *adj.* greater; more important. MAJOR *n.* an army officer, in rank between captain and lieutenant-colonel.

majority *n.* the greater number; the larger part.

make *v.* 1 to construct or shape something. 2 to compel. 3 to add up to. 4 to bring about. MAKE *n.* origin or type of manufactured object.

malaria *n.* a fever caused by mosquito bites.

male *n.* 1 a man or boy. 2 an animal or plant of the male sex. MALE *adj.*

malice *n.* spite; bad feeling. MALICIOUS *adj.*

malinger *v.* to pretend to be ill in order to avoid work. MALINGERER *n.*

mallet *n.* a wooden hammer.

malt *n.* barley or other grain prepared for brewing.

mammal *n.* an animal that produces milk on which it feeds its young.

mammoth *n.* a large elephant, now extinct. MAMMOTH *adj.* huge; gigantic.

man *n.* 1 a human being; mankind. 2 an adult male person.

manage *v.* 1 to be in charge of or to control. 2 to succeed in doing.

manager *n.* the person in charge of a business, hotel or shop. *fem.* MANAGERESS.

mane *n.* the long hair on the neck of a horse, a lion and some other animals.

manger *n.* a feeding-trough for horses and cattle.

mangle *v.* to tear or crush to pieces.

manhood *n.* the state of being an adult man.

maniac *n.* a mad person.

manicure *n.* care of the hands and nails. MANICURE *v.* to care for the hands and nails.

manifest *adj.* easily seen or understood; obvious. MANIFEST *v.* to show clearly.

manifesto *n.* a public declaration of what a ruler or group intends to do.

manipulate *v.* to control, manage or work (something) skilfully.

mankind *n.* the human race.

manly *adj.* strong and brave.

man-made *adj.* made by humans; not natural; synthetic.

manner *n.* 1 the way a thing is done. 2 the way in which a person behaves.

mannerism *n.* an unusual or characteristic way of speaking or behaving.

manoeuvre *n.* 1 a planned movement or rehearsal by armed forces. 2 a clever plan or movement. MANOEUVRE *v.* to carry out such a movement.

manor *n.* 1 the land belonging to a lord or squire. 2 a large country house.

mansion *n.* a large house.

manslaughter *n.* killing a person unlawfully but without the intention of doing so.

mantel *n.* the shelf over a fireplace.

mantle *n.* a loose, sleeveless cloak.

manual *adj.* done with the hands. MANUAL *n.* a book of instructions or information; a handbook.

manufacture *v.* to make by machinery. MANUFACTURE *n.* the making of articles or material in large quantities.

manure *n.* any substance that enriches and fertilises the land.

manuscript *n.* a book or paper written by hand. MANUSCRIPT *adj.* written by hand.

many *adj.* a large number of; numerous. MANY *n.* a large number.

map *n.* a drawing showing the shape and features of a continent, country or area, usually indicating rivers, roads, hills, etc. MAP *v.* to make a map or plan of.

maple *n.* a tree similar to the sycamore, some kinds of which give a syrup.

marble *n.* 1 a fine limestone which takes a high polish and is used for buildings and statues. 2 a small stone or glass ball used in various games.

March *n.* the third month of the year.

march *v.* 1 to walk with a regular step. 2 to make a person walk like this. MARCH *n.* 1 the act of marching or the distance marched. 2 a piece of music suitable for marching to.

mare *n.* a female horse. *masc.* STALLION.

margarine *n.* a substance resembling butter and made from animal or vegetable fats.

margin *n.* 1 an edge; a border; the brink. 2 an amount to spare.

marine *adj.* to do with the sea. MARINE *n.* a soldier serving aboard a ship.

mariner *n.* a sailor; a seaman.

maritime *adj.* having to do with the sea or ships.

mark *n.* 1 a stain, spot or pattern on something. 2 a target; a thing aimed at. 3 a number or symbol given as an award. MARK *v.* 1 to make a mark on something. 2 to observe. 3 to give marks.

market *n.* 1 a public place for buying and selling. 2 the demand for a certain class of goods. MARKET *v.* to buy and sell in a market.

market town *n.* a town which grew up around the market based or visiting there.

marmalade *n.* a jam made from oranges, lemons or grapefruit.

maroon *n.* 1 a warning rocket. 2 a brownish-red colour. MAROON *v.* to abandon (a person) in a deserted place.

marquee *n.* a large tent.

marriage *n.* 1 the life together of a husband and wife. 2 a wedding ceremony.

married *adj.* joined together as man and wife.

marry *v.* 1 to take a person as husband or wife. 2 to perform the marriage ceremony.

Mars *n.* 1 a planet lying between Earth and Jupiter. 2 the Roman god of war.

marsh *n.* wet, low-lying ground. MARSHY *adj.*

martyr *n.* a person who suffers because of his or her beliefs or cause.

marvel *v.* to be filled with wonder or astonishment. MARVEL *n.* a wonderful or astonishing thing.

marvellous *adj.* extraordinary, astonishing. MARVELLOUSLY *adv.*

mascot *n.* an object or person believed to bring good luck.

masculine *adj.* opposite of feminine; belonging to men; concerning men.

mash *n.* a mixture of bran, meal, etc., pulped as a food for animals. MASH *v.* to pound into a pulp.

mask *n.* 1 a covering to disguise the face. 2 a model of a face. MASK *v.* to cover with a mask; to conceal.

mason *n.* a worker in stone.

masquerade *v.* to be in disguise. MASQUERADE *n.* a masked ball.

mass *n.* 1 a lump, piece or large quantity. 2 the main body. 3 a crowd. MASS *v.* to form into a mass.

massacre *n.* a great slaughter. MASSACRE *v.* to slaughter many.

massage *n.* the rubbing and kneading of parts of the body to remove pain or stiffness. MASSAGE *v.* to rub and knead parts of the body to remove pain or stiffness.

massive *adj.* large and heavy.

mast *n.* a pole supporting a ship's sails or a flag; a radio, telephone or television aerial.

master *n.* 1 an employer. 2 a male teacher. *fem.* MISTRESS. 3 the captain of a ship. 4 an expert.

masticate *v.* to chew.

mat *n.* 1 a small rug or piece of carpet. 2 a thin pad to protect a surface. MAT *v.* to twist and tangle. MATTED *adj.*

matt *adj.* dull; not glossy.

match *n.* 1 anything which agrees with or suits another thing. 2 an equal. 3 a game or contest. 4 a marriage. 5 a small piece of wood tipped with a substance which burns easily when rubbed. MATCH *v.* to be equal or similar to.

mate *n.* 1 a friend; a husband or wife. 2 one of a mated pair of animals or birds. 3 a ship's officer who is second in command. MATE *v.* to marry; to pair for breeding.

material *n.* any substance from which something can be made. MATERIAL *adj.* 1 essential; important. 2 real; actual.

maternal *adj.* motherly; having to do with a mother.

maternity *n.* motherhood.

mathematics, maths *n.* the science which deals with numbers and measurements. MATHEMATICAL *adj.* MATHEMATICIAN *n.*

matrimony *n.* marriage.

matter *n.* 1 the material; the substance a thing is made of. 2 a subject written or spoken about. MATTER *v.* to be important.

mattress *n.* a large, flat, oblong cushion for sleeping on.

mature *adj.* fully grown; ripe. MATURE *v.* to ripen.

maul *v.* to hurt by handling roughly.

mauve *n.* a pale purple colour. MAUVE *adj.*

maximum *n.* the greatest number or quantity. MAXIMUM *adj.* greatest.

May *n.* the fifth month of the year.

may *v.* am/is/are able (to do something); can (possibly).

maybe *adv.* perhaps; possibly.

mayor *n.* the chief citizen of a town or metropolis.

mayoress *n.* 1 the wife of a mayor. 2 a female mayor.

maze *n.* an intricate and puzzling network of lines and paths; a labyrinth.

meadow *n.* a field of grass.

meal *n.* 1 food taken at one time; the food that is eaten. 2 grain ground to powder.

mean *v.* 1 to intend, to plan. 2 to be a sign of, to show. MEAN *adj.* 1 shabby, poor. 2 average. MEAN *n.* the middle, average; in maths, the number or measurement that is found by adding the data and dividing the total by the number of data.

meaning *n.* what is meant; an explanation.

meaningless *adj.* without meaning; senseless; useless.

means *n.* 1 method; way of doing something. 2 a person's money and possessions.

measles *n.* an infectious disease that causes red spots on the body.

measure *n.* 1 an instrument used for measuring. 2 an amount, quantity or size. MEASURE *v.* to find the amount, quantity or size (of something) by using a measure.

measurement *n.* the amount, quantity or size of anything.

meat *n.* flesh used as food.

mechanic *n.* a person skilled in the making, repairing or use of machinery.

mechanical *adj.* 1 concerned with machinery. 2 automatic; done without thinking.

mechanism *n.* a working part of a machine.

medal *n.* a piece of metal shaped like a disc, cross or star awarded for bravery, merit, or to commemorate a special event.

meddle *v.* to interfere.

median *n.* the middle number or measurement when a set of data is put in order.

mediate *v.* to act as a peacemaker; to try to help settle disputes.

medical *adj.* concerning healing and doctors.

medicine *n.* 1 a liquid or tablet intended to cure or heal. 2 the science of healing.

medieval *adj.* of the Middle Ages.

medium *adj.* mid-way; average; moderate. MEDIUM *n.* the means by which something is done; in art, the material used, e.g. paint or pencil. *pl.* MEDIA.

medley *n.* a mixture.

meek *adj.* mild and gentle. MEEKLY *adv.* MEEKNESS *n.*

meet *v.* 1 to come face to face (with). 2 to assemble. 3 to satisfy. MEET *n.* a gathering of huntsmen and hounds.

meeting *n.* 1 a gathering; an assembly. 2 an encounter.

mellow *adj.* 1 soft and ripe. 2 pleasant; mature. MELLOW *v.* to ripen; to mature.

melody *n.* an arrangement of musical notes; an air or tune.

melon *n.* a large, juicy fruit.

melt *v.* 1 to change a substance from solid to liquid. 2 to soften.

member *n.* 1 a person who belongs to a family, club, society, group, etc. 2 a limb of the body.

membership *n.* all the members of a group.

memento *n.* an object kept as a keepsake or souvenir.

memoir *n.* a record of events, a written personal account of what has happened.

memorable *adj.* worthy of being remembered.

memorial *n.* something which reminds people of a person or an event; a monument.

memory *n.* the ability to remember; something remembered.

menace *v.* to threaten. MENACE *n.* a threat or danger. MENACING *adj.*

menagerie *n.* a collection of wild animals.

mend *v.* to repair something; to put back into good order. MEND *n.* a mended part.

mensuration *n.* the measurement of lengths, areas and volumes.

mental *adj.* to do with the mind. MENTALLY *adv.*

mention *v.* to speak of or refer to. MENTION *n.* a remark about or a reference to.

menu *n.* a list of the food to be served at a meal or available in a hotel or restaurant.

mercantile *adj.* to do with buying, selling and trade.

mercenary *n.* a soldier hired to fight for a foreign country. MERCENARY *adj.* working only for money.

merchant *n.* a wholesale trader.

merciful *adj.* showing mercy; lenient.

merciless *adj.* without mercy; unforgiving.

mercury *n.* a heavy, silvery liquid metal.

Mercury *n.* the planet nearest to the sun.

mercy *n.* compassion; forgiveness; leniency, unwillingness to hurt. *pl.* MERCIES.

mere *n.* a pond or lake. MERE *adj.* simple; not more than.

merely *adv.* simply; only.

merge *v.* 1 to be joined together. 2 to become part of; to single.

merger *n.* a joining together into one.

meridian *n.* 1 an imaginary line passing through the North and South Poles and cutting the equator at right angles. 2 the highest point in the sun's path.

merit *n.* excellence; worth.

mermaid *n.* an imaginary creature with the body of a woman and the tail of a fish.

merry *adj.* happy; cheerful; full of fun.

mesh *n.* the space between the threads of a net. MESH *v.* 1 to interlock; to engage. 2 to catch in a net.

mess *n.* 1 disorder; confusion. 2 a meal taken with others. MESS *v.* 1 to make a mess of. 2 MESS WITH to eat a meal with others.

message *n.* news or information sent from one person to another.

messenger *n.* a person who carries a message.

Messiah *n.* the promised deliverer of the Jews whom Christians believe to be Christ.

metal *n.* a substance such as gold, silver, iron, tin, copper, lead, etc.

metaphor *n.* a way of describing something by comparing it to something else, but without using the words 'as' or 'like' (see SIMILE).

meteorology *n.* the study of the Earth's weather and atmosphere. METEOROLOGIST *n.*

meter *n.* an instrument for measuring the amount of electricity, gas or water used.

method *n.* 1 a way or means of doing something. 2 orderliness.

methodical *adj.* orderly; done according to a plan or system.

metre *n.* 1 the main unit of length in the metric system, 1 metre = 100 cm = 1000 mm (39.37 inches). 2 the regular arrangement of syllables in a verse.

metric *adj.* to do with the decimal system of measurement.

metropolis *n.* the capital or chief city of a country.

microbe *n.* a very tiny living thing; a germ.

microchip *n.* a small chip of material, containing many circuits, which makes a computer work.

microphone *n.* an instrument which enables sounds to be made louder, broadcast or recorded.

microscope *n.* an instrument for magnifying small objects. MICROSCOPIC *adj.*

microwave *n.* 1 a short wave of electricity used for radio messages and for cooking. 2 a type of oven that cooks or heats food quickly using microwaves.

mid *adj.* middle. MID *prep.* amid; among.

midday *n.* the middle of the day; noon.

middle *n.* a point at equal distance from each end or side; the central point. MIDDLE *adj.* in the middle; mid; central.

midge *n.* an insect; a gnat.

midnight *n.* the middle of the night; twelve o'clock at night.

might *n.* great power or strength.

mighty *adj.* strong; very great.

migrant *n.* a migrating animal, bird or person.

migrate *v.* to move from one place to another, esp. from one part of the world to another. MIGRATION *n.*

mild *adj.* gentle; not severe or harsh. MILDLY *adv.*

mile *n.* an imperial measure of distance, 1760 yards (1.61 kilometres).

mileage *n.* the distance in miles.

militant *adj.* aggressive; ready to fight.

military *adj.* having to do with soldiers or with warfare. MILITARY *n.* the army.

milk *n.* a white fluid produced by female mammals to feed their young. MILK *v.* to obtain milk from a cow or other animal.

mill *n.* 1 a machine for grinding or crushing. 2 a building which contains machines for grinding and crushing or for spinning and weaving.

miller *n.* a person who grinds corn into flour.

milligram *n.* a metric unit of mass (weight), one thousandth part of a gram.

millilitre *n.* a metric unit of capacity; one thousandth part of a litre.

millimetre *n.* a metric unit of length, one thousandth part of a metre.

million *n.* a thousand thousands, the number 1 000 000.

mime *n.* a play in which actions or dancing take the place of speaking. MIME *v.* to act without speaking.

mimic *v.* to imitate, esp. in a mocking way. MIMIC *n.* a person who imitates or copies.

mince *v.* to cut or chop into small pieces. MINCE *n.* meat chopped into small pieces.

mind *n.* 1 the mental powers by which a person thinks, feels and understands. 2 an opinion. 3 memory. MIND *v.* 1 to look after something. 2 to watch out for. 3 to object to.

mine *n.* 1 a place where coal or other minerals are dug from the ground. 2 an explosive hidden under ground or water. MINE *v.* 1 to dig for coal or minerals. 2 to place explosives under ground or water.

mine *pron.* belonging to me.

miner *n.* a worker in a mine.

mineral *n.* any substance obtained by mining, such as rocks, coal, iron, etc. MINERAL *adj.*

mingle *v.* to mix together.

miniature *adj.* very small; made on a small scale.

minim *n.* a note in music, written ♩.

minimum *n.* the smallest possible quantity. MINIMUM *adj.* smallest; least. MINIMAL *adj.* very minute or slight.

minister *adj.* 1 a clergyman or woman. 2 the head of a government department. MINISTER (TO) *v.* to give help or service to.

minor *adj.* smaller; less important. MINOR *n.* a person under 18 years of age.

minster *n.* a large church; a cathedral.

minstrel *n.* a wandering musician or singer.

mint *n.* 1 a place where coins are made. 2 a plant whose leaves are used for flavouring. MINT *v.* to make coins. MINT *adj.* in new condition.

minus *adj.* less than nothing; negative. MINUS *n.* the sign (–) for subtraction.

minute *n.* (pron. MINIT) 1 a unit of time, 1/60 of an hour. 2 a unit of angle measurement, 1/60 of a degree. MINUTE *adj.* (pron. my-NUTE) very small; very exact.

miracle *n.* a wonderful happening beyond human power; a wonderful event.

mirage *n.* an optical illusion which causes distant objects to be seen in the air.

mirror *n.* a polished surface that produces a reflected image. MIRROR *v.* to reflect.

mirth *n.* merriment; laughter.

misadventure *n.* an unfortunate accident or happening.

misbehave *v.* to behave badly. MISBEHAVIOUR *n.*

miscalculate *v.* to calculate wrongly.

miscellaneous *adj.* mixed, made up of several kinds; various.

mischief *n.* 1 harm or injury done intentionally. 2 childish pranks.

mischievous *adj.* harmful; annoying; fond of playing pranks.

misconduct *n.* bad behaviour.

miscount *v.* to count wrongly.

misdirect *v.* to give the wrong information or directions to.

miser *n.* a person who saves money and spends as little as possible because of greed.

miserable *adj.* wretched and unhappy.

misery *n.* great unhappiness; suffering.

misfortune *n.* bad luck.

misgiving *n.* a feeling of fear or doubt.

mishap *n.* an unfortunate accident.

misinform *v.* to give wrong information to.

misinterpret *v.* to misunderstand.

misjudge *v.* to judge (someone or something) wrongly.

mislead *v.* to deceive.

misplace *v.* to put in the wrong place.

misprint *n.* a mistake in printing.

misrepresent *v.* to give a wrong meaning or impression of.

miss *n.* a young girl; an unmarried woman. MISS *v.* 1 to fail to hit, reach, meet or catch. 2 to regret the absence of (someone or something).

missile *n.* a weapon thrown or fired, or launched by a rocket.

missing *adj.* lost; absent.

mission *n.* 1 an expedition or journey with a special purpose. 2 a task or duty undertaken. 3 a place where missionaries work.

missionary *n.* a person sent to preach a religion.

mist *n.* a cloud of very fine water drops seen in the air. MIST *v.* to turn misty; to cloud.

mistake *n.* an error; a misunderstanding. MISTAKE *v.* to make a mistake about; to misunderstand.

mistletoe *n.* a plant that bears white, sticky berries and grows on apple and other trees.

mistress *n.* 1 a woman in charge or control. 2 a female teacher (*masc.* MASTER).

mistrust *v.* not to trust (someone or something). MISTRUST *n.* doubt; suspicious.

misty *adj.* hazy; covered with mist.

misunderstand *v.* to misinterpret words or actions.

misuse *v.* to use (something) for a wrong purpose or in a wrong way.

mitre *n.* 1 a bishop's tall head-dress. 2 a joint in woodwork fitting at an angle of 45°.

mix *v.* 1 to combine or blend two or more things. 2 to meet and mingle with other people. 3 to stir or shake things together.

mixture *n.* a number of things or substances combined together.

mnemonic *n.* a way of remembering things such as spellings, e.g. there is a rat in separate.

moan *n.* a low sound of pain or grief. MOAN *v.* to utter a low sound of pain or grief.

moat *n.* a deep defensive ditch round a castle.

mob *n.* an unruly and disorderly crowd. MOB *v.* to crowd around.

mobile *adj.* able to move freely; changing quickly. MOBILE *n.* 1 *abbrev.* mobile telephone. 2 hanging decoration.

mock *v.* to make fun of (someone or something). MOCK *adj.* imitation; not real.

mode *n.* 1 the way in which something is done. 2 custom, fashion or method. 3 the number or measurement which appears most often in a set of data.

model *n.* 1 an example or pattern. 2 a small copy or version of something. 3 a person who poses for an artist or photographer or who displays clothing. MODEL *v.* 1 to make a copy of. 2 to work as a model.

moderate *v.* to make less violent or severe. MODERATE *adj.* avoiding extremes; reasonable.

modern *adj.* belonging to the present time.

modest *adj.* humble, not boastful.

modify *v.* to change or vary (something).

moist *adj.* damp, slightly wet.

moisten *v.* to make or become damp,

moisture *n.* dampness.

molar *n.* a back tooth.

mole *n.* 1 a dark spot on the skin. 2 a small furry burrowing animal. 3 a massive wall or object built to break force of waves; an artificial harbour. 4 a spy.

molecule *n.* the smallest possible part of a substance; a small particle.

mollusc *n.* a soft-bodied invertebrate animal (snail, oyster, octopus, etc.).

molten *adj.* melted; liquefied by heat.

moment *n.* 1 a very short period of time. 2 importance or value.

monarch *n.* a king, queen, emperor or empress.

monastery *n.* a building where monks live or lived. *pl.* MONASTERIES.

Monday *n.* the second day of the week.

monetary *adj.* having to do with money.

money *n.* coins and notes used for making payment; wealth.

monitor *n.* a computer or television screen.

monk *n.* a man who takes religious vows and is a member of a community living in a monastery.

monkey *n.* an animal resembling man, usually with a long tail.

monologue *n.* a long speech made by one speaker or character.

monoplane *n.* an aeroplane with one pair of wings.

monotonous *adj.* 1 tedious; with no variation. 2 boring; dull.

monsoon *n.* a wind that blows in the Indian Ocean bringing heavy rain in summer and dry weather in winter.

monster *n.* a large, frightening creature. MONSTER *adj.* very large.

month *n.* 1 any of the twelve parts into which the year is divided. 2 the period in which the moon makes a complete revolution and a complete rotation.

monument *n.* a memorial to a person or event.

mood *n.* a state of mind or feeling.

moon *n.* the heavenly body which travels round the Earth once each month, and reflects light from the sun.

moor *n.* an area of rough land often covered with heather. MOORLAND *n.*

moor *v.* to secure (a boat) to a buoy or quayside.

mooring *n.* a place to moor a boat.

mop *n.* a bundle of coarse wool or cloth fastened to a handle and used for cleaning floors. MOP *v.* to use a mop.

moraine *n.* debris carried and deposited by a glacier.

moral *adj.* 1 concerned with right and wrong behaviour. 2 good; virtuous. MORAL *n.* the lesson taught by a story or fable.

more *adj.* greater in number. MORE *adv.* to a greater extent.

morning (**morn**) *n.* the first part of the day; the time before noon.

Morse *n.* a code of signals made up of dots and dashes.

mortar *n.* 1 the mixture of cement, sand and water used for laying bricks. 2 a short gun that fires shells at a high angle. 3 a basin in which substances are finely ground.

mortgage *n.* an agreement for borrowing money to buy a house or land.

mortuary *n.* a building where dead bodies are kept before burial.

mosaic *n.* a design made with small pieces of glass or stone.

mosque *n.* a Muslim place of worship.

mosquito *n.* a blood-sucking insect that may carry malaria. *pl.* MOSQUITOES.

moss *n.* a small plant found in damp places.

most *n.* the greatest quantity, extent or number. MOST *adv.* in the greatest or highest degree. MOST *adj.* greatest.

motel *n.* a hotel for motorists.

moth *n.* a winged insect usually seen at night.

mother *n.* a female parent. MOTHER *v.* to act like a mother to.

motion *n.* 1 movement. 2 a plan put before a meeting.

motif *n.* a picture or symbol on something; a repeated shape in a pattern.

motive *n.* a reason for doing something.

motor *n.* an engine that provides power. MOTOR *v.* to travel in a car.

motorway *n.* a road for fast long-distance traffic.

motto *n.* a wise saying.

mould *n.* 1 a hollow pattern which gives its shape to whatever is poured or pressed into it. 2 a plant growth found in damp places. MOULD *v.* to shape and model.

moult *v.* to shed fur, feathers, hair, etc.

mound *n.* a bank of earth or stones; a small hill.

mount *n.* 1 a mountain or hill. 2 an animal on which a person rides. MOUNT *v.* 1 to climb; to get on to. 2 to rise or increase. 3 to prepare something for display. MOUNTED *adj.*

mountain *n.* a high hill. MOUNTAINOUS *adj.*

mountaineer *n.* a person who climbs mountains.

mourn *v.* to grieve; to be sorrowful.

mouse *n.* 1 a small rodent, usually with a long tail. 2 a pointing device used with a computer. *pl.* MICE.

mousse *n.* a foam; a light, foamy dessert.

moustache *n.* hair grown on the upper lip.

mouth *n.* 1 the opening in the head containing the teeth and the tongue. 2 an opening or entrance.

movable *adj.* that can be moved; not fixed.

move *v.* 1 to change from one position to another. 2 to set in motion. MOVE *n.* the act of moving.

movement *n.* 1 moving; motion. 2 mechanism of a watch or clock. 3 a group of people who support a particular cause.

moving *adj.* 1 causing movement; in motion. 2 affecting the emotions.

mow *v.* to cut down.

mower *n.* 1 a machine that mows. 2 a person who mows.

much *n.* a great quantity or amount. MUCH *adj.* great in quantity or amount. MUCH *adv.* to a large extent.

mud *n.* a soft mixture of earth and water. MUDDY *adj.*

muddle *v.* 1 to mix things up. 2 to confuse or bewilder. MUDDLE *n.* disorder; confusion.

muffle *v.* to make (a sound) quieter. MUFFLER *n.*

mug *n.* 1 a large cup used without a saucer. 2 a fool. MUG *v.* to attack or rob (someone).

mule *n.* 1 a cross between a horse and an ass. 2 an obstinate person. 3 a type of spinning machine.

mullion *n.* the vertical division between the lights of a window.

multiple *adj.* having many parts. MULTIPLE *n.* a number or quantity which contains another an exact number of times, e.g. 100 is a multiple of 10.

multiply *v.* to increase; to increase a number a given number of times.

multiracial *adj.* of many races or people.

multitude *n.* a crowd; a great number.

mumble *v.* to speak indistinctly.

mumps *n.* a disease that causes the glands of the neck to swell.

municipal *adj.* having to do with a city or town.

munitions *n. pl.* military weapons, ammunition and supplies.

mural *adj.* to do with a wall. MURAL *n.* a wall painting.

murder *n.* the unlawful and intentional killing of a human being. MURDER *v.* to kill a human being unlawfully and intentionally.

murmur *n.* a low continuous sound; a mutter. MURMUR *v.* 1 to speak in a low voice. 2 to make a low continuous sound; to mutter.

muscle *n.* fibres in the body which produce movement.

museum *n.* a building in which old, interesting and valuable objects are displayed.

mushroom *n.* a fungus which can be eaten. MUSHROOM *v.* to grow quickly.

music *n.* an arrangement of pleasing sounds made by singing or by playing musical instruments.

musician *n.* a person skilled in composing or playing music.

Muslim *n.* a person who follows the religion of Islam.

mussel *n.* a small, edible shellfish.

must *v.* am/are/is obliged to do (something).

mustard *n.* a plant whose seeds are ground and used as a hot flavouring for food.

muster *v.* to assemble; to gather together. MUSTER *n.* an assembly; a rally.

mute *adj.* dumb; silent. MUTE *n.* a person who is unable to speak.

mutilate *v.* to damage (something) by tearing, breaking or cutting; to disfigure.

mutineer *n.* a person who takes part in a mutiny.

mutiny *n.* a revolt, in the armed forces, against authority. MUTINY *v.* to revolt against authority.

mutter *v.* to murmur or speak in a low voice.

mutton *n.* the flesh of the sheep.

mutual *adj.* shared (feelings or actions); done by each to the other.

mysterious *adj.* puzzling; difficult to explain.

mystery *n.* a secret; something which cannot be explained.

mystify *v.* to bewilder; to puzzle; to hoax.

myth *n.* a story handed down from ancient times; a legend.

N

nag *v.* to find fault (with) or scold continually. NAG *n.* a small horse or pony.

nail *n.* 1 the hard covering on the tips of fingers and toes. 2 a sharp metal spike driven in with a hammer to secure pieces of wood, etc. NAIL *v.* to fasten with nails.

naïve *adj.* (pron. na-EEV) simple in manner, thought or speech; immature.

naked *adj.* unclothed; uncovered; nude. NAKEDNESS *n.*

name *n.* 1 the word by which a person, place or thing is known or called. 2 a person's reputation. NAME *v.* 1 to give a name to (someone or something). 2 to mention by name.

namesake *n.* a person or thing having the same name as another.

nap *n.* a short sleep. NAP *v.* to have a short sleep.

narrate *v.* to tell or relate a story.

narrative *n.* a spoken or written account of what happened.

narrator *n.* the character or person telling the story in a book, play or film.

narrow *adj.* 1 of small width compared to length. 2 selfish and unsympathetic towards another person's point of view. NARROW *v.* to make or become less in breadth.

nasal *adj.* 1 relating to the nose. 2 sounded through the nose. NASALLY *adv.*

nasty *adj.* 1 unpleasant to the taste or smell. 2 dirty. 3 difficult to deal with. NASTILY *adv.* NASTINESS *n.*

nation *n.* 1 all the people of one country. 2 a tribe or large group of people who have the same customs, history, language, etc.

national *adj.* belonging to a nation or race.

nationality *n.* one's nation; a membership of a particular nation.

nationally *adv.* throughout a nation.

native *adj.* natural; possessed from birth. NATIVE *n.* a person born in a particular place; a local inhabitant.

nativity *n.* birth, esp. the birth of Jesus Christ.

natural *adj.* 1 found in nature. 2 usual and normal. 3 simple and unaffected.

naturally *adv.* 1 simply and normally. 2 of course.

nature *n.* 1 the world of plants, trees, animals, land and sea, weather, etc. 2 the qualities and character of a person or thing.

naughty *adj.* badly behaved. NAUGHTILY *adv.*

nautical *adj.* to do with ships and sailors.

naval *adj.* to do with the navy.

nave *n.* the middle, or main, part of a church.

navel *n.* the small hollow in the centre of a person's abdomen.

navigable *adj.* suitable for ships to sail through.

navigate *v.* to control and direct the course of an aircraft, ship or spacecraft. NAVIGATION *n.*

navigator *n.* a person who navigates.

navy *n.* a fleet of warships and the people who sail in them. *pl.* NAVIES.

near *adj.* 1 not far away in place or time. 2 closely related.

nearly *adv.* almost; closely.

neat *adj.* 1 smart and tidy. 2 cleverly done. 3 undiluted.

necessary *adj.* that cannot be done without; essential; unavoidable. NECESSARY *n.* something that cannot be done without.

necessity *n.* something that cannot be done without; a great need.

neck *n.* 1 the part of the body joining the head to the shoulders. 2 the narrow top of a bottle, vase, etc.

necklace *n.* a string of beads, etc., worn around the neck.

need *v.* to be in want of; to require. NEED *n.* 1 a want or a requirement. 2 poverty; distress.

needle *n.* 1 a thin, pointed instrument used in sewing and knitting. 2 the pointer in a compass or on a dial.

needy *adj.* very poor; in need.

negative *adj.* meaning or saying "no". NEGATIVE *n.* 1 the words "no" and "not". 2 in maths, a sign indicating quantities to be subtracted. 3 a number below zero. 4 a photographic film on which light and dark areas are reversed.

neglect *v.* to fail to give proper attention or care to; to disregard. NEGLECT *n.* a failure in attention or care; disregard.

negligence *n.* carelessness.

negligent *adj.* careless. NEGLIGENTLY *adv.*

negligible *adj.* not important; very small.

negotiate *v.* 1 to discuss and try to come to an agreement about (something). 2 to get by or over (something). NEGOTIATION *n.*

neighbour *n.* a person who lives near to another. NEIGHBOURING *adj.* nearby; adjoining.

neighbourhood *n.* the surrounding district.

neither *adv.* not either. NEITHER *adj.* & *pron.* not one nor the other.

neolithic *adj.* of the later Stone Age.

nephew *n.* the son of one's brother or sister.

nerve *n.* 1 a fibre which carries feeling between the brain and all parts of the body. 2 courage; boldness. NERVE *v.* to give strength or courage to.

nervous *adj.* 1 timid; fearful. 2 of the nerves.

nest *n.* the place where birds lay their eggs and rear their young; the home of certain animals and insects. NEST *v.* to build a nest; to make a home in a certain place.

nestle *v.* to lie or sit closely together.

net *n.* 1 a mesh of cord, wire or nylon for catching birds, butterflies, fish, etc. 2 a piece of this material for enclosing a goal or dividing a court. 3 an unfolded 3-D shape with all the faces laid flat. 4 THE NET *n.* an abbreviation for the internet. NET *v.* to catch in a net.

net *adj.* that remaining after necessary deductions from the original price, profit or weight.

netting *n.* material for nets.

nettle *n.* a common stinging weed. NETTLE *v.* to provoke and annoy.

network *n.* a system which connects people, places or things; a system of connected computers. NETWORK *v.* to connect.

neutral *adj.* 1 not taking sides in a quarrel or war. 2 not distinctly marked or coloured. NEUTRAL *n.* a person or nation taking no part in a dispute or war.

neutron *n.* a neutral part of an atom, that is, one that is electrically uncharged.

never *adv.* not ever; at no time.

new *adj.* recently bought or made; different; novel; changed; unused. NEWNESS *n.*

newly *adv.* recently.

news *n.* a report or information about recent events.

newspaper *n.* a daily or weekly printed publication containing news, notices and advertisements.

newt *n.* a small amphibious creature, lizard-like in appearance, but in the frog family, which lives in water but can survive on land.

newton *n.* a unit which measures force.

next *adj.* nearest; immediately after or following. NEXT *n.* the nearest one; the one after or following. NEXT *adv.* near; nearest.

nice *adj.* 1 pleasing; kind; friendly. 2 careful and exact. NICELY *adv.*

niece *n.* the daughter of one's brother or sister.

night *n.* the period of darkness between sunset and sunrise.

nil *n.* nothing; nought; zero.

nimble *adj.* light and quick in movement; skilful.

nimbus *n.* 1 a rain cloud. 2 the circle of light or halo round the sun or moon; the halo round the head of a saint.

nine *n.* the number one more than eight; the symbol 9.

nip *v.* to pinch or bite sharply. NIP *n.* 1 a small pinch or bite. 2 a small drink.

nitrogen *n.* a colourless, tasteless, odourless gas which makes up four-fifths of the air.

no *adj.* not any; not one. NO *adv.* not at all. NO *n.* a negative, denial or refusal.

noble *n.* a person of high rank, birth or title; a lord or peer. NOBLE *adj.* 1 of high rank, birth or title. 2 great and splendid; brave.

nobody *pron.* no person; no one. NOBODY *n.* a person of no importance.

nocturnal *adj.* of or in the night. NOCTURNALLY *adv.*

nod *v.* 1 to bend the head forward in agreement or greeting. 2 to droop the head forward in sleep. NOD *n.* a forward movement of the head.

noise *n.* 2 any kind of sound. 2 a loud or harsh sound. NOISE *v.* NOISE ABROAD to make public; to make known widely.

noisy *adj.* making a lot of noise. NOISILY *adv.*

nomad *n.* a member of a wandering group or tribe; a wanderer. NOMADIC *adj.*

nominate *v.* to appoint; to propose a person for a position or election.

none *pron.* no one; nothing. NONE *adj.* not one; not any. NONE *adv.* by no amount; not at all.

nonsense *n.* words or behaviour which do not mean anything, or do not make sense.

noon *n.* midday; twelve o'clock in the middle of the day.

noose *n.* a running loop in a rope which tightens when pulled.

nor *conj.* and not; and no more.

Norse *adj.* Viking. NORSE *n.* Viking language. NORSEMAN *n.* another name for a Viking.

norm *n.* a standard or typical example to compare other things with.

normal *adj.* ordinary; typical; usual.

north *n.* in the Northern Hemisphere, the direction opposite to the sun at midday; in the Southern Hemisphere, the direction of the sun at midday. NORTH *adj.* in or from the north. NORTH *adv.* towards the north. NORTHERN *adj.*

Norwegian *adj.* belonging to Norway or its people. NORWEGIAN *n.* the language or one of the people of Norway.

nose *n.* 1 the part of the face containing the nostrils; the organ of smell. 2 the front end of anything. NOSE *v.* to detect by smell; to search and pry.

nostril *n.* one of the two openings in the nose.

not *adv.* a word expressing denial or refusal.

notable *adj.* remarkable; famous; worth taking note of.

note *n.* 1 a short letter. 2 a single sound in music. 3 something written down as a reminder. 4 a piece of paper money. 5 fame or renown. NOTE *v.* 1 to notice. 2 to set down in writing; to make a note.

nothing *n.* 1 not anything. 2 a thing of no importance. NOTHING *adv.* not at all.

notice *v.* to observe something; to note. NOTICE *n.* 1 a written or printed announcement. 2 a warning. 3 attention.

notify *v.* to make something known to (someone); to give notice to.

notion *n.* an idea or opinion.

notorious *adj.* well known for bad reasons.

noun *n.* a word naming a person or thing.

nourish *v.* to help keep well by feeding; to care for.

nourishment *n.* food; nutrition.

novel *adj.* new and original. NOVEL *n.* a long fiction story, usually filling a whole book. NOVELIST *n.* the writer of a novel.

novelty *n.* a new or unusual item.

November *n.* the eleventh month of the year.

novice *n.* a beginner or learner.

now *adv.* at the present time; immediately.

nozzle *n.* the nose or spout fitted to a hose.

nuclear *adj.* concerning atomic energy; of the energy released when the nuclei of atoms are split or combined.

nucleus *n.* 1 the centre around which a number of persons or things collect; a core. 2 the central point of an atom. *pl.* NUCLEI.

nudge *v.* to push or poke gently. NUDGE *n.* a gentle push or poke.

nugget *n.* a small rough lump of native gold.

nuisance *n.* a person or thing that annoys.

null *adj.* of no effect; cancelled.

numb *adj.* without the power to feel.

number *n.* 1 a word or figure showing how many. 2 a crowd; a quantity or amount. 3 one issue of a magazine or newspaper. NUMBER *v.* 1 to count. 2 to amount to.

numeral *n.* a figure; a number; a digit.

numerator *n.* the number above the line in a vulgar fraction.

numerous *adj.* many; great in number.

nun *n.* a woman who has taken religious vows and usually lives in a convent.

nurse *n.* 1 a person trained to look after sick or injured people. 2 a woman specially trained to care for young children. NURSE *v.* 1 to look after a baby. 2 to look after sick or injured people.

nut *n.* 1 a fruit consisting of a seed within a hard shell. 2 a small block of metal for screwing onto a bolt.

nutrient *n.* any substance which animals or plants need to live and grow.

nutrition *n.* 1 the process of taking in and using food. 2 the study of food.

nutritious *adj.* nourishing; efficient as food.

nylon *n.* a synthetic plastic substance made into clothes, moulded objects, etc.

O

oak *n.* a large hardwood tree bearing acorns.

oar *n.* a pole with a flat blade used for rowing boats. OARSMAN *n.*

oasis *n.* a fertile place in the desert where water is found.

oath *n.* 1 a solemn promise to speak the truth. 2 a swear word.

oats *n. pl.* a cereal grown as food.

obedience *n.* doing, or being ready and willing to do, as told. OBEDIENT *adj.* OBEDIENTLY *adv.*

obey *v.* to do as told (by); to submit to.

obituary *n.* a notice of someone's death.

object *n.* (pron. OB-ject) 1 a thing that can be seen or touched. 2 an aim or purpose. OBJECT *v.* (pron. ob-JECT) to protest; to disapprove.

objection *n.* an expression of disapproval or dislike. OBJECTOR *n.*

objective *n.* a thing which a person aims to do; a place which a person is trying to reach. OBJECTIVE *adj.* real, actual.

oblige *v.* 1 to do (someone) a favour; to help. 2 to force or compel.

obliging *adj.* willing to help. OBLIGINGLY *adv.*

oblique *adj.* 1 slanting. 2 greater or less than a right angle.

obliterate *v.* 1 to destroy. 2 to leave no clear traces of.

oblong *n.* a rectangle; a four-sided, right-angled figure greater in length than breadth.

oboe *n.* a wood-wind instrument.

obscene *adj.* indecent; disgusting. OBSCENITY *n.*

obscure *adj.* 1 dark; unclear; hidden. 2 not easily understood; unknown. OBSCURE *v.* to darken; to make less clear. OBSCURITY *n.*

observant *adj.* 1 quick to notice things. 2 obedient to.

observation *n.* 1 noticing or being noticed. 2 obedience. 3 a remark or comment.

observatory *n.* a building from which astronomers study the heavens.

observe *v.* 1 to see; to watch carefully. 2 to obey. 3 to comment.

obsession *n.* a thought or intention which occupies the mind continually.

obsolete *adj.* out of date; no longer in use.

obstacle *n.* anything that gets in the way and hinders or stops progress.

obstinate *adj.* stubborn; not easily overcome. OBSTINATELY *adv.*

obstruct *v.* to get in the way; to block.

obstruction *n.* 1 blocking or being blocked. 2 something that hinders.

obtain *v.* to buy or acquire. OBTAINABLE *adj.*

obvious *adj.* plain to see or understand; unmistakable. OBVIOUSLY *adv.*

occasion *n.* 1 a particular time. 2 a special time or event.

occasional *adj.* happening now and then; not regular or frequent. OCCASIONALLY *adv.*

occupant *n.* a person who occupies a house, flat, etc.

occupation *n.* 1 an activity. 2 a person's business or work; a job.

occupy *v.* 1 to live in (house, etc.). 2 to take up space or time. 3 OCCUPY ONESELF WITH to keep busy.

occur *v.* 1 to happen. 2 to be found. 3 to come into the mind.

occurrence *n.* a happening or event.

ocean *n.* 1 the water surrounding the land of the globe. 2 a great area of sea.

o'clock *adv.* by the clock.

octagon *n.* an eight-sided shape. OCTAGONAL *adj.*

octave *n.* 1 a span of eight musical notes. 2 the interval between a note and the eighth above or below it.

October *n.* the tenth month of the year.

octopus *n.* a sea creature with eight arms.

odd *adj.* 1 not even; not divisible by two. 2 strange; unusual.

oddments *n. pl.* odds-and-ends; things left over; scraps.

ode *n.* a short poem or song giving praise.

odour *n.* a smell. ODOURLESS *adj.* without smell.

offence *n.* 2 an unlawful act; the breaking of a law or rule. 2 hurting of the feelings.

offend *v.* 1 to commit an offence; to break a law or rule. 2 to hurt a person's feelings. OFFENDER *n.*

offensive *adj.* 1 disgusting; causing hurt feelings. 2 used for attack, as of weapons. OFFENSIVE *n.* an attack.

offer *v.* 1 to hold out or put forward for acceptance or refusal. 2 to suggest a price. OFFER *n.* 1 an expression of readiness to do or give something. 2 the thing which is offered.

offering *n.* 1 something offered or given. 2 the act of offering.

office *n.* 1 a room or building used as a place of business. 2 a government department. 3 an official position.

officer *n.* 1 a person in a position of command in the army, navy, air force, police, etc. 2 the holder of a public appointment; the president, chairman, treasurer, etc., of a club, society, etc.

official *n.* a person who holds a position of responsibility and authority. OFFICIAL *adj.* done or said with authority.

offspring *n.* descendant(s); person's child or children; animal's young.

often *adv.* many times; frequently.

oil *n.* a greasy liquid used for cooking, fuel, lubrication, etc. OIL *v.* to apply oil to make something run smoothly; to lubricate.

ointment *n.* a greasy substance for healing cuts and sores.

old *adj.* 1 having lived for a long time; elderly. 2 not new; worn; made a long time ago. 3 of age.

olden *adj.* in past times.

olive *n.* an evergreen tree; one of its small, oily berries. OLIVE *adj.* yellowish-green.

Olympic *adj.* 1 of or at Olympia in Greece, and the games once held there every four years. 2 about similar international games held in the present day.

Ombudsman *n.* an official appointed to consider the grievances of individuals.

omelet, omelette *n.* beaten eggs, fried and folded, often flavoured with herbs, cheese, ham, etc.

omission *n.* 1 something left out or not done. 2 neglect.

omit *v.* to leave out or leave undone.

once *adv.* for one time; on one occasion. AT ONCE *adv.* immediately. ONCE *conj.* as soon as. ONCE *n.* one time.

one *n. & pron.* a single thing or person. ONE *adj.* single.

onion *n.* an edible bulb with a strong smell and flavour.

onlooker *n.* a spectator.

only *adj.* alone; by itself. ONLY *adv.* not more than; singly. ONLY *conj.* but then.

onomatopoeia *n.* the use of words which sound like their meaning, e.g. woof, miaow, hiss. ONOMATOPOEIC *adj.*

onslaught *n.* a fierce attack.

onward *adj.* forward. ONWARD *adv.* further on.

opaque *adj.* not able to be seen through; not allowing light through; not transparent.

open *adj.* 1 not closed; not covered. 2 not enclosed. 3 frank; clear. OPEN *v.* 1 to make (a thing) open; to unfasten. 2 to begin; to start.

opening *n.* 1 a gap; a space. 2 a beginning; an opportunity.

openly *adv.* not secretly; in full view.

opera *n.* a musical drama where the words are sung.

operate *v.* 1 to work; to cause (something) to work. 2 to perform an operation.

operation *n.* 1 the process or method of working. 2 a military campaign. 3 surgical treatment.

opinion *n.* a view or judgement; a person's belief.

opponent *n.* a rival; an adversary; someone on the opposite side.

opportunity *n.* a good chance or occasion to do something.

oppose *v.* 1 to fight or play against. 2 to be against (something); to resist.

opposite *adj.* 1 facing. 2 entirely different. OPPOSITE *n.* one of two things as different as possible.

opposition *n.* 1 resistance. 2 those who resist or oppose.

oppress *v.* to treat cruelly or to govern harshly.

opt *v.* 1 OPT FOR to choose. 2 OPT OUT OF to choose not to do (something).

optical *adj.* to do with the eyes or sight.

optician *n.* a person who makes and supplies spectacles or optical instruments.

optimist *n.* a person who takes a hopeful and cheerful view of things. OPTIMISTIC *adj.*

option *n.* 1 a choice. 2 a right to choose. OPTIONAL *adj.*

oral *adj*. 1 spoken; verbal. 2 by or for the mouth.

orange *n*. 1 a round, juicy fruit with a thick, reddish-yellow skin. 2 a reddish-yellow colour. ORANGE *adj*.

orbit *n*. the path in which a planet, satellite or spacecraft moves round another body.

orchard *n*. a piece of ground where fruit trees are gown.

orchestra *n*. a large group of musicians who play together.

ordeal *n*. a severe test of courage, character or endurance.

order *n*. 1 a command. 2 a request for the supply of something. 3 the manner in which things are arranged in relation to one another.

orderly *adj*. 1 well arranged; methodical. 2 well behaved.

ordinal (number) *n*. a number which shows the position of something in a list, e.g. first, second, tenth.

ordinary *adj*. 1 usual; normal. 2 plain; uninteresting.

ore *n*. a rock or solid mineral from which metals or other valuable substances may be extracted.

organ *n*. 1 a part of the body with particular work to do. 2 a large musical wind instrument.

organise *v*. to arrange (something); to plan. ORGANISER *n*.

organism *n*. an animal or plant.

organist *n*. a person who plays an organ.

oriental *adj*. of the East. ORIENTAL *n*. a person from an Eastern country.

origin *n*. the beginning; the point where something began.

original *adj*. earliest; first; not copied; not imitation. ORIGINAL *n*. 1 a model from which others are made. 2 a genuine work of art.

originality *n*. inventiveness; freshness.

ornament *n*. an object or decoration that adds beauty to something. ORNAMENT *v*. to adorn or beautify.

ornate *adj*. elaborately or richly decorated.

ornithology *n*. the study of birds. ORNITHOLOGIST *n*. an expert in ornithology.

orphan *n*. a child who has lost one or both parents through death.

ostrich *n*. a large, fast-running African bird that cannot fly.

other *adj*. not the same (as already mentioned); different. OTHER *pron*. not the same person or thing; other person or thing. OTHER *adv*. otherwise.

otherwise *adv*. in another or different way. OTHERWISE *conj*. or else. OTHERWISE *adj*. in a different state.

otter *n*. a fish-eating mammal that lives by a river or stream.

ought *v*. should; must.

ounce *n*. an imperial measure of weight, one sixteenth of a pound (28.3 grams).

our *adj*. belonging to us.

out *adv*. 1 away from a place or not in it. 2 in the open air. 3 without. OUT *prep*. out of.

outbreak *n*. a sudden beginning or breaking-out.

outburst *n*. a sudden bursting-out of something, esp. sound or feelings.

outcome *n*. the result or consequence of something.

outcry *n*. 1 a loud wail of anger. 2 a protest.

outfit *n*. the clothes and equipment needed for a special purpose.

outing *n*. a pleasure trip.

outlet *n*. a way out; an exit.

outlook *n*. 1 a view. 2 what seems likely to happen; a forecast.

output *n*. the quantity of things produced.

outrage *n*. a violent or cruel action. OUTRAGE *v*. to shock; to offend.

outside *n*. the outer part or surface of something. OUTSIDE *adj., prep*.

outspoken *adj*. frank and bold in speech.

outstanding *adj*. prominent; superior; excellent; easily seen.

outward *adj*. 1 on the outside. 2 on the way out.

ova *n. pl*. see OVUM.

oval *adj*. shaped like an egg.

ovary *n*. in animals, the female reproductive organ, which produces the eggs or ova.

ovation *n*. cheering and applause; an enthusiastic reception.

oven *n*. a heated box for baking or roasting things, esp. food.

over *prep.* 1 covering all or part of. 2 across; from side to side. 3 higher than (in position, authority, value, etc.) OVER *adv.* 1 on the opposite side; across. 2 more than required. 3 ended; finished. OVER *adj.* upper; outer. OVER *n.* a number of balls bowled in succession from one end of the pitch in cricket.

overboard *adv.* over the side of a boat. OVERDUE *adj.* beyond the stated time of arrival or payment, etc.; late.

overflow *v.* to flow over; to flood. OVERFLOW *n.* what overflows.

overhaul *v.* 1 to examine and repair thoroughly. 2 to overtake.

overlap *v.* partly to cover another thing; to overhang. OVERLAP *n.* the overhanging part.

overture *n.* 1 a piece of orchestral music performed at the beginning of a concert or opera. 2 an offer or proposal.

overturn *v.* 1 to turn over; to upset. 2 to overthrow.

overwhelm *v.* 1 to overcome completely. 2 to flood or sweep away.

ovule *n.* a small female part of a plant, which contains the egg cell and develops into the seed after fertilisation.

ovum *n.* an unfertilised egg cell. *pl.* OVA.

owe *v.* to be in debt.

owl *n.* a night-flying bird of prey.

own *v.* 1 to possess. 2 OWN UP to admit; to confess. OWN *adj.* belonging to a certain person.

oxygen *n.* a gas without colour, taste or smell, forming part of the air and without which plants and animals would die.

oyster *n.* an edible shellfish.

P

pace *n.* 1 a single step in walking. 2 speed of walking or moving. PACE *v.* 1 to walk with regular steps. 2 PACE OUT to measure a distance in paces.

pacifist *n.* a person who is opposed to war.

pacify *v.* to make calm and peaceful.

pack *n.* 1 a bag or bundle of things wrapped together for carrying. 2 a group of animals herding or hunting together. 3 a set of playing cards. PACK *v.* 1 to gather together in a box, bag or case. 2 to crowd together. 3 to compress tightly.

package *n.* a bundle or parcel.

pact *n.* an agreement or treaty.

pad *n.* 1 soft material used as a protection against damage or injury. 2 sheets of paper fastened together at one edge. 3 the sole of the foot in some quadrupeds. 4 a guard for parts of the body when playing games. PAD *v.* 1 to fill or cover with padding. 2 to walk with a soft tread.

paddle *n.* a short oar with a broad blade. PADDLE *v.* 1 to propel with a paddle. 2 to walk with bare feet in shallow water.

paddock *n.* 1 a small grass enclosure for horses. 2 an area where horses or racing cars assemble before a race.

padlock *n.* a detachable lock with a hinged loop. PADLOCK *v.* to secure with a padlock.

pagan *n.* a person belonging to a religion which worships many gods and is older than Christianity; a heathen. PAGAN *adj.*

page *n.* 1 one side of a sheet, or leaf, of paper in a book. 2 a boy attendant.

pageant *n.* 1 an outdoor performance based on people and events from history. 2 a colourful parade or show. PAGEANTRY *n.*

pail *n.* a bucket.

pain *n.* mental or physical suffering.

painful *adj.* of pain or suffering. PAINLESS *adj.*

paint *n.* a colouring substance. PAINT *v.* 1 to cover with paint. 2 to make a picture in paint.

painter *n.* 1 a person who paints. 2 a rope for mooring a boat.

painting *n.* a painted picture.

pair *n.* two things of the same kind; a couple; a set of two. PAIR *v.* to form pairs.

Pakistani *adj.* belonging to Pakistan or its people. PAKISTANI *n.* one of the people of Pakistan.

palace *n.* the official residence of the ruler of a country, a bishop, or a person of high rank.

palate *n.* 1 the roof of the mouth. 2 the sense of taste.

palatial *adj.* splendid; like a palace.

pale *adj.* whitish and having little colour. PALE *v.* to turn white. PALELY *adv.*

pale *n.* a wooden stake for a fence.

palette *n.* a board on which an artist mixes colours.

palindrome *n.* a word or phrase which is the same read forwards or backwards e.g. mum, dad, madam.

pallid *adj.* pale.

pallor *n.* paleness.

palm *n.* 1 a tropical tree with broad, spreading leaves. 2 the flat of the hand. PALM *v.* to conceal in the palm of the hand.

paltry *adj.* trivial; of little value.

pamper *v.* to indulge; to spoil with too much kindness. PAMPERED *adj.*

pamphlet *n.* a small booklet.

pan *n.* a container used in cooking.

pandemonium *n.* a scene of confusion and uproar.

pane *n.* a sheet of glass in a window.

panel *n.* 1 a flat piece of wood, metal or other material forming part of a door, wall, etc. 2 a group of people answering questions.

pang *n.* a sudden sharp pain or feeling of sadness.

panic *n.* a sudden and great fear sometimes affecting a number of people.

panorama *n.* a wide and complete view of a landscape.

pant *v.* to take short, quick gasps of breath.

pantomime *n.* a Christmas entertainment usually based on a fairy story.

paper *n.* 1 a material made from wood-pulp, rags, etc., and used for wrapping, for writing and for printing on. 2 a newspaper. PAPER *adj.* made of paper.

parable *n.* a story which teaches a lesson.

parachute *n.* an umbrella-shaped apparatus, made of nylon, which enables a person or object to descend safely from an aircraft in flight. PARACHUTE *v.* to descend by parachute. PARACHUTIST *n.*

parade *n.* 1 a procession or display moving past spectators. 2 a military display or inspection. PARADE *v.* to assemble for a parade; to march in a procession.

paradise *n.* 1 the Garden of Eden; heaven. 2 a place or state of complete happiness.

paraffin *n.* an oil obtained from petroleum and shale and used as a fuel and lubricant and for making candle wax.

paragraph *n.* 1 a distinct passage or section in a book or piece of writing. 2 a separate short item in a newspaper. PARAGRAPH *v.* to divide into paragraphs.

parallel *adj.* 1 alike; similar. 2 continuously the same distance apart. PARALLEL *n.* 1 a line marking latitude. 2 a comparison or similarity.

parallelogram *n.* a four-sided shape with its opposite sides parallel and equal.

paralyse *v.* to affect with paralysis; to make helpless or powerless.

paralysis *n.* a state of being unable to move or feel anything.

paramount *adj.* supreme; above all others.

parapet *n.* a low wall at the edge of a balcony, bridge, etc.

parasite *n.* an animal or plant that grows and lives on another.

parcel *n.* a small bundle or package wrapped and tied up for carrying or posting.

parch *v.* to make (something) become hot and dry. PARCHED *adj.*

pardon *v.* to forgive; to excuse. PARDON *n.* forgiveness.

pare *v.* to trim or reduce by cutting away the edge or surface of.

parent *n.* a father or mother. PARENTAL *adj.*

parenthesis *n.* see BRACKET. *pl.* PARENTHESES.

parish *n.* 1 the smallest unit of local government. 2 an area with its own church and clergy.

parity *n.* equality.

parliament *n.* a body of people responsible for making the laws of their country. PARLIAMENTARY *adj.*

parody *n.* a piece of writing, music or speech, often comical, which copies the style or form of another. PARODY *v.*

parole *n.* word of honour; a solemn promise.

parrot *n.* a bird with brilliant feathers and a hooked bill, often able to imitate the human voice.

part *n.* 1 a portion or share; some, but not all. 2 a piece of something. 3 a character in a play. PART *v.* to separate or divide. PARTLY *adv.*

partial *adj.* incomplete; forming only a part of.

partial (to) *adj.* favouring; fond of.

participate *v.* to take part or have a share in. PARTICIPATION *n.*

particle *n.* a very small amount; the smallest possible amount.

particular *n.* a single point or detail. PARTICULAR *adj.* 1 having to do with one person or thing. 2 special; important.

partisan *n.* 1 a keen supporter of a party or cause. 2 a guerrilla; a member of a resistance movement.

partition *v.* 1 to divide into parts. 2 to separate by means of a partition. 3 in maths, to split a number into parts in order to work out a sum, e.g. $34 + 11 = 30 + 4 + 10 + 1$. PARTITION *n.* 1 a dividing wall or screen. 2 the act of dividing into parts.

partly *adj.* to some extent; not completely.

partner *n.* 1 one of two people who share or do things together. 2 a person who shares in a business. 3 a husband or wife. PARTNER *v.* to associate with another person as a partner. PARTNERSHIP *n.*

partridge *n.* a game-bird.

party *n.* 1 a group of people with the same ideas or interests. 2 a social gathering of people usually celebrating a special occasion. *pl.* PARTIES.

pass *v.* 1 to go past; to travel. 2 to succeed. 3 to disappear. 4 to declare something to be suitable. 5 to hand (something) to someone. PASS *n.* 1 the act of passing. 2 a narrow way over hills and mountains. 3 a permit.

passable *adj.* 1 fairly good; acceptable. 2 that can be crossed or travelled over.

passage *n.* 1 a narrow corridor. 2 a way through. 3 a journey by air or sea. 4 a short extract from a book, speech or piece of music.

passenger *n.* a person travelling in a train, bus, ship, aircraft, etc.; a person being driven in a car.

passion *n.* 1 a strong feeling of emotion or love. 2 an enthusiasm for something. PASSIONATE *adj.*

passport *n.* an official document showing identity and carried by a person travelling abroad.

past *adj.* gone by; previous. PAST *n.* time already gone. PAST *prep.* 1 beyond. 2 up to and beyond.

pasta *n.* 1 a type of food made of flour paste, e.g. macaroni, lasagne.

paste *n.* 1 a mixture for sticking together paper, card, etc. 2 any sticky mixture. PASTE *v.* to stick with paste.

pastel *n.* 1 a coloured chalk crayon. 2 a picture drawn with pastels. PASTEL *adj.* pale in shade or colour.

pastime *n.* a sport, recreation or hobby that helps to pass the time away.

pastry *n.* a mixture of flour, fat and water baked in an oven.

pasture *n.* grassland for grazing sheep or cattle. PASTURE *v.* to put sheep or cattle out to graze.

pat *n.* a light tap with the hand or with a flat object. PAT *v.* to tap lightly. PAT *adv.* ready for the right moment.

patch *n.* 1 a piece of material used to repair clothing, etc. 2 a small area of ground. PATCH *v.* to mend or repair.

patent *adj.* obvious; easily seen. PATENT *n.* a right given to an inventor to prevent anyone using his invention without payment. PATENT *v.* to obtain a patent for.

paternal *adj.* 1 fatherly. 2 related on the father's side.

path *n.* 1 a track to walk along. 2 a course or line along which a person or thing moves.

pathologist *n.* a specialist in the study of diseases.

pathway *n.* a track for pedestrians.

patience *n.* enduring pain or inconvenience without complaint.

patient *adj.* having or showing patience. PATIENT *n.* a person receiving medical attention. PATIENTLY *adv.*

patriot *n.* a person who loves and serves his/her own country. PATRIOTIC *adj.*

patrol *v.* to keep watch by marching or sailing to and fro. PATROL *n.* a person, or persons, or ship or aircraft on patrol.

pattern *n.* 1 a model; an example to be copied. 2 a decorative design.

pause *n.* a short stop or interval. PAUSE *v.* to stop for a short time.

pave *v.* 1 to cover an area with flat stones; to make a pavement. 2 to prepare the way.

pavement *n.* a paved footpath.

pavilion *n.* a building for spectators or players of outside games.

paw *n.* an animal's clawed foot. PAW *v.* to scrape with a paw.

pay *v.* 1 to give money in return for goods bought, work done or services received. 2 to be profitable. 3 PAY FOR to be punished for; to suffer. PAY *n.* money earned, wages, salary.

payment *n.* 1 the act of paying. 2 the money paid.

pea *n.* a climbing plant with round seeds in pods; the seed of the pea-plant.

peace *n.* 1 freedom from war, violence and disorder. 2 quietness and calm.

peaceful *adj.* calm; quiet; full of peace.

peach *n.* a tree with soft-skinned, fleshy fruit with a rough stone.

peacock *n.* a male bird with long, colourful, spreading tail feathers. *fem.* PEAHEN.

peak *n.* 1 the pointed top of a hill or mountain. 2 the highest level or point of something. 3 the brim of a cap.

peal *n.* 1 a continuous ringing of bells. 2 a loud outburst of sound. PEAL *v.* 1 to ring loudly. 2 to thunder; to roll like thunder.

pear *n.* a soft, tapering fruit.

pearl *n.* a smooth, round, silvery-white granule formed in the shell of an oyster.

peasant *n.* in some countries, a person who works on the land.

peat *n.* decaying vegetable matter cut from bogs and used in gardening or as fuel.

pebble *n.* a small smooth stone.

peculiar *adj.* 1 odd; unusual. 2 particular; individual.

pedal *v.* to work with the foot; to use a pedal. PEDAL *n.* a lever worked by the foot.

peddle *v.* to go from place to place selling goods.

pedestal *n.* the base of a column or statue.

pedestrian *n.* a person who goes on foot; a walker. PEDESTRIAN *adj.* concerned with walking.

pedigree *n.* a list of a person's or animal's ancestors. PEDIGREE *adj.* pure-bred.

pedlar *n.* a person who goes from place to place selling goods.

peel *n.* the skin or rind of many fruits. PEEL *v.* 1 to remove the skin or rind of. 2 to come off in flakes.

peep *v.* 1 to look through a narrow opening. 2 to glance quickly.

peer *n.* 1 a person's equal. 2 a nobleman; a member of the House of Lords. *fem.* PEERESS.

peer *v.* to look at or closely into.

peg *n.* 1 a wooden pin. 2 a pin for fastening or hanging things on. PEG *v.* to fasten or secure with a peg.

pellet *n.* a small hard ball or pill.

pelvis *n.* the set of wide bones at the base of a person's back, to which the leg bones are joined. PELVIC *adj.*

pen *n.* 1 an instrument for writing with. 2 an enclosure for animals. PEN *v.* 1 to write. 2 to enclose in a pen.

penal *n.* having to do with punishment.

penalty *n.* 1 a fine or other punishment. 2 a disadvantage imposed for breaking a rule in sport.

pence *n. pl.* pennies or their amount in value. 100p = £1.

pencil *n.* an instrument containing graphite, for writing and drawing.

pendant *n.* an ornament hanging from a necklace or chain.

pending *adj.* awaiting a decision; undecided.

pendulum *n.* a freely-swinging weight, esp. in a clock.

penetrate *v.* 1 to make or find a way through. 2 to find out or see through. PENETRATION *n.*

penguin *n.* an Antarctic sea-bird that can swim under water but cannot fly.

penicillin *n.* a drug for preventing the growth of many disease bacteria.

peninsula *n.* an area of land almost surrounded by water.

penitent *adj.* feeling or showing sorrow and regret.

pennant *n.* a long, tapering flag.

penny *n.* a coin worth one hundredth of a pound.

pension *n.* a regular payment of money to a retired person. PENSIONER *n.*

people *n.* 1 men, women and children. 2 the persons composing a community or nation.

pepper *n.* 1 a plant whose seeds are ground into a hot spice for flavouring. 2 a bright green or red vegetable. PEPPER *v.* to season with pepper.

perceive *v.* to see; to understand.

percentage *n.* the rate or portion per hundred.

perception *n.* the ability to see and understand.

perch *n.* 1 a freshwater fish. 2 a roosting place for a bird. PERCH *v.* to roost; to rest; to alight.

percussion *n.* the striking together of two objects and the sound produced.

perennial *adj.* 1 lasting for many years. 2 of plants that carry on growing year after year.

perfect *adj.* (pron. PER-fect) complete; without fault; excellent. PERFECT *v.* (pron. per-FECT) to make perfect; to complete.

perforate *v.* to pierce with a hole or holes. PERFORATED *adj.* PERFORATION *n.* a hole.

perform *v.* 1 to do (something); to carry out. 2 to entertain an audience.

performance *n.* 1 the carrying out of a duty, command, etc. 2 the presentation of a play, exhibition, demonstration, etc. PERFORMER *n.*

perfume *n.* 1 a sweet smell. 2 a liquid with a fragrant smell. PERFUME *v.* to put scent on; to give fragrance to.

perhaps *adv.* possibly; it may be.

peril *n.* a great danger or risk. PERILOUS *adj.* very dangerous; risky. PERILOUSLY *adv.*

perimeter *n.* 1 the line around a shape; the circumference. 2 the boundary of something.

period *n.* 1 a length of time. 2 the time during which something takes place.

periodical *adj.* happening at regular intervals. PERIODICAL *n.* a magazine or journal which is published at regular intervals.

periscope *n.* a device with mirrors for viewing objects above the surface or above eye-level.

perish *v.* 1 to die. 2 to decay; to wither.

perjure *v.* to give false evidence under oath. PERJURY *n.*

permanent *adj.* 1 long lasting; intended to last for ever. 2 fixed; not to be moved. PERMANENTLY *adv.*

permeable *adj.* allowing water or gas to pass through.

permissible *adj.* allowable.

permission *n.* consent given.

permit *v.* (pron. per-MIT) to allow (something) to be done. PERMIT *n.* (pron. PER-mit) written permission to do something; a pass.

perpendicular *adj.* standing upright at right angles to the base; vertical.

perpetrate *v.* to commit (a blunder, crime or wrongdoing).

perpetual *adj.* 1 unceasing, everlasting. 2 frequently repeated.

persecute *v.* to treat cruelly; to oppress or torment. PERSECUTED *adj.*

persecution *n.* ill-treatment; oppression.

perseverance *n.* a constant effort to achieve something. PERSEVERE *v.*

Persian *adj.* belonging to Persia or its people. PERSIAN *n.* the language or one of the people of Persia (now called Iran).

persist *v.* to persevere; to go on in spite of difficulties.

person *n.* an individual human being; a man, woman or child.

personal *adj.* 1 belonging to a particular person. 2 private. 3 referring to an individual.

personality *n.* 1 the qualities making up a person's character. 2 a well-known person.

personification *n.* a form of metaphor which gives animals or objects human qualities or feelings, e.g. love is blind.

personnel *n. pl.* the employees of a business or organisation.

perspective *n.* 1. the art of drawing scenes or objects as they appear to the eye. 2 a particular way of looking at or considering something; an opinion or point of view.

perspire *v.* to sweat. PERSPIRATION *n.*

persuade *v.* to cause or influence (someone to do or believe something). PERSUASION *n.* PERSUASIVE *adj.*

perturb *v.* to upset; to make anxious.

pervade *v.* to spread through or penetrate all parts of.

pessimist *n.* a person who always expects the worst to happen. PESSIMISTIC *adj.*

pest *n.* 1 a troublesome or destructive insect or animal. 2 a nuisance.

pester *v.* to annoy and worry (somebody) continually.

pet *n.* a tame animal kept and treated with fondness; a favourite child. PET *v.* to fondle.

petal *n.* one of the brightly-coloured leaves in a flowerhead.

petition *n.* 1 an appeal. 2 a written request signed by many people.

petrify *v.* 1 to turn to stone. 2 to paralyse with fear and horror. PETRIFIED *adj.*

petrol *n.* a fuel used in motor-car engines.

petroleum *n.* a mineral oil found in various parts of the world.

petty *adj.* unimportant; trivial.

pew *n.* a long wooden bench with a high back, used in churches.

phantom *n.* a ghost; an apparition.

pharmacist *n.* a person qualified to prepare medicines; a chemist; a dispenser; a druggist.

pharmacy *n.* 1 the work of dispensing medicines. 2 a chemist's shop.

phase *n.* a stage in the development of something.

pheasant *n.* a long-tailed game-bird.

phenomenal *adj.* remarkable; uncommon.

phial *n.* a small glass bottle.

philatelist *n.* a collector of postage stamps.

philately *n.* the collection and study of postage stamps. PHILATELIC *adj.*

philosopher *n.* a teacher or student of philosophy.

philosophy *n.* the study of the meaning and understanding of life.

phoneme *n.* a sound; the smallest unit of sound in a word.

photograph *n.* a picture taken by means of a camera. PHOTOGRAPHER *n.* PHOTOGRAPHY *n.* the science and art of taking photographs. PHOTOGRAPHIC *adj.*

photosynthesis *n.* the process by which plants convert carbon dioxide and water into food, using light energy (see CHLOROPHYLL). PHOTOSYNTHESISE *v.*

phrase *n.* 1 a small group of words without a verb and forming part of a sentence. 2 a short sequence of musical notes. PHRASE *v.* to say in words.

physical *adj.* 1 having to do with the body. 2 that can be touched and seen; to do with the laws of nature; natural. PHYSICAL FEATURES *n. pl.* in geography, parts of the landscape which occur naturally, e.g. mountains, rivers. PHYSICALLY *adv.*

physician *n.* a doctor; a person qualified to practise medicine.

physics *n. pl.* the scientific study of heat, light, sound, electricity, magnetism and mechanics.

pianist *n.* a person who plays the piano.

piano *n. abbrev.* pianoforte, a musical instrument played by striking keys with the fingers.

pick *v.* 1 to choose; to select. 2 to pull or pluck. 3 to use a pickaxe. PICK *n.* 1 a choice; a selection. 2 a tool for breaking hard ground.

picket *n.* 1 a group of strikers who try to dissuade others from working. 2 a group of soldiers on guard duty. PICKET *v.* to position a group of people or soldiers as pickets.

pickle *n.* food preserved in salt, vinegar, etc., esp. vegetables. PICKLE *v.* to preserve in salt or vinegar.

picnic *n.* a meal eaten for pleasure out of doors.

pictogram *n.* a graph in which pictures stand for things.

pictorial *adj.* illustrated by pictures.

picture *n.* 1 a drawing, painting or photograph. 2 a vivid description of something. PICTURE *v.* to imagine.

picturesque *adj.* 1 like a picture. 2 charming or vivid in description.

pie *n.* meat, fish or fruit covered with pastry and baked.

piece *n.* 1 a part or fragment of something. 2 a single item. 3 an instance or example. PIECE *v.* to put parts together to make a whole.

pier *n.* 1 a structure built out into the sea as a protection, landing-stage or promenade. 2 a bridge or arch support.

pierce *v.* to bore a hole through something; to penetrate.

piercing *adj.* 1 penetrating. 2 shrill. 3 cold and bitter.

pig *n.* 1 a swine. 2 a block of metal cast in a mould.

pigeon *n.* a bird in the dove family.

pigment *n.* any substance that gives colour to something.

pike *n.* 1 a large, fierce, freshwater fish. 2 a spear with a long shaft and a sharp head.

pilchard *n.* a small sea-fish in the herring family.

pile *n.* 1 a number of things on top of each other; a mound. 2 a post of concrete, steel or wood driven into the ground as a support for a building, bridge, etc. PILE *v.* to to make into a heap. 2 to drive piles into the ground.

pilfer *v.* to steal (things) in small quantities. PILFERER *n.*

pilgrim *n.* a person who makes a journey to a shrine or holy place.

pilgrimage *n.* a pilgrim's journey.

pill *n.* medicine made up into a tablet.

pillar *n.* 1 an upright column supporting a roof or an arch. 2 a monument or landmark.

pillion *n.* a seat for a passenger on a motor cycle or horse.

pillow *n.* a cushion for the head.

pilot *n.* 1 the person who controls an aircraft during flight. 2 a person who steers ships in and out of harbour. PILOT *v.* to act as a pilot.

pin *n.* a piece of thin, stiff wire with a point and a head, used for fastening papers or material together. PIN *v.* to fasten with a pin.

pinch *v.* 1 to nip with the finger and thumb; to squeeze. PINCH *n.* 1 a nip or sharp squeeze. 2 a small amount.

pine *n.* an evergreen, cone-bearing tree. PINE *v.* 1 to waste away from sickness or grief. 2 PINE FOR or AFTER to long for.

pink *n.* 1 a pale red colour. 2 a garden flower. 3 IN THE PINK in excellent condition. PINK *adj.*

pint *n.* an imperial measure for liquids, one eighth of a gallon (0.57 litre).

pioneer *n.* an original explorer or settler; a person who tries a new method, idea or enterprise. PIONEER *v.* to be the first to explore, investigate or develop something.

pipe *n.* 1 a long hollow tube for conveying water, gas, etc. 2 a bowl with a hollow stem for smoking tobacco. 3 a musical wind instrument. PIPE *v.* 1 to convey through a pipe. 2 to play music on a pipe.

piping *n.* 1 a system of pipes for conveying gas, water, etc. 2 the sound of pipes playing.

piracy *n.* robbery at sea.

pirate *n.* a person who robs a ship at sea. PIRATICAL *adj.*

pistil *n.* the female part of a flower which produces seeds.

pistol *n.* a small gun, held in one hand when firing.

piston *n.* 1 the part of an engine which moves inside the cylinder. 2 a valve on a musical instrument.

pit *n.* 1 a deep hole in the ground. 2 a coal-mine. 3 the ground floor of a theatre.

pitch *v.* 1 to throw or fling something. 2 to rise and fall with the waves. 3 to erect (a tent). PITCH *n.* 1 an area of ground on which a game is played. 2 the highness or lowness of a musical note. 3 the angle of slope of a roof. 4 a tarry substance.

piteous *adj.* pitiful; arousing or deserving pity.

pith *n.* the white spongy substance in the stems of plants or in fruit peel.

pitiful *adj.* 1 showing or arousing pity. 2 deserving contempt.

pitiless *adj.* showing no pity; merciless.

pitted *adj.* marked with shallow holes or scars.

pity *n.* 1 a feeling of sorrow and sympathy for the troubles and sufferings of others. 2 the cause of someone feeling sorrow or regret. PITY *v.* to feel sorry for.

pivot *n.* a point or pin on which something turns. PIVOT *v.* to rotate on a point or pin.

placard *n.* a poster or notice. PLACARD *v.* to stick up a poster or notice.

place *n.* 1 a particular spot, position, town, locality, etc. 2 a job; a position. 3 somewhere to sit. PLACE *v.* 1 to put in a certain spot or position. 2 to appoint. 3 PLACE AN ORDER to give an order for goods.

placid *adj.* calm; peaceful; not easily ruffled. PLACIDLY *adv.*

plague *n.* a widespread deadly disease or affliction. PLAGUE *v.* to pester; to tease.

plaice *n.* a broad, flat sea-fish.

plaid *n.* (pron. PLAD) a length of tartan woollen cloth.

plain *adj*. 1 easily seen or understood. 2 simple; undecorated. 3 straightforward; honest. PLAIN *n*. a large area of flat country. PLAINLY *adv*.

plait *v*. (pron. PLAT) to form into a plait; to fold. PLAIT *n*. a braid of hair or other material formed by twisting three or more strands together; a fold. PLAITED *adj*.

plan *n*. 1 a scheme, arrangement or proposal to do something and the method of doing this. 2 a map, drawing or diagram of a building, street, town, etc. PLAN *v*. 1 to think out and prepare a scheme or proposal. 2 to draw a plan.

plane *n*. 1 a level surface. 2 a joiner's tool for smoothing wood. 3 an aircraft or an aircraft wing. 4 a tree with broad leaves. PLANE *v*. 1 to smooth wood with a plane. 2 to glide; to skim over water.

planet *n*. a heavenly body which moves in orbit round the sun.

plank *n*. a long flat piece of timber.

plant *n*. 1 any living thing that is not an animal. 2 the machinery and equipment of a factory. PLANT *v*. 1 to place plants and seeds in the soil so that they will grow. 2 to position firmly.

plantation *n*. 1 an area of land planted with trees. 2 an estate for growing cotton, rubber, sugar, tobacco, etc.

plaster *n*. 1 a mixture of lime, sand and water for spreading on walls and ceilings to form a smooth surface. 2 a dressing for a wound. PLASTER *v*. to cover with plaster. PLASTERER *n*.

plastic *adj*. 1 easily moulded into shape. 2 made of plastic.

plastic *n*. a synthetic substance made from chemicals.

plate *n*. 1 a round, shallow dish for holding food. 2 a flat sheet of metal. 3 articles of gold or silver. PLATE *v*. to cover with a thin plating of metal.

plateau *n*. an area of high, level land. *pl*. PLATEAUX, PLATEAUS.

platform *n*. 1 a stage or raised floor in a hall. 2 a raised surface for passengers at a railway station.

platinum *n*. a heavy and very valuable greyish-white metal.

plausible *adj*. 1 apparently honest, probable and reasonable. 2 good at giving reasons.

play *v*. 1 to frisk or move about in a lively, happy manner. 2 to take part in a game. 3 to perform upon a musical instrument. 4 to act a play. PLAY *n*. 1 a game; an amusement. 2 a story for acting.

playwright *n*. a person who writes plays; a dramatist.

plea *n*. 1 a request. 2 in a court of law, a defendant's answer to the charge against him or her. 3 an excuse.

plead *v*. 1 to answer a charge in a court of law. 2 to offer as an excuse. 3 PLEAD WITH to beg; to entreat.

pleasant *adj*. agreeable; giving pleasure; enjoyable. PLEASANTLY *adv*.

please *v*. 1 to give joy or pleasure to. 2 to choose; to be willing. 3 word used when making a polite request. PLEASING *adj*.

pleasure *n*. 1 a feeling of happiness or delight. 2 something that gives happiness.

pleat *n*. a fold made in cloth. PLEAT *v*. to fold into pleats.

pledge *n*. 1 a solemn promise; an agreement. 2 something given as security. PLEDGE *v*. 1 to promise; to guarantee. 2 to give as security.

plenty *n*. as much as or more than is needed; a large number or quantity. PLENTY *adv*. quite enough; in abundance. PLENTIFUL *adj*.

pliable *adj*. 1 easily bent; flexible. 2 easily influenced.

pliers *n. pl*. a tool for gripping things, like a small pair of pincers.

plod *v*. to travel slowly and steadily; to trudge.

plot *n*. 1 a small piece of ground. 2 a secret plan. 3 the main outline of a story or play. PLOT *v*. to scheme; to draw up a plan.

plough *n*. 1 a farming implement for turning the soil. 2 a similar implement for moving snow. PLOUGH *v*. to use a plough.

pluck *n*. bravery; courage. PLUCK *v*. 1 to pick or gather (flowers or fruit). 2 pull the feathers off a dead bird. 3 to snatch.

plucky *adj*. brave and courageous. PLUCKILY *adv*.

plug *n*. 1 a piece of metal, wood or rubber used as a stopper. 2 a fitting to connect an appliance to the electrical supply. PLUG *v*. to stop up a hole or gap.

plumage *n.* the feathers on a bird.

plumb *adj.* upright; vertical. PLUMB *n.* a lead weight attached to a string used to test the uprights in building work. PLUMB *v.* 1 to test whether a wall or other object is vertical. 2 to find the depth of water.

plumber *n.* a person who installs and repairs water-pipes, taps, etc.

plump *adj.* fat and rounded.

plunder *v.* to steal by force. PLUNDER *n.* loot; booty; stolen goods.

plunge *v.* to thrust or dive into water. PLUNGE *n.* a dive.

plural *adj.* more than one.

plus *n.* the sign (+), the symbol of addition. PLUS *prep.* with the addition of.

plutonium *n.* a radioactive element made from uranium.

pneumatic *adj.* 1 filled with air. 2 operated by compressed air.

pneumonia *n.* inflammation of the lungs.

poach *v.* 1 to cook food gently in a liquid. 2 to catch game or fish unlawfully.

poacher *n.* a person who catches game or fish unlawfully. POACHING *n.*

pocket *n.* a small bag or pouch sewn into a piece of clothing for carrying small articles. POCKET *v.* to place in a pocket.

pod *n.* a long seed-case on some plants.

poem *n.* a piece of rhythmic verse or poetry.

poet *n.* a person who writes poetry. *fem.* POETESS.

poetry *n.* a poet's thoughts and feelings usually arranged in lines and verses, often with a regular rhythm and pattern of lines.

point *n.* 1 the sharp end or tip of something. 2 an aim or purpose. 3 a place or position. 4 a headland or cape. 5 an idea or item. 6 a mark in scoring. POINT *v.* 1 to sharpen. 2 POINT OUT to direct attention to. 3 POINT AT to aim at. POINTED *adj.*

pointillism *n.* a painting technique in which pictures are formed from small dots of colour against a white background.

points *n. pl.* movable rails for transferring a train from one track to another.

poise *n.* balance, assurance, self-confidence. POISE *v.* to balance or hover.

poison *n.* 1 a substance which can cause death or serious illness to living things. 2 a harmful influence. POISON *v.* 1 to give poison to. 2 to corrupt or infect. POISONOUS *adj.*

poke *v.* to prod or thrust at, or into, with a finger or stick, etc. POKE *n.* a prod or thrust.

polar *adj.* concerning the North and South Poles.

pole *n.* 1 a long round piece of wood or metal, a tall post. 2 the North or South Pole, the Earth's most northern or southern point. 3 each of the opposite ends of a magnet.

police *n.* the body of men and women appointed to enforce and maintain law and order. POLICE *v.* to maintain law and order by means of the police.

policy *n.* 1 a plan or course of action. 2 an insurance agreement.

polish *v.* to make something smooth by polishing. POLISH *n.* 1 a substance used for polishing. 2 smoothness; gloss. POLISHED *adj.*

Polish *adj.* belonging to Poland or its people. POLE *n.* an inhabitant of Poland. POLISH *n.* the language of Poland.

polite *adj.* courteous; having good manners. POLITELY *adv.*

political *adj.* concerning politics, government or the state.

politician *n.* a person engaged in politics.

politics *n. pl.* 1 political matters. 2 the study and art of government.

poll *n.* 1 the voting at an election; the counting of voters; the number of votes. 2 an attempt to estimate public opinion. POLL *v.* to receive votes at an election.

pollen *n.* the tiny yellow fertilising grains found in flowers.

pollinate *v.* to put pollen on the stigma of a flower; to fertilise a plant. POLLINATION *n.* the process of putting pollen on the stigma of a flower; fertilisation in plants.

pollute *v.* to make (a thing) dirty or impure; to contaminate. POLLUTION *n.*

polo *n.* a game, like hockey, played on horseback.

polygamy *n.* the practice of having two or more wives or husbands at the same time.

polygon *n*. a shape with many angles and only straight sides.

polythene *n*. a tough, thin, plastic material used for bags, wrappings, etc.

pomp *n*. a splendid display; splendour.

pompous *adj*. self-important; displaying exaggerated pride and dignity.

pond *n*. a pool of standing water; a small lake.

ponder *v*. to consider something; to think about.

pontoon *n*. a flat-bottomed boat.

pony *n*. a small horse.

pool *n*. a pond; a puddle; a deep place in a river.

poor *adj*. 1 having little or no money; having few possessions. 2 inferior; of low quality. 3 weak; feeble.

poorly *adj*. ill; in bad health. POORLY *adv*. in a poor way; badly.

Pope *n*. the head of the Roman Catholic Church.

poplar *n*. a tall, quick-growing tree.

poppy *n*. a wild or cultivated flower, usually red or scarlet in colour. *pl*. POPPIES.

popular *adj*. well liked by many people; favourite. POPULARITY *n*.

population *n*. the total number of people living in one place. POPULATED *adj*.

porcelain *n*. a fine kind of glazed china.

porch *n*. a covered entrance to a building.

pore *n*. the small opening of a sweat gland in the skin.

pore (over) *v*. to look closely at; to study hard.

pork *n*. the flesh of a pig.

porous *adj*. having pores; not watertight.

porridge *n*. oatmeal boiled in water or milk.

port *n*. 1 a harbour. 2 a town with a harbour. 3 the left-hand side of a ship or aircraft. 4 a dark-red wine from Oporto in Portugal.

portable *adj*. convenient for carrying; movable.

porter *n*. 1 a gatekeeper or door-keeper. 2 a worker employed to carry luggage or loads.

portion *n*. a part, share or helping of something. PORTION *v*. to divide into parts or portions.

portmanteau word *n*. a word made up of two others, e.g. smoke + fog = smog.

portrait *n*. a drawing, painting or photograph of a person; a vivid description.

portray *v*. to paint or draw a picture of; to describe in words.

Portuguese *adj*. belonging to Portugal or its people. PORTUGUESE *n*. the language of Portugal and Brazil.

pose *n*. 1 an assumed position or attitude. 2 an unnatural attitude. POSE *v*. 1 to assume a certain position or attitude. 2 to behave in an unnatural way.

position *n*. 1 a place or spot where something is or should be. 2 a job or situation. 3 an attitude or posture. POSITION *v*. to put in the proper position.

positive *adj*. 1 definite; certain. 2 in maths, greater than zero. 3 beyond doubt.

possess *v*. to have, to own, to control. POSSESSOR *n*.

possession *n*. the act of possessing; something owned or occupied.

possibility *n*. something that may happen.

possible *adj*. that can happen; that can be done.

possibly *adv*. maybe; perhaps.

post *n*. 1 an upright pole of wood, metal or concrete. 2 a job, a situation. 3 the collection and delivery of letters and parcels. POST *v*. to send through the post. POSTAL *adj*.

postage *n*. the charge made for sending letters and parcels by post.

poster *n*. a placard or advertisement displayed in a public place.

postpone *v*. to put (something) off until a later date; to defer. POSTPONED *adj*. POSTPONEMENT *n*.

pot *n*. a bowl or jar made of earthenware, glass or metal for containing things. POT *v*. to put in a pot; to plant in a pot.

potato *n*. a plant with tubers which are used for food. *pl*. POTATOES.

potential *adj*. possible at some future time.

pottery *n*. 1 pots, cups, dishes and other articles made of baked clay. 2 the place where these things are made.

poultry *n*. hens, ducks, geese and all farmyard fowls.

pounce (upon) *v*. to sweep and attack something; to leap upon. POUNCE *n*. a sudden swoop.

pound *n*. 1 an imperial unit of weight, 16 ounces (454 grams). 2 a unit of money, 100 pence. POUND *v*. 1 to beat into powder or very small pieces. 2 to beat with heavy blows.

pour *v.* 1 to flow or to make something flow. 2 to rain heavily.

poverty *n.* the state of being poor; scarcity of.

powder *n.* very fine particles; anything crushed or ground into dust. POWDER *v.* 1 to make into powder. 2 to sprinkle powder on.

power *n.* 1 the ability to do something. 2 the right or the authority to do something. 3 strength, force, energy.

powerful *adj.* having or producing great power; strong, influential.

powerless *adj.* without power; weak, helpless.

practicable *adj.* that can be done or used.

practical *adj.* 1 concerned with doing or making something. 2 skilled and efficient at doing or making things. 3 useful; workable.

practically *adv.* 1 in a practical way. 2 nearly; almost.

practice *n.* 1 a habit or custom. 2 an action done repeatedly. 3 action as opposed to theory. 4 the business of doctor, solicitor, etc.

practise *v.* 1 to do something regularly in order to become skilful. 2 to do something as a habit. 3 to work in the legal or medical professions.

prairie *n.* a large treeless area of grassland.

praise *v.* 1 to speak highly of (a person or thing); to commend. 2 to worship. PRAISE *n.* 1 the act of praising; approval. 2 worship.

prawn *n.* a shellfish similar to a large shrimp.

pray *v.* 1 to ask earnestly. 2 to offer praise and prayer (to God).

prayer *n.* 1 the act of praying. 2 a request or thanksgiving to God.

preach *v.* 1 to deliver a sermon. 2 to proclaim and make known. PREACHER *n.*

precarious *adj.* 1 doubtful, depending on chance. 2 uncertain; risky. PRECARIOUSLY *adv.*

precaution *n.* care or action taken beforehand.

precede *v.* to come or go before in time, place or importance. PRECEDENCE *n.*

precedent *n.* a past action or pattern which may serve as an example or rule in the future.

precious *adj.* 1 of great price or worth; valuable. 2 loved; prized.

precipice *n.* the very steep face of a cliff or mountain.

precise *adj.* 1 clear in meaning; definite; exact. 2 very particular. PRECISELY *adv.* PRECISION *n.*

predator *n.* an animal that hunts prey.

predecessor *n.* 1 the former holder of an office or position. 2 something that has been replaced by a similar thing.

predicament *n.* a difficult, an awkward or a dangerous situation.

predicate *n.* the part of a sentence which gives information about the SUBJECT.

predict *v.* to foretell; to forecast.

preen *v.* 1 to make the feathers clean with the beak. 2 to show pride in and satisfaction with oneself.

prefabricate *v.* to manufacture sections and units in a factory so that they can be assembled or erected elsewhere.

preface *n.* an introduction to a book.

prefer *v.* to like better; to choose (one thing) before others. PREFERABLE *adj.* PREFERENCE *n.*

prefix *n.* 1 a syllable or another (shorter) word placed at the beginning of a word to change its meaning. 2 a title placed before a name, e.g. Dr, Mr. PREFIX *v.* to place at the beginning.

pregnant *adj.* 1 fruitful. 2 carrying a foetus in the womb. 3 imaginative; suggestive.

prehistoric *adj.* belonging to a time before history was recorded.

prejudice *n.* an opinion formed without full consideration of the facts; bias. PREJUDICE *v.* to fill with prejudice.

preliminary *n.* the first or introductory stage. PRELIMINARY *adj.* introductory; preparing for what follows.

premier *adj.* first in position, order or importance. PREMIER *n.* 1 the first. 2 the Prime Minister.

premises *n. pl.* houses, buildings and their grounds.

premium *n.* 1 an extra charge. 2 a regular payment on an insurance policy.

premonition *n.* a foreboding; a feeling that something is going to happen.

preparation *n.* 1 things done to make ready. 2 a medicine or mixture already made up.

preparatory *adj.* preliminary; introductory.

prepare *v.* to get ready, to make ready. PREPARED *adj.*

preposition *n.* a word placed before a noun or pronoun, and together with it forming a phrase: e.g. to, for, with, after, etc.

prescribe *v.* to order (someone) to use; to give directions; to lay down as a rule or guide.

prescription *n.* 1 a doctor's instructions for the dispensing of medicine. 2 the medicine prescribed.

presence *n.* being present; a personal appearance.

present *n.* (pron. PREZ-ent) a gift. PRESENT *adj.* now; being in a particular place.

present *v.* (pron. pre-ZENT) 1 to give, to offer. 2 to introduce.

presentation *n.* a giving, an offering.

presently *adv.* soon; shortly; before long.

preservation *n.* protection; a preserved condition.

preserve *v.* 1 to keep (something) safe. 2 to keep something in good condition. PRESERVE *n.* a conserve – jam, pickles, etc.

preside *v.* to take control; to chair a meeting.

president *n.* a person who presides; the head of a state or republic.

press *v.* 1 to push; to crush; to urge. 2 to make (something) flat or smooth. PRESS *n.* 1 a device for pressing things. 2 a printing machine. 3 the newspapers.

pressure *n.* 1 a force which presses or pushes. 2 strong influence or persuasion.

presumably *adv.* as may be supposed; probably.

presume *v.* to take for granted; to suppose (something) to be true.

pretence *n.* pretending; a false claim.

pretend *v.* to sham; to claim falsely.

pretext *n.* an excuse; a false reason.

pretty *adj.* attractive to eye or ear. PRETTY *adv.* fairly; moderately.

prevail *v.* 1 to win. 2 PREVAIL UPON to persuade.

prevalent *adj.* common; usual; widespread.

prevent *v.* to stop; to hinder. PREVENTION *n.*

previous *adj.* earlier in time; former. PREVIOUSLY *adv.*

prey *n.* 1 an animal or bird that is hunted, killed and eaten by another. 2 a victim. PREY (UPON) *v.* to hunt; to plunder.

price *n.* the money asked or paid for anything sold; the cost. PRICE *v.* to fix the price of.

prick *v.* to pierce slightly; to make a small hole. PRICK *n.* the small hole made by pricking.

pride *n.* 1 too high an opinion of oneself; arrogance. 2 something which gives a feeling of pleasure. 3 a group of lions. PRIDE *v.* PRIDE ONESELF ON to be proud of.

priest *n.* 1 a clergyman or clergywoman. 2 a religious leader.

primary *adj.* first; most important; original.

primary source *n.* in research, a text, picture or artefact that is original, not copied (see SECONDARY SOURCE).

primate *n.* an archbishop.

prime *adj.* 1 first in importance, rank or time. 2 of highest quality. 3 see PRIME (NUMBER). PRIME *n.* the time of greatest health and strength. PRIME *v.* 1 to prepare (something) for use by filling. 2 to apply first coat of paint.

prime (number) *n.* in maths, a number which cannot be divided exactly by another whole number.

primitive *adj.* 1 ancient; early. 2 rough; crude; simple.

prince *n.* the son of a king or queen; a ruler. *fem.* PRINCESS.

principal *adj.* chief; most important. PRINCIPAL *n.* the head teacher of a school or college.

principally *adv.* chiefly; mainly.

principle *n.* a rule of conduct; a fixed rule or law.

print *v.* to mark letters and pictures on paper by means of a printing press. PRINT *n.* 1 a mark made by pressure. 2 a photograph produced from a negative. 3 printed lettering. PRINTER *n.* PRINTING *n.*

prior *adj.* earlier; previous. PRIOR TO *prep.* before. PRIOR *n.* head of a monastery or convent.

priority *n.* the right to be first; the right to do something before others.

prism *n.* 1 a 3-D shape with two congruent and parallel end faces. 2 a transparent object shaped so that it reflects and disperses light.

prison *n*. a place where criminals are detained.

prisoner *n*. a person kept in prison; a captive.

privacy *n*. seclusion; being private.

private *adj*. 1 concerning one person or group; personal. 2 hidden from view; secret. PRIVATE *n*. lowest rank of soldier.

privilege *n*. a right or advantage enjoyed by a limited number of people.

prize *n*. a reward; an honour; an award for success. PRIZE *v*. 1 to value something highly. 2 to force open or apart.

probable *adj*. likely to be; likely to happen.

probably *adv*. very likely.

probation *n*. 1 testing a person's ability or character. 2 a period of test or trial.

probe *v*. 1 to investigate (something) deeply. 2 to examine with a probe. PROBE *n*. an instrument or piece of equipment used for probing.

problem *n*. something hard to understand or deal with.

procedure *n*. the way in which something is usually done; the method.

proceed *v*. 1 to move forward; to continue or resume.

proceeds *n.pl*. the money taken; the profit.

process *n*. 1 the method of manufacture. 2 a series of events which bring about change and development.

procession *n*. a body of people, vehicles, etc., moving forward in order.

proclaim *v*. to make a public announcement, to declare openly. PROCLAMATION *n*. an official or public announcement.

procure *v*. to obtain (something); to bring about.

produce *v*. (pron. pro-DUCE) 1 to bring forward. 2 to create or make. 3 to prepare (a play) for performance. PRODUCE *n*. (pron PRO-duce) 1 the quantity. 2 goods.

producer *n*. 1 the person who produces anything. 2 the person supervising the presentation of a stage, film or television performance. 3 in science, a green plant which produces its own food from nutrients, rather than eating other living things.

product *n*. 1 something produced by a natural process or by manufacture. 2 the number obtained by multiplying two numbers together.

production *n*. 1 the act of producing. 2 the quantity or thing produced.

productive *adj*. fertile; able to produce.

productivity *n*. efficiency in production.

profess *v*. 1 to declare strongly. 2 to claim.

profession *n*. 1 an occupation which requires high educational qualifications (doctor, lawyer, etc.). 2 a declaration.

professional *adj*. 1 connected with a profession. 2 earning a living by skill in a sport, as a musician, etc.

professor *n*. a teacher of high rank, usually in a university.

proficiency *n*. skill; ability.

proficient *adj*. skilled; expert. PROFICIENTLY *adv*.

profile *n*. a side view; an outline of something.

profit *n*. a financial gain; benefit. PROFIT (BY or FROM) *v*. to gain profit or benefit from. PROFITABLE *adj*.

profuse *adj*. plentiful; abundant; extravagant. PROFUSION *n*. plentifulness; great abundance. PROFUSELY *adv*.

programme *n*. 1 a list of events which are to take place; a plan. 2 details of an entertainment. 3 a broadcast on television or radio.

progress *n*. (pron. PRO-gress) 1 forward movement. 2 an advance, improvement or development. PROGRESS *v*. (pron. pro-GRESS) to move forward.

prohibit *v*. to forbid; to prevent.

prohibitive *adj*. too costly; intended to prevent.

project *n*. (pron. PRO-ject) a plan, scheme or undertaking. PROJECT *v*. (pron. pro-JECT) 1 to throw forwards. 2 to jut out.

projectile *n*. something thrown or shot through the air; a missile.

projecting *adj*. sticking or jutting out.

projector *n*. an apparatus for projecting slides or films on to a screen.

profile *adj*. producing abundantly; very fruitful.

prologue *n*. an introduction to a play, poem, book or event.

prolong *v*. to make longer; to cause to continue. PROLONGED *adj*.

promenade *n*. 1 a place set aside for walking. 2 a short walk for pleasure or display. PROMENADE *v*. to walk for pleasure or display.

prominent *adj*. 1 clearly seen; standing out. 2 famous, important. PROMINENCE *n*.

promise *n*. 1 an assurance that a person will do or will not do something. 2 a sign of something to come. PROMISE *v*. to give an assurance (to do or not to do something).

promising *adj*. full of promise; encouraging.

promontory *n*. a headland; a cape.

promote *v*. 1 to raise to a high rank or position. 2 to help; to encourage; to support. PROMOTER *n*.

promotion *n*. a rise in rank or position; an advancement.

prompt *adj*. acting quickly; without delay. PROMPT *v*. 1 to encourage or cause (a person to do something). 2 to help an actor or speaker who has forgotten his words. PROMPTLY *adv*.

prone *adj*. 1 lying face downwards. 2 inclined or liable (to do something).

prong *n*. a point of a fork.

pronoun *n*. a word used instead of a noun: e.g. I, you, he, this, etc.

pronounce *v*. 1 to utter; to speak (a word) distinctly. 2 to make a public declaration.

pronunciation *n*. the way in which a word is pronounced.

proof *n*. 1 a test or trial. 2 evidence of the truth. 3 a printer's trial copy. PROOF (AGAINST) *adj*. safe against something; resisting.

proofread *v*. to check a text for mistakes before publication.

propaganda *n*. the spreading of ideas and information (sometimes false) in an attempt to persuade people.

propagate *v*. 1 to multiply or increase by saving, grafting or breeding. 2 to spread.

propel *v*. to drive on or push forward.

propeller *n*. a revolving shaft with blades which turns rapidly to propel a ship or aircraft.

proper *adj*. 1 right, correct, suitable. 2 respectable. PROPERLY *adj*.

property *n*. 1 something owned; possessions; 2 land or buildings. 3 a special quality or ability.

prophecy *n*. a prediction; something foretold. *pl*. PROPHECIES.

prophesy *v*. to make a prophecy; to foretell.

prophet *n*. 1 a person who foretells the future. 2 a person who interprets God's will. *fem*. PROPHETESS.

proportion *n*. 1 a comparison of the quantity, size or importance of one thing with that of another. 2 a relative part or share.

proposal *n*. a suggestion; something put forward for consideration; an offer.

propose *v*. to suggest; to offer. PROPOSER *n*.

proposition *n*. something proposed; a scheme; a suggestion.

proprietor *n*. an owner. *fem*. PROPRIETRESS.

propulsion *n*. a driving forward; the force that propels.

prose *n*. language as it is spoken or written and not in verse.

prosecute *v*. to take legal action against. PROSECUTION *n*.

prospect *n*. (pron. PROS-pect) 1 something expected or hoped for. 2 a wide view. PROSPECT *v*. (pron. pros-PECT) to explore; to search for minerals.

prospector *n*. a person who searches for mineral deposits.

prosper *v*. to succeed; to flourish. PROSPERITY *n*.

prosperous *adj*. successful; flourishing.

protect *v*. to defend from danger; to shield. PROTECTOR *n*. PROTECTION *n*.

protected *adj*. defended; guarded; fortified.

protein *n*. a substance found in eggs, meat, milk, etc., which is an essential part of the diet and is used by the body for growth and repair.

protest *v*. (pron. pro-TEST) to raise an objection; to express disapproval. PROTEST *n*. (pron. PRO-test) an objection; a complaint. PROTESTER *n*.

Protestant *n*. a member of any of the Christian bodies that broke away from the Church of Rome at the time of the Reformation.

proton *n*. an atomic charge of positive electricity.

prototype *n*. the first model or example made to test a new design.

protract *v*. to draw out; to lengthen; to prolong.

protractor *n*. an instrument for measuring angles.

protrude *v*. to stick out; to project.

proud *adj.* 1 having a proper pride or dignity. 2 conceited; arrogant. PROUDLY *adv.*

prove *v.* 1 to test; to verify. 2 to show that something is true.

proverb *n.* a short, wise saying in general use.

provide *v.* 1 to supply; to give. 2 to get ready in advance.

provided *conj.* on condition that; if.

province *n.* 1 a large division of a country. 2 the extent of a person's duty or authority.

provincial *adj.* belonging to a province. PROVINCIAL *n.* a person not living in the capital city of a country.

provision *n.* 1 what is provided. 2 preparation for future need.

provisional *adj.* temporary; for the time being.

provisions *n. pl.* supplies of food and drink.

proviso *n.* a condition on which something is done.

provocative *adj.* intentionally irritating; annoying.

provoke *v.* to make angry; to annoy.

prow *n.* the front part of a boat or ship; bow.

prowl *w.* to go about stealthily. PROWLER *n.* PROWLING *adj.*

proximity *n.* nearness.

prune *v.* 1 to trim by cutting away unwanted branches, shoots, etc. 2 to cut out or get rid of unnecessary parts.

prune *n.* a dried plum.

pry (into) *v.* 1 to look and peer inquisitively. 2 to be over-curious about other people's affairs. PRYING *adj.*

psalm *n.* a sacred song; a hymn.

pseudonym *n.* an assumed name.

psychiatry *n.* the study and treatment of mental and nervous disorders. PSYCHIATRIST *n.*

psychology *n.* the study of the mind. PSYCHOLOGIST *n.*

puberty *n.* the time when a child's body changes into an adult's.

public *adj.* 1 concerning the community as a whole; for general use. 2 open; well known. PUBLIC *n.* people in general; the community.

publication *n.* a published book, journal, magazine, etc.

publicity *n.* 1 the condition of being well known to the public. 2 advertising.

publicly *adv.* in public; openly.

publish *v.* 1 to make known generally. 2 to prepare and issue copies of a book, paper, magazine, etc., for sale. PUBLISHER *n.*

pudding *n.* 1 a mixture of fat, sugar, eggs and flour baked or boiled. 2 the sweet course of a meal.

puddle *n.* a small pool of water.

pull *v.* 1 to draw or move towards. 2 to pluck; to tear. PULL *n.* the act of pulling; a strain.

pullet *n.* a young hen.

pulley *n.* a wheel with a grooved rim in which runs a rope or chain for raising weights.

pulp *n.* a mass of soft, often juicy, substance. PULP *v.* to make into pulp.

pulpit *n.* a raised structure from which the preacher in a church or chapel gives the sermon.

pulsate *v.* to throb; to expand and contract rhythmically.

pulse *n.* 1 the regular beat or throb of the arteries as the blood is pumped through them. 2 a steady beat.

pump *n.* 1 a machine for pumping air or liquids through a pipe. 2 a soft, light shoe. PUMP *v.* to use a pump; to make a pumping action.

pun *n.* an amusing use of a word or phrase which has two meanings; a play on words, e.g. I'm on a seafood diet: I see food and I eat it.

punch *n.* 1 a blow with the fist. 2 a tool for making holes. PUNCH *v.* 1 to hit with the fist. 2 to make a hole with a punch.

punctual *adj.* coming at the appointed time; in good time, not late. PUNCTUALLY *adv.*

punctuate *v.* to mark the pauses and emphasis in writing with full stops, commas, exclamation marks, etc. PUNCTUATION *n.*

puncture *n.* a prick; a hole made by a sharp point. PUNCTURE *v.* to make a hole using a sharp point.

punish *v.* to make a person suffer for a crime or offence they have committed. PUNISHMENT *n.*

punt *n.* a flat-bottomed boat propelled by a long pole. PUNT *v.* to move a boat along using a long pole.

pupa *n*. the chrysalis stage in certain insects. *pl*. PUPAE. PUPAL *adj*.

pupil *n*. 1 a person who is being taught. 2 the round opening in the iris of the eye.

puppet *n*. 1 a doll or other figure with jointed limbs worked by strings. 2 a person whose actions are controlled by others.

purchase *v*. to buy. PURCHASE *n*. the buying of something; anything bought. PURCHASER *n*.

pure *adj*. 1 clean; unmixed with anything else. 2 free from faults. PURELY *adv*.

purge *v*. 1 to make clean or pure. 2 to get rid of someone or something unwanted.

purify *v*. to make pure; to cleanse.

purity *n*. pureness; cleanness.

purple *n*. a deep reddish-blue made by mixing red and blue. PURPLE *adj*.

purpose *n*. an aim; a plan or intention. PURPOSELY *adv*.

purr *n*. the sound a cat makes when pleased. PURR *v*.

purse *n*. a small bag for carrying money.

purser *n*. the officer on a ship responsible for the accounts and money.

pursue *v*. 1 to chase; to try to catch up with (something or someone). 2 to continue discussing or going on with (something). PURSUER *n*.

pursuit *n*. 1 a chase or hunt. 2 a person's business or occupation.

push *v*. 1 to press against (something) in order to move it. 2 to urge on; to make an effort. PUSH *n*. 1 the act of pushing. 2 enterprise; drive.

put *v*. 1 to place (something) in a particular position. 2 to express in words.

putt *v*. to tap a golf-ball towards a hole. PUTT *n*. the stroke made in golf. PUTTER *n*. a golf-club used in putting.

putty *n*. a paste of ground chalk and linseed oil used to fix glass into position.

puzzle *n*. 1 a problem or question which is difficult to solve. 2 a game to test a person's skill. PUZZLE *v*. 1 to bewilder (someone); to set someone a problem. 2 PUZZLE OVER to try to find the answer to a problem.

pygmy *n*. a member of a dwarf race in Central Africa. PYGMY *adj*. small; dwarf-like.

pyjamas *n. pl*. a loose-fitting jacket and trousers for sleeping in.

pylon *n*. a steel tower which supports electrical cables.

pyramid *n*. a 3-D shape with three or more equal triangular sides which meet at a point at the top.

pyrotechnics *n. pl*. the art of making and displaying fireworks.

python *n*. a large snake that kills its prey by coiling round it and crushing it.

Q

quadrangle *n*. 1 a figure with four sides, as a square or a rectangle. 2 a courtyard; a lawn with buildings round it.

quadrant *n*. 1 a quarter of a circle or its circumference. 2 an instrument used for measuring angles.

quadrilateral *n*. a four-sided shape. QUADRILATERAL *adj*. four-sided.

quadruped *n*. a four-footed animal.

quadruple *n*. an amount four times as great. QUADRUPLE *v*. to multiply by four. QUADRUPLE *adj*. fourfold.

quadruplet *n*. one of four children born of the same mother at the same birth.

quaint *adj*. odd; unusual; old-fashioned. QUAINTLY *adv*.

quake *v*. to shake; to tremble. QUAKING *adj*.

Quaker *n*. a member of the Society of Friends, a religious group.

qualification *n*. 1 proof of training or skill. 2 fitness; suitability.

qualified *adj*. 1 having the qualifications; authorised; licensed. 2 fitted; suitable.

qualify *v*. 1 to reach an acceptable standard, usually by examination, to follow a profession or trade. 2 to modify.

quality *n*. 1 the character or nature of anything. 2 the degree of goodness or badness. *pl*. QUALITIES.

quandary *n*. a puzzling position; a state of uncertainty.

quantity *n*. amount, measure or size. *pl*. QUANTITIES.

quarantine *n*. a period of isolation for animals, people or ships to prevent the spread of disease.

quarrel *n.* a dispute or angry argument.
QUARREL *v.* to dispute or argue angrily.

quarry *n.* 1 a place where stone or slate is cut and dug. 2 a hunted animal. QUARRY *v.* to dig from a quarry. QUARRYING *n.*

quart *n.* an imperial liquid measure equal to two pints (about 1.14 litres).

quarter *n.* 1 a fourth part. 2 a period of three months. 3 a district in a town or city.
QUARTER *v.* to divide into four equal parts.

quarterly *adj.* once every three months.
QUARTERLY *n.* a periodical published every three months.

quartet *n.* 1 a group of four musicians or singers. 2 a piece of music for four musicians or singers.

quartz *n.* a solid mineral containing silica.

quash *v.* to cancel; to put an end to.

quaver *n.* a musical note equal to half a crotchet, written ♪. QUAVER *v.* to shake; to tremble, esp. voice.

quay *n.* (pron. KEE) a place for the loading and unloading of ships; a wharf.

queen *n.* 1 a female ruler. 2 the wife of a king. 3 a piece in chess.

queer *adj.* strange; unusual.

quell *v.* to suppress; to crush.

quench *v.* 1 to extinguish; to put out a fire. 2 to satisfy a thirst.

query *n.* 1 a question. 2 a question mark. 3 an inquiry. QUERY *v.* 1 to ask a question. 2 to doubt.

quest *n.* a search.

question *v.* 1 to ask questions of. 2 to have doubts about. QUESTION *n.* 1 a sentence requesting information and requiring an answer. 2 a subject for discussion. QUESTIONER *n.*

questionable *adj.* doubtful; not reliable.

questionnaire *n.* a list of questions to be answered.

queue *n.* a line of people, vehicles, etc., waiting their turn for something. QUEUE *v.* to form, or wait in, a queue.

quick *adj.* 1 fast moving; rapid. 2 lively; bright; alert. 3 hasty; impulsive. QUICKLY *adv.*
QUICKNESS *n.*

quicken *v.* to make or become quicker.

quiet *adj.* 1 without sound; silent. 2 without movement; calm. 3 kept secret. QUIETLY *adv.*
QUIETNESS *n.*

quieten *v.* to calm or become calm; to make quiet.

quilt *n.* a light, padded bed-cover. QUILT *v.* to stitch together pieces of material with padding between.

quintet *n.* 1 a group of five musicians or singers. 2 a piece of music for five musicians or singers.

quire *n.* a measure of paper, 25 sheets.

quit *v.* to go away; to leave.

quite *adv.* 1 completely; entirely. 2 to a certain extent.

quiver *v.* to tremble; to shake. QUIVER *n.* 1 a tremble; a shudder. 2 a sheath to hold arrows.

quiz *n.* a test of general knowledge or a panel-game. QUIZ *v.* to question closely.

quoit *n.* a flat metal or rubber ring used in quoits and similar games.

quota *n.* a share to be given to or received by each member of a group; an allowance.

quotation *n.* 1 the repeating of something said or written. 2 a price stated.

quote *v.* 1 to repeat something said or written by another person. 2 to give or state a price.

quotient *n.* the number of times one number divides into another.

R

rabbi *n.* a Jewish religious leader.

rabbit *n.* a small burrowing animal of the hare family.

rabble *n.* a mob; a disorderly, noisy crowd.

race *n.* 1 a group of people or animals having the same origin and characteristics. 2 a contest of speed. RACE *v.* to run or move very fast.

racial *adj.* having to do with races and their differences.

rack *n.* 1 a framework for holding and supporting articles. 2 an instrument of torture.

racket *n.* 1 a stringed bat for playing tennis, badminton, etc. 2 an uproar; a noise.

radar *n.* an electronic navigational device that detects distant objects that come within its range.

radial *adj.* radiating from the centre.

radiant *adj.* 1 giving out light or heat. 2 joyful; happy. RADIANCE *n.*

radiate *v.* 1 to send out rays of light and heat. 2 to spread out in all directions. RADIATION *n.*

radiator *n.* 1 an apparatus for radiating heat using hot water, oil or electricity. 2 an apparatus for keeping a petrol engine cool.

radio *n.* the sending and receiving of sound messages by means of electrical waves; an apparatus for receiving radio broadcasts. RADIO *v.* to communicate by means of radio waves.

radioactive *adj.* giving off radiant energy by the breakdown of unstable atomic nuclei. RADIOACTIVITY *n.*

radium *n.* a rare radioactive metal which gives out rays that are used in the treatment of some diseases.

radius *n.* the distance from the centre to the circumference of a circle. *pl.* RADII.

raft *n.* a floating platform, usually wooden.

rafter *n.* a sloping beam supporting a roof.

rag *n.* a torn piece of cloth.

rage *n.* violent anger. RAGE *v.* to be furious or angry. RAGING *adj.*

raid *n.* a sudden attack. RAID *v.* to make a sudden attack upon. RAIDER *n.*

rail *n.* 1 a wooden or metal bar forming the top part of a fence. 2 a steel bar forming part of a railway track. RAIL *v.* to use angry language. RAILING *n.*

railway *n.* 1 the track on which trains run. 2 a railway system.

rain *n.* condensed moisture falling in drops from the sky. RAIN *v.* to fall in drops as or like rain. RAINY *adj.*

rainbow *n.* a coloured arch formed in the sky by the sun shining through raindrops.

rainfall *n.* the amount of rain that falls in a given time at a particular place.

raise *v.* 1 to lift up; to move up. 2 to construct; to create. 3 to bring up children or animals. 4 to collect (an army, money, etc.).

raisin *n.* a dried grape.

rake *n.* a long-handled tool with several prongs for smoothing or scraping soil. RAKE *v.* to scrape or collect with a rake.

rally *v.* 1 to bring or come together again; to reassemble. 2 to recover partly; to revive. RALLY *n.* 1 an assembly of people. 2 a recovery. 3 a competition among motorists, cyclists, etc.

ram *n.* 1 a male sheep. *fem.* EWE. 2 something used for hammering with great force. RAM *v.* to strike heavily with repeated blows.

ramble *v.* 1 to walk or wander for pleasure. 2 to talk in a confused way. RAMBLE *n.* a walk for pleasure. RAMBLER *n.*

ramp *n.* a slope joining two levels; an incline.

rampage *v.* to rush about in a violent and unruly manner. RAMPAGE *n.* violent and unruly behaviour.

rampart *n.* a defensive wall or mound.

ranch *n.* a large cattle farm. RANCHER *n.*

rancid *adj.* smelling or tasting stale or sour.

random *adj.* haphazard; without aim or purpose. RANDOM *n.* a chance; a hazard.

range *n.* 1 a line; a row. 2 the choice or variety of anything. 3 the distance over which something can operate. 4 a piece of ground with targets for shooting. RANGE *v.* 1 to set in a line. 2 to wander. 3 to vary between limits.

rank *n.* 1 a row or line. 2 a class or order of something. RANK *v.* to classify.

ransack *v.* to plunder; to search thoroughly.

ransom *n.* a sum of money paid or demanded for the release of a captive. RANSOM *v.* to buy release or freedom.

rap *n.* 1 a sharp, light blow. 2 a form of poetry with a strong rhythm and quick pace. RAP *v.* to strike a sharp, light blow.

rapid *adj.* quick, speedy. RAPIDLY *adv.*

rapids *n. pl.* a part of a river where the water flows rapidly over rocks.

rapture *n.* great delight, joy or ecstasy. RAPTUROUS *adj.*

rare *adj.* scarce; uncommon; unusual. RARELY *adj.* RARENESS *n.*

rarity *n.* a rare or an uncommon thing. *pl.* RARITIES.

rascal *n.* 1 a rogue. 2 a naughty or mischievous person.

rash *n.* an outbreak of spots on the skin. RASH *adj.* hasty; reckless. RASHLY *adv.*

rasher *n.* a slice of bacon.

rasp *n*. 1 a coarse file. 2 a harsh grating sound. RASP *v*. to scrape; to grate.

raspberry *n*. a small, soft, red fruit. *pl*. RASPBERRIES.

rat *n*. a gnawing rodent, resembling a large mouse.

rate *n*. 1 a relative speed. 2 a local tax on property. 3 a fixed price. RATE *v*. 1 to estimate the value of. 2 to value.

rather *adv*. more willingly; to a greater extent.

ratio *n*. the proportion of one thing to another.

ration *n*. a fixed allowance or share. RATION *v*. to share something out in fixed quantities.

rational *adj*. reasonable; sensible. RATIONALLY *adv*.

rattle *v*. to make a series of sharp sounds. RATTLE *n*. 1 a series of sharp sounds. 2 a baby's plaything.

raucous *adj*. hoarse; harsh-sounding. RAUCOUSLY *adv*.

ravage *v*. to plunder; to devastate.

rave *v*. 1 to talk wildly. 2 to talk enthusiastically.

ravel *v*. to entangle; to confuse.

raven *n*. a large black bird of the crow family.

ravenous *adj*. very hungry. RAVENOUSLY *adv*.

ravine *n*. a deep narrow valley.

raw *adj*. 1 not cooked. 2 not trained or experienced. 3 cold and damp. RAWNESS *n*.

ray *n*. a narrow beam of light or heat.

rayon *n*. artificial silk.

razor *n*. an instrument for shaving.

reach *v*. 1 to stretch. 2 to arrive at. REACH *n*. 1 the distance a person can reach with the arm. 2 a straight stretch of river.

react *v*. 1 to act or behave in response to something said or done. 2 to act in opposite ways.

reaction *n*. a response caused by some person, thing or event.

read *v*. to look at and understand the meaning of printed or written words. READER *n*. READING *n*.

readily *adv*. 1 quickly; promptly. 2 willingly. READINESS *n*.

ready *adj*. 1 prepared; prompt. 2 willing.

real *adj*. 1 actual; genuine. 2 actually existing.

realise *v*. 1 to understand. 2 to sell for a price.

realism *n*. 1 an awareness or acceptance of reality, the way things are. 2 a style of art which copies real life.

realistic *adj*. like the real thing. REALISTICALLY *adv*.

really *adv*. truly; without doubt.

realm *n*. a kingdom.

reap *v*. to cut and gather grain crops.

reappear *v*. to appear again.

rear *n*. the back of something; the point furthest from the front. REAR *v*. 1 to bring up (young children or animals). 2 to rise up on the hind legs.

rearrange *v*. to arrange in a new order. REARRANGEMENT *n*.

reason *n*. 1 an explanation or excuse. 2 a cause. 3 the capacity to understand. REASON *v*. to think or talk over sensibly. REASONING *n*.

reasonable *adj*. sensible; moderate; fair.

reassure *v*. to remove (someone's) doubts and fears; to encourage. REASSURING *adj*. REASSURANCE *n*.

rebate *n*. a deduction or discount.

rebel *n*. (pron. REB-el) a person who resists authority or control. REBEL (against) *v*. (pron. rib-EL) to resist; to oppose.

rebellion *n*. a revolt; open resistance to authority or control.

rebellious *adj*. taking part in a rebellion; defiant.

rebound *v*. (pron. ri-BOUND) to spring or bounce back; to recoil. REBOUND *n*. (pron. REE-bound) a bounce back.

rebuild *v*. to build again; to reconstruct.

rebuke *v*. to reproach or criticise. REBUKE *n*. a reproach.

recall *v*. 1 to call back. 2 to remember. RECALL *n*. 1 a call to return. 2 the ability to remember.

recapture *v*. 1 to capture again; to retake. 2 to recall.

recede *v*. to go back or shrink back; to retreat. RECEDING *adj*.

receipt *n*. 1 the fact of receiving or being received. 2 a written acknowledgement that something has been received.

receive *v*. 1 to take or accept something that is offered. 2 to welcome (someone).

receiver *n.* 1 a person who receives. 2 the earpiece of a telephone. 3 a radio set.

recent *adj.* new; having happened a short time ago. RECENTLY *adv.*

receptacle *n.* a container for holding things.

reception *n.* 1 a welcome. 2 a formal meeting of welcome. 3 the quality of radio sound or television sound and picture.

recess *n.* 1 an alcove. 2 a break or interval in work; a holiday.

recipe *n.* 1 a list of the ingredients and directions for preparing a dish. 2 directions for doing something successfully.

recital *n.* 1 a musical performance of playing or singing. 2 a detailed account of facts.

recite *v.* 1 to repeat aloud from memory. 2 to mention in order. RECITER *n.*

reckless *adj.* careless; not caring or thinking of the consequences of what one is doing. RECKLESSLY *adv.*

reckon *v.* to calculate; to consider.

reclaim *v.* 1 to claim (something) back. 2 to recover; to improve. RECLAMATION *n.*

recline *v.* to lean or lie back; to rest.

recluse *n.* a person who lives in solitude.

recognition *n.* the act of knowing or remembering what has been seen before.

recognise *v.* 1 to know again or remember. 2 to acknowledge; to admit.

recollect *v.* to remember. RECOLLECTION *n.*

recommence *v.* to start again.

recommend *v.* 1 to suggest; to advise. 2 to speak well of (something or someone). RECOMMENDATION *n.*

reconcile *v.* 1 to make friendly again after a quarrel. 2 RECONCILE ONESELF TO to accept.

reconnaissance *n.* a preliminary inspection or survey before taking action.

reconnoitre *v.* to inspect or survey.

reconsider *v.* to think again about.

reconstruct *v.* 1 to build again. 2 to restore; to remake.

record *v.* (pron. re-KORD) 1 to write (something) down. 2 to make a reproduction of. RECORD *n.* (pron. RE-kord) 1 a written account. 2 a disc on which music or sound has been recorded. 3 an unbeaten performance. RECORDED *adj.*

recorder *n.* 1 a person who keeps a record of events. 2 the judge who presides at quarter sessions. 3 a simple form of flute. 4 TAPE RECORDER an apparatus for recording sound on tape.

recount *v.* (pron. re-COUNT) to tell; to describe in detail.

re-count *v.* (pron. RE-count) to count over again. RECOUNT *n.* the second or further counts.

recover *v.* 1 to regain; to get back. 2 to return to normal health. RECOVERY *n.*

recreation *n.* games, sports, hobbies and other leisure interests.

recruit *n.* a person who has just joined the armed forces; a new member. RECRUIT *v.* to obtain recruits.

rectangle *n.* a shape with four straight sides and four right angles; a square or oblong. RECTANGULAR *adj.*

rectify *v.* to put right; to correct. 2 to purify. RECTIFIED *adj.*

rector *n.* 1 a clergyman or clergywoman having the care of a parish. 2 the head of a Scottish university.

recuperate *v.* to recover from illness.

recur *v.* to happen again; to be repeated. RECURRENCE *n.*

recycle *v.* to collect and process rubbish so that it can be used again.

red *n.* 1 a colour ranging from crimson to orange. 2 IN THE RED in debt. RED *adj.*

redeem *v.* 1 to buy back. 2 to save; to rescue.

redirect *v.* to direct again; to re-address.

reduce *v.* 1 to make less or smaller. 2 to weaken. REDUCTION *n.*

redundant *adj.* more than is necessary; no longer useful or needed. REDUNDANCY *n.*

reed *n.* 1 a tall plant that grows in or near water. 2 a vibrating strip in some wind instruments.

reef *n.* a ridge of rocks or coral just above or below the surface of the sea.

reek *v.* to give off an unpleasant smell. REEK *n.* an unpleasant smell.

reel *n.* 1 a cylinder, drum or bobbin on which wire, thread, cotton, paper, etc., is wound. 2 a lively Scottish dance. 3 a stagger. REEL *v.* 1 to wind on a reel. 2 to stagger or walk unsteadily.

refer (to) *v.* 1 to go to (someone or something) for help, a decision or information. 2 to mention or speak about. 3 to indicate.

referee *n.* 1 a person who controls a game according to the rules. 2 a person chosen to decide between opposing parties.

reference *n.* 1 the referring of a matter to someone for decision or settlement. 2 a book where information can be found. 3 a letter concerning the character or ability of a person; a testimonial.

refine *v.* to purify; to improve. REFINED *adj.*

refinery *n.* a place where materials are purified.

refit *v.* to fit again; to restore. REFIT *n.* the process of refitting.

reflect *v.* 1 to throw back (light, heat, etc.). 2 to show an image as in a mirror. 3 to think matters over; to consider. REFLECTION *n.*

reflector *n.* a surface which thrown back light, heat, radio signals, etc.

reform *v.* to change for the better; to improve. REFORM *n.* an improvement or amendment. REFORMED *adj.* REFORMER *n.*

Reformation *n.* the period in the 16th century when Protestant churches were established (in England, under King Henry VIII).

refrain *v.* to hold back; to abstain (from doing something). REFRAIN *n.* the chorus of a song; a tune.

refresh *v.* to freshen; to give new strength to. REFRESHING *adj.*

refreshment *n.* food and drink.

refrigerate *v.* to freeze or to chill (something).

refrigerator *n.* a device for keeping things chilled or frozen.

refuge *n.* a place of shelter.

refugee *n.* a person who leaves his or her home or country to seek safety from disaster, danger or persecution.

refusal *n.* a rejection; the opportunity to accept or decline something.

refuse *v.* (pron. re-FUZE) to decline or to reject. REFUSE *n.* (pron. REF-use) rubbish; anything rejected as worthless.

regain *v.* to get back; to recover (something).

regard *v.* 1 to look at. 2 to consider. 3 to respect. REGARD *n.* 1 a look; a gaze. 2 concern, care. 3 respect.

regarding *prep.* concerning; about.

regardless *adj.* not considering; without caring.

regards *n. pl.* kind wishes; friendly feelings.

regatta *n.* a race meeting for boats and yachts.

regiment *n.* an army unit consisting of several companies or battalions.

region *n.* a district; an area; part of a country or of the world. REGIONAL *adj.*

register *n.* 1 an official record book. 2 the range between the highest and lowest notes of a voice or instrument. REGISTER *v.* to record official information. REGISTERED *adj.*

regret *v.* to be sorry or sad about. REGRET *n.* sorrow.

regular *adj.* 1 normal; according to rule. 2 evenly spaced. REGULARLY *adv.*

regulate *v.* 1 to control. 2 to adjust. REGULATED *adj.* REGULATOR *n.*

regulation *n.* a rule or order.

rehearsal *n.* a practice in preparation for a performance.

rehearse *v.* to practise something to be performed. REHEARSED *adj.*

reign *n.* the period of time during which a king or queen rules. REIGN *v.* to rule.

rein *n.* a narrow strap for guiding and controlling a horse. REIN *v.* to guide; to control.

reindeer *n.* a kind of deer living in cold regions.

reinforce *v.* 1 to strengthen. 2 to send further troops or supplies to. REINFORCEMENT *n.*

reinstate *v.* to replace in the position held before.

reject *v.* (pron. ri-JECT) to refuse; to discard. REJECT *n.* (pron. RE-ject) something discarded. REJECTED *adj.* REJECTION *n.*

rejoice *v.* 1 to feel joy or gladness. 2 to make joyful or glad. REJOICING *n.*

rejoin *v.* 1 to join again. 2 to say in answer.

relapse *v.* to fall back (into a former condition). RELAPSE *n.* a return to a former condition or ways.

relate *v.* 1 to tell; to give an account of. 2 to join; to connect.

relation *n.* 1 any connection between persons or things. 2 a relative; a member of the same family.

relative *n.* a family relation. RELATIVE *adj.* having some relation; connected with.

relax *v.* 1 to become less tense or strict. 2 to rest.
relay *n.* a race involving successive runners.
RELAY *v.* to pass on.
release *v.* to set free; to let go. RELEASE *n.* freedom; relief.
relegate *v.* to transfer to a lower position. RELEGATION *n.*
relent *v.* to become less severe; to yield.
relevant *adj.* to do with the matter being discussed. RELEVANCE *n.*
reliable *adj.* trustworthy; to be relied on; dependable. RELIABLY *adv.*
reliance *n.* trust, confidence. RELIANT *adj.*
relic *n.* something which has survived from a long time ago.
relief *n.* 1 help; assistance. 2 the easing of pain or worry. 3 a design which stands out from the surface. 4 a person who releases another from duty. RELIEVE *v.*
religion *n.* a particular set of beliefs and worship; the worship of God or of gods. RELIGIOUS *adj.*
relish *v.* to enjoy; to like the taste of. RELISH *n.* 1 enjoyment; a good taste. 2 a sauce.
reluctant *adj.* unwilling to do something.
rely (on or **upon)** *v.* to depend on; to have trust in.
remain *v.* 1 to stay; to continue. 2 to survive.
remainder *n.* the part left over or unused.
remand *v.* to send back to prison to await trial.
remark *v.* 1 to say; to comment. 2 to notice; to observe. REMARK *n.* a comment; something said.
remarkable *adj.* unusual; exceptional.
remedy *n.* a cure. REMEDY *v.* to cure or heal. REMEDIAL *adj.*
remember *v.* 1 to recall to mind; to recollect. 2 to reward.
remind *v.* to cause (someone) to remember (something).
remit *v.* 1 to pardon; to excuse. 2 to pay.
remnant *n.* a small amount or piece left over.
remorse *n.* deep regret or repentance for a fault or wrongdoing.
remote *adj.* 1 far away; distant. 2 slight; faint. REMOTELY *adv.* REMOTENESS *n.*

removal *n.* 1 a dismissal. 2 a transfer; being removed. 3 an extraction.
remove *v.* 1 to take from one place to another; to transfer. 2 to take from its place. 3 to take off; to uncover. REMOVED *adj.*
remunerate *v.* to pay for something done; to reward. REMUNERATION *n.*
rend *v.* 1 to tear apart. 2 to split.
rendezvous *n.* a meeting-place. RENDEZVOUS *v.* to meet at a certain place.
renew *v.* 1 to make new. 2 to restore; to replace. RENEWAL *n.*
renounce *v.* to give up; to reject.
renovate *v.* to make something like new; to restore. RENOVATION *n.*
renown *n.* fame; glory; honour. RENOWNED *adj.*
rent *n.* 1 a payment made by a tenant to a landlord for the occupation of property or land. 2 a tear; a split.
re-open *v.* to open again.
repair *v.* to mend; to restore. REPAIR *n.* a mend; a restoration.
repatriate *v.* to send or bring a person back to his own country.
repay *v.* 1 to pay back. 2 to return a kindness. REPAYMENT *n.*
repeat *v.* 1 to say or do again. 2 to recite. REPEATEDLY *adv.*
repel *v.* to push (something) back or away.
repent *v.* to feel sorry for what has been done or left undone. REPENTANCE *n.*
repercussion *n.* 1 an echo. 2 the effect of something that has happened.
repetition *n.* repeating or being repeated.
replace *v.* 1 to put back in its place. 2 to take the place of (something or someone); to substitute. REPLACEMENT *n.*
replenish *v.* to fill again; to restock.
replica *n.* an exact copy; a duplicate.
reply *v.* to answer; to respond. REPLY *n.* an answer; a response. *pl.* REPLIES.
report *v.* 1 to give an account of; to give information about. 2 to announce that one has arrived for duty. 3 to make a complaint. REPORT *n.* 1 an account or statement. 2 the sound of an explosion.

reporter *n.* a person who collects news and information for a newspaper, radio or television.

represent *v.* 1 to show. 2 to describe. 3 to act for somebody. 4 to claim to be. REPRESENTATION *n.* REPRESENTATIVE *n.*

repress *v.* to keep down; to restrain.

reprieve *v.* 1 to delay; to postpone. 2 to cancel or reduce punishment. REPRIEVE *n.* a delay; a postponement. REPRIEVED *adj.*

reprimand *n.* a rebuke. REPRIMAND *v.* to rebuke.

reprint *v.* to print again; to print a further or new edition of a book. REPRINT *n.* a further or new edition of a book.

reprisal *n.* an act of revenge or retaliation.

reproach *v.* to speak disapprovingly to; to blame. REPROACH *n.* blame or disapproval; a reprimand.

reproduce *v.* 1 to produce again; to copy; to imitate. 2 to produce young. REPRODUCTION *n.*

reptile *n.* a crawling, vertebrate animal such as a snake, lizard, crocodile, etc.

republic *n.* a country which has an elected government but no king or queen.

repulse *v.* to drive back; to repel; to reject.

repulsive *adj.* disgusting; loathsome.

reputable *adj.* worthy; well thought of.

reputation *n.* what is generally said or thought about a person's character.

request *v.* to ask; to require. REQUEST *n.* something asked for.

require *v.* to want; to need. REQUIREMENT *n.*

rescue *v.* to free or save from attack, danger or captivity. RESCUE *n.* an act which saves from attack, danger or captivity. RESCUER *n.*

research *n.* a careful search or inquiry; a scientific study to discover new facts. RESEARCH *v.* to make researches; to investigate.

resemble *v.* to be like or similar to (someone or something). RESEMBLANCE *n.*

resent *v.* to feel or show bitterness or anger about something. RESENTFUL *adj.* RESENTMENT *n.*

reserve *v.* to keep or store for a special purpose or person. RESERVE *n.* 1 an emergency supply. 2 shyness. 3 an area of land set aside for certain animals or people to live in. RESERVED *adj.*

reservoir *n.* a place, often an artificial lake, where water is stored.

reside (**at** or **in**) *v.* to live in a place.

residence *n.* a house; a dwelling-place.

resident *n.* an occupant; a permanent inhabitant. RESIDENTIAL *adj.*

residual *adj.* remaining or left over.

residue *n.* the remainder; what is left over.

resign *v.* 1 to give up; to relinquish. 2 RESIGN ONESELF TO to be ready to accept or endure.

resilience *n.* elasticity; buoyancy. RESILIENT *adj.*

resist *v.* to oppose; to struggle against; to offer resistance. RESISTANCE *n.*

resistant *adj.* opposing; offering resistance.

resolute *adj.* firm; determined. RESOLUTELY *adv.*

resolution *n.* 1 firmness; determination. 2 a decision; a purpose.

resolve *v.* to make a decision; to intend. RESOLVE *n.* a decision; an intention. RESOLVED *adj.*

resort *n.* 1 a place frequently visited. 2 something turned to for help. RESORT (TO) *v.* 1 to visit frequently. 2 to turn to for help.

resound *v.* to echo; to fill with sound.

resource *n.* 1 a source of help; useful material. 2 enterprise; ingenuity. RESOURCEFUL. *adj.*

respect *v.* to esteem; to show regard for. RESPECT *n.* esteem; regard.

respectable *adj.* 1 deserving respect or honour. 2 decent. RESPECTABILITY *n.*

respectful *adj.* courteous; showing regard and esteem. RESPECTFULLY *adv.*

respective *adj.* individual; concerning each one.

respiration *n.* the intake of air; breathing. RESPIRE *v.*

respirator *n.* a mask worn over the mouth and nose to aid breathing or to purify the air breathed in.

respond *v.* 1 to answer; to reply. 2 to react.

response *n.* 2 an answer; a reply. 2 a reaction. RESPONSIVE *adj.*

responsible *adj.* 1 answerable or liable for. 2 trustworthy and reliable. RESPONSIBILITY *n.*

rest *n.* 1 a pause; a stop. 2 sleep. 3 a support or prop. 4 the remainder. REST *v.* 2 to pause or stop. 2 to sleep.

restaurant *n.* a place where meals may be bought and eaten.

restful *adj.* quiet; peaceful.

restless *adj.* uneasy; impatient.

restoration *n.* a renewal; the act or process of restoring.

restore *v.* 1 to give back; to bring back. 2 to repair.

restrain *v.* to hold back; to keep under control. RESTRAINT *n.*

restrict *v.* to keep within certain limits; to confine. RESTRICTION *n.*

result *n.* the outcome; the consequence. RESULT *v.* to happen because of other actions or events. RESULTING *adj.*

resume *v.* to begin again.

resurrect *v.* to revive; to bring back to life. RESURRECTION *n.*

retail *v.* 1 to sell in small quantities. 2 to sell to others. RETAILER *n.*

retain *v.* 1 to keep; to hold. 2 to employ. RETAINING *adj.*

retaliate *v.* to repay (injury or insult) in the same way. RETALIATION *n.*

retard *v.* to delay; to make slow or late.

reticent *v.* cautious; reserved; saying little. RETICENCE *n.*

retire *v.* 1 to withdraw. 2 to cease active employment. 3 to go to bed. RETIREMENT *n.*

retrace *v.* to go back over something.

retreat *v.* to move back; to retire. RETREAT *n.* 1 a withdrawal or retirement. 2 a quiet, peaceful place.

retrieve *v.* 1 to recover anything lost. 2 to regain.

retriever *n.* a dog trained to find and bring in game that has been shot.

return *v.* 1 to come or go back. 2 to send or to give back. RETURN *n.* 1 a coming or going back. 2 a sending or giving back. 3 a profit; an account. 4 a two-way travel ticket.

reunion *n.* reuniting; a gathering of friends.

reunite *v.* to come together again.

reveal *v.* 1 to show what was hidden. 2 to make known; to disclose.

revenge *v.* to do harm to another person in return for harm done by him; to retaliate. REVENGE *n.* a harmful repayment; a retaliation. REVENGEFUL *adj.*

revenue *n.* income of an individual, business or nation.

reverence *n.* a deep feeling of respect. REVERENT *adj.* REVERENTLY *adv.*

reverse *v.* 1 to turn something the other way round or inside out. 2 to go backwards. 3 to undo or to cancel (a decision). REVERSE *n.* 1 the opposite; the other side of. 2 a defeat or failure. REVERSE *adj.* opposite; backward. REVERSIBLE *adj.* able to be reversed or changed back.

review *v.* 1 to re-examine. 2 to inspect. 3 to give an opinion of. REVIEW *n.* 1 a re-examination. 2 an inspection. 3 a criticism of a book, play, film, etc.

revise *v.* 1 to examine and correct faults and mistakes. 2 to study again. REVISED *adj.* REVISION *n.*

revive *v.* to bring back to life or health.

revolt *v.* 1 to rebel. 2 to fill with disgust or horror. REVOLT *n.* a rebellion. REVOLTING *adj.*

revolution *n.* 1 a rebellion or uprising. 2 a turn or rotation. 3 a complete change in opinion, fashion, etc. REVOLUTIONARY *adj.*

revolve *v.* to turn round; to rotate.

revolver *n.* a pistol that will fire several shots without reloading.

revulsion *n.* disgust; a change of feeling.

reward *n.* something given or received for service or merit. REWARD *v.* to give a reward.

rhetoric *n.* (pron. RE-toric) writing or speech intended to persuade or sound important. RHETORICAL *adj.* (pron. re-TOR-ical)

rheumatism *n.* a disease which causes pain and swollen joints.

rhyme *n.* a similarity of sound in endings of words or verse lines. RHYME *v.* to use similar-sounding words.

rhythm *n.* a regular beat or accent in music or speech. RHYTHMIC *adj.*

rib *n.* 1 one of the curved bones round the upper part of the body. 2 a spar of wood which strengthens the hull of a ship.

ribcage *n.* the structure of ribs that protects the heart and lungs.

ribbon *n.* a long narrow strip of material.

rice *n.* 1 a cereal plant grown in marshy ground in warm climates. 2 the white grain of the rice plant used as food.

rich *adj.* 1 wealthy; having much money or many possessions. 2 full of goodness or colour.

rid *v.* to make free from; to remove something.

riddle *n.* 1 a question or statement, sometimes in rhyme, which forms a puzzle. 2 a large sieve. RIDDLE *v.* to sieve; to fill with holes.

ride *v.* 1 to be carried by an animal or vehicle. 2 to travel; to drive. RIDE *n.* a journey on an animal or in a vehicle. RIDER *n.*

ridge *n.* a raised part between furrows; a mountain range.

ridicule *v.* to make fun of; to mock or laugh at. RIDICULE *n.* mockery.

ridiculous *adj.* absurd; very silly. RIDICULOUSLY *adv.*

rife *adj.* common; found everywhere.

rifle *n.* a gun having a long spirally grooved barrel. RIFLE *v.* to rob and plunder.

rift *n.* 1 a crack or split. 2 quarrel.

rig *v.* 1 to provide a ship with sails, ropes and gear. 2 to fit out with clothes or equipment. RIG *n.* 1 the way in which a ship's sails, ropes, etc., are arranged. 2 the platform or equipment for drilling an oil-well.

rigging *n.* the sails and ropes of a ship.

right *n.* 1 that which is right. 2 something allowed by law or custom. 3 correctness. RIGHT *adj.* 1 just and true. 2 proper; correct. 3 the opposite of left. RIGHT *adv.* correctly; exactly. RIGHTLY *adv.*

rigid *adj.* 1 stiff; unbending. 2 strict. RIGIDLY *adv.*

rigorous *adj.* very strict; severe; harsh. RIGOROUSLY *adv.*

rim *n.* the outer edge; the brim.

rind *n.* the peel of fruit, skin of bacon, crust of cheese, etc.

ring *n.* 1 a circle of gold, or other metal, worn on a finger. 2 any circular object. 3 an area where boxing matches are fought or where a circus performs. 4 a sound like a bell. RING *v.* 1 to encircle. 2 to make a sound like a bell.

rink *n.* a stretch of ice prepared for ice sports; an area used for roller-skating.

rinse *v.* to wash out; to remove soapy water.

riot *n.* a violent disturbance of the peace by a crowd. RIOT *v.* to join in a riot. RIOTER *n.* RIOTOUS *adj.*

rip *v.* to tear violently; to pull apart. RIP *n.* a tear.

ripe *adj.* mature; fully-developed; ready for eating or harvesting. RIPEN *v.*

ripple *n.* a slow, gentle wave or movement in water.

rise *v.* 1 to stand. 2 to go up; to ascend. 3 to swell; to increase. 4 to rebel. RISE *n.* 1 an upward slope. 2 an increase in pay or price.

risk *n.* a chance of loss, injury or danger. RISK *v.* to take a chance with. RISKY *adj.*

rite *n.* a religious or solemn ceremony.

rival *n.* an opponent; a competitor. RIVAL *v.* to oppose; to compete against. RIVALRY *n.*

river *n.* a large stream of water flowing into another river, a lake or the sea.

rivet *n.* a metal pin for fastening metal plates together. RIVET *v.* to join together with rivets.

roach *n.* a freshwater fish in the carp family.

road *n.* a highway for traffic.

roam *v.* to wander about. ROAMER *n.*

roar *n.* a loud, deep, hoarse sound. ROAR *v.* to make a loud, deep, hoarse sound.

roast *v.* to cook in an oven or over a fire. ROAST *n.* a joint of meat, etc. for roasting.

rob *v.* 1 to steal from. 2 to plunder with violence. ROBBER *n.* ROBBERY *n.*

robe *n.* a long loose garment. ROBE *v.* to dress.

robin *n.* a small bird with a red breast.

robot *n.* a machine designed to work like a person.

robust *adj.* strong and healthy.

rock *n.* 1 a large piece of stone. 2 a hard sweet. 3 a style of music. ROCK *v.* to move backwards and forwards or from side to side.

rocket *n.* 1 a firework or signal which is fired into the air. 2 a spacecraft or missile launcher.

rod *n.* a straight, slender stick or bar.

rodent *n.* an animal that gnaws, such as a rat, squirrel, etc.

roe *n.* 1 the eggs of a fish. 2 a kind of small deer.

rogue *n.* 1 a rascal; a scoundrel. 2 a mischievous person.

role *n.* 1 what a person has undertaken to do. 2 the part played by an actor.

role-play *n.* an activity in which a person plays a part in order to learn or practise something.

roll *v.* 1 to turn over and over. 2 to flatten with a roller. 3 to rock and sway. ROLL *n.* 1 a turning over and over. 2 a bundle made by rolling. 3 a rocking and swaying movement. 4 a register. 5 the rapid beat of a drum. 6 a small loaf.

Roman *adj.* belonging to Rome or its people. ROMAN *n.* a resident of Rome.

romance *n.* 1 an imaginary story with happenings that have little to do with real life. 2 a love affair. ROMANCE *v.* to exaggerate or embroider the truth. ROMANTIC *adj.*

roof *n.* 1 the upper covering of a house or building. 2 the upper part of the mouth. ROOF *v.* to cover with a roof.

rook *n.* a large black bird of the crow family. ROOKERY *n.* a colony of rooks.

room *n.* 1 a part of a house or building enclosed by walls, floor and ceiling. 2 the space anything occupies.

roost *n.* a bird's resting place. ROOST *v.* to settle for sleep.

root *n.* 1 that part of the plant growing in the soil. 2 a base or source from which something grows, e.g. a root word. ROOT *v.* 1 to take root. 2 to fix firmly.

rope *n.* a thick cord made of twisted strands of hemp, nylon, etc. ROPE *v.* to tie with a rope.

rose *n.* a prickly shrub bearing beautiful and usually fragrant flowers.

rosette *n.* a badge, shaped like a rose, made of ribbons.

rot *v.* to decay; to go bad. ROT *n.* 1 decay; badness. nonsense; rubbish.

rota *n.* a list of duties to be taken in turn.

rotate *v.* to revolve; to turn like a wheel.

rotary *adj.* moving round like a wheel. ROTATION *n.*

rotten *adj.* bad; decayed; corrupt.

rough *adj.* 1 uneven; not smooth or level. 2 wild; stormy. 3 harsh; unpleasant. ROUGHNESS *n.*

roughen *v.* to make rough. ROUGHLY *adv.*

round *adj.* shaped like a ball; circular; spherical. ROUND *n.* 1 a circle. 2 a part-song. 3 a visit to one person after another. 4 a bullet or cartridge. 5 a period in a boxing match, a game of golf, etc.

round *v.* 1 to make round. 2 to raise or lower a number to its nearest whole number, ten, hundred, etc.

rouse *v.* to wake up; to stir into action. ROUSING *adj.*

rout *n.* a complete and utter defeat. ROUT *v.* to put to flight.

route *n.* the course to be followed; the way travelled.

routine *n.* 1 a fixed and regular way of doing certain things. 2 a regular procedure or method.

row *n.* 1 a line of persons or things. 2 a trip in a rowing-boat. ROW *v.* to move a boat by using oars.

row *n.* 1 a noise; a noisy quarrel or disturbance.

rowan *n.* the mountain ash tree.

rowdy *adj.* rough and noisy. ROWDYISM *n.*

royal *adj.* 1 having to do with a king or queen. 2 regal; splendid. ROYALTY *n.*

rub *v.* 1 to move one thing over the surface of another. 2 to clean or polish.

rubber *n.* a tough, elastic substance obtained from a tropical tree.

rubbish *n.* 1 refuse; waste matter. 2 nonsense.

rubble *n.* waste fragments of brick, stone, concrete, etc.

rucksack *n.* a bag carried on the back by walkers and climbers.

rudder *n.* the device by which a boat or aircraft is steered.

rude *adj.* 1 impolite; insolent. 2 not decent; vulgar. 3 primitive; roughly made. RUDELY *adv.* RUDENESS *n.*

ruffian *n.* a brutal, violent person.

ruffle *v.* to disturb the smoothness of something; to annoy or irritate. RUFFLE *n.* a frill.

rug *n.* 1 a mat for the floor. 2 a thick blanket.

rugby *n.* a football game played with an oval ball which maybe handled and carried.

rugged *adj.* 1 rough; uneven. 2 robust; sturdy.

ruin *v.* 1 to spoil; to destroy. 2 to make poor. RUIN *n.* 1 the remains of an old or derelict building. 2 destruction; downfall. RUINED *adj.*

rule *n.* 1 a law, regulation or custom. 2 government. 3 a measuring device. RULE *v.* 1 to govern. 2 to make a decision. 3 to draw a straight line using a rule.

ruler *n.* 1 a person who rules or governs. 2 a drawing and measuring instrument.

ruling *n.* a decision; a judgement. RULING *adj.*

rumble *n.* a low rolling sound like thunder. RUMBLING *n.*

rumour *n.* general talk or gossip that may not be true. RUMOUR *v.* to spread a report by rumour.

run *v.* 1 to move on foot with quick steps. 2 to flow. 3 to travel; to go. 4 to manage (a business etc.). RUNNING *adj.* RUN *n.* 1 a race. 2 a journey; a voyage; a route. 3 a score made in cricket.

runes *n. pl.* the letters of the Anglo-Saxon and Viking alphabets. RUNIC *adj.*

rung *n.* the step of a ladder.

runner *n.* a person who runs.

rural *adj.* belonging to the countryside.

ruse *n.* a trick.

rush *v.* 1 to run or move forward violently or speedily. 2 to attack suddenly. RUSH *n.* 1 a violent or sudden forward movement. 2 a marsh plant.

Russian *adj.* belonging to Russia or its people. RUSSIAN *n.* the language or one of the people of Russia.

rust *n.* a yellowish-brown coating formed on iron by the action of moisture; corrosion. RUSTY *adj.*

rut *n.* 1 a groove made in the ground by a wheel; a furrow. 2 a fixed method or routine.

ruthless *adj.* without pity or mercy. RUTHLESSLY *adv.*

rye *n.* a cereal grain used for making flour or used as fodder.

S

sabbath *n.* a weekly day for rest and prayer: Saturday for Jews, Sunday for Christians.

sabotage *n.* damage done intentionally to equipment, machinery, etc. SABOTAGE *v.* to damage intentionally.

sack *n.* 1 a large bag made of coarse material. 2 the attack on and looting of a town. 3 THE SACK dismissal from employment. SACK *v.* 1 to attack and loot a town. 2 to dismiss from employment.

sacred *adj.* holy; belonging to God or dedicated to some person or purpose.

sacrifice *n.* 1 something given up or a loss suffered for the sake of somebody or something else. 2 an offering to a god; the thing offered. SACRIFICE *v.* 1 to give up (something that is valued). 2 to offer something to a god.

sad *adj.* unhappy; full of sorrow. SADLY *adv.* SADDEN *v.* SADNESS *n.*

saddle *n.* a seat for the rider of a horse or bicycle. SADDLE *v.* 1 to put a saddle on. 2 SADDLE WITH to put a burden or load on (someone).

safari *n.* an expedition to see or to hunt big game.

safe *adj.* 1 secure from danger. 2 not dangerous. 3 careful; cautious. SAFE *n.* a steel chest for the storage of valuables. SAFELY *adv.*

safety *n.* security; freedom from danger or risks.

sag *v.* to sink or droop in the middle due to weight or pressure. SAGGING *n.*

saga *n.* a long story with many events; a story told in Viking times.

sail *n.* 1 a canvas or nylon sheet which spreads to catch the wind and moves a boat forward. 2 the arm of a windmill. 3 a short voyage. SAIL *v.* 1 to be moved along by means of sails. 2 to begin a sea voyage. SAILING *n.*

sailor *n.* a seaman; a member of a ship's crew.

saint *n.* 1 a holy person. 2 a person officially given the title of saint after death.

salad *n.* a mixture of vegetables or fruit served raw.

salary *n.* a periodic payment in return for work.

sale *n.* 1 the exchange of goods for money. 2 a time when goods are offered at reduced prices.

saliva *n.* fluid formed in the mouth.

sallow *adj.* pale and sickly in colour.

salmon *n.* a large fish with pink flesh.

saloon *n.* a large reception hall or public room.

salt *n.* sodium chloride, a white crystalline substance used for flavouring and preserving food.

salute *n.* a gesture of respect, courtesy or friendship. SALUTE *v.* to make such a gesture.

salvage *v.* 1 to save (a wrecked or damaged ship). 2 to recover (goods or materials) from fire, flood, shipwreck or destruction. SALVAGED *adj.*

salvation *n.* a rescue from sin or danger.

salvo *n.* a great burst of guns, bombs or clapping.

same *adj.* alike; identical; unchanging.

sample *n.* a specimen; an example; a pattern. SAMPLE *v.* to test.

sanction *n.* 1 the approval or permission of someone. 2 a penalty imposed. SANCTION *v.* to approve or give permission for.

sanctuary *n.* 1 a holy place. 2 a place of refuge.

sand *n.* fine grains of rock. SAND *v.* 1 to sprinkle with sand. 2 to smooth with sandpaper.

sandal *n.* a sole strapped to the foot.

sandpaper *n.* a tough paper with a coating of sand for smoothing wood.

sandwich *n.* two slices of bread with a filling between them. *pl.* SANDWICHES. SANDWICH *v.* to put (something) between or among other things.

sane *adj.* of sound mind; sensible. SANITY *n.*

sanitary *adj.* free from dirt and infection; clean. SANITATION *n.*

sap *n.* the juice circulating in plants. SAP *v.* to drain of sap; to weaken.

sapling *n.* a young tree.

sarcasm *n.* a bitter, scornful and hurtful remark. SARCASTIC *adj.* SARCASTICALLY *adv.*

sardine *n.* a small fish of the herring kind, usually canned in oil.

sash *n.* 1 a strip of material worn over the shoulder or round the waist. 2 a window frame that slides up and down.

satellite *n.* 1 a body (usually a moon) which moved in orbit round a planet. 2 a spacecraft or other man-made object sent travelling in orbit round a planet.

satin *n.* a silky material, shiny on one side.

satisfaction *n.* a feeling of pleasure or contentment.

satisfactory *adj.* good enough; suitable; adequate.

satisfy *v.* 1 to please; to gratify. 2 to be enough for the needs of (someone or something). SATISFIED *adj.* SATISFACTORILY *adv.*

saturate *v.* to soak thoroughly; to fill with moisture. SATURATED *adj.* SATURATION *n.*

Saturday *n.* the seventh day of the week.

sauce *n.* 1 a liquid flavouring for food. 2 impertinence.

saucer *n.* a shallow dish to hold a cup.

sauna *n.* a steam bath.

saunter *v.* to stroll leisurely. SAUNTER *n.* a leisurely stroll.

sausage *n.* minced and seasoned meat enclosed in a skin.

savage *adj.* wild; fierce and cruel. SAVAGE *n.* a person from a primitive tribe. SAVAGELY *adv.*

save *v.* 1 to rescue or preserve from harm or danger. 2 to keep for future use; to reserve. 3 to be economical. SAVE *prep.* except.

savings *n. pl.* money saved up.

saviour *n.* 1 a person who rescues or saves. 2 THE SAVIOUR Jesus Christ.

savour *v.* to appreciate the taste of; to enjoy. SAVOURY *adj.*

saw *n.* a tool with a toothed edge for cutting wood, metal, etc. SAW *v.* to cut with a saw.

Saxon *n.* 1 one of a people from northern Germany who invaded and conquered Britain in the fifth and sixth centuries. 2 the language of this people. SAXON *adj.*

say *v.* to speak; to express; to give an opinion.

saying *n.* a well-known remark or proverb.

scabbard *n.* a sheath for a bayonet, dagger or sword.

scaffold *n.* 1 a framework of metal or wood supporting a platform on which people can work when a building is being built, repaired or painted. 2 a platform erected for carrying out an execution.

scald *v.* 1 to injure with hot liquid or steam. 2 to cook or clean in steam. SCALD *n.* an injury caused by hot liquid or steam. SCALDED *adj.*

scale *n.* 1 a series of graduated marks on a ruler, thermometer, map, etc. 2 a succession of musical notes. 3 a weighing instrument. 4 a thin flake of skin. SCALE *v.* 1 to climb. 2 to flake the scales off.

scalp *n.* the skin and hair on top of the head.

scan 1. to examine carefully. 2 to look quickly through (a text) to find information by looking for key words. 3 in poetry, to have same rhythm as the rest of the poem.

scandal *n.* 1 a shameful or disgraceful action. 2 malicious gossip. SCANDALOUS *adj.*

Scandinavian *adj.* belonging to Scandinavia. SCANDINAVIAN *n.* a native of Scandinavia.

scar *n.* 1 the mark left by a healed wound. 2 a cliff; a crag. SCAR *v.* to mark with a scar.

scarce *adj.* not plentiful; in short supply. SCARCELY *adv.* hardly; not quite. SCARCITY *n.*

scare *v.* to frighten; to strike with terror. SCARE *n.* a state of fear; a fright.

scarf *n.* a length of material worn round the neck or shoulders.

scarlet *n.* a bright red colour. SCARLET *adj.*

scarp *n.* the steep slope of a hill.

scatter *v.* to throw things in different directions; to disperse. SCATTERED *adj.*

scavenge *v.* to collect, or live on, refuse.

scene *n.* 1 the place where an action happens. 2 a view. 3 a part of a play; a stage set for a play. 4 a display of temper.

scenery *n.* 1 a view of the countryside. 2 painted scenes used for a stage play.

scent *v.* 1 to discover by smell. 2 to suspect. SCENT *n.* 1 a smell; a perfume. 2 a trail or track. SCENTED *adj.*

sceptre *n.* a decorated stick carried by a king or queen.

schedule *n.* 1 a programme; a catalogue. 2 a list of details. SCHEDULE *v.* 1 to plan a programme. 2 to make a list of details.

scheme *n.* 1 a plan; a design. 2 a plot. SCHEMING *n.*

scholar *n.* 1 a pupil or student. 2 a learned person. SCHOLARLY *adj.*

school *n.* 1 a place for the education of children. 2 a shoal of fish or whales. SCHOOL *v.* to teach.

schooner *n.* a two-masted sailing ship.

science *n.* the knowledge of natural laws and truths based on observation, experiment, measurement and deduction. SCIENTIST *n.*

scientific *adj.* according to rules laid down by science. SCIENTIFICALLY *adv.*

scissors *n.* a cutting instrument with two blades.

scold *v.* to find fault with or blame noisily.

scone *n.* a small flat cake.

scoop *n.* 1 a bowl-shaped shovel or spoon. 2 special news printed by one newspaper before another. SCOOP *v.* 1 to move something with a scoop. 2 to obtain news before rivals do.

scope *n.* 1 the opportunity to do something. 2 range of plans and aims.

scorch *v.* to burn, dry up or singe a surface. SCORCHED *adj.* SCORCHING *adj.*

score *n.* 1 a scratch or cut. 2 points made in a game. 3 a copy of music showing vocal and instrumental parts. 4 twenty. SCORE *v.* 1 to scratch or cut. 2 to gain points in a game. 3 to arrange the parts in a piece of music.

scorn *n.* contempt. SCORN *v.* to show contempt for.

Scot *n.* a native of Scotland.

Scottish, Scotch, Scots *adj.* belonging to Scotland or its people.

scoundrel *n.* a rogue; an unscrupulous person.

scour *v.* to clean and polish by rubbing. SCOURING *n.* cleaning; polishing.

scout *n.* 1 a person sent out to spy or to obtain information. 2 a member of the Scout movement. SCOUT *v.* 1 to spy. 2 to explore.

scowl *v.* to frown; to look sullen. SCOWL *n.* a frown; a sullen look. SCOWLING *adj.*

scramble *v.* 1 to climb or crawl awkwardly. 2 to mix or jumble (something). SCRAMBLE *n.* 1 a rough climb. 2 a race over rough country.

scrap *n.* 1 a small piece; a fragment. 2 waste material. SCRAP *v.* to discard or throw away.

scrape *v.* 1 to rub with something hard or sharp. 2 to injure or damage by scraping. 3 to manage with difficulty. SCRAPE *n.* 1 the act or sound of scraping. 2 damage caused by scraping. 3 an awkward or dangerous situation.

scratch *v.* 1 to mark (a surface) with something sharp. 2 to rub with the nails to relieve itching. 3 to withdraw from a race or competition. SCRATCH *n.* a mark or injury caused by scratching. SCRATCH *adj.* hurriedly gathered together.

scrawl *v.* to write hurriedly or hastily; to scribble. SCRAWL *n.* hurried, untidy writing.

scream *v.* to utter a loud, sharp cry of pain or terror. SCREAM *n.* a loud cry or shriek.

scree *n.* an area of small, loose stones covering a mountain side.

screech *v.* to utter a harsh, shrill cry or sound. SCREECH *n.* a harsh, shrill cry or sound.

screen *n*. 1 a partition used to give protection from draughts, heat, light or view. 2 anything that conceals or gives protection or shelter. 3 a white or silver surface onto which slides or films may be projected. SCREEN *v*. 1 to protect, shelter or conceal from view. 2 to sieve. 3 to examine or pass through a test.

screw *n*. 1 a kind of nail with a spiral thread used for gripping wood or metal. 2 the propeller of a ship. SCREW *v*. 1 to fasten with a screw. 2 to twist.

scribble *v*. to write hurriedly and untidily; to scrawl. SCRIBBLE *n*. a piece of careless and untidy writing.

scribe *n*. 1 a writer of manuscripts. 2 a teacher of Jewish law.

script *n*. 1 handwriting. 2 the text of a film, play, radio or television programme.

Scriptures *n. pl*. the Bible; sacred writings.

scroll *n*. a roll of parchment or paper.

scrounge *v*. to obtain (money, goods, etc.) by begging, theft or without payment.

scrub *v*. to rub hard or clean with a stiff brush. SCRUB *n*. 1 a good cleaning. 2 bushes or stunted trees.

scruple *n*. a feeling of doubt or hesitation about whether it is right to do something. SCRUPLE *v*. to doubt or hesitate (whether to do something).

scrutiny *n*. a close inspection or thorough examination of something.

sculptor *n*. a person who carves or models in wood, stone, metal, etc. *fem*. SCULPTRESS. SCULPT *v*.

sculpture *n*. the art of carving in wood, stone or metal; something so carved. SCULPTURED *adj*.

scuttle *v*. 1 to hurry away. 2 to sink a ship intentionally.

scythe *n*. an implement with a long handle and a long curved blade for cutting grass by hand.

sea *n*. 1 the expanse of salt water that covers most of the Earth's surface. 2 an area of salt water. 3 a large area or quantity of something.

seal *n*. 1 a furry sea animal. 2 a design stamped on wax, lead, etc., and used for sealing a document, a packet, etc. SEAL *v*. 1 to attach a seal. 2 to close and fasten something firmly. 3 to make a thing airtight.

seam *n*. 1 the line formed where two pieces of material are sewn or joined together. 2 a layer of coal, metal ore, etc. SEAM *v*. to join by a seam.

seaman *n*. a sailor; a mariner.

seamanship *n*. skill in sailing and navigating a ship or boat.

search (for) *v*. 1 to look carefully for (something or someone). 2 to seek. SEARCH *n*. 1 an attempt to find. 2 an investigation. SEARCHER *n*. SEARCHING *adj*.

seaside *n*. a town or place beside the sea. SEASIDE *adj*.

season *n*. 1 one of the four divisions of the year, spring, summer, autumn, winter. 2 a proper, suitable or favourable time for a particular activity. SEASON *v*. 1 to bring into mature condition. 2 to flavour. SEASONING *n*.

seasonal *adj*. depending upon or changing with the seasons. SEASONABLE *adj*.

seat *n*. 1 something for sitting on. 2 the place where something is situated. SEAT *v*. to provide seats for.

seaworthy *adj*. in a suitable condition to sail on the sea.

seclude *v*. to keep apart from others; to isolate. SECLUDED *adj*.

second *n*. 1 the next after the first in order, time, position, etc. 2 a helper for a fighter in a boxing match or duel. 3 a sixtieth part of a minute or of a degree. SECOND *v*. to aid; to support.

secondary *adj*. coming second; of less importance. SECONDARY SOURCE *n*. in research, a text, picture or artefact that is not original, a copy or imitation (see PRIMARY SOURCE).

secret *adj*. 1 kept hidden; not generally known. 2 secluded; quiet. SECRET *n*. something hidden; something not to be generally known. SECRETLY *adv*. SECRECY *n*.

secretary *n*. a person who deals with correspondence, records and arrangements for an individual, firm, organisation or society, etc. SECRETARIAL *adj*.

secrete *v*. 1 to hide; to conceal. 2 to produce a juice or liquid.

secretive *adj*. in the habit of keeping things secret.

section *n*. a part or division of something. SECTIONAL *adj*.

sector *n*. 1 a part of a circle between two radii. 2 a particular area of activity.

secure *adj*. 1 safe; free from danger. 2 firmly fastened or established. SECURE *v*. 1 to succeed in getting. 2 to fasten firmly. SECURELY *adj*.

security *n*. 1 freedom from anxiety or danger. 2 a guarantee or assurance.

sediment *n*. solid matter that settles at the bottom of a liquid.

see *v*. 1 to perceive; to use the eyes to recognise. 2 to understand. 3 to examine; to look at. 4 to consult.

seed *n*. the grain or nut from which a new plant grows.

seek *v*. to look for; to try to find.

seem *v*. to appear to be; to look as if. SEEMING *adj*.

seep *v*. to trickle; to ooze.

seethe *v*. 1 to boil; to bubble. 2 to be agitated; to be annoyed. SEETHING *adj*.

segment *n*. (pron. SEG-ment) a part cut off; a distinct part. SEGMENT *v*. (pron. seg-MENT) to cut or divide into segments; to break up a word into its sounds in order to read or spell it, e.g. c-a-t. SEGMENTED *adj*.

seize *v*. 1 to grasp or grip suddenly. 2 to take by force. SEIZURE *n*.

seldom *adv*. rarely; not often.

select *v*. to pick; to choose carefully. SELECT *adj*. carefully chosen; choice. SELECTED *adj*. SELECTIVE *adj*.

selection *n*. a choice; whatever is selected.

self *n*. a person's own nature or character.

selfish *adj*. lacking in consideration for others; disregarding others. SELFISHLY *adv*. SELFISHNESS *n*.

sell *v*. to exchange (goods or property) for money.

semaphore *n*. a code of signalling by using movements of the arms.

semi- prefix meaning "half" or "to some extent".

semi-colon *n*. a punctuation mark (;) used to separate clauses in a sentence.

send *v*. to cause (something or somebody) to go or move somewhere.

senile *adj*. sick and feeble due to old age; having to do with old age.

senior *adj*. 1 older. 2 higher in rank or authority. SENIOR *n*. an older person; a person senior in rank or authority. SENIORITY *n*.

sensation *n*. 1 a feeling. 2 an event causing great excitement. SENSATIONAL *adj*.

sense *n*. 1 the ability to hear, see, smell, taste and feel. 2 a feeling; an appreciation. 3 the meaning. SENSE *v*. to be aware of; to feel.

sensible *adj*. 1 having or showing good sense. 2 practical; useful. SENSIBLY *adv*.

sensitive *adj*. 1 having feelings and emotions that are easily affected. 2 easily upset.

sentence *n*. 1 a number of words which together form a complete statement. 2 the penalty imposed on a guilty person. SENTENCE *v*. to pronounce sentence on.

sentinel *n*. a sentry; a soldier on guard.

sentry *n*. a guard.

separate *v*. to divide; to make or become separate. SEPARATE *adj*. SEPARATELY *adv*.

separation *n*. a parting or division.

September *n*. the ninth month of the year.

sequel *n*. 1 something that follows as the result of something else; a result. 2 a book or film that continues the story of an earlier one.

sequence *n*. the arrangement in which things follow one another.

serene *adj*. calm; clear and peaceful. SERENITY *n*.

sergeant *n*. a non-commissioned officer in the army and the air force; a police officer below the rank of inspector.

serial *adj*. forming a series; in successive parts or instalments.

series *n*. a number of things arranged in order; a sequence.

serious *adj*. 1 thoughtful; earnest; responsible. 2 grave; dangerous. SERIOUSLY *adv*.

serpent *n*. a snake.

serration *n*. a notch or a tooth on a saw-like edge. SERRATED *adj*.

servant *n*. 1 a person who serves. 2 a person who carries out the orders of a particular person or organisation.

serve *v.* 1 to work for. 2 to place food on the table for a meal. 3 to attend to customers in a shop. 4 to hit the ball into play at tennis.

service *n.* 1 working for others; acting as a servant. 2 an organisation supplying some special need. 3 a form of worship. 4 a set of cups, saucers, etc.

serviceable *adj.* strong; useful and hard-wearing.

session *n.* 1 the time spent at a particular activity. 2 a sitting of a meeting or conference.

set *v.* 1 to put; to place; to arrange. 2 to become solid. 3 to sink below the horizon. SET *n.* 1 a group of people with the same interests. 2 a group of things of the same kind. 3 a radio or television receiver. SET *adj.* fixed; regular.

settle *v.* 1 to come to rest. 2 to sink to the bottom. 3 to agree upon. 4 to decide. 5 to make a home in one place. SETTLED *adj.* SETTLEMENT *n.* a town, village or city; a place where people have made their homes. SETTLE *n.* a wooden seat with a high back.

settler *n.* a person who makes a home in a new country.

seven *n.* the number one more than six, the symbol 7.

sever *v.* to cut through; to separate.

several *adj.* 1 a few more than one or two; not very many. 2 separate; various.

severe *adj.* 1 strict; harsh. 2 serious; violent. 3 plain. SEVERELY *adv.* SEVERITY *n.*

sew *v.* to fasten together using a needle and thread; to stitch. SEWING *n.*

sewage *n.* water and waste matter carried away by a sewer.

sewer *n.* an underground drain for sewage. SEWERAGE *n.*

sextant *n.* an instrument for measuring the angle between two distant objects used in navigation and surveying.

shabby *adj.* 1 worn; threadbare. 2 mean; unfair. SHABBILY *adv.*

shackle *n.* a metal loop or staple; a link or chain. SHACKLE *v.* to fasten with a shackle.

shade *v.* 1 to shield from strong light. 2 to change colour gradually. SHADE *n.* 1 an area shaded from bright light; something that shuts out bright light. 2 a slight difference of colour.

shadow *n.* 1 an area of shade. 2 the shape of something obstructing the light. SHADOW *v.* 1 to darken. 2 to watch; to follow. SHADOWY *adj.*

shaft *n.* 1 a pole; a long handle. 2 the vertical opening to a mine; the space containing a lift. 3 a pillar or column. 4 a ray of light. 5 an arrow.

shake *v.* 1 to move something quickly to and fro or up and down. 2 to tremble; to shiver. 3 to wave; to brandish. SHAKE *n.* a shudder, shock or jolt.

shale *n.* a rock formed from clay, which splits easily into thin layers or flakes.

shallow *adj.* 1 not deep. 2 superficial; trivial. SHALLOWNESS *n.*

sham *v.* to pretend to be. SHAM *n.* a pretence; a counterfeit. SHAM *adj.* false; imitation.

shamble *v.* to walk clumsily; to shuffle. SHAMBLE *n.* a clumsy; shuffling walk. SHAMBLES *n. pl.* 1 a slaughter-house. 2 a place of bloodshed and slaughter. 3 a muddle.

shame *n.* a feeling of disgrace or guilt. SHAME *v.* to disgrace.

shampoo *v.* to lather and wash the hair thoroughly. SHAMPOO *n.* a lotion for washing the hair.

shamrock *n.* a small three-leaved plant, resembling clover; the national emblem of Ireland.

shank *n.* 1 the part of the leg from knee to ankle. 2 the shaft or handle on some tools or instruments.

shape *n.* the form or outline of anything. SHAPE *v.* to make (something) into a particular shape.

share *n.* 1 one of the portions of something which is divided among several people or things. 2 the blade of a plough. SHARE *v.* 1 to divide among. 2 to use something jointly.

shareholder *n.* a person who holds shares in a business or company.

shark *n.* a large, ferocious sea-fish.

sharp *adj.* 1 having a thin cutting edge or fine point. 2 quick at understanding. 3 painful; intense. 4 a semi-tone above the natural note in music. SHARP *n.* the mark (#) in music showing that a note is to be raised by a semi-tone. SHARPLY *adv.*

sharpen *v.* to make sharper.

shatter *v.* to break suddenly and violently into pieces. SHATTERING *adj.*

shave *v.* 1 to remove hair with a razor. 2 to scrape or graze lightly. SHAVE *n.* 1 shaving; being shaved. 2 a narrow miss or escape.

shaving *n.* 1 the act of shaving. 2 a thin slice or flake.

shear *v.* 1 to cut with shears or a blade. 2 to clip the wool off a sheep. SHEARING *n.*

shears *n. pl.* a cutting tool with two movable blades.

sheath *n.* 1 a close-fitting cover. 2 a case, or scabbard, for a sword or dagger.

sheathe *v.* to place in a sheath.

shed *v.* 1 to throw off. 2 to let something fall or flow. SHED *n.* a hut or small building.

sheep *n.* an animal raised for its wool and flesh (mutton). *pl.* SHEEP.

sheer *adj.* 1 complete; thorough. 2 very steep. 3 very thin and transparent. SHEER *v.* to turn aside; to go away.

sheet *n.* 1 a flat, thin piece of any material such as paper, glass, metal, ice, etc. 2 a flat area of anything. 3 a piece of linen, cotton or nylon used as a bed cover and to sleep under.

shelf *n.* 1 a board or ledge on a wall or in a cupboard for placing things on. 2 a ridge of rock in the sea; a reef. *pl.* SHELVES.

shell *n.* 1 a hard outer covering or case; a pod or husk. 2 a metal case filled with explosive. 3 the outer walls of an unfinished or damaged building. SHELL *v.* 1 to remove the shell from. 2 to fire shells at.

shellfish *n.* a sea creature with a hard outer shell. (e.g. oyster, whelk).

shelter *n.* 1 a shield or protection against cold, wind, hardship, etc. 2 a building or shield that gives protection. SHELTER *v.* to protect or shield.

shelve *v.* 1 to place on a shelf. 2 to set aside or postpone. 3 to slope.

shepherd *n.* a person who looks after sheep. SHEPHERD *v.* to tend and look after; to direct and guide.

sheriff *n.* the chief law-officer of a county.

shield *v.* to protect; to shelter. SHIELD *n.* 1 a piece of armour carried to protect the body. 2 a protection or safeguard.

shift *v.* to alter position; to move. SHIFT *n.* 1 a change or alteration. 2 a relay or change of workers.

shimmer *v.* to shine with a quivering light; to gleam.

shin *n.* the front of the leg between the knee and the ankle. SHIN *v.* to climb.

shine *v.* 1 to give out or reflect light. 2 to polish. 3 to be bright and lively. SHINE *n.* brightness; gloss; polish. SHINING *adj.*

shingle *n.* 1 pebbles and gravel. 2 a flat piece of wood used as a roof tile.

ship *n.* a large boat or sea-going vessel. SHIP *v.* to send by ship. SHIPPING *n.*

shipwreck *n.* the sinking or destruction of a ship.

shirk *v.* to avoid duty, responsibility or work.

shirt *n.* a thin garment worn on the upper part of the body.

shiver *v.* to shake or tremble from cold or fear. SHIVER *n.* 1 a tremor. 2 a shudder caused by cold or fear. SHIVERING *n.*

shoal *n.* 1 a large group of fish swimming together. 2 a shallow place over a sandbank in the sea.

shock *n.* 1 a fright or unpleasant surprise. 2 a violent knock or collision. SHOCK *v.* 1 to cause fright or surprise. 2 to fill with disgust or horror. SHOCKING *adj.* SHOCKINGLY *adv.*

shoe *n.* 1 an outer covering worn on the foot. 2 a metal rim nailed to a horse's hoof. SHOE *v.* to fit a horse with shoes.

shoot *v.* 1 to fire a bullet, shell or missile. 2 to wound or kill by shooting. 3 to move very quickly. 4 to aim the ball at the goal in football, etc. 5 to sprout or grow. SHOOT *n.* 1 a sprout or bud. 2 a shooting match.

shop *n.* a place where goods are sold. SHOP *v.* to buy in shops. SHOPPING *n.*

shore *n.* 1 the coast; the beach. 2 a prop or support. SHORE (UP) *v.* to prop or to support.

short *adj.* 1 less than normal length or height. 2 not lasting very long. 3 brief; concise. 4 insufficient. 5 curt; abrupt.

shortage *n.* a lack of; an insufficiency.

shorten *v.* to make or become shorter.

shortly *adv.* soon; briefly.

shot *n.* 1 the sound made by a gun. 2 lead pellets. 3 a marksman.

shoulder *n*. the part of the body between the neck and the upper arm. SHOULDER *v*. 1 to push with the shoulder. 2 to accept responsibility.

shout *v*. to call loudly. SHOUT *n*. a loud call. SHOUTING *n*.

shove *v*. to push roughly; to thrust. SHOVE *n*. a push or thrust.

shovel *n*. a broad spade used for lifting coal and other loose materials. SHOVEL *v*. to use a shovel.

show *v*. 1 to cause or allow (something) to be seen. 2 to appear; to be visible. 3 to make something clear. SHOW *n*. 1 a display; an entertainment; an exhibition. 2 a pretence.

shower *n*. a brief fall of hail, rain, snow, bullets, stones, arrows, etc. SHOWER *n*. 1 to send or come down in a shower. 2 to give liberally.

shred *v*. to cut or tear into small pieces. SHRED *n*. a thin piece or strip.

shrew *n*. 1 a small animal like a mouse. 2 a quarrelsome, bad-tempered woman.

shrewd *adj*. 1 wise; clever. 2 cutting; astute. SHREWDLY *adv*.

shriek *v*. to scream; to screech. SHRIEK *n*. a scream; a screech.

shrill *adj*. having a piercing and high-pitched sound. SHRILLY *adv*.

shrink *v*. 1 to become or make smaller. 2 to move away quickly; to recoil.

shrivel *v*. to make or become dry and wrinkled.

shroud *v*. to cover; to hide. SHROUD *n*. the cover in which a dead body is wrapped.

shrub *n*. a small bush. SHRUBBERY *n*.

shrug *v*. to lift the shoulders slightly. SHRUG *n*. a slight lift of the shoulders.

shudder *v*. to tremble; to shiver. SHUDDER *n*. a tremble; a shiver.

shuffle *v*. 1 to move about dragging and scraping the feet. 2 to mix up.

shun *v*. to avoid; to keep away from.

shut *v*. to close (a door, window, lid, etc.).

shuttle *n*. 1 a device which carries the weft thread through the warp on a weaving loom. 2 a train or bus service between two places. 3 a reusable space vehicle. SHUTTLE *v*.

shy *adj*. reserved; timid in company; bashful. SHY *v*. 1 to throw; to hurl. 2 SHY AWAY FROM to take fright at something. SHYLY *adv*. SHYNESS *n*.

sibling *n*. 1 a brother or sister. 2 a near relative.

sick *adj*. 1 ill; unwell. 2 wanting to vomit. 3 tired of; disgusted. SICKEN *v*. SICKENING *adj*.

sickle *n*. a tool with a short handle and a long curved blade for cutting grass by hand.

sickness *n*. 1 an illness; a disease. 2 vomiting.

side *n*. 1 one of the flat surfaces of an object. 2 the part between the front and back of an object. 3 the part of the body between the hip and shoulder. 4 a team of players. SIDE EFFECT *n*. an unwanted effect caused e.g. by a drug.

siding *n*. a short length of track leading off a main railway line.

siege *n*. the surrounding of a town by troops in an attempt to make it surrender.

sieve *n*. a mesh used to separate the coarse parts of a liquid or solid. SIEVE *v*. to sift through a sieve.

sift *v*. 1 to pass through a sieve. 2 to examine closely.

sigh *v*. to draw a deep breath showing sadness, weariness, relief, etc. SIGH *n*. the act or sound of sighing. SIGHING *n*.

sight *n*. 1 the ability to see. 2 seeing or being seen. 3 something interesting or unusual to see. 4 the aiming device on a gun. SIGHT *v*. 1 to see, to observe. 2 to aim a gun.

sign *n*. 1 a mark or object used to convey a meaning. 2 a gesture. 3 an indication or warning. 4 a board with a name or instruction on it. SIGN *v*. 1 to make a sign. 2 to write a signature.

signal *n*. 1 a message sent by means of signs. 2 a set of lights or signs giving instructions. 3 a gesture; an indication. SIGNAL *v*. to send a message by signs.

signature *n*. a person's name written by himself or herself.

significant *adj*. having meaning; important. SIGNIFICANCE *n*. SIGNIFICANTLY *adv*.

signify *v*. to mean; to denote.

Sikh *n*. a member of a religious sect founded in Northern India in the sixteenth century.

silage *n*. a green crop preserved in a silo.

silence *n*. 1 being silent. 2 quietness; absence of sound. SILENCE *v*. to quieten; to make soundless.

silent *adj*. making no sound. SILENTLY *adv*.

silhouette *n.* a shadow shape, usually black on a white background.

silica *n.* a mineral substance in sand and quartz.

silk *n.* 1 a strong, fine thread spun by silkworms. 2 a fabric woven from silk thread.

sill *n.* a piece of wood or stone at the bottom of a door or window.

silly *adj.* foolish; stupid. SILLINESS *n.*

silo *n.* a tower for storing grain or crops for use as fodder.

silt *n.* a sediment of fine soil or sand deposited by water. SILT (UP) *v.* to block or fill with silt.

silver *n.* 1 a soft, white precious metal. 2 articles and coins made from silver. SILVER *adj.* made of silver or silver in colour.

similar *adj.* like; of the same sort. SIMILARLY *adv.*

similarity *n.* a likeness; a resemblance.

simile *n.* a way of describing something by comparing it to something else, e.g. <u>as</u> white <u>as</u> snow; a voice <u>like</u> thunder; a comparison.

simmer *v.* to boil gently. 2 to be in a state of suppressed anger or indignation.

simple *adj.* 1 plain; easy; not complicated. 2 easily deceived. SIMPLICITY *n.*

simplify *v.* to make easy and simple. SIMPLIFICATION *n.*

simply *adv.* 1 in simple manner. 2 merely.

simulate *v.* to pretend; to imitate.

simultaneous *adj.* happening at the same time. SIMULTANEOUSLY *adv.*

since *adv.* from then until now. SINCE *conj.* as; because; from when. SINCE *prep.* after.

sincere *adj.* genuine; true; honest. SINCERELY *adv.* SINCERITY *n.*

sing *v.* to make musical sounds with the voice. SINGING *n.*

singe *v.* to scorch or burn on the surface. SINGE *n.* a slight scorch or burn. SINGED *adj.*

singer *n.* a person who sings.

single *adj.* 1 one only. 2 unmarried. 3 for the use of one person only. SINGLE *n.* a one-way travel ticket. SINGLE (OUT) *v.* to pick one at a time. SINGLY *adv.*

singular *adj.* 1 one only. 2 odd; unusual; exceptional.

sinister *adj.* evil; threatening.

sink *v.* 1 to go under water; to submerge. 2 to move slowly downwards. 3 to bore; to dig. 4 to lose strength. SINK *n.* a basin with a drain to take away water. SINKING *n.*

sip *v.* to drink in small quantities; to taste. SIP *n.* a small drink; a taste.

siphon, syphon *n.* a bent tube for drawing off liquid from a container. SIPHON *v.* to transfer liquid using a siphon.

sir *n.* 1 a title of respect given to a man. 2 the title of a knight or baronet.

siren *n.* 1 a device which makes a hooting or wailing sound; a warning whistle. 2 a mythical creature, half woman, half bird, whose song lured sailors to destruction.

sister *n.* 1 one of the daughters of the same parent. 2 a senior hospital nurse. 3 a nun.

sit *v.* 1 to be seated (upon). 2 to cause to sit. 3 to hold a meeting. SITTING *n.*

site *n.* 1 a place chosen for some purpose. 2 the place where a town or building is or has been.

situated *adj.* in a particular place. SITUATE *v.*

situation *n.* 1 a site; a position. 2 a position in employment; a job. 3 circumstances.

six *n.* the number one more than five, the symbol 6.

size *n.* 1 the largeness or smallness of something. 2 a particular measurement. 3 a weak glue.

skate *n.* 1 a steel blade fixed to a boot for gliding on ice. 2 a roller skate. 3 a kind of flat-fish. SKATE *v.* to move on skates. SKATER *n.*

skeleton *n.* 1 the bony framework of a body. 2 a framework or outline.

sketch *n.* 1 a quickly-made drawing. 2 a short, comic play. SKETCH *v.* to make a sketch.

ski *n.* a long, narrow strip of wood fastened to the foot for travelling over snow. SKI *v.* to travel on skis. SKIER *n.* SKIING *n.*

skid *v.* to slip or slide accidentally. SKID *n.* 1 a side-slip. 2 a piece of wood acting as a brake on a wheel.

skill *n.* the ability to do something well, expertly or efficiently. SKILFUL *adj.*

skim *v.* 1 to remove something from the surface of a liquid. 2 to move quickly and lightly over a surface. 3 to read (a text) quickly to get an idea of what it is about.

skin *n*. 1 the outer layer of the body of a person or animal. 2 the outer covering or layer. SKIN *v*. to remove the skin from; to peel.

skip *v*. 1 to leap; to frisk. 2 to jump repeatedly over a turning rope. 3 to miss out pieces when reading.

skipper *n*. the captain of a ship, aircraft or team. SKIPPER *v*. to command or captain.

skirmish *n*. a fight between small groups of people. SKIRMISH *v*. to take part in a skirmish.

skirt *n*. part of a woman's outer garment that hangs from the waist. SKIRT *v*. to move along the edge of.

skittles *n. pl.* a game in which wooden pins are bowled at; ninepins.

skull *n*. the bony framework of the head.

sky *n*. the cloud region surrounding the Earth. *pl*. SKIES.

slab *n*. a thick, flat piece of wood, stone, etc.

slack *adj*. 1 not firmly held; loose. 2 slow; lazy. SLACKEN *v*. SLACKNESS *n*.

slag *n*. the waste material from a smelting furnace, mine, etc.

slam *v*. to shut, or put down, violently. SLAM *n*. the sound of slamming.

slander *n*. words spoken to harm a person's character. SLANDER *v*. to utter a false statement intended to harm someone. SLANDEROUS *adj*.

slang *n*. words and phrases in common use but not regarded as standard English.

slant *n*. a slope; a tilt. SLANT *v*. to slope; to lean. SLANTING *adj*.

slap *v*. to smack with an open hand. SLAP *n*. a smack.

slash *v*. 1 to make long cuts in; to slit. 2 to reduce drastically. SLASH *n*. a long cut.

slate *n*. a rock that splits easily into thin sheets and is used for roofing. SLATE *adj*. made of slate; coloured like slate. SLATE *v*. to cover with slates.

slaughter *v*. 1 to kill animals for food. 2 to kill or massacre many people or animals. SLAUGHTER *n*. the killing of many animals or people.

Slav *n*. a member of an East European race speaking a Slavonic language – a Russian, a Pole, a Czech, etc. SLAVONIC *adj*.

slave *n*. a person who is the property of another and is bound to obey and serve him or her. SLAVE *v*. to work like a slave. SLAVERY *n*.

sledge *n*. 1 a vehicle with runners for sliding on snow or grass; a toboggan. 2 a heavy hammer with a long handle. SLEDGE *v*. to travel on a sledge.

sleek *adj*. soft, smooth and glossy.

sleep *v*. to rest in a natural state of unconsciousness; to slumber. SLEEP *n*. a natural state of unconsciousness; slumber; repose.

sleeper *n*. 1 a sleeping person. 2 a wooden or concrete beam supporting railway lines. 3 a berth in a railway sleeping carriage.

sleet *n*. a mixture of rain and hail or snow.

sleeve *n*. 1 the part of a garment covering the arm. 2 the outer cover for a record, etc.

sleigh *n*. a horse-drawn sledge.

slender *adj*. 1 narrow; thin. 2 slim; slight. SLENDERNESS *n*. SLENDERLY *adv*.

slice *n*. a thin piece cut off something. SLICE *v*. to cut in slices.

slide *v*. to glide or move smoothly over a surface, esp. over snow or ice. SLIDE *n*. 1 a smooth surface used for sliding. 2 a frame holding a photograph for use in a projector. 3 a clip to hold hair in place.

slight *adj*. 1 small; not important. 2 slender; slim. SLIGHT *n*. an insult; a snub. SLIGHT *v*. to insult; to ignore.

slim *adj*. thin; slender. SLIM *v*. to reduce weight by diet or exercise.

slime *n*. soft, sticky mud; sludge.

sling *n*. 1 a strap or device for hurling stones. 2 a support for an injured arm. 3 a rope or chain for lifting heavy objects. SLING *v*. 1 to throw something. 2 to lift with a sling.

slink *v*. to move stealthily, to prowl.

slip *v*. 1 to slide accidentally, to fall. 2 to make a mistake. 3 to move quietly or stealthily; to escape. SLIP *n*. 1 a slide or fall. 2 a mistake. 3 a piece of paper.

slipper *n*. a light shoe to wear indoors.

slit *n*. a long tear, cut or opening. SLIT *v*. to cut open; to make a slit.

slogan *n*. a short, catchy phrase.

sloop *n*. a one-masted sailing-ship.

slope *n.* an incline; a slant. SLOPING *adj.*

slot *n.* a narrow opening; a slit or groove. SLOT (INTO) *v.* to put in place.

slouch *n.* an ungainly, stooping manner in standing or walking. SLOUCH *v.* to move in an ungainly, stooping manner. SLOUCHING *n.* & *adj.*

slow *adj.* 1 taking a long time. 2 behind time; late. 3 not quick to learn. SLOWLY *adv.* SLOWNESS *n.*

sluice *n.* a gate or sliding door for controlling the volume or flow of water. SLUICE *v.* to flood or clean with water.

slum *n.* an area of a town where the houses are in a poor condition, overcrowded and unhealthy.

slump *v.* 1 to collapse. 2 to decrease suddenly. SLUMP *n.* 1 a collapse. 2 a sudden or continuous fall in price, value, demand, etc.

slur *v.* 1 to speak indistinctly by running one's words together. 2 PUT A SLUR UPON to discredit (someone). 3 SLUR OVER to pass over lightly. SLUR *n.* 1 the act of speaking indistinctly. 2 a discredit. 3 in music, a curved line under or over notes to be slurred. SLURRED *adj.*

slush *n.* mud; thawing snow. SLUSHY *adj.*

sly *adj.* cunning; underhand. SLYLY *adv.*

smack *n.* 1 a sharp slap; a blow; the sound of a blow. 2 a slight flavour. 3 a small fishing boat. SMACK *v.* to slap; to make a sound like a blow.

small *adj.* 1 little; not large. 2 not important.

smart *v.* to feel or cause a sharp pain; to sting. SMART *adj.* 1 quick; sharp. 2 well-dressed; neat. SMARTEN *v.* SMARTNESS *n.*

smash *v.* 1 to break into pieces; to shatter. 2 SMASH INTO to collide (with). SMASH *n.* a breakage; a collision.

smear *v.* 1 to spread with something sticky. 2 to slander. SMEAR *n.* 1 a greasy mark; a daub. 2 a slander.

smell *n.* 1 the sense of smell. 2 an odour; a fragrance. SMELL *v.* 1 to be aware of an odour. 2 to give off an odour or scent. SMELLY *adj.*

smelt *v.* to melt a metal ore in a furnace. SMELTING *n.*

smile *v.* to express joy, pleasure, amusement, etc., by parting or drawing up the lips. SMILE *n.* the act of smiling. SMILING *adj.*

smock *n.* a loose garment worn over other clothes.

smog *n.* a dense, smoky fog.

smoke *n.* the mixture of gas and carbon that rises from a fire. SMOKE *v.* 1 to give off smoke. 2 to inhale tobacco smoke. SMOKER *n.*

smooth *adj.* 1 having an even surface. 2 having no difficulties in the way. 3 without lumps. 4 pleasing; persuasive. SMOOTHLY *adv.* SMOOTH *v.* to make smooth.

smother *v.* 1 to suffocate. 2 to cover thickly.

smoulder *v.* to burn slowly without flame.

smuggle *v.* to take goods or persons illegally from one country to another. SMUGGLER *n.*

snack *n.* a quick, small meal.

snag *n.* 1 a jagged object. 2 a difficulty. SNAG *v.* to damage by catching on something sharp.

snail *n.* a small, soft-bodied, crawling, invertebrate animal with a shell; a mollusc.

snake *n.* a long, legless, creeping reptile.

snap *v.* 1 to make a quick, sudden bite. 2 to break or crack. 3 to speak sharply. SNAP *n.* 1 the act or sound of snapping; 2 a bite.

snare *n.* 1 a trap for catching animals; a noose of wire. 2 a temptation.

snarl *v.* 1 to growl and show the teeth. 2 to tangle up. SNARL *n.* a tangle. SNARLING *adj.*

snatch *v.* to grab something quickly. SNATCH *n.* a quick grab.

sneak *v.* 1 to move quietly and furtively. 2 to act as an informer. SNEAK *n.* 1 a petty thief. 2 an underhand person; an informer.

sneer *v.* to show contempt and scorn. SNEER *n.* an expression of contempt and scorn.

sneeze *n.* an uncontrollable burst of air from the mouth and nose. SNEEZE *v.* to have an uncontrollable burst of air from the mouth and nose.

sniff *v.* to draw air in noisily through the nose; to smell. SNIFF *n.* the act or sound of sniffing.

snore *v.* to breathe noisily during sleep. SNORE *n.*

snow *n.* white flakes of frozen water vapour. SNOW *v.* to fall as snow.

snub *v.* to treat with contempt. SNUB *n.* an action showing contempt.

snug *adj.* warm and comfortable; cosy; sheltered. SNUGLY *adv.*

so *adv.* 1 in this or that manner. 2 to such an extent. 3 very. SO *conj.* therefore; for that reason.

soak *v.* to drench; to wet through. SOAKING *n.*

soap *n.* a washing and cleansing material made from fats and oils. SOAP *v.* to wash or rub with soap.

soar *v.* to rise in the air; to float in the sky.

sob *v.* to cry and gulp noisily. SOB *n.* the sound of crying. SOBBING *n.*

sober *adj.* 1 not drunk. 2 calm; serious.

soccer *n.* Association football.

sociable *adj.* friendly; enjoying the company of other people. SOCIABLY *adj.* SOCIABILITY *n.*

social *adj.* 1 living in, or concerning, groups or societies. 2 in society. 3 friendly. SOCIAL *n.* a gathering or party.

society *n.* 1 the system of living together in groups; a community. 2 a group of people with the same interests.

sock *n.* a short stocking.

socket *n.* a hollow into which something fits; a holder for an electrical plug or bulb.

soda *n.* a mineral substance used in baking, washing, and the manufacture of glass.

soft *adj.* 1 easily pressed into another shape. 2 not hard; yielding. 3 gentle; tender. SOFTEN *v.* SOFTLY *adv.*

soil *n.* the ground; the top layer of the earth in which plants grow. SOIL *v.* to make dirty; to stain; soiled *adj.*

solar *adj.* concerning the sun.

soldier *n.* a member of an army.

sole *n.* 1 the underside of a foot, boot or shoe. 2 a flat sea-fish. SOLE *adj.* single, one and only. SOLELY *adv.*

solemn *adj.* 1 serious; thoughtful. 2 earnest; grave. SOLEMNLY *adv.*

solicit *v.* to ask for earnestly and repeatedly.

solicitor *n.* a lawyer; a legal adviser.

solid *adj.* 1 of substance throughout; not liquid or fluid. 2 rigid, hard and compact. 3 not hollow. SOLID *n.* a substance which is hard right through.

solidify *v.* to make or become solid; to harden.

solitary *adj.* 1 alone or lonely. 2 without companions. 3 single.

solitude *n.* being solitary; isolation.

solo *n.* 1 a piece of music for one singer or player. 2 something undertaken by one person. SOLOIST *n.*

soluble *adj.* 1 that can be dissolved in a liquid. 2 that can be solved.

solution *n.* 1 a liquid having something dissolved in it. 2 the answer to a problem.

solve *v.* to find an answer to or explanation for.

solvent *n.* a liquid which will dissolve other substances. SOLVENT *adj.* able to pay all debts. SOLVENCY *n.*

some *adj.* more or less; unspecified in number or quantity; about. SOME *pron.* a little; a few; a certain number of persons or things.

somebody *n.* 1 an unspecified person. 2 an important person.

somersault *n.* a jump and a turn heels over head before landing on the feet. SOMERSAULT *v.* to turn a somersault.

son *n.* a male child of a parent.

song *n.* 1 a piece of music for singing; something which is sung. 2 words set to music.

sonic *adj.* to do with sound or sound waves.

sonnet *n.* a poem containing fourteen lines of equal length.

soon *adv.* 1 in a short time. 2 early. 3 readily; willingly.

soot *n.* a black substance in the smoke of wood, coal, oil, etc. SOOTY *adj.*

soothe *v.* 1 to make calm. 2 to reduce pain. SOOTHING *adj.*

soprano *n.* 1 the highest singing voice of a female or boy. 2 a person having such a voice.

sordid *adj.* dirty; mean; squalid.

sore *adj.* 1 painful, hurting when touched or used. 2 sad; annoyed. SORE *n.* a painful or inflamed place on the skin. SORELY *adv.*

sorrow *n.* 1 sadness; grief. 2 regret; disappointment. SORROW *v.* to feel sorrow. SORROWFUL *adj.* SORROWFULLY *adv.*

sorry *adj.* feeling grief, pity or regret.

sort *v.* to arrange into groups or sets. SORT *n.* a kind; a class. SORTER *n.*

soul *n.* the spiritual, non-material part of a person thought of as immortal.

sound *adj.* 1 healthy; in good condition.
2 sensible; reliable. SOUNDLY *adv.* SOUND *v.* 1 to
make a sound. 2 to examine; to question.
SOUND *n.* 1 something that can be heard. 2 a
strait; a channel.

soup *n.* a liquid food made from meat and/or
vegetables.

sour *adj.* 1 having a sharp taste; bitter. 2 surly;
bad-tempered.

source *n.* 1 the place or thing from which
something starts; the origin. 2 a spring. 3 a text,
picture or artefact that provides a model for
future work or gives information.

south *n.* a cardinal point of the compass opposite
to north. SOUTH *adj.* in or towards the south.
SOUTH *adv.* towards the south. SOUTHERN *adj.*

southerly *adj.* towards or in the south.

souvenir *n.* something given, bought or kept as a
reminder of a person, place or event.

sovereign *n.* 1 a monarch; a king or queen. 2 a
gold coin formerly worth one pound.
SOVEREIGN *adj.* supreme; excellent.

sow *n.* (pron. like HOW) a female pig. *masc.* BOAR.

sow *v.* (pron. SO) to scatter or plant seed; to
spread. SOWER *n.*

spa *n.* a place where there is a mineral spring.

space *n.* 1 the distance between objects. 2 an
empty gap or area. 3 the immeasurable expanse
in which the planets and stars move. 4 a period
of time. SPACE *v.* to arrange at intervals.
SPACED *adj.*

spacious *adj.* wide; roomy; extensive.

spade *n.* a tool with a broad flat blade and
handle, used for digging.

span *n.* 1 the breadth of anything. 2 the part of a
bridge between its supports. 3 a period of time.
4 the maximum distance between the tips of the
little finger and the thumb, nine inches (about
22 centimetres). SPAN *v.* to stretch across from
one side to the other.

Spaniard *n.* a native of Spain.

Spanish *adj.* belonging to Spain or its people.

spanner *n.* a tool for turning nuts and bolts.

spar *n.* a strong pole; a ship's mast. SPAR (WITH)
v. 1 to fight with the fists. 2 to argue.

spare *adj.* 1 extra; kept in reserve. 2 thin.
SPARE *v.* 1 to allow to go unharmed. 2 to do
without or use in small quantities. SPARING *adj.*

spark *n.* 1 a fiery particle. 2 a small flash of light
or electricity. SPARK *v.* to make sparks.

sparkle *v.* to flash or glitter. SPARKLE *n.*
brightness. SPARKLING *adj.*

sparrow *n.* a small, common, brownish bird
which nests in hedges or houses.

sparse *adj.* scanty; thinly scattered.
SPARSELY *adv.*

spasm *n.* a sudden pain; a sudden jerking
movement which a person cannot prevent.
SPASMODIC *adj.*

spate *n.* 1 a sudden river flood. 2 a sudden rush.

spatial *adj.* relating to space.

spawn *n.* the eggs of fish, frogs and other water
animals.

speak *v.* 1 to say in words; to talk. 2 to make a
speech. SPEAKER *n.* SPEAKING *adj.*

spear *n.* a weapon with a sharp point on a long
shaft. SPEAR *v.* to pierce with a spear.

special *adj.* 1 of a particular or rare kind.
2 reserved for a particular person, occasion or
purpose. SPECIALLY *adv.*

specialist *n.* an expert in a particular subject.

species *n.* a group of plants or animals which
have common characteristics.

specific *adj.* detailed; exact; precise.
SPECIFICALLY *adv.*

specification *n.* a detailed and full description of
something to be made or undertaken. SPECIFY *v.*

specimen *n.* an example or sample; a pattern.

speck *n.* a small spot or particle.

spectacle *n.* an exciting or impressive display.

spectacles *n. pl.* a pair of lenses in a frame to
correct faulty vision.

spectator *n.* a person who watches or looks on.

spectrum *n.* the band of colours seen in a
rainbow or through a glass prism.

speech *n.* 1 the ability to speak; spoken words.
2 a language; a dialect. 3 a talk given to an
audience.

speechless *adj.* unable to speak; dumb.

speed *n.* 1 rapid movement; swiftness. 2 the rate
at which something moves. SPEED *v.* to move
rapidly.

spell *v.* to arrange letters in a particular order to
form a word. SPELL *n.* 1 a short period of time;
a continuous period. 2 a charm or influence.

spend *v.* 1 to pay out money. 2 to use up. 3 to pass time.

spent *adj.* used up; exhausted.

sphere *n.* 1 a ball; a globe. 2 a solid having all points of its surface at an equal distance from the centre. 3 a person's daily activity and influence. SPHERICAL *adj.*

sphinx *n.* 1 a fabled monster with the body of a lion and the head of a woman. 2 a person who is silent and secretive.

spice *n.* 1 a vegetable substance, such as nutmeg, cloves or pepper, used to flavour food. 2 something that adds interest or excitement. SPICY *adj.*

spider *n.* a small invertebrate animal with eight legs that spins webs.

spike *n.* 1 a sharp projecting point. 2 a long, pointed nail. 3 a cluster of flowers growing from a single stem. SPIKE *v.* to pierce with a spike. SPIKED *adj.* SPIKY *adj.*

spill *v.* 1 to fall or flow from a container. 2 to cause to fall or flow from a container. SPILL *n.* 1 a fall or tumble. 2 a thin strip of paper or wood used to light a fire, etc.

spin *v.* 1 to twist (yarn, cotton, nylon, etc), into a thread. 2 to turn round and round rapidly. SPIN *n.* a rapid, turning movement.

spindle *n.* 1 a rod used to twist and wind thread in spinning. 2 the shaft on which something revolves.

spine *n.* 1 the backbone. 2 a sharp, pointed thorn. SPINAL *adj.*

spiral *adj.* coiled round and round like a spring or the thread of a screw.

spire *n.* a tapering structure built on top of a tower; a steeple.

spirit *n.* 1 the soul; the personality. 2 a ghost. 3 courage; enthusiasm. 4 alcohol.

spit *n.* 1 a revolving rod on which meat is roasted. 2 a narrow piece of land projecting into the sea. SPIT *v.* to eject saliva, etc., from the mouth.

spite *n.* a desire to harm someone; malice. SPITE *v.* to harm or annoy (someone) maliciously. SPITEFUL *adj.*

splash *v.* to bespatter with liquid. SPLASH *n.* the act or sound of splashing.

splendid *adj.* magnificent; excellent; glorious. SPLENDIDLY *adv.* SPLENDOUR *n.*

splice *v.* 2 to join ropes by weaving the ends of their strands together. 2 to join two pieces of wood together by overlapping their ends. SPLICE *n.* the joining of two pieces of wood, rope, etc.

splint *n.* a rigid piece of material used to keep a broken bone firmly in position.

splinter *n.* a small, sharp, broken fragment of wood, metal, glass, etc. SPLINTER *v.* to break into splinters.

split *v.* 1 to cut, break or come apart lengthways. 2 to divide into shares. SPLIT *n.* 1 the act or process of splitting. 2 a crack; a division; a separation.

spoil *v.* 1 to make or become damaged or useless. 2 to plunder. SPOIL *n.* plunder; loot.

spoke *n.* a radiating rod or bar joining the rim of a wheel to the hub.

sponge *n.* 1 a simple sea creature. 2 a light, porous, absorbent pad used in washing and cleaning. 3 a light cake or pudding. SPONGE *v.* to wash with a sponge. SPONGY *adj.*

sponsor *n.* a person who becomes responsible for another person.

spontaneous *adj.* happening or done naturally and freely.

spool *n.* a reel or small cylinder on which thread, film, ribbon, etc., is wound.

spoon *n.* a utensil with a shallow bowl and a handle used in serving and eating food. SPOON *v.* to serve with a spoon. SPOONFUL *n.*

spoor *n.* the track and scent of an animal.

sport *n.* 1 fun; amusement. 2 games and pastimes such as football, athletics, fishing, cricket, etc. SPORTSMAN *n.*

spot *n.* 1 a small, round mark or stain. 2 a particular place. 3 a small quantity. SPOT *v.* 1 to make a small mark or stain. 2 to notice or catch sight of.

spout *n.* 1 a pipe or mouth from which liquid flows. 2 a jet of liquid. SPOUT *v.* to pour or gush out.

sprain *v.* 1 to injure by twisting or spraining. 2 to twist or wrench a joint. SPRAIN *n.* an injury caused by a twist or wrench.

sprawl *v.* 1 to sit or lie with arms and legs spread out. 2 to spread out over a wide area. SPRAWL *n.* a sprawling attitude or movement. SPRAWLING *adj.*

spray *n.* 1 liquid carried through the air in small drops. 2 a device for spraying liquid. 3 a bunch of flowers. SPRAY *v.* to scatter liquid in small drops; to sprinkle.

spread *v.* 1 to stretch out; to extend. 2 to scatter; to distribute. 3 to make known. SPREAD *n.* 1 a covering. 2 an increase.

spreadsheet *n.* a computer program for working with data, especially numbers, in rows and columns.

spring *n.* 1 a place where water flows from the ground. 2 a coil of metal or wire. 3 a leap or jump. 4 the season of the year between winter and summer. SPRING *v.* 1 to flow (from). 2 to recoil. 3 to leap or jump. 4 to come up; to sprout.

sprinkle *v.* to scatter or shower in small drops or particles. SPRINKLING *n.*

sprint *v.* to run a short distance at full speed. SPRINT *n.* a short, fast run or race. SPRINTER *n.*

sprout *v.* to begin to grow; to shoot. SPROUT *n.* 1 a shoot; a new growth. 2 a vegetable of the cabbage family.

spur *n.* 1 a sharp instrument worn on a horse-rider's heel. 2 a projecting ridge in a mountain range. 3 anything urging a person on. SPUR *v.* to urge on.

spurt *v.* 1 to gush or spout out. 2 to speed up suddenly. SPURT *n.* 1 a sudden gush. 2 a short, sudden effort.

spy *n.* a person collecting and reporting secret information. SPY *v.* 1 to see. 2 to obtain secret information. 3 SPY OUT to observe or explore secretly.

squabble *v.* to bicker or quarrel noisily. SQUABBLE *n.* a petty quarrel.

squad *n.* a small group of trained people.

squadron *n.* a section of a fleet, regiment or air force.

squall *n.* a sudden violent gust of wind. SQUALLY *adj.*

square *n.* 1 a shape having four equal sides and four right angles; anything shaped like this. 2 an open space with buildings on four sides. 3 the product of a number multiplied by itself. SQUARE *adj.* 1 square-shaped. 2 honest; fair.

squash *v.* 1 to crush; to squeeze. 2 to silence or repress. SQUASH *n.* 1 a crush; a crowd. 2 a crushed-fruit drink.

squat *v.* 1 to sit on the heels. 2 to take possession of land or buildings without permission. SQUAT *adj.* short and stocky.

squeak *v.* to make a short, shrill cry. SQUEAK *n.* a short, shrill cry. SQUEAKY *adj.*

squeal *v.* to make a long, shrill cry. SQUEAL *n.* a long, shrill cry.

squeeze *v.* 1 to press tightly; to crush. 2 to pack tightly. SQUEEZE *n.* 1 a firm grip; an embrace. 2 a tight fit.

squirrel *n.* a small rodent, with a bushy tail, which lives in trees.

squirt *v.* to shoot out a jet of liquid. SQUIRT *n.* 1 a jet of liquid. 2 a syringe.

stab *v.* to pierce, or thrust, with a short pointed weapon. STAB *n.* a wound caused by stabbing.

stability *n.* steadiness; firmness.

stable *n.* a building in which horses are kept. STABLE *v.* to keep or put a horse in a stable. STABLE *adj.* steady; firm; reliable.

stack *n.* 1 a large pile; a heap. 2 the part of a chimney which projects above the roof. STACK *v.* to heap or pile (something) up.

stadium *n.* a sports arena.

staff *n.* 1 a stick or pole used as a support, weapon or symbol of office. 2 a group of persons employed in a business, school, etc. STAFF *v.* to provide (a business) with staff.

stag *n.* a male deer. *fem.* DOE.

stage *n.* 1 a raised platform. 2 a regular stopping place. 3 a point or step in the development of something. STAGE *v.* to produce on the stage.

stagger *v.* 1 to reel; to walk or stand unsteadily. 2 to shock; to amaze. 3 to arrange in alternate order.

stagnate *v.* 1 to become motionless; to cease to flow. 2 to be dull and stale. STAGNANT *adj.* STAGNATION *n.*

stain v. 1 to discolour; to mark in patches. 2 to colour. STAIN n. 1 a dirty mark or patch. 2 a paint or dye. 3 a blemish. STAINED adj.

stair n. a number of steps between the floors of a building; one of these steps.

staircase n. a flight or series of stairs within a building.

stake n. 1 a strong, pointed post. 2 money risked in gambling. STAKE v. 1 to support with stakes. 2 to risk (money). 3 STAKE OUT to mark out with stakes.

stalactite n. a crystalline deposit hanging from the roof of a cave and formed by the dripping of water containing lime.

stalagmite n. a crystalline deposit rising from the floor of a cave and formed by the dripping of water containing lime.

stale adj. 1 not fresh; musty. 2 uninteresting; dull.

stalk v. to follow stealthily. STALK n. the stem of a plant. STALKER n.

stall n. 1 a stand for displaying goods. 2 a division for one animal in a stable or cattle shed. 3 a seat in a theatre. STALL v. 1 to stop; to halt. 2 to lose flying speed in an aircraft and fall out of control.

stallion n. a male horse. *fem.* MARE.

stalwart adj. strong; reliable; determined.

stamen n. the male reproductive part of a flower which produces the pollen.

stamina n. the power of endurance.

stammer v. to stutter and hesitate when speaking.

stamp v. 1 to put a foot down heavily on the ground. 2 to print a mark on (something). 3 to stick a postage stamp on (a letter or parcel). STAMP n. 1 a heavy tread. 2 something used to make a mark. 3 a postage stamp.

stampede n. a sudden flight of animals or people caused by fright, fear or panic. STAMPEDE v. to run or cause to run in fear or panic.

stand v. 1 to be in an upright position. 2 to rise to the feet. 3 to endure. STAND n. 1 the act of standing. 2 a stall. 3 a support. 4 a raised structure for spectators.

standard n. 1 a flag or banner. 2 a measure. 3 average quality. STANDARD adj. of the usual type; of the normal kind.

standing n. 1 rank or position. 2 reputation. STANDING adj. 1 upright. 2 permanent.

stanza n. a verse in poetry.

star n. 1 a tiny bright body seen in the sky at night. 2 a pattern with five or six points representing a star. 3 a famous or popular entertainer, sportsperson, etc. STAR v. to play the leading part.

starboard n. the right-hand side of a ship or aircraft.

starch n. a substance found in foods such as potatoes and rice and which is a source of energy.

stare v. to look continuously with a fixed gaze. STARE n. a fixed gaze.

starling n. a common bird with glossy bluish-black feathers.

start v. 1 to begin; to commence; to make the first move. 2 to make a quick, sudden movement. START n. 1 a beginning. 2 a quick sudden movement. 3 an advantage.

startle v. to surprise or frighten (somebody or something). STARTLING adj.

starve v. to suffer or die from hunger. STARVATION n.

state n. 1 the condition of someone or something. 2 a nation. STATE v. to say; to declare. STATESMAN, STATESWOMAN n.

stately adj. dignified; imposing; grand.

statement n. 1 something said or written. 2 an account.

static adj. at rest; not changing or moving.

station n. 1 a stopping place for trains and buses with buildings for passengers and staff. 2 a headquarters for policemen, firemen or troops. STATION v. to place in position.

stationary adj. remaining in one place; not moving.

stationer n. a person who sells writing materials. STATIONERY n. writing materials.

statistics n. pl. facts and figures collected, classified and arranged to give information. STATISTICAL adj.

statue n. a figure carved from stone or cast in metal.

status n. rank or social position.

staunch adj. reliable; loyal.

stave *n*. 1 one of the narrow strips of wood forming the side of a cask. 2 the lines on which notes of music are written.

stay *v*. 1 to remain. 2 to live in a place temporarily. STAY *n*. a prop; a support.

steady *adj*. 1 firm; not moving. 2 regular. 3 constant and reliable. STEADILY *adv*. STEADINESS *n*.

steak *n*. a thick slice of meat or fish.

steal *v*. 1 to take (something) dishonestly. 2 to move stealthily. STEALING *n*.

stealth *n*. secrecy; a furtive and secret manner. STEALTHY *adj*. STEALTHILY *adv*.

steam *n*. the vapour produced by boiling water. STEAM *v*. 1 to give off steam. 2 to use steam power. 3 to cook in steam.

steel *n*. a hard metal made from iron, carbon, and other minerals.

steep *adj*. sloping sharply. STEEP *v*. to soak in a liquid. STEEPNESS *n*.

steeple *n*. a spire built on a tower.

steer *v*. to guide; to direct. STEER *n*. a bullock; a young ox.

stem *n*. 1 the stalk of a plant. 2 the forepart of a ship. STEM *v*. to stop or hold back; to dam up.

stencil *n*.a sheet of metal or card with a pattern cut out. STENCIL *v*. to decorate or make a picture using a stencil. STENCILLING *n*.

sterilise *v*. to free from germs. STERILISER *n*.

sterling *n*. British currency. STERLING *adj*. 1 of standard quality. 2 true; genuine.

stern *adj*. strict; severe; grim; harsh. STERN *n*. the rear part of a ship. STERNLY *adv*.

stereotype *n*. a fixed idea or image of a type of person or thing, which is often not entirely true. STEREOTYPE *v*. STEREOTYPICAL *adj*.

stew *v*. to cook by slow boiling. STEW *n*. meat and vegetables that have been cooked gently.

steward *n*. a person who caters for a club or college; a person who manages an estate, a race-course, etc.; an attendant on a ship or aircraft. *fem*. STEWARDESS.

stick *n*.1 a straight, thin branch cut from a tree. 2 a slender piece of wood cut for a particular purpose. 3 a piece of celery, chalk, etc. STICK *v*. 1 to pierce; to thrust into. 2 to glue (one thing to another).

stiff *adj*. 1 hard to bend, stir or move. 2 difficult. 3 strong; rigid. STIFFEN *v*.

stifle *v*. 1 to smother; to suffocate. 2 to keep back; to suppress.

stigma *n*. the top of the female part of a flower, which receives pollen (see STAMEN, CARPEL).

stile *n*. a step or steps to enable people to climb over a wall or fence.

still *adj*. 1 calm; without movement. 2 silent; quiet. STILL *adv*. 1 up to and including the present time. 2 nevertheless. STILL *n*. an apparatus for making spirits.

stilts *n*. *pl*. a pair of poles with foot-rests which enable the user to walk above ground level.

stimulant *n*. something which increases physical or mental activity.

stimulate *v*. to arouse thought, action, interest or excitement.

stimulus *n*. something that arouses activity or energy.

sting *n*. a sharp-pointed weapon in some insects, animals and plants. STING *v*. 1 to wound with a sting. 2 to feel or cause acute pain.

stipulate *v*. to make conditions; to insist upon. STIPULATION *n*.

stir *v*. 1 to start or keep moving. 2 to excite; to arouse. STIR *n*. a slight movement or activity. STIRRING *adj*.

stirrups *n*. *pl*. supports, hanging from a saddle, for the horse-rider's feet.

stitch *n*. 1 a loop of thread made in sewing or knitting. 2 a single, complete movement in sewing or knitting. 3 a sudden pain in the side. STITCH *v*. to sew with a needle and thread.

stoat *n*. a small animal similar to the weasel and ferret; the ermine.

stock *n*. 1 a supply or store of goods for sale or use. 2 the animals on a farm; livestock. 3 family or ancestry. 4 a handle. STOCK *v*. 1 to store goods for sale. 2 to supply or obtain animals for a farm.

stocking *n*. a close-fitting covering for the foot and leg.

stocks *n*. *pl*. 1 the framework on which a ship rests when it is being built. 2 a wooden frame, set up in a public place, where offenders were fixed by the ankles.

stoke *n*. to feed (a fire or furnace) with fuel. STOKER *n*.

stole *n*. 1 a narrow band of silk worn round the neck and shoulders by a priest. 2 a woman's shoulder wrap.

stomach *n*. the organ of the body that receives and digests food.

stone *n*. 1 a small piece of rock; a piece of building stone. 2 the hard seed of fruits, such as the plum, apricot, etc. 3 an imperial weight of 14 pounds (6.4 kilograms). STONE *v*. 1 to throw stones at. 2 to remove stones from fruit. STONE *adj*. made of stone.

stool *n*. a low seat without a back.

stoop *v*. to bend forwards and downwards. STOOP *n*. a forward bending of the body.

stop *v*. 1 to cease; to bring to an end. 2 to prevent; to hinder. 3 to come to rest; to halt. 4 to remain. STOP *n*. 1 a halt; stopping or being stopped. 2 a short stay. 3 a punctuation mark. 4 a mechanism in a musical instrument which regulates its sounds.

storage *n*. the placing of goods in store; the charge for storing goods.

store *n*. 1 a stock of something kept for future use. 2 a place where goods are kept. 3 a large shop selling a variety of goods. STORE *v*. 1 to put aside for future use. 2 to place in a warehouse or storage place.

storey, story *n*. one level or floor of a building.

storm *n*. 1 a sudden disturbance of the air with thunder, strong wind, heavy rain or snow. 2 a sudden, violent attack. STORM *v*. 1 to attack suddenly and violently. 2 to display violent anger. STORMY *adj*.

story *n*. an account of real or imaginary happenings. *pl*. STORIES.
STORY BOARD *n*. a plan for a video or film which shows the events through a sequence of pictures.

stout *adj*. 1 strong and thick. 2 fat. 3 brave. STOUT *n*. a kind of strong beer.

stove *n*. an apparatus used for cooking or heating.

stow *v*. to pack and store something away.

stowaway *n*. a person who hides in a ship or aircraft to avoid paying the fare.

straggle *v*. to fall behind or wander away from the main party. STRAGGLER *n*.

straight *adj*. 1 without a bend or curve. 2 neat and tidy. 3 honest; direct. STRAIGHTEN *v*.

straightforward *adj*. direct; uncomplicated; honest.

strain *v*. 1 to stretch tightly. 2 an injury caused by straining. STRAINED *adj*.

strait *n*. a narrow channel of water connecting two seas. STRAITS *n*. *pl*. difficulty or hardship.

strand *n*. 1 a single thread or fibre of a wire or rope. 2 a shore or beach. STRAND *v*. 1 to leave in a difficult or dangerous situation. 2 to run aground. STRANDED *adj*.

strange *adj*. 1 unusual; not familiar or well known. 2 odd; peculiar. STRANGELY *adv*.

stranger *n*. 1 a person not known before. 2 a person in unfamiliar surroundings.

strap *n*. a strip of leather or material used for holding things together. STRAP *v*. to fasten or hit with a strap.

strategy *n*. the planning of a campaign.

stratum *n*. a layer. *pl*. STRATA.

straw *n*. 1 the dry cut stalks of corn. 2 a thin tube for drinking through.

stray *v*. to wander; to lose the way. STRAY *n*. a lost person or animal.

streak *n*. a line or stripe of contrasting colour. STREAK *v*. 1 to mark with stripes. 2 to move quickly. STREAKY *adj*.

stream *n*. 1 a small river or brook. 2 a flow of water, light, air, people, traffic, etc. STREAM *v*. to move or flow freely.

street *n*. a road lined with buildings.

strength *n*. being strong; power. STRENGTHEN *v*.

strenuous *adj*. needing great effort; vigorous.

stress *n*. 1 pressure; tension; strain. 2 emphasis; importance. STRESS *v*. to emphasise.

stretch *v*. 1 to make (something) wider, longer or tighter by pulling. 2 to strain; to extend; to spread. STRETCH *n*. 1 the act of stretching or being stretched. 2 a continuous length of time or space.

stretcher *n*. a light, folding framework with handles at each end for carrying a sick or injured person.

strict *adj.* 2 exact; precise. 2 severe; stern. STRICTNESS *n.*

stride *v.* to walk with long steps.

strife *n.* conflict; struggle.

strike *v.* 1 to hit; to attack suddenly. 2 to refuse to work because of a dispute. 3 to sound. STRIKE *n.* a hit. 2 a refusal to work because of a dispute. 3 a sound produced by striking. STRIKING *adj.*

string *n.* 1 a thin cord used for tying things. 2 a length of stretched wire or cord used to sound a note in a musical instrument. 3 a series of things linked together. STRING *v.* 1 to put on a string. 2 to provide with a string. STRINGED *adj.*

strip *v.* 1 to remove the outer covering from. 2 to undress. 3 to deprive of. STRIP *n.* 1 a narrow piece. 2 a footballer's shirt.

stripe *n.* 1 a long narrow mark. 2 a marking on a uniform indicating the rank of the wearer. STRIPE *v.* to mark with stripes. STRIPED *adj.*

strive *v.* to try very hard; to struggle.

stroke *n.* 1 a blow. 2 a sweep of an oar in rowing; a movement of the arms in swimming. 3 a mark made with a pencil, brush or pen. 4 a sudden paralysis. STROKE *v.* to smooth with the hand.

strong *adj.* 1 having great power; not easily broken or damaged. 2 very powerful in flavour or smell. 3 glaring; dazzling.

stronghold *n.* a fortress.

structure *n.* 1 something that has been built. 2 the way in which something is built or put together.

struggle *v.* 2 to make great efforts. 2 STRUGGLE WITH or AGAINST to fight. STRUGGLE *n.* an effort; a fight.

stubble *n.* short stalks of corn left in the ground after reaping.

stubborn *adj.* obstinate; inflexible. STUBBORNNESS *n.*

stud *n.* 1 a short nail with a flat head. 2 a fastener for attaching a collar to a shirt. 3 a reflecting road marker. 4 animal(s), esp. horse(s), kept for breeding purposes.

student *n.* a person who studies.

studied *adj.* deliberate; carefully planned.

studio *n.* 1 a workroom for an artist or photographer. 2 a place for making sound recordings, films or broadcasts.

study *v.* 2 to give time and thought to acquiring information, knowledge and learning. 2 to examine carefully. STUDY *n.* 2 the learning of a subject. 2 a private room used when studying. STUDIOUS *adj.*

stuff *n.* 1 the material from which something is made. 2 objects; belongings. STUFF *v.* to fill tightly. STUFFED *adj.*

stumble *v.* 1 to trip up. 2 to move or speak hesitatingly. STUMBLE *n.* a trip; a fall.

stump *n.* 1 the projecting part of a felled or fallen tree. 2 the remaining part of a cut or broken pencil, tooth, etc. 3 one of the three uprights forming the wicket in cricket. STUMP *v.* 1 to walk clumsily and heavily. 2 to break down the wicket whilst a batsman is out of his crease.

stun *v.* 1 to knock senseless. 2 to amaze; to confuse.

stunt *v.* to check the growth or development of. STUNT *n.* something done to attract attention or to gain publicity. STUNTED *adj.*

stupid *adj.* foolish; lacking intelligence. STUPIDLY *adv.* STUPIDITY *n.*

sturdy *adj.* robust; strong; vigorous. STURDILY *adv.*

stutter *v.* to stammer. STUTTER *n.* a stammer.

sty *n.* 1 an enclosure for keeping pigs. 2 an inflamed swelling on the eyelid. *pl.* STIES.

style *n.* 1 the way or manner in which something is done, written or spoken. 2 fashion in dress, furnishing, etc. 3 in flowering plants, the long, thin stalk which holds the stigma. STYLISH *adj.*

subconscious *adj.* 1 not fully conscious. 2 about those mental activities of which a person is not fully aware.

subject *adj.* (pron. SUB-ject) 1 under the power of another. 2 liable to or conditional upon. SUBJECT *n.* 1 a member of a particular state or country. 2 a topic of conversation; a theme. 3 who or what a sentence is about. SUBJECT *v.* (pron. sub-JECT) to subdue.

submarine *n*. a ship which can travel under water. SUBMARINE *adj*. living or growing under the sea.

submerge *v*. to go under water or beneath the surface of a liquid; to cause something to do this.

submission *n*. a surrender; obedience.

submit *v*. 1 to surrender; to yield. 2 to suggest; to propose.

subordinate *adj*. lower in rank or importance. SUBORDINATE *n*. a person who is lower in rank or importance. SUBORDINATE *v*. to regard as less important; to put into a subordinate position.

subscribe *v*. to make a contribution; to help towards something. SUBSCRIBER *n*. SUBSCRIPTION *n*.

subsequent *adj*. following; coming later.

subside *v*. to sink or settle down; to grow less. SUBSIDENCE *n*.

subsidy *n*. a financial grant or aid.

substance *n*. 1 any kind of matter; anything that is real and not imaginary. 2 a drug. 3 wealth and possessions. 4 the meaning or importance of something. SUBSTANTIAL *adj*.

substitute *v*. to use (something or someone) in place of (another). SUBSTITUTE *n*. something or someone used in place of another. SUBSTITUTION *n*.

subterranean *adj*. underground.

subtle *adj*. 1 fine and delicate. 2 ingenious; clever. SUBTLY *adv*.

subtract *v*. to take one number or quantity from another; to deduct. SUBTRACTION *n*.

suburb *n*. an area of houses on the edge of a town or city. SUBURBAN *adj*.

subway *n*. an underground passage for pedestrians.

succeed *v*. 1 to be successful; to achieve a purpose. 2 to come after; to take the place of; to inherit.

success *n*. 1 achievement; prosperity. 2 a person who achieves success. SUCCESSFUL *adj*. SUCCESSFULLY *adv*.

successive *adj*. coming one after another in turn.

successor *n*. a person or thing coming after another.

such *adj*. 1 of the same kind as. 2 denoting a particular person or thing. 3 so great.

suck *v*. to draw (liquid or air) into the mouth.

suction *n*. a sucking or drawing of liquid or air from something.

sudden *adj*. happening or done quickly and unexpectedly. SUDDENLY *adv*. SUDDENNESS *n*.

sue *v*. to plead; to take legal action against.

suffer *v*. 1 to undergo pain or experience loss, grief or punishment. 2 to tolerate; to allow. SUFFERER *n*. SUFFERING *n*.

sufficient *adj*. enough; adequate. SUFFICIENTLY *adv*.

suffix *n*. a syllable or another (shorter) word placed at the end of a word to change its meaning.

suffocate *v*. to have difficulty in breathing. 2 to smother or choke. SUFFOCATION *n*.

sugar *n*. a sweet, energy-giving substance obtained from plants, esp. sugar-cane and sugar-beet.

suggest *v*. 1 to put forward an idea or proposal. 2 to hint. SUGGESTION *n*.

suicide *n*. intentional self-killing.

suit *n*. 1 a set of clothes of the same material and colour. 2 one of the four sets in a pack of playing-cards. 3 an action in a law court. SUIT *v*. 1 to meet the needs of. 2 to look well on; to be good for.

suitable *adj*. appropriate for the purpose or occasion. SUITABLY *adv*.

suite *n*. 1 a set of furniture. 2 a set of rooms. 3 a musical composition in several parts.

sulk *v*. to be sullen and silent. SULKY *adj*.

sullen *adj*. morose and gloomy.

sum *n*. the total obtained when adding numbers, quantities or items. SUM *v*. to add together.

summary *n*. a short account of a story, book, article, speech, etc. SUMMARISE *v*.

summer *n*. the warmest season of the year.

summit *n*. the highest point; the top; the highest degree.

summon *v*. 1 to call together; to command someone to appear. 2 to order to appear in court.

summons *n*. an order to appear in court. SUMMONS *v*. to serve with a summons.

sun *n.* the heavenly body giving light and heat to the Earth.

Sunday *n.* the first day of the week.

sundry *adj.* various; several; SUNDRIES *n.*

sunken *adj.* 1 submerged; below ground level. 2 hollow.

sunlight *n.* the light given by the sun. SUNLIT *adj.*

sunshine *n.* the direct light of the sun.

superb *adj.* splendid; magnificent.

superficial *adj.* on the surface; shallow; not thorough.

superfluous *adj.* more than needed or required.

superintend *v.* to supervise; to control. SUPERINTENDENT *n.*

superior *adj.* greater, higher or better than others. SUPERIOR *n.* a person of higher rank or better than others. SUPERIORITY *n.*

supermarket *n.* a large self-service store selling goods of all kinds.

supersede *v.* to take the place of (another); to replace.

superstition *n.* a belief in magic and supernatural powers. SUPERSTITIOUS *adj.*

supervise *v.* to direct and control work or performance. SUPERVISION *n.*

supervisor *n.* a person who supervises; a manager.

supper *n.* an evening meal.

supple *adj.* easily bent; flexible.

supplement *v.* to add something to; to assist. SUPPLEMENT *n.* an addition.

supply *v.* to provide what is needed. SUPPLY *n.* 1 a stock of something. 2 something which is supplied. *pl.* SUPPLIES.

support *v.* 1 to hold up; to keep in place. 2 to provide for. 3 to encourage. SUPPORT *n.* a person or thing that supports.

suppose *v.* 1 to assume; to think. 2 to imagine. SUPPOSED *adj.*

suppress *v.* 1 to crush; to put an end to. 2 to hold back; to keep secret.

supreme *adj.* highest in authority, rank or power. SUPREMELY *adv.*

sure *adj.* 1 certain; confident. 2 safe; reliable.

surf *n.* the foam of breaking waves.

surface *n.* the outside of something; the exterior. SURFACE *v.* to come to the surface.

surfeit *n.* an excess of something.

surge *v.* to move up and down or to and fro. SURGE *n.* a surging motion.

surgeon *n.* a doctor who performs operations.

surgery *n.* 1 the treatment of disease and injury by operations on the body. 2 the room where a dentist or doctor sees his patients.

surly *adj.* sullen; morose; sulky.

surmise *v.* to suppose; to imagine. SURMISE *n.* something that is supposed; a guess.

surmount *v.* to overcome (difficulties).

surname *n.* a family name.

surpass *v.* to outdo; to exceed.

surplus *n.* the amount left over when the required amount has been used; the excess. SURPLUS *adj.* needless; unnecessary.

surprise *n.* 1 an unexpected happening. 2 the feeling a person has about an unexpected happening. SURPRISE *v.* to cause a feeling of surprise in; to startle. SURPRISING *adj.*

surrender *v.* 1 to give in to; to yield. 2 to give up possession of. SURRENDER *n.* the act of surrendering.

surround *v.* to encircle; to be round (something) on all sides.

surroundings *n. pl.* the things and places which are around a person or place; a neighbourhood.

survey *v.* (pron. sur-VEY) 1 to look at and consider. 2 to measure. 3 to make a map or a plan of. SURVEY *n.* (pron. SUR-vey) 1 a view or inspection. 2 a map or plan of an area. 3 a collection of information or opinions.

surveyor *n.* a person qualified to survey land and buildings.

survive *v.* to remain alive or to outlive. SURVIVOR *n.*

suspect *v.* (pron. sus-PECT) 1 to have suspicions or doubts about. 2 to suppose; to imagine. SUSPECT *n.* (pron. SUS-pect) a suspected person. SUSPECT *adj.* arousing suspicion.

suspend *v.* 1 to hand (something) up. 2 to delay or postpone. SUSPENSION *n.*

suspense *n.* uncertainty; strain; doubt.

suspicion *n.* 1 a feeling that something is wrong. 2 a slight trace; a very small amount.

suspicious *adj.* doubtful; distrustful. SUSPICIOUSLY *adv.*

sustain *v.* 1 to support; to maintain; to keep going. 2 to give strength to.

sustainable *adj.* able to be maintained or kept going. SUSTAINABILITY *n.*

swab *v.* to wash with a mop; to clean. SWAB *n.* 1 a mop for cleaning floors and decks. 2 a pad of cotton wool for medical use.

swallow *n.* 1 a swift-flying, migratory bird with a forked tail. 2 a gulp. SWALLOW *v.* 1 to allow food or drink to pass down the throat. 2 to believe readily.

swamp *v.* to flood; to sink; to overwhelm. SWAMP *n.* a marsh; boggy land.

swan *n.* a large, white, long-necked water bird.

swarm *n.* 1 a large group of insects. 2 a crowd or multitude. SWARM *v.* 1 to move in a large group. 2 SWARM OVER or UP to climb by using arms and legs.

sway *v.* 1 to move or swing from side to side. 2 to control; to influence. SWAY *n.* 1 a swinging movement. 2 control; influence.

swear *v.* 1 to take an oath. 2 to use bad language. SWEARING *n.*

sweat *v.* to perspire. SWEAT *n.* perspiration; condensation.

swede *n.* a yellow variety of turnip.

Swede *n.* an inhabitant of Sweden.

Swedish *adj.* belonging to Sweden or its people. SWEDISH *n.* the language of Sweden.

sweep *v.* 1 to clean with a brush. 2 to travel over quickly. 3 to clear everything away quickly or forcefully. SWEEP *n.* 1 a long, swift movement. 2 a person who cleans chimneys. SWEEPING *adj.*

sweet *adj.* 1 having a taste like sugar. 2 pleasant; attractive. SWEET *n.* 1 a small piece of something sweet made from sugar or chocolate. 2 a pudding. SWEETNESS *n.*

sweetheart *n.* a loved one.

swell *v.* 1 to grow larger or louder. 2 to rise and fall like waves. SWELLING *n.*

swerve *v.* to change direction suddenly. SWERVE *n.* a sudden change of direction.

swift *adj.* fast; speedy; quick. SWIFT *n.* a small, swift-flying migratory bird in the swallow family.

swill *v.* 1 to clean with water. 2 to drink greedily. SWILL *n.* waste food given to pigs.

swim *v.* 1 to move through the water by moving limbs or fins. 2 to cross water by swimming. 3 to feel dizzy. SWIM *n.* time spent swimming.

swindle *v.* to cheat; to defraud. SWINDLE *n.* a fraud. SWINDLER *n.*

swine *n.* a pig or pigs.

swing *v.* 1 to move to and fro. 2 to turn suddenly. SWING *n.* 1 a swinging movement. 2 a suspended seat for swinging on.

Swiss *n.* an inhabitant of Switzerland. SWISS *adj.* belonging to Switzerland or its people.

switch *n.* 1 a device for turning electricity on or off. 2 a sudden change. SWITCH *v.* 1 to operate a switch. 2 to change direction suddenly.

swoop *v.* 1 to descend steeply and swiftly. 2 to make a sudden attack. SWOOP *n.* a sudden descent or attack.

sword *n.* a weapon with a long, steel blade and hilt.

sycamore *n.* a large deciduous tree.

syllable *n.* a whole word or part of a word containing one vowel sound.

syllabus *n.* the programme for a course of study.

symbol *n.* a sign or mark which represents something else; an emblem.

symmetrical *adj.* having exactly corresponding shapes on each side.

symmetry *n.* 1 the state of being equally balanced on each side. 2 a balance; harmony.

sympathy *n.* 1 sharing the feelings of others. 2 understanding; agreement. SYMPATHETIC *adj.*

symphony *n.* a musical composition in several movements for orchestra.

symptom *n.* 1 a change in a person's condition that indicates illness. 2 a sign; an indication.

synagogue *n.* a building for Jewish worship and teaching.

syndicate *n.* a group of people or firms working together.

synonym *n.* a word or phrase which has the same meaning as another, e.g. big = large (see ANTONYM).

synopsis *n.* a short outline of a text or speech; a summary.

syntax *n.* the grammar of a sentence.

synthetic *adj.* produced artificially.

syringe *n.* an instrument for squirting or injecting liquids. SYRINGE *v.* to squirt; to spray.

syrup *n.* 1 a thick fluid obtained in the refining of sugar. 2 a solution of sugar in water or fruit juice.

system *n.* 1 a regular method or planned way of doing things. 2 a number of things working together for a purpose. SYSTEMATIC *adj.* SYSTEMATICALLY *adv.*

T

tab *n.* a small flap of cloth or leather.

table *n.* 1 a piece of furniture with a flat top supported on legs. 2 a statement of facts or figures set out in columns; a chart.

tablet *n.* 1 a flat piece of stone with words cut on it. 2 a small pill. 3 a piece of soap.

tabulate *v.* to arrange figures or words in a table or index. TABULATION *n.*

tacit *adj.* permitted and understood but not spoken. TACITLY *adv.*

taciturn *adj.* in the habit of saying very little.

tack *n.* 1 a short, broad-headed nail. 2 a long, loose stitch. 3 a zigzag course against the wind in sailing. TACK *v.* 1 to fasten with tacks. 2 to stitch loosely. 3 to sail a zigzag course.

tackle *n.* 1 equipment needed for a particular activity. 2 an arrangement of ropes and pulleys for lifting loads. 3 the grasping or holding of an opponent. TACKLE *v.* 1 to deal with a problem or task. 2 to grasp; to hold.

tact *n.* the ability to speak and act without causing offence. TACTFUL *adj.* TACTLESS *adj.*

tactical *adj.* according to plan; concerned with tactics.

tactics *n. pl.* 1 the management of military forces in battle. 2 the plan for achieving a purpose. TACTICIAN *n.*

tadpole *n.* a frog or toad in the first stage after hatching.

tag *n.* 1 a tie-on label. 2 the metal point at the end of a lace. TAG *v.* to fix a label to.

tail *n.* 1 the projecting part at the rear end of the bodies of animals, birds and fish. 2 anything sticking out behind or at the rear.

tailor *n.* a person who makes suits and other garments. *fem.* TAILORESS. TAILOR *v.* to make garments.

taint *v.* to infect; to corrupt. TAINT *n.* a trace of something unpleasant or bad.

take *v.* 1 to get hold of. 2 to grasp; to seize. 3 to guide; to accompany. 4 to photograph. 5 to consider; to suppose.

takings *n. pl.* money received; the total receipts.

tale *n.* a true or fictitious story. 2 a mischievous report.

talent *n.* a special skill or ability. TALENTED *adj.*

talk *v.* 1 to speak; to hold a conversation. 2 TALK OVER or ABOUT to discuss. TALK *n.* 1 a conversation or discussion. 2 a lecture. 3 gossip.

tall *adj.* 1 of more than average height. 2 of a particular height.

tallow *n.* animal fat melted down for use in making candles, soap, etc.

talon *n.* the claw of a bird of prey, such as an eagle or hawk.

tambourine *n.* a small, one-sided drum with bells round its side.

tame *adj.* 1 not wild; domesticated. 2 gentle and obedient. TAME *v.* to make tame; to subdue.

tamper (**with**) *v.* to meddle with; to interfere.

tan *v.* to make an animal skin into leather by treating with acid. 2 to become brown by exposure to the sun. TAN *n.* 1 oak bark used for tanning. 2 sunburn. 3 a yellowish-brown colour. TANNED *adj.* TANNING *n.*

tandem *n.* a bicycle for two riders.

tang *n.* a sharp or strong taste.

tangent *n.* a straight line which touches a curve at a point but does not cross it.

tangerine *n.* a small, sweet orange.

tangible *adj.* 1 that can be touched. 2 real; definite.

tangle *v.* 1 to become confused and muddled. 2 to twist or jumble together. TANGLE *n.* a muddle; a mix-up.

tank *n.* 1 a container for a liquid or a gas. 2 an armoured fighting vehicle moving on caterpillar tracks.

tanka *n.* a Japanese poem based on HAIKU with two extra lines and a total of 31 syllables.

tankard *n.* a large drinking mug.

tanker *n.* a ship or road vehicle for carrying liquids.

tantalise *v.* to tease or torment.

tantrum *n.* a fit of bad temper.

tap *n.* 1 a device for controlling the flow of a liquid or gas. 2 a light pat or touch. TAP *v.* 1 to draw off liquid by means of a tap. 2 to pat or touch.

tape *n.* 1 a narrow strip of cloth. 2 a magnetic ribbon used to make sound recordings. TAPE *v.* 1 to fasten with tape. 2 to record (sound) on tape.

taper *v.* 1 to become narrower towards one end. 2 to make thinner towards one end. TAPER *n.* 1 a narrowing. 2 a long thin candle.

tapestry *n.* a piece of cloth with patterns or pictures woven into it.

tapioca *n.* a white, starchy food obtained from cassava root.

tar *n.* a thick, black substance obtained from coal and used for road surfacing and wood preservation. TAR *v.* to coat with tar.

tare *n.* 1 a weed found growing among corn. 2 the weight of a container or vehicle when empty.

target *n.* 1 a mark or object for shooting at. 2 something to be aimed at.

Tarmac *n.* a mixture of tar and gravel used on road surfaces, playgrounds, etc.

tarn *n.* a small, mountain lake.

tarnish *v.* to make or become dull and discoloured. TARNISHED *adj.*

tarpaulin *n.* a large, thick, canvas sheet, coated with tar, etc. to make it waterproof.

tart *n.* a piece of pastry containing fruit or jam; a shallow pie. TART *adj.* sharp or sour in taste.

tartan *n.* woollen cloth woven in the colours of a Scottish Highland clan.

task *n.* a piece of work set to be done.

taste *n.* 1 the ability to taste. 2 flavour. 3 a person's judgement in liking things. 4 a small quantity. TASTE *v.* 1 to distinguish a taste or flavour. 2 to test a small quantity. TASTEFUL *adj.* TASTELESS *adj.* TASTY *adj.*

tasty *adj.* of pleasant flavour; savoury.

tattoo *n.* 1 a military display at night. 2 a drumbeat calling soldiers together. 3 a design on the skin made by pricking it and applying dyes. TATTOO *v.* to prick a design into the skin.

taunt *v.* to mock or sneer at; to ridicule. TAUNT *n.* mockery; ridicule.

taut *adj.* tightly stretched. TAUTLY *adv.*

tautology *n.* the use of an extra word or phrase which is not needed, e.g. the big elephant was enormous.

tavern *n.* an inn; a public house.

tax *n.* a contribution levied on a person, property or business by the Government for the payment of national expenses. TAX *v.* 1 to demand or impose a tax. 2 to accuse; to charge. TAXATION *n.*

taxable *adj.* liable to be taxed.

taxi *n.* a motor car and driver that may be hired. TAXI *v.* to move an aircraft along the ground before or after flying.

taxidermy *n.* the art of stuffing the skins of animals, birds and fish to make them look life-like. TAXIDERMIST *n.*

tea *n.* 1 the dry leaves of a shrub grown in Asia. 2 a hot drink made by pouring water on these leaves. 3 an afternoon meal at which tea is usually drunk.

teach *v.* 1 to pass on knowledge or skill. 2 to give instruction in a particular subject. TEACHING *n.*

teacher *n.* a person who teaches.

teak *n.* 1 a tree from the Far East. 2 its timber.

teal *n.* a kind of small, wild duck.

team *n.* 1 a group of people playing or working together. 2 two or more animals harnessed together.

tear *v.* (pron. TARE) 1 to pull apart by force; to pull to pieces. 2 to rush along. TEAR *n.* a rip; a rent. TEARING *adj.*

tear *n.* (pron. TEER) a drop of water in or flowing from the eye. TEARFUL *adj.*

tease *v.* 1 to make fun of or to annoy and torment somebody. 2 to separate the fibres of wool or other material using a comb or teasel.

teasel *n.* a plant with large prickly heads used in combing or dressing cloth; a device used as a substitute for the plant.

technical *adj.* concerning some particular art, craft or science.

technicality *n.* a technical detail or point.

technique *n*. 1 the way of doing something. 2 the skill required by an artist, musician, etc.

technology *n*. the practical uses of scientific knowledge.

tedious *adj*. wearisome; long and boring.

teem *v*. 1 to swarm; to be abundant. 2 to rain heavily. TEEMING *adj*.

telegram *n*. a message sent by telegraph.

telegraph *n*. an electrical apparatus for sending messages or signals over long distances.

telephone *n*. an electrical apparatus for transmitting sound and speech over long distances. TELEPHONIC *adj*.

telescope *n*. an instrument fitted with lenses for making distant objects seem nearer and larger. TELESCOPE *v*. to make (something) shorter by sliding one section inside another. TELESCOPIC *adj*.

television *n*. 1 the radio transmission of a picture which is reproduced on a screen. 2 the apparatus for receiving such pictures. TELEVISION *adj*. concerned with television.

tell *v*. 1 to give an account of; to relate. 2 to reveal. 3 to order; to command. 4 TELL THINGS APART to distinguish one thing from another.

temper *n*. 1 a person's state of mind or mood. 2 the degree of hardness in metal. 3 a fit of anger or annoyance. TEMPER *v*. 1 to toughen and harden (metal) by heating and cooling. 2 to make less severe; to calm.

temperament *n*. a person's nature, character and state of mind.

temperate *adj*. 1 moderate; avoiding extremes. 2 neither very hot nor very cold.

temperature *n*. 1 the hotness or coldness of something as shown by a thermometer.

tempest *n*. a violent storm.

template *n*. 1 a pattern cut out in wood, card, plastic, etc., used to draw round. 2 in word processing, a document that provides a pattern on which to base new documents.

temple *n*. 1 a place of religious worship. 2 the part of the head between forehead and ear.

temporary *adj*. lasting only for a short time. TEMPORARILY *adv*.

tempt *v*. 1 to try to persuade; to entice. 2 to attract; to allure. TEMPTING *adj*.

temptation *n*. 1 tempting or being tempted. 2 an attraction; a bait.

ten *n*. the number one more than nine; the symbol 10.

tenacious *adj*. holding firmly; clinging tightly. TENACITY *n*.

tenancy *n*. 1 the use of a building, house or land in return for rent. 2 the period of such use.

tenant *n*. a person who rents a building, house or land.

tend *v*. 1 to look after; to take care of. 2 to move or be directed in a certain direction; to incline towards.

tendency *n*. a leaning towards; a trend.

tender *n*. 1 a small supply vehicle or vessel. 2 an offer to do work or to supply goods at a fixed price. TENDER *v*. to make an offer. TENDER *adj*. 1 soft; easily damaged. 2 easily cut or chewed. 3 loving; kindly. 4 sore; painful. TENDERNESS *n*.

tendon *n*. a strong cord connecting a bone to a muscle.

tendril *n*. a shoot by which a climbing plant attaches itself to a support.

tenement *n*. a large building divided into several dwellings.

tennis *n*. a game for two or four players played with rackets and a ball on a grass or hard court.

tenor *n*. 1 the male voice between baritone and alto. 2 the musical part for a tenor voice; a man with such a voice. 3 a general course of direction.

tense *adj*. stretched tight; strained. TENSE *n*. the form taken by a verb to indicate time – past, present and future.

tension *n*. 1 stretching or being stretched. 2 mental strain or excitement.

tent *n*. a portable shelter, made of canvas or nylon and supported by poles and ropes.

tentacle *n*. the long slender feeler of certain animals and insects.

tentative *adj*. done as a trial; experimental. TENTATIVELY *adv*.

tepid *adj*. slightly warm; lukewarm.

term *n*. 1 a period of time. 2 a division of the school or university year. 3 a word having a precise meaning. TERMS *n. pl*. conditions; tone of expression. TERM *v*. to name; to describe.

terminal *n*. 1 a connecting point for electrical apparatus. 2 an airport building, container depot or railway station at which journeys begin or end. TERMINAL *adj*. occurring at the end.

terminate *v*. to stop; to bring to an end. TERMINATION *n*.

terminus *n*. the end of a railway or bus route; a station at the end of a route.

tern *n*. a small sea-bird with pointed wings and forked tail.

terrace *n*. 1 a raised, level piece of ground. 2 a row of houses built in one block.

terrestrial *adj*. 1 living on the ground. 2 belonging to the Earth.

terrible *adj*. 1 causing great fear or terror. 2 awful; dreadful. TERRIBLY *adv*.

terrier *n*. a small, lively dog that will dig to reach its prey.

terrific *adj*. 1 causing terror. 2 very great; excellent. TERRIFICALLY *adv*.

terrify *v*. to frighten; to fill with terror.

territory *n*. 1 a large area of land. 2 land belonging to an individual or to a particular country; an area dominated by certain animals or birds. TERRITORIAL *adj*.

terror *n*. 1 great fear. 2 a terrifying thing or person.

terse *adj*. short and concise. TERSELY *adv*.

tessellate *v*. to fit together without gaps. TESSELLATION *n*.

test *n*. an examination of something or somebody. TEST *v*. to examine or try the qualities, nature or ability of (someone or something). TESTED *adj*.

testament *n*. 1 a will; a written statement. 2 one of the two main parts of the Bible.

testify *n*. to give evidence; to declare.

testimonial *n*. 1 a written statement giving an opinion about a person's character and abilities. 2 a gift presented as a token of appreciation and respect.

testimony *n*. evidence; a written or oral statement made under oath.

tether *n*. a rope, chain or halter for tying up an animal. TETHER *v*. to fasten with a tether.

text *n*. 1 the actual words spoken or written by someone. 2 a short passage from the Bible, quoted as the subject for a sermon. 3 any piece of writing.

textile *n*. woven material, cloth or fabric. TEXTILE *adj*. concerned with fabrics and weaving.

texture *n*. 1 the manner in which something is woven. 2 the quality of something according to taste or feel.

than *conj*. a word used when making comparisons.

thank *v*. to express gratitude to. THANKFUL *adj*.

thanks *n. pl*. an expression of gratitude.

that *pron. & adj*. the person or thing already named. *pl*. THOSE.

thatch *n*. straw or reeds used to make a roof. THATCH *v*. to cover (a roof or building) with straw or reeds.

thaw *v*. 1 to become unfrozen; to unfreeze (something). 2 to become more relaxed and genial.

theatre *n*. 1 a place where plays are performed. 2 a room where surgical operations are performed. THEATRICAL *adj*.

theft *n*. stealing; robbery.

their *pron. pl*. belonging to them.

them *pron. pl*. persons already spoken about.

theme *n*. 1 a subject or topic. 2 a repeated melody, with variations.

then *adv*. 1 at that time. 2 after that; next. 3 for this reason. THEN *conj*. in that case; therefore.

theodolite *n*. a surveying instrument for measuring horizontal and vertical angles.

theology *n*. the study of God and religion.

theorem *n*. an idea or statement which needs to be proved by reasoning.

theory *n*. 1 a set of assumptions or hypotheses that produce an explanation. 2 the general ideas and principles of some activity.

therapy *n*. healing; the treatment of disease or illness.

there *adv*. at, in or to that place.

thermal *adj*. of heat; determined, operated or measured by heat. THERMAL *n*. a rising current of warm air.

thermometer *n.* an instrument for measuring temperature.

thermostat *n.* an automatic device for controlling temperature.

thesaurus *n.* a type of dictionary which lists words with similar meanings; a dictionary of synonyms.

these *pron. pl.* plural of this.

thick *adj.* 1 of great or specified depth from one side to the other. 2 crowded; packed. 3 dense; hard to see through. 4 stiff; flowing slowly. THICKLY *adv.* THICKNESS *n.*

thicken *v.* to make or become denser, stiffer or thicker.

thief *n.* a person who steals.

thieve *v.* to steal.

thigh *n.* the part of the leg between the hip and the knee.

thimble *n.* a small metal or plastic cap to protect the finger when sewing.

thin *adj.* 1 having opposite surfaces close together. 2 of small diameter; not thick; narrow. 3 slim; slender. 4 weak; watery. THIN *v.* 1 to make or become thin. 2 to reduce in bulk or number.

thing *n.* 1 an object; an article. 2 an action or happening.

think *v.* 1 to reason; to have an opinion. 2 to consider; to imagine. THINKING *n.*

third *adj.* the next after second; the last of three. THIRD *n.* one of three equal parts.

thirst *n.* a strong desire or need to drink. THIRST (FOR or AFTER) *v.* to desire strongly. THIRSTY *adj.*

thirteen *n.* the number one more than twelve, the symbol 13.

thirty *n.* three times ten, the symbol 30.

this *pron. & adj.* the person or thing near or just mentioned. *pl.* THESE.

thistle *n.* a wild plant with prickly leaves and purple flowers.

thorax *n.* the chest.

thorn *n.* 1 a sharp, pointed growth on a plant. 2 a prickly shrub or tree.

thorough *adj.* 1 complete; with attention to every part or detail. 2 careful; conscientious. THOROUGHLY *adv.* THOROUGHNESS *n.*

thoroughbred *adj.* of pure breed.

thoroughfare *n.* a through road; a public road.

those *pron. pl.* plural of that.

though *adv.* however; nevertheless. THOUGH *conj.* although; in spite of the fact that.

thought *n.* 1 the process of thinking or reasoning. 2 an idea or opinion.

thoughtful *adj.* 1 thinking deeply. 2 considerate.

thoughtless *adj.* lacking in thought and consideration.

thousand *n.* ten times a hundred, the symbol 1000.

thrash *v.* 1 to beat and hit repeatedly. 2 THRASH ABOUT to move about violently. THRASHING *n.*

thread *n.* 1 a length of cotton, silk or nylon. 2 the spiral ridge on a screw or inside a nut. 3 the connection between points in a talk or story. THREAD *v.* to pass thread through a needle or opening. 2 to find a way through.

threat *n.* 1 a warning sign of trouble or danger. 2 a source of trouble or danger. THREATEN *v.* THREATENING *adj.*

three *n.* the number one more than two, the symbol 3. THREE-DIMENSIONAL *adj.* (abbrev. 3-D) having or seeming to have length, breadth and depth.

thresh *v.* to separate the grain from the husks in ears of corn.

thrift *n.* careful management of goods or money in order to save. THRIFTY *adj.*

thrill *n.* a sudden feeling of excitement. THRILL *v.* to cause excitement in someone; to feel excitement.

thrive *v.* to grow vigorously; to prosper. THRIVING *adj.*

throat *n.* the front of the neck; the gullet and the windpipe.

throb *v.* to beat with a steady rhythm; to vibrate. THROB *n.* a heat; a vibration.

throne *n.* the seat of a king, queen or bishop.

throttle *v.* 1 to struggle; to choke. 2 to regulate the flow of. THROTTLE *n.* a valve for regulating the flow of air or steam.

through *prep.* 1 from end to end; from the beginning to the end of. 2 as a result of. THROUGH *adv.* all the way.

throughout *adv.* in every part. THROUGHOUT *prep.* from end to end of.

throw v. to fling or hurl. THROW n. 1 the act of throwing. 2 the distance something is thrown.

thrush n. a song-bird with a brown back and speckled breast.

thrust v. to push suddenly or violently; to pierce. THRUST n. a sudden or violent push.

thud n. a dull, low sound. THUD v.

thumb n. the short, thick digit on the hand. THUMB v. to handle or mark with the thumb.

thump v. to hit or beat heavily. THUMP n. a heavy blow or fall.

thunder n. 1 the loud sound that follows lightning. 2 any loud rumbling noise. THUNDER v. to make a sound like thunder; to roll; to rumble loudly.

Thursday n. the fifth day of the week.

thus adv. in this or that way.

thyme n. (pron. TIME) a sweet-smelling herb used in cookery.

tick n. 1 a light regular sound; the sound made by a watch or clock. 2 the mark ✔. TICK v. 1 to make a ticking sound. 2 to make the mark ✔.

ticket n. a piece of card or paper giving the right to be admitted, travel, etc.

tickle v. 1 to touch a person's skin lightly, often producing laughter. 2 to amuse. TICKLE n. 1 the act of tickling. 2 an irritation.

tidal adj. affected by or concerned with the tides.

tide n. 1 the regular rise and fall of the sea. 2 a time or season. 3 something which ebbs and flows.

tidings n. pl. news.

tidy adj. neat; carefully arranged. TIDILY adv. TIDINESS n.

tie v. 1 to fasten with a string or cord. 2 to score equally in a competition or game. TIE n. 1 a link or connection. 2 an equal score. 3 a necktie. TIED adj.

tier n. one of several rows of benches, chairs, etc., placed above and below each other.

tiger n. a large, fierce, striped animal of the cat family. fem. TIGRESS.

tight adj. 1 firmly fastened or stretched. 2 closely fitted or crowded together. TIGHTEN v.

tile n. a thin piece of baked clay or other material for covering roofs, floors or walls. TILE v. to cover with tiles.

till n. a drawer or register for money in a shop. TILL v. to plough and cultivate the land.

tiller n. a lever used to turn the rudder of small boats.

tilt v. to slope to one side; to lean. TILT n. a slant.

timber n. 1 wood used in building, carpentry, etc. 2 trees providing such wood. TIMBERED adj.

time n. 1 the measure or duration of the past, present and future. 2 a particular moment in time. 3 a period of time. 4 the rhythm and speed of a piece of music. TIME v. to measure the time taken to do something. TIME adj. concerned with time.

timid adj. shy; easily frightened. TIMIDLY adv.

timorous adj. timid.

tin n. 1 a soft, silvery-white metal. 2 a can or container made of tin-plate. TIN v. 1 to pack something into tins. 2 to coat with tin.

tinge v. to colour slightly. TINGE n. a faint colouring. TINGED adj.

tingle v. to have a prickly sensation on the skin.

tint n. a shade of colour; a hue. TINT v. to colour; to tinge.

tiny adj. very small.

tip n. 1 the point or end of something. 2 a useful piece of advice. 3 a place where rubbish is dumped. 4 gratuity for service. TIP v. 1 to tilt or overturn. 2 to give a gratuity to. 3 to touch lightly.

tirade n. a long outburst or speech.

tire v. 1 to become or to make weary. 2 TIRE OF to lose interest in. TIRED adj. TIREDNESS n.

tireless adj. never becoming weary; never resting. TIRELESSLY adv.

tiresome adj. annoying; making weary.

tissue n. 1 a fine woven fabric. 2 a paper handkerchief. 3 the substance of which living things are made.

tithe n. 1 a tax of one tenth of the produce of a farm, formerly paid to support the clergy and the church. 2 a tenth part.

title n. 1 the name of a book, play, film or piece of music. 2 a word which shows a person's rank, position or profession. TITLED adj.

toad n. a warty amphibian of the frog family.

toadstool n. an umbrella-shaped kind of fungus, often poisonous.

toast *v.* 1 make (food) crisp and brown by grilling it. 2 to drink to a person's health. TOAST *n.* 1 toasted bread. 2 the act of drinking to a person's health.

tobacco *n.* the dried leaves of the tobacco plant prepared for smoking in cigarettes, cigars and pipes. TOBACCONIST *n.*

toboggan *n.* a long, narrow sledge for use in snow. TOBOGGAN *v.* to travel on a toboggan.

today *n.* this present day.

toe *n.* 1 a digit of the foot. 2 the front part of a shoe, sock or boot.

toffee *n.* a sweet made from boiled sugar, butter, etc.

together *adv.* 1 in company. 2 at the same time.

toil *v.* to work hard. TOIL *n.* heavy work; labour.

toilet *n.* 1 a lavatory. 2 the act of washing, dressing, etc.

token *n.* 1 a sign; a symbol. 2 a piece of metal or plastic used as a coin or ticket.

tolerable *adj.* 1 that can be borne or endured. 2 fairly good.

tolerant *adj.* willing to tolerate opinions and behaviour different from one's own. TOLERANCE *n.*

tolerate *v.* to put up with; to endure. TOLERATION *n.*

toll *n.* 1 a charge made for the use of some roads and bridges. 2 loss and suffering. TOLL *v.* to ring a bell slowly.

tomato *n.* a red, pulpy edible fruit. *pl.* TOMATOES.

tomb *n.* a grave; a burial place.

tomorrow *n.* the day after today.

ton *n.* an imperial measure of weight, 2240 pounds (about 1010 kilograms).

tone *n.* 1 a musical sound. 2 a quality indicating the character of something. 3 a shade or tint of colour. TONE *v.* 1 to give tone or colour to. 2 to blend colours to.

tongue *n.* 1 the movable, fleshy organ in the mouth used in speaking, tasting and swallowing. 2 a language.

tonic *n.* a medicine or influence which improves the health.

tonight *n.* this night.

tonne *n.* a metric unit of mass (weight), 1000 kilograms.

tonsil *n.* one of the two small organs at the back of the throat. TONSILLITIS *n.*

too *adv.* 1 also; in addition. 2 more than is wanted.

tool *n.* an instrument or implement required for doing work.

tooth *n.* 1 one of the bone-like structures rooted in the gums and used for biting and chewing. 2 a tooth-like projection on a comb, gear-wheel or saw. *pl.* TEETH.

toothache *n.* a pain in a tooth or the teeth.

toothless *adj.* without teeth.

top *n.* 1 the highest part of anything. 2 the upper surface. 3 the person or thing in the highest position. 4 spinning toy.

topic *n.* a subject for discussion, study or writing. TOPICAL *adj.*

topography *n.* the physical features of a district or landscape.

tor *n.* a small, rocky hill.

torch *n.* 1 a small portable electric lamp. 2 a piece of blazing material carried to give light.

torment *v.* (pron. tor-MENT) to torture; to cause great suffering. TORMENT *n.* (pron TOR-ment) severe physical or mental suffering. TORMENTOR *n.*

tornado *n.* a violent whirlwind.

torpedo *n.* a self-propelled underwater missile. *pl.* TORPEDOES. TORPEDO *v.* to attack with torpedoes.

torrent *n.* 1 a rushing stream. 2 a heavy downpour of rain. 3 a rush of words. TORRENTIAL *adj.*

torso *n.* the human body without head or limbs; the trunk.

tortoise *n.* a four-legged slow-moving reptile with a hard body shell.

tortuous *adj.* 1 full of twists or turns. 2 devious; not straightforward.

torture *n.* the infliction of severe bodily or mental pain. TORTURE *v.* to inflict such pain upon.

Tory *n.* a member or supporter of the Conservative Party.

toss *v.* 1 to throw lightly, easily or carelessly. 2 to move restlessly from side to side. TOSS *n.* the act of tossing.

total *n.* the full amount; the total number. TOTAL *v.* to find the total; to add up. TOTAL *adj.* whole; complete. TOTALLY *adv.*

touch *v.* 1 to be in contact with; to feel. 2 to obtain the sympathy of. TOUCH *n.* 1 the act of touching. 2 the sense enabling a person to feel. TOUCHING *adj.*

tough *adj.* 1 strong; not easily broken. 2 hard to bite or cut. 3 rough; violent. 4 difficult. TOUGHEN *v.* TOUGHNESS *n.*

tour *n.* a journey from place to place. TOUR *v.* to travel from place to place. TOURISM *n.* travel for pleasure. TOURIST *n.*

tournament *n.* 1 a series of games or contests. 2 formerly, a combat on horseback.

tow *v.* to pull along using a rope or chain. TOW *n.* 1 anything towed. 2 coarse flax.

toward, towards *prep.* in the direction of; approaching.

towel *n.* a cloth for drying things.

tower *n.* a tall, narrow building rising high above others, often part of a church or fortress. TOWER *v.* to rise high above others.

town *n.* 1 a place, larger than a village, with houses, shops, churches, schools, etc. 2 the people living in a town.

toy *n.* a child's plaything. TOY (WITH) *v.* to play frivolously with; to consider idly.

trace *v.* 1 to seek and find. 2 to copy by using transparent paper. TRACE *n.* 1 a mark, sign or piece of evidence. 2 a small quantity. 3 a strap by which a horse pulls a vehicle.

tracery *n.* a delicate pattern of lines.

track *n.* 1 a path or trail made by regular use. 2 a railway line. 3 a series of marks left by a person, animal or vehicle. TRACK *v.* to follow tracks.

tract *n.* 1 a large area or stretch of land. 2 a short pamphlet or book.

traction *n.* the power used in pulling something.

tractor *n.* a motor vehicle for pulling heavy loads.

trade *n.* 1 the buying, selling or exchanging of goods. 2 business. 3 a particular craft or occupation. TRADE *v.* to buy, sell or deal. TRADER *n.*

tradesman *n.* 1 a shopkeeper. 2 a man skilled in a particular trade or craft. *fem.* TRADESWOMAN.

tradition *n.* the ideas, customs, music and stories passed on from one generation to another. TRADITIONAL *adj.* TRADITIONALLY *adv.*

traffic *n.* 1 the movement of people, vehicles, ships and aircraft. 2 trading and dealing. TRAFFIC *v.* to trade, esp. illegally.

tragedy *n.* 1 a tragic event or misfortune. 2 a play with an unhappy ending. *pl.* TRAGEDIES.

tragic *adj.* concerned with tragedy and sadness. TRAGICALLY *adv.*

trail *v.* 1 to drag or pull along. 2 to walk wearily behind. 3 to follow the tracks of. TRAIL *n.* 1 the track left by something. 2 a rough path.

trailer *n.* 1 a vehicle pulled by another. 2 extracts from a film shown to advertise it.

train *v.* to give (to someone) instruction and practice in doing something. 2 to prepare for a particular activity. TRAIN *n.* 1 a number of coaches or wagons drawn by a locomotive. 2 the trailing part of a long dress.

trained *adj.* skilled and efficient through training.

trainer *n.* a person who prepares athletes, horses, etc., for races.

training *n.* practical instruction and education.

trait *n.* a feature of a person's character or personal habits.

traitor *n.* a person who betrays a trust or his country. *fem.* TRAITRESS.

tramp *v.* 1 to walk heavily. 2 to walk for a long distance. TRAMP *n.* 1 a heavy tread. 2 a long walk. 3 a homeless person who walks from place to place. 4 a cargo ship without a regular route.

trample *v.* to tread heavily on.

trance *n.* a sleep-like state; a hypnotic state.

tranquil *adj.* peaceful; quiet; untroubled. TRANQUILLY *adv.* TRANQUILLITY *n.*

transact *v.* to do; to carry through; to carry out (business). TRANSACTION *n.*

transcend *v.* 1 to rise above; to exceed. 2 to go beyond.

transept *n.* an arm of a cross-shaped church, at right angles to the nave.

transfer *v.* (pron. trans-FER) 1 to move a person or thing from one place to another. 2 to give legal possession (of something) to another. TRANSFER *n.* (pron. TRANS-fer) 1 a movement from one place to another. 2 a change of ownership. 3 a small picture that can be transferred from one surface to another.

transform *v.* to make a considerable change in the appearance or shape of. TRANSFORMATION *n.*

transformer *n.* a device that changes electrical voltage.

transfuse *v.* 1 to transfer liquid from one thing to another. 2 to transfer blood from one person's body to that of another person. TRANSFUSION *n.*

transgress *v.* to break the law; to go beyond the limit.

transient *adj.* brief; passing quickly.

transistor *n.* an electronic device used in radio, television, etc.

transit *n.* 1 a passing across. 2 the carrying of passengers, goods, etc., from one place to another.

translate *v.* to turn what is said or written from one language into another. TRANSLATION *n.* TRANSLATOR *n.*

translucent *adj.* almost transparent; allowing some light through, so able to be seen through, but not clearly.

transmission *n.* 1 the act of sending from one person to another. 2 a radio or television broadcast programme.

transmit *v.* 1 to pass on; to communicate. 2 to send out radio or television signals. TRANSMITTER *n.*

transparency *n.* 1 being transparent. 2 a photograph on a transparent film.

transparent *adj.* able to be seen through; allowing light through; not opaque. 2 clear; obvious.

transplant *v.* to plant in another place; to remove to another place.

transport *v.* (pron. trans-PORT) 1 to convey from one place to another. 2 to carry away by strong emotion; to delight. TRANSPORT *n.* (pron. TRANS-port) 1 the act of transporting. 2 vehicles, ships or aircraft used for carrying passengers or goods.

trap *n.* 1 a device for catching wild animals. 2 a plan or trick for catching a person unawares. 3 a small horse-drawn carriage with two wheels. TRAP *v.* to catch in a trap.

trapeze *n.* a swinging bar used by gymnasts and acrobats.

trapper *n.* a person who traps wild animals.

trash *n.* rubbish; refuse.

travel *v.* 1 to make a journey. 2 to move. TRAVEL *n.* 1 movement. 2 a journey. TRAVELLED *adj.* TRAVELLING *n.*

traverse *v.* to go across; to pass through. TRAVERSING *adj.*

trawl *n.* a wide-mouthed net used in fishing. TRAWL *v.* to drag a net along the sea bed.

trawler *n.* a fishing-boat which drags a trawl.

tray *n.* a flat piece of wood, metal or plastic, with raised edges, for carrying things.

treacherous *adj.* 1 deceptive; unreliable. 2 disloyal; not to be trusted.

treachery *n.* betrayal; disloyalty.

treacle *n.* a thick, sweet syrup obtained from sugar.

tread *v.* 1 to walk; to step. 2 TREAD UPON to trample. TREAD *n.* 1 the act of stepping. 2 the horizontal part of a step or a stair. 3 the moulded part of a tyre which touches the road.

treason *n.* 1 disloyalty to a cause or friend. 2 the betrayal of a country or its secrets to an enemy.

treasure *n.* 1 a store of valuables. 2 anything of great value. TREASURE *v.* to value highly.

treasurer *n.* a person responsible for the funds and accounts of a club, society or business.

treasury *n.* 1 a storage place for valuables. 2 a Government department which is responsible for the nation's finances.

treat *v.* 1 to deal with in a certain way. 2 to give medical attention to somebody. 3 to pay for food, drink or entertainment for (somebody).

treatment *n.* 1 a particular way in which anything is dealt with. 2 the method of treating a patient or disease.

treaty *n.* an agreement between nations.

treble *n.* 1 the highest part in music. 2 a boy with a high singing voice. TREBLE *v.* to multiply by three. TREBLE *adj.* three times as much; three times as many.

tree *n.* a large plant having a wooden trunk from which leaf-bearing branches grow.

trek *v.* to make a long and exhausting journey. TREK *n.* a long and exhausting journey.

tremble *v.* to shake; to shudder with anger, cold, fear, etc. TREMBLE *n.* a shake; a shudder.

tremendous *adj.* 1 very great or powerful. 2 dreadful; fearful.

tremor *n.* a shudder; a vibration; a quiver.

tremulous *adj.* trembling; timid. TREMULOUSLY *adv.*

trench *n.* a long narrow ditch cut in the ground.

trend *n.* the general direction or tendency; a fashion. TRENDY *adj.* fashionable.

trepidation *n.* fear; alarm; anxiety.

trespass *v.* 1 to sin. 2 TRESPASS UPON to enter (another person's property) without permission. 3 to intrude upon. TRESPASS *n.* 1 an act of trespassing. 2 a sin. TRESPASSER *n.* 1 a person who enters property without permission. 2 a sinner.

trestle *n.* a movable frame for supporting a table top, bench or platform.

trial *n.* 1 a test; an experiment. 2 a law-court hearing. 3 an affliction or hardship.

triangle *n.* 1 a shape with three sides and three angles. 2 a percussion instrument shaped like a triangle. TRIANGULAR *adj.*

tribe *n.* a group of families or a race of people ruled by a chief. TRIBAL *adj.*

tribunal *n.* 1 a court of justice. 2 a court appointed to deal with a particular type of problem or a specific question.

tributary *n.* a stream or river flowing into another. TRIBUTARY *adj.* paying tribute.

tribute *n.* 1 something said, done or given to show respect or admiration. 2 a tax paid by one nation to another.

trick *n.* 1 a deceitful act or scheme. 2 a clever act meant to amuse or entertain. 3 the cards played in one round of whist, etc. TRICK *v.* to deceive by a trick; to cheat.

trickle *v.* to flow in drops or a small stream. TRICKLE *n.* a small stream.

tricky *adj.* 1 artful; cunning. 2 difficult. TRICKILY *adv.*

tricycle *n.* a cycle with three wheels.

trident *n.* a spear with three prongs.

tried *adj.* tested and proved.

trifle *n.* 1 something of very little importance. 2 a small amount. 3 a sweet dish made of cake, jam, cream, custard, etc. TRIFLE (WITH) *v.* to treat (something) lightly.

trigger *n.* the catch or lever which fires a gun.

trigonometry *n.* the branch of mathematics dealing with the relationship between the sides and angles of a triangle.

trigraph *n.* three letters representing one sound, e.g. s<u>igh</u>, ju<u>dge</u>.

trim *adj.* neat and tidy. TRIM *v.* 1 to make neat and tidy. 2 to decorate. 3 to balance a boat or aircraft. TRIM *n.* fitness; condition.

trio *n.* 1 a group of three musicians or singers. 2 a piece of music for three musicians or singers.

trip *v.* 1 to stumble. 2 to step lightly and quickly. TRIP *n.* 1 a stumble. 2 a light, quick step. 3 a journey; an outing.

tripe *n.* part of the stomach of an ox or a cow used as food.

triple *adj.* 1 having three parts. 2 three times as much or as many. TRIPLE *v.* to multiply by three.

triplet *n.* one of three children born to the same mother at one birth.

tripod *n.* a stand or support having three legs.

triumph *n.* victory; a great success. TRIUMPH *v.* to win a victory; to be very successful. TRIUMPHAL *adj.*

triumphant *adj.* victorious; successful. TRIUMPHANTLY *adv.*

trivial *adj.* of small value or importance. TRIVIALITY *n.*

trolley *n.* 1 a small truck or handcart. 2 a small table on wheels.

trombone *n.* a large brass wind instrument with a sliding tube for changing notes.

troop *n.* 1 a group of people or animals. 2 a company of soldiers. TROOP *v.* to move in a large group.

trophy *n.* 1 a prize. 2 something kept as a souvenir of a victory or success.

tropic *n.* one of the two imaginary circles around the Earth between the equator and the poles. TROPICS *n. pl.* the hot regions between the Tropic of Cancer and the Tropic of Capricorn.

tropical *adj.* 1 of or from (one of) the tropics. 2 hot. 3 exotic.

trot *v.* to run at a moderate pace. TROT *n.* 1 a moderate run. 2 a horse's pace between a walk and a gallop.

trouble *n.* 1 worry; vexation. 2 grief; difficulty. 3 disturbance; discontent. TROUBLE *v.* 1 to worry or be worried. 2 to disturb or be disturbed. TROUBLED *adj.* TROUBLESOME *adj.*

trough *n.* 1 a long, narrow receptacle for animals to drink or feed from. 2 the hollow between two waves. 3 an area of low barometric pressure.

trousers *n. pl.* a garment with two legs covering the body from waist to ankles.

trousseau *n.* (pron. TROO-so) a bride's outfit of clothes.

trout *n.* a small freshwater fish, held in high regard as food and game.

trowel *n.* 1 a flat-bladed tool used for laying bricks. 2 a small hand tool for use in a garden.

truancy *n.* the act of being absent from school without permission.

truant *n.* a pupil who is absent from school without permission.

truce *n.* an agreement to cease fighting for a time.

truck *n.* 1 a lorry; a heavy goods vehicle. 2 an open railway wagon. 3 a trolley; a barrow.

truculent *adj.* very aggressive and critical.

trudge *v.* to walk with weary, heavy steps. TRUDGE *n.* a long, weary walk.

true *adj.* 1 real; genuine; in accordance with fact. 2 loyal; faithful. 3 reliable; trustworthy. TRULY *adv.*

trumpet *n.* a brass wind instrument.

truncate *v.* to cut the top or end off.

truncheon *n.* a short club or cudgel as carried by the police.

trundle *v.* to roll or push along.

trunk *n.* 1 the main stem of a tree. 2 a torso; a body without head or limbs. 3 a large chest or box with a hinged lid. 4 the long nose of an elephant.

truss *n.* 1 a bundle of hay or straw. 2 a bandage for support. 3 supporting structure of a roof or bridge. TRUSS (UP) *v.* to tie up in a bundle.

trust *v.* 1 to rely upon; to believe in. 2 to hope. TRUST *n.* 1 confidence or faith in. 2 responsibility. 3 property placed in the care of a trustee.

trustee *n.* a person to whom property is entrusted.

truth *n.* whatever is true; reality; fact. TRUTHFUL *adj.*

try *v.* 1 to attempt; to make an effort. 2 to test or examine (something). 3 to put on trial. TRYING *adj.*

tube *n.* 1 a hollow length of metal or flexible material for carrying water, gas, petrol, etc. 2 a soft container for toothpaste, ointment, etc., which can be squeezed out. 3 an underground railway in London.

tuck *v.* to fold in or under. TUCK *n.* a fold made in a garment or a piece of material.

Tudor *n.* an English royal family which ruled between 1485 and 1603. TUDOR *adj.* of the Tudor period.

Tuesday *n.* the third day of the week.

tuft *n.* a bunch of feathers, hair or grass growing together.

tug *v.* 1 to give a sudden pull. 2 to pull along, to drag. TUG *n.* 1 a sudden pull. 2 a small, powerful boat which tows larger vessels.

tuition *n.* teaching; instruction.

tulip *n.* a bell-shaped flower which grows from a bulb.

tumble *v.* 1 to fall. 2 to perform acrobatics. TUMBLE *n.* a fall.

tumbler *n.* 1 an acrobat. 2 a drinking-glass.

tumour *n.* a swelling; a growth in the body.

tumult *n.* an uproar; a great disorder. TUMULTUOUS *adj.*

tumulus *n.* an ancient burial mound. *pl.* TUMULI.

tundra *n.* a vast, treeless plain with arctic climate and vegetation.

tune *n.* a musical melody or air. TUNE *v.* 1 to correct the pitch of (a musical instrument). 2 to adjust (an engine or other mechanism) to give maximum performance. TUNEFUL *adj.* TUNELESS *adj.*

tunic *n.* 1 a uniform jacket worn by policemen, members of the forces, etc. 2 loose garment hanging from the shoulders to the hips.

tunnel *n*. an underground passage. TUNNEL *v*. to dig or bore a tunnel; to burrow. TUNNELLING *n*.

turban *n*. a man's head-dress made by winding a long cloth round the head, worn by Muslims, Hindus and Sikhs.

turbine *n*. an engine which is operated by a jet of gas, steam or air.

turf *n*. a layer of soil with grass growing on it. TURN *v*. to cover with turf.

turkey *n*. a large bird reared as food.

Turkish *adj*. belonging to Turkey or its people. TURKISH *n*. the language of the Turks. TURK *n*.

turmoil *n*. agitation; tumult; confusion.

turn *v*. 1 to change direction. 2 to revolve; to rotate. 3 to alter; to convert. 4 TURN ON to switch on. TURN *n*. 1 a change of direction. 2 a revolution; a rotation. TURNING *n*.

turnip *n*. a large root vegetable.

turquoise *n*. 1 a precious stone, greenish-blue in colour. 2 a greenish-blue colour.

turret *n*. 1 a small tower, often on top of a castle or building. 2 a revolving protection for mounted guns.

turtle *n*. a sea reptile with a hard shell and flippers.

tusk *n*. a long, pointed tooth projecting beyond the mouth as in the elephant, walrus, etc.

tutor *n*. a teacher; an instructor. TUTORIAL *adj*.

tweed *n*. a heavy, woven, woollen cloth.

tweezers *n. pl*. small pincer-like instrument for picking up small objects or plucking out hairs.

twelve *n*. the number one more than eleven, the symbol 12; one dozen.

twenty *n*. the number one more than nineteen, the symbol 20.

twice *adv*. two times; on two occasions.

twig *n*. a small shoot or branch of a shrub or tree.

twilight *n*. the faint light before sunrise and after sunset.

twill *n*. a woven fabric with diagonal lines or ribs on the surface.

twin *n*. one of two children born to the same mother at one birth.

twine *n*. strong cord made of strands twisted together. TWINE *v*. to twist together; to wind round one another.

twinkle *v*. 1 to sparkle. 2 to shine with a light that comes and goes. TWINKLE *n*. a sparkle or shine.

twirl *v*. to whirl or spin round rapidly. TWIRL *n*. a whirling or rapid spin.

twist *v*. 1 to turn (something) round. 2 to turn and curve. 3 to bend out of shape. TWIST *n*. twisting or being twisted.

twitch *v*. to jerk; to move jerkily. TWITCH *n*. a sudden jerk.

two *n*. the number one more than one, the symbol 2.

type *n*. 1 a kind; a sort; a species. 2 an example; a specimen. 3 a letter or symbol, usually in metal, for printing. TYPE *v*. to use a typewriter.

typewriter *n*. a machine with a keyboard, for printing letters on paper.

typhoid *n*. an infectious disease, producing a fever, caused by germs in contaminated water or food.

typhoon *n*. a violent hurricane or whirlwind.

typhus *n*. a dangerous disease transmitted by small parasitic insects.

typical *adj*. serving as an example or type; normal; usual.

typist *n*. a person skilled in the use of a typewriter.

tyranny *n*. the rule of a tyrant. TYRANNICAL *adj*. acting like a tyrant.

tyrant *n*. a cruel, harsh ruler or person.

tyre *n*. 1 an air-filled rubber tube round a vehicle wheel. 2 a metal or rubber rim round a wheel.

U

Note: some words beginning with UN have not been included. UN is a prefix which usually means *not* **or** *the opposite of.* **For instance,** *unashamed* **means** *not ashamed.* **You would, therefore, look up the word** *ashamed.*

udder *n*. the bag or glands of a cow, goat or sheep where the milk is made and stored.

ugly *adj*. 1 unpleasant or repulsive in appearance. 2 dangerous; threatening. UGLINESS *n*.

ulcer *n*. an open sore on the external or internal surface of the body.

ultimate *adj*. the last of all; final. ULTIMATELY *adv*.

ultimatum *n.* a final offer or demand.

ultrasonic *adj.* beyond the normal hearing range.

umbrella *n.* 1 a light, folding, metal framework, covered with fabric to give protection against rain. 2 a protective canopy or covering.

umpire *n.* 1 a referee in certain games. 2 a person appointed to decide a question of dispute. UMPIRE *v.* to referee; to judge.

unable *adj.* not able to; powerless.

unabridged *adj.* complete; not shortened or censored.

unacceptable *adj.* not acceptable; unwelcome.

unaccepted *adj.* refused; rejected.

unaccompanied *adj.* alone; not escorted.

unaccountable *adj.* not able to be explained; not responsible.

unaccustomed *adj.* not used to; unusual; strange.

unaided *adj.* without help; single-handed.

unaltered *adj.* unchanged; remaining the same.

unanimous *adj.* with the agreement of everyone; all of one mind. UNANIMOUSLY *adv.*

unarmed *adj.* without weapons.

unassuming *adj.* modest; humble.

unattached *adj.* independent; free.

unattainable *adj.* that cannot be obtained or reached.

unavoidable *adj.* certain; not able to be avoided. UNAVOIDABLY *adv.*

unaware *adj.* not knowing; ignorant of.

unbearable *adj.* that cannot be borne or endured. UNBEARABLY *adv.*

unbecoming *adj.* not suitable; not appropriate.

unbelieving *adj.* not believing; doubting. UNBELIEVABLE *adj.*

unbounded *adj.* without bounds or limits.

unbroken *adj.* 1 continuous; uninterrupted. 2 whole; entire.

uncanny *adj.* mysterious; strange; weird. UNCANNILY *adv.*

unceasing *adj.* continual; endless. UNCEASINGLY *adv.*

uncertain *adj.* doubtful; not reliable; changeable. UNCERTAINLY *adv.* UNCERTAINTY *n.*

unchanging *adj.* fixed; consistent.

uncivilised *adj.* primitive; rough.

uncle *n.* the brother of a mother or father; the husband of an aunt.

unclean *adj.* dirty; impure.

uncomfortable *adj.* lacking comfort; uneasy. UNCOMFORTABLY *adv.*

uncommon *adj.* rare; unusual; remarkable. UNCOMMONLY *adv.*

unconcern *n.* lack of worry, anxiety or care. UNCONCERNED *adj.*

unconditional *adj.* without conditions; complete. UNCONDITIONALLY *adv.*

unconscious *adj.* 1 not conscious. 2 not aware. UNCONSCIOUSLY *adv.* UNCONSCIOUSNESS *n.*

uncontrollable *adj.* unmanageable; beyond control; unruly. UNCONTROLLABLY *adv.*

unconvincing *adj.* uncertain; not easy to believe. UNCONVINCINGLY *adv.*

uncouth *adj.* clumsy; awkward; vulgar; rough.

uncover *v.* to expose; to reveal; to remove a cover.

undaunted *adj.* fearless; not dismayed.

undecided *adj.* 1 not decided; not certain. 2 hesitating; doubtful.

undeniable *adj.* that cannot be denied; certain. UNDENIABLY *adv.*

under *prep.* beneath; below. UNDER *adv.* in a lower position. UNDER *adj.* lower.

undercharge *v.* to charge less or too little.

undercurrent *n.* a current flowing beneath the surface.

undergo *v.* to suffer; to bear.

underground *adj.* 1 below the ground. 2 secret or concealed. UNDERGROUND *n.* 1 an underground railway. 2 a secret movement.

undergrown *adj.* not fully grown; undersized.

undergrowth *n.* shrubs or small trees growing under larger ones.

underline *v.* 1 to draw a line under (a word). 2 to emphasise; to stress.

underlying *adj.* lying under; forming the basis of.

undermine *v.* 1 to dig beneath and weaken. 2 to weaken or wear out slowly.

underneath *adv.* beneath; below; lower. UNDERNEATH *prep.* beneath; below.

underrate *v.* to underestimate; to rate too low.

understand *v.* 1 to know the meaning of. 2 to have a thorough knowledge of. 3 to comprehend.

understandable *adj.* 1 clear; easily understood. 2 excusable; forgivable.

understanding *n.* 1 the ability to see the full meaning; intelligence. 2 an agreement.

understatement *n.* 1 an insufficient description. 2 less than the truth.

understudy *n.* a person who is able to take the part or place of another.

undertake *v.* 1 to promise to do something. 2 to attempt.

undertaker *n.* a person who makes funeral arrangements.

undertaking *n.* 1 something which is being attempted. 2 a business. 3 a promise.

undeserved *adj.* not deserved.

undesirable *adj.* not wanted; unpleasant; unwelcome. UNDESIRABLY *adv.*

undisciplined *adj.* unruly; lacking discipline.

undiscovered *adj.* not found; hidden.

undisturbed *adj.* 1 not altered. 2 not troubled; calm.

undivided *adj.* complete; whole.

undo *v.* 1 to untie or unfasten. 2 to reverse; to destroy.

undoubted *adj.* certain; without any doubt or question. UNDOUBTEDLY *adv.*

undulating *adj.* 1 having the appearance of waves. 2 gently rising and falling.

unduly *adv.* too much; more than is necessary.

unearned *adj.* not earned; not gained by work or service.

unearth *v.* 1 to dig up. 2 to discover; to find by searching.

uneasy *adj.* restless; uncomfortable. UNEASILY *adv.* UNEASE *n.*

unemployed *adj.* 1 out of work. 2 not being used.

uneven *adj.* 1 not smooth or level. 2 not of the same length. 3 not of the same quality throughout.

unexpected *adj.* 1 not expected or foreseen. 2 surprising. UNEXPECTED *adv.*

unfair *adj.* unjust; not impartial. UNFAIRLY *adv.*

unfaithful *adj.* disloyal; deceitful.

unfamiliar *adj.* strange; uncommon; not well known.

unfavourable *adj.* not encouraging; adverse. UNFAVOURABLY *adv.*

unfeeling *adj.* unsympathetic; without feeling.

unfit *adj.* 1 not suitable. 2 not fit; unhealthy.

unfold *v.* 1 to open out. 2 to tell; to reveal.

unfortunate *adj.* 1 unlucky; unhappy. 2 unsuccessful. UNFORTUNATELY *adv.*

unfounded *adj.* 1 without foundation; not based on facts. 2 untrue.

unfriendly *adj.* hostile; unkind.

ungainly *adj.* clumsy; awkward.

ungrateful *adj.* showing no gratitude or thanks. UNGRATEFULLY *adv.*

unguarded *adj.* 1 without a guard; unprotected. 2 careless; heedless.

unhappy *adj.* 1 sad; sorrowful. 2 unfortunate; unsuitable. UNHAPPILY *adv.*

unhealthy *adj.* 1 damaging to health. 2 sickly; diseased.

unheeded *adj.* ignored; not noticed.

unhesitating *adj.* 1 without hesitation. 2 prompt; ready. UNHESITATINGLY *adv.*

uniform *adj.* always the same; not changing. UNIFORM *n.* the official clothing worn by members of a team, the police, military forces etc.

uninhabited *adj.* not lived in; deserted.

unintelligible *adj.* not able to be understood.

unintentional *adj.* not intended; accidental. UNINTENTIONALLY *adv.*

union *n.* 1 the joining together as one; being united. 2 an association of workers.

unique *adj.* being the only one of its kind; having no likeness or equal. UNIQUELY *adv.*

unison *n.* a tune in which everyone sings the same notes; agreement.

unit *n.* 1 a single thing or person; one. 2 a quantity or amount used as a basis for measurement.

unite *v.* 1 to join together. 2 to make or become one; to combine. UNITED *adj.*

unity *n.* 1 one; oneness; being one, single or individual. 2 harmony; agreement.

universal *adj.* concerning everything and everybody. UNIVERSALLY *adv.*

universe *n.* all existing things; the whole of creation.

university *n.* a place of learning and research. *pl.* UNIVERSITIES.

unjust *adj.* not fair; not just. UNJUSTLY *adv.*

unkind *adj.* not kind; harsh; cruel. UNKINDNESS *n.*

unknown *adj.* 1 undiscovered; unexplored. 2 not identified.

unlawful *adj.* not permitted by law; illegal. UNLAWFULLY *adv.*

unless *conj.* if not; except when.

unlike *adj.* not like; different from.

unlikely *adj.* improbable.

unlimited *adj.* very numerous; without limit.

unloosen *v.* to unfasten; to set free.

unlucky *adj.* unfortunate; unsuccessful. UNLUCKILY *adj.*

unmanageable *adj.* unruly; difficult to control or handle.

unmannerly *adj.* rude; impolite.

unmentionable *adj.* not fit to be spoken of; unspeakable.

unmerciful *adj.* cruel; inhuman.

unmerited *adj.* not deserved.

unmistakable *adj.* certain; undoubted; obvious. UNMISTAKABLY *adv.*

unmoved *adj.* firm; calm; not affected by emotion.

unnatural *adj.* strange; artificial; not according to nature.

unnecessary *adj.* not needed; superfluous. UNNECESSARILY *adv.*

unnerve *v.* to frighten; to weaken.

unnoticed *adj.* not seen; ignored; overlooked.

unobservant *adj.* not seeing; not noticing.

unobtrusive *adj.* modest; not prominent; reserved.

unperturbed *adj.* calm; not upset.

unpleasant *adj.* disagreeable; not pleasing.

unpopular *adj.* disliked; not in favour. UNPOPULARITY *n.*

unpromising *adj.* not showing promise; unfavourable.

unquestionable *adj.* certain; beyond doubt.

unravel *v.* to disentangle; to solve a problem.

unreasonable *adj.* 1 absurd; foolish. 2 excessive.

unreliable *adj.* not trustworthy; uncertain.

unrest *n.* a state of trouble or discontent; disturbance.

unrivalled *adj.* unequalled; without rivals.

unruly *adj.* disorderly; badly behaved; hard to control. UNRULINESS *n.*

unsatisfactory *adj.* poor; not good enough. UNSATISFACTORILY *adv.*

unsatisfied *adj.* discontented; not convinced.

unscrupulous *adj.* without any regard for rightness, honesty or detail.

unseen *adj.* unnoticed; invisible.

unselfish *adj.* generous; showing concern for others.

unsettle *v.* to upset; to disturb; to make restless.

unsightly *adj.* ugly; not pleasing to see.

unskilled *adj.* not trained, experienced or skilled.

unstable *adj.* not steady; not secure.

unsuccessful *adj.* not able to achieve aims; unfortunate.

unsuspecting *adj.* having no suspicions; trusting.

unsympathetic *adj.* lacking sympathy; unkind.

untidiness *n.* a lack of neatness and order.

untidy *adj.* not neat and orderly; careless.

until *conj.* till; up to the time when. UNTIL *prep.* till; up to the time of.

untiring *adj.* persistent; tireless.

unto *prep.* to.

untrue *adj.* 1 false; inaccurate. 2 not faithful. 3 not straight, level or exact. UNTRULY *adv.*

untruth *n.* a lie; a falsehood. UNTRUTHFUL *adj.*

unusual *adj.* uncommon; remarkable; strange. UNUSUALLY *adv.*

unvarying *adj.* not changing; steady; reliable.

unwary *adj.* incautious.

unwell *adj.* ill; not in good health.

unwind *v.* to undo; to uncoil.

unwise *adj.* foolish; showing bad judgement.

unworthy *adj.* without merit; dishonourable. UNWORTHILY *adv.* UNWORTHINESS *n.*

unwrap *v.* to undo; to take out of the wrapping.

unyielding *adj.* firm; determined.

up *adv.* 1 to a higher place; in a high place. 2 out of bed and dressed. 3 completely; absolutely. 4 finished.

uphold *v.* to defend; to support; to maintain.

upholster *v.* to pad and cover chairs and other seats. UPHOLSTERY *n.* UPHOLSTERER *n.*

upkeep *n.* 1 the cost of keeping something in good repair. 2 maintenance.

upon *prep.* on.

upper *adj.* higher in place. UPPER *n.* the upper part of a shoe or boot.

uppermost *adj.* the highest in rank or place.

upright *adj.* 1 vertical; erect. 2 honest; honourable. UPRIGHT *n.* a vertical post or support.

uprising *n.* a revolt; a mutiny.

uproar *n.* shouting; disturbance; tumult.

uproot *v.* to pull out by the roots.

upset *v.* 1 to overturn. 2 to disarrange; to confuse. 3 to disturb the temper or digestion. UPSET *n.* disorder; confusion.

upstairs *adv.* on a higher floor.

upthrust *n.* 1 an upward push or thrust. 2 in water or air, a force which balances gravity and keeps objects afloat or airborne.

upward *adj.* going up towards something higher or overhead.

upwards *adv.* in an upward direction; more.

uranium *n.* a radioactive metal used as a source of atomic energy.

urban *adj.* belonging to a city or large town.

urge *v.* 1 to drive on. 2 to try to persuade. URGE *n.* a strong desire; a longing.

urgency *n.* the need to act immediately.

urgent *adj.* needing immediate attention or action. URGENTLY *adv.*

urine *n.* a pale-yellow liquid, containing bodily waste, filtered from the blood by the kidneys and discharged via the bladder.

usable *adj.* that can be used.

usage *n.* 1 the method of using. 2 the custom or habit.

use *v.* (pron. YOOZ) 1 to do something with; to employ. 2 to consume. USE *n.* (pron. YOOS) 1 the work done; employment. 2 the ability or right to use. USEFUL *adj.* USEFULNESS *n.*

useless *adj.* 1 serving no useful purpose. 2 having no effect. USELESSLY *adv.* USELESSNESS *n.*

usual *adj.* common; normal; happening often. USUALLY *adv.*

utensil *n.* an instrument; a tool; a dish or pan.

utilise *v.* to make use of.

utility *n.* 1 usefulness. 2 something useful. 3 a useful service.

utmost *adj.* 1 the farthest; the most distant. 2 the greatest; the strongest.

utter *adj.* complete; total. UTTER *v.* 1 to speak. 2 to issue false coins or banknotes. UTTERANCE *n.*

utterly *adv.* fully; completely.

V

vacancy *n.* 1 emptiness. 2 an unfilled job or post.

vacant *adj.* 1 empty; not filled or occupied. 2 dreamy; stupid.

vacate *v.* 1 to leave empty. 2 to give up possession of.

vacation *n.* a holiday.

vaccinate *v.* to inoculate with a vaccine to obtain protection against smallpox and other diseases. VACCINATION *n.*

vaccine *n.* a substance containing a virus introduced into the body by inoculation to obtain immunity to a disease.

vacuum *n.* a space that is completely empty; a space from which all air has been removed.

vagabond *n.* a wanderer; a tramp.

vagrant *n.* a wanderer; a tramp or beggar.

vague *adj.* not clear; not certain. VAGUELY *adv.* VAGUENESS *n.*

vain *adj.* 1 useless; unsuccessful. 2 proud and conceited. VAINLY *adj.*

vale *n.* a valley.

valentine *n.* a card sent anonymously on St. Valentine's Day, 14th February; a sweetheart chosen on this day.

valiant *adj.* brave; courageous. VALIANTLY *adv.*

valid *adj.* 1 sound; good. 2 legally acceptable.

valley *n.* lowland between hills or mountains.

valour *n.* personal courage, etc. in battle; bravery.

valuable *adj.* 1 of great value. 2 precious; very useful.

valuation *n.* an estimation of the value of something.

value *n.* 1 the amount something is worth in money. 2 the importance or worth of something. VALUE *v.* 1 to estimate the worth of (something). 2 to have a high opinion of. VALUED *adj.* VALUELESS *adj.*

valve *n.* 1 a device for controlling the flow of air, gas or liquid through a pipe. 2 an electronic device used in radios, etc.

vampire *n.* 1 a legendary spirit that sucked the blood of sleeping people. 2 a species of bat.

van *n.* 1 a vehicle for carrying goods. 2 *abbrev.* of VANGUARD *n.* the leading part of an army or a fleet.

vandal *n.* a person who deliberately spoils or destroys things. VANDALISM *n.*

vane *n.* 1 a weathercock. 2 the blade of a propeller or water-wheel; the sail of a windmill.

vanilla *n.* the flavouring obtained from the pod of vanilla, a tropical plant, used in cakes, ice cream and chocolate.

vanish *v.* to disappear; to pass out of sight.

vanity *n.* conceit; excessive pride.

vanquish *v.* to defeat; to overcome.

vapour *n.* 1 the gas into which most liquids and solids can be turned by heat. 2 steam; mist.

variable *adj.* changeable.

variation *n.* change; alteration.

varied *adj.* different; of various sorts.

variegated *adj.* marked with different colours. VARIEGATE *v.* VARIEGATION *n.*

variety *n.* 1 the absence of monotony or sameness. 2 a number of different things. VARIETY SHOW an entertainment consisting of singing, dancing, comedy, etc.

various *adj.* 1 different. 2 of many kinds. VARIOUSLY *adj.*

varnish *n.* a clear liquid which gives a hard, glossy surface to canvas, wood, paint, etc. VARNISH *v.* to coat with varnish.

vary *v.* 1 to make or become different. 2 to differ; to disagree.

vase *n.* a jar of glass, pottery, etc., used as an ornament or for holding cut flowers.

vast *adj.* immense; huge; very great. VASTNESS *n.*

vat *n.* a large tub or container for liquids.

vault *n.* 1 an arched ceiling. 2 a cellar. 3 a leap or spring over something. VAULT *v.* to leap or spring over (something). VAULTED *adj.*

veal *n.* the flesh of a calf as food.

veer *v.* to change direction. VEERING *adj.*

vegetable *n.* a plant grown for food. VEGETABLE *adj.* concerning or made from plants.

vegetarian *n.* a person who eats no flesh or animal food.

vegetation *n.* plant life.

vehicle *n.* 1 any conveyance that carries passengers or goods over land or in space. 2 the means by which something is done.

veil *n.* 1 a piece of light material used to hide or protect the face. 2 a curtain. VEIL *v.* to conceal; to cover.

vein *n.* 1 blood vessel through which blood flows back to the heart. 2 the small rib of a leaf. 3 a seam of mineral in rock.

velocity *n.* 1 speed. 2 rate of motion in a given direction.

velvet *n.* a closely-woven fabric with a thick, short pile. VELVETY *adj.*

vendetta *n.* a quarrel or feud between families, often started by a murder.

veneer *v.* to cover (a piece of wood) with a thin layer of finer quality. VENEER *n.* 1 a thin layer of wood. 2 outward show or appearance.

vengeance *n.* revenge; infliction of punishment for wrong done.

venison *n.* the flesh of a deer as food.

venom *n.* 1 the poison from snakes and other poisonous animals. 2 spite; hatred.

vent *n.* 1 a hole or slit to allow air, liquid or smoke to pass through. 2 an outlet. VENT *v.* to pour out or give outlet to feelings.

ventilate *v.* 1 to allow fresh air to circulate freely. 2 to discuss (something) freely. VENTILATION *n.* VENTILATOR *n.*

ventriloquist *n.* a person who can make his/her voice appear to come from some other person or place. VENTRILOQUISM *n.*

venture *n.* an adventurous or risky undertaking. VENTURE *v.* to risk; to dare.

venue *n.* a meeting-place.

Venus *n.* 1 a bright planet which moves round the sun. 2 in Roman mythology, the goddess of beauty and love.

veranda *n.* an open platform, running alongside a house, with a roof supported on pillars.

verb *n.* the word in a sentence that tells what a thing does or what is done to it.

verbal *adj.* spoken; not written. VERBALLY *adv.*

verbatim *adv.* word for word.

verdict *n.* 1 the decision given by a jury in a court of law. 2 a decision; a judgement.

verge *n.* 1 the border, brink or edge. 2 the grass border alongside a road or path. VERGE (ON) *v.* to border on.

verify *v.* to prove the truth or accuracy of (a statement, evidence, etc.). VERIFICATION *n.*

vermilion *n.* a bright red colour.

vermin *n.* small destructive animals, such as mice, rats, fleas, lice, etc. VERMINOUS *adj.*

verruca *n.* a type of wart, usually on the foot.

versatile *adj.* turning easily from one subject or task to another; adaptable. VERSATILITY *n.*

verse *n.* 1 a group of rhymed lines in a poem or song. 2 poetry.

version *n.* 1 a description; an account. 2 a translation of a book.

versus *prep.* against.

vertebra *n.* each of the segments forming the backbone or spine. *pl.* VERTEBRAE.

vertebrate *n.* an animal which has a backbone or spine.

vertex *n.* in maths, a corner; the highest point. *pl.* VERTICES.

vertical *adj.* upright; perpendicular. VERTICALLY *adv.*

very *adj.* real; true. VERY *adv.* to a great extent; extremely.

vessel *n.* 1 a container for holding liquids. 2 a ship or boat.

vest *n.* 1 an undergarment worn next to the skin. 2 a waistcoat.

vestige *n.* a small trace or sign of something.

vestment *n.* a robe esp. one worn by clergy during church services.

vestry *n.* a room in a church where vestments, robes, registers, etc., are kept.

veteran *n.* a person who has had long experience or service. VETERAN *adj.* old and experienced.

veterinary *adj.* concerned with the diseases and injuries of domestic animals.

veto *v.* to forbid or reject. VETO *n.* the power or right to forbid or reject a legal instruction or proposed law.

vex *v.* to annoy; to irritate. VEXED *adj.*

via *prep.* by way of; through.

viaduct *n.* a long bridge built on a series of arches to carry a road or railway.

vibrate *v.* to throb; to tremble; to quiver. VIBRATION *n.*

vicar *n.* a clergyman or clergywoman responsible for a parish. VICARAGE *n.* the house of a vicar.

vice *n.* 1 evil; wickedness. 2 a sin; a wicked habit. 3 an appliance with two jaws which can grip and hold tightly. VICE *(prefix)* in place of; second in rank e.g. vice-president, vice-admiral.

vicinity *n.* the surrounding area; the neighbourhood.

vicious *adj.* spiteful; evil. VICIOUSLY *adv.*

victim *n.* 1 a killed or injured person or creature. 2 a person who suffers injury or loss.

victor *n.* a person who wins a contest; a conqueror.

victory *n.* success in a contest or battle. VICTORIOUS *adj.* VICTORIOUSLY *adv.*

victuals *n. pl.* food; provisions.

videophone *n.* a telephone equipped for transmitting pictures of the speakers.

videotape *n.* a magnetic tape used to record television pictures.

view *n.* 1 a scene; a sight of anything. 2 an opinion. VIEW *v.* to look at; to examine.

viewpoint *n.* perspective; point of view.

vigil *n.* a time of watching and waiting.

vigilant *adj.* watchful; wakeful; cautious.

vigour *n.* 1 strength; energy. 2 healthy growth. VIGOROUS *adj.* VIGOROUSLY *adv.*

Viking *n.* a Scandinavian sea-adventurer of the eighth to tenth centuries.

vile *adj.* 1 shameful; disgusting. 2 unpleasant; bad.

village *n.* a group of houses in a country area. VILLAGER *n.*

vindicate *v.* to clear of blame; to prove (someone or something) to be right, just or innocent. VINDICATION *n.*

vindictive *adj.* revengeful; spiteful.

vine *n.* any climbing plant with a slender stem, but esp. one that bears grapes.

vinegar *n.* an acid liquid obtained from wine, malt, etc., and used for flavouring and pickling food. VINEGARY *adj.*

vineyard *n*. a plantation of grape-vines.

viola *n*. 1 a stringed musical instrument like a large violin. 2 the family of plants to which violets and pansies belong.

violate *v*. 1 to break an agreement or treaty. 2 to break in upon.

violence *n*. 1 brutal conduct or physical force. 2 intense force.

violent *adj*. 1 using or having great physical force. 2 strong; wild. VIOLENTLY *adv*.

violet *n*. a small, purplish-blue flower.

violin *n*. a musical instrument with four strings played with a bow. VIOLINIST *n*.

viper *n*. a small poisonous snake; an adder.

virtue *n*. goodness; excellence. VIRTUOUS *adj*.

virus *n*. 1 a microscopic organism that causes many diseases. 2 in computers, a hidden instruction that causes problems or errors and can be transmitted to other computers.

visa *n*. an official mark on a passport allowing the holder to enter or leave a particular country.

viscount *n*. a nobleman ranking between an earl and a baron. *fem*. VISCOUNTESS.

visibility *n*. 1 being visible; the possibility of being seen determined by the conditions of light and atmosphere. 2 the distance at which something can be seen under particular weather conditions.

visible *adj*. that can be seen. VISIBLY *adv*.

vision *n*. 1 the power of seeing; sight. 2 imagination. 3 something seen in a dream or a trance.

visit *v*. 1 to go to see (a person or place). 2 to stay with a person or at a place. VISITOR *n*.

visor *n*. the movable front part of a helmet, protecting the face.

visual *adj*. to do with sight. VISUALLY *adv*.

vital *adj*. 1 essential to life. 2 very important. VITALLY *adv*.

vitamins *n. pl*. any of a number of substances occurring in foods which are essential for health and normal growth.

vivacious *adj*. lively; animated. VIVACITY *n*.

vivarium *n*. a place for keeping animals in their natural state.

vivid *adj*. 1 bright; intense. 2 lively; clear. VIVIDLY *adv*.

vixen *n*. 1 a female fox. 2 a bad-tempered woman.

vocabulary *n*. 1 the words used in a language or by a person. 2 a list of words with their meanings.

vocal *adj*. to do with the voice; spoken or sung. VOCALIST *n*.

vogue *n*. the popular fashion.

voice *n*. 1 sound that comes from the mouth in speaking, shouting, singing, etc. 2 an opinion. VOICE *v*. 1 to speak. 2 to give an opinion.

void *adj*. 1 empty; vacant. 2 not valid. VOID *n*. an empty space.

volcano *n*. a mountain with openings through which ash, lava and gases sometimes erupt or flow. *pl*. VOLCANOES. VOLCANIC *adj*.

vole *n*. a small, mouse-like rodent with short ears and a long tail.

volley *n*. 1 a shower of missiles. 2 a sudden rush of words, questions, etc. 3 in ball games, the return of the ball before it touches the ground.

volt *n*. a unit for measuring electricity. VOLTAGE *n*.

voluble *adj*. talkative; speaking with a great flow of words. VOLUBLY *adv*.

volume *n*. 1 a book or one of a set of books. 2 the amount of space occupied. 3 the amount of sound produced.

voluntary *adj*. done willingly, freely and without compulsion. VOLUNTARILY *adv*.

volunteer *n*. a person who voluntarily offers service. VOLUNTEER *v*. to offer to serve without being asked.

vomit *v*. to reject food from the stomach through the mouth; to be sick.

vortex *n*. a whirlpool or whirlwind.

vote *v*. to express an opinion or choice. VOTE *n*. 1 an opinion or choice. 2 the right to vote. VOTER *n*.

vouch (for) *v*. to confirm; to guarantee.

voucher *n*. a receipt; a ticket.

vow *n*. a promise or oath. VOW *v*. to promise.

vowel *n*. a simple speech sound – a, e, i, o, u.

voyage *n*. a journey by sea. VOYAGE *v*. to go on a journey by sea.

vulgar *adj*. coarse in manners; rude. VULGARLY *adv*. VULGARITY *n*.

vulnerable *adj*. 1 defenceless; open to attack. 2 easily damaged or wounded.

vulture *n*. a large bald-headed bird of prey that feeds on decaying flesh.

W

wad *n*. a pad of soft material. WADDING *n*.

wade *v*. to walk through water, mud, snow, etc.

wader *n*. 1 a person who wades. 2 a long-legged bird that wades.

waders *n. pl*. high waterproof boots for wading.

wafer *n*. a thin, crisp biscuit.

wage *n*. a regular payment for work done. WAGE *v*. to carry on (war or a battle).

wager *n*. a bet. WAGER *v*. to bet.

wagon, waggon *n*. 1 a railway truck. 2 a large four-wheeled cart.

wagtail *n*. a small bird with a long tail.

wail *v*. to cry or moan loudly. WAIL *n*. a long, loud cry or moan.

waist *n*. the part of the body between the hips and the ribs.

waistcoat *n*. a short sleeveless and collarless garment usually worn under a jacket.

wait *v*. 1 to remain in place. 2 to delay doing something. 3 WAIT UPON to serve food. WAIT *n*. time spent in remaining at one place. WAITING *n*.

waiter *n*. a man who serves food or drink in a restaurant, hotel, etc. *fem*. WAITRESS.

wake *v*. 1 to rouse from sleep. 2 to cease sleeping. WAKE *n*. the track left by a ship in the water. WAKEN *v*. WAKENING *n*.

walk *v*. to travel on foot. WALK *n*. 1 the act of walking. 2 a journey on foot. 3 a pathway. 4 WALK OF LIFE occupation; profession. WALKER *n*.

wall *n*. a side of a house, room or building; a stone or brick fence.

wallet *n*. a folding case for holding papers and money, and carried in the pocket or handbag.

wallow *v*. to roll about in mud or water.

walnut *n*. a tree whose wood is used for making furniture; the edible nut of this tree.

walrus *n*. a large, furry sea mammal with two large tusks, and of the seal family.

waltz *n*. a dance with a graceful, flowing melody. WALTZ *v*. to dance a waltz.

wander *v*. 1 to roam aimlessly. 2 to stray from the point. WANDERER *n*. WANDERING *adj*.

wane *v*. 1 to become less bright. 2 to weaken or decrease. WANING *n*.

want *v*. 1 to need or require. 2 to wish for; to desire. 3 to be without. WANT *n*. 1 shortage; scarcity. 2 a need.

war *n*. an armed struggle and fighting between armies or countries. WARFARE *n*. WARLIKE *adj*.

ward *n*. 1 a room for patients in a hospital. 2 a child in the care of a guardian. 3 a division of a town or area for election purposes. WARD (OFF) *v*. to protect (oneself or someone else) from.

warden *n*. 1 a person in charge of a hostel, college or other institution. 2 a person with particular duties, such as a traffic warden.

warder *n*. a prison officer.

wardrobe *n*. 1 a large cupboard in which clothes are hung. 2 all of a person's clothes.

ware *n*. a general name for manufactured articles.

warehouse *n*. a building for the storage of goods.

warm *adj*. 1 containing heat; fairly hot. 2 enthusiastic; affectionate. WARM *v*. to make or become warm. WARMTH *n*.

warn *v*. 1 to give notice or caution of danger. 2 to give advance notice to. WARNING *n*.

warp *v*. 1 to twist or distort. 2 to haul a ship with a rope. WARP *n*. 1 a twist or distortion. 2 a rope. 3 the lengthwise threads in woven material. WARPED *adj*.

warrant *n*. an official document giving authority. WARRANT *v*. to authorise; to guarantee.

warren *n*. an area containing many rabbit burrows.

warrior *n*. a soldier; a fighting man.

wart *n*. a small, hard growth on the skin.

wary *adj*. cautious; watchful. WARILY *adv*.

wash *v*. 1 to clean with water. 2 to flow against. 3 WASH AWAY to be carried away by water. WASH *n*. 1 the act of washing. 2 things to be washed. 3 the action and sound of water. 4 a thin covering of paint. WASHING *n*.

washer *n*. a rubber or metal ring that seals a joint or fits under a nut to keep it tight.

wasp *n.* a small black and yellow winged insect with a sting.

waste *v.* 1 to spend carelessly; to squander; to use extravagantly. 2 to become thinner or weaker. WASTE *n.* 1 refuse; rubbish. 2 uncultivated or barren land. 3 extravagance. WASTEFUL *adj.*

watch *v.* 1 to look at (something) closely. 2 to guard. 3 to be wakeful. WATCH *n.* 1 the act of watching. 2 a small type of clock for the wrist or pocket. 3 a spell of duty on board a ship, etc. WATCHFUL *adj.*

watchmaker *n.* a person who makes or repairs watches.

watchman *n.* a person employed to guard property.

watchword *n.* a password; a slogan.

water *n.* 1 a colourless, tasteless, odourless liquid. 2 an expanse of lake, sea or river. WATER *v.* 1 to supply or provide with water. 2 to add water to. WATERY *adj.*

watercress *n.* a small plant which grows in streams and is used in salads.

waterfall *n.* a stream or river of water falling over a ledge of rock.

waterfowl *n.* birds which live and nest near water.

waterlogged *adj.* saturated or filled with water.

watermark *n.* a faint design or mark in a sheet of paper indicating the maker's name.

waterproof *adj.* not allowing water to pass through. WATERPROOF *n.* a raincoat or other garment which is impervious to water. WATERPROOF *v.* to make something proof against water.

watershed *n.* the area of high land dividing two river basins.

watt *n.* a unit of electrical power.

wattle *n.* 1 a fence of woven twigs and sticks. 2 the fleshy crest on the head of a fowl; the fleshy lump on the throat of a turkey.

wave *n.* 1 a moving ridge of water. 2 something shaped like a wave. 3 a sign made with the hand. 4 a vibration of electricity, heat, light or sound. WAVE *v.* 1 to move up and down or to and fro. 2 to make a waving movement with the hand. 3 to curl (the hair).

waver *v.* to hesitate; to move unsteadily. WAVERING. *adj.*

wax *n.* 1 a fatty substance produced by bees. 2 any of various substances resembling beeswax. WAX *v.* 1 to smear with wax . 2 to increase in size or strength.

way *n.* 1 a road, track, path or route. 2 distance travelled. 3 a method, plan, habit, custom or manner of behaving.

weak *adj.* 1 feeble; fragile; frail. 2 having little will-power. 3 watery; thin. WEAKLY *adv.* WEAKNESS *n.*

weaken *v.* to make or to become weak.

weal *n.* a raised mark on the skin caused by a blow.

wealth *n.* riches; large possessions. WEALTHY *adj.*

wean *v.* 1 to accustom a baby to food other than its mother's milk. 2 to break away from a habit.

weapon *n.* an instrument used in war or fighting to kill or injure people or to destroy property.

wear *v.* 1 to have something on the body; to be clothed in. 2 to attach something to the clothes. 3 to last a long time. 4 WEAR OUT to use or be used until no longer usable. WEAR *n.* 1 clothing. 2 damage from continual use.

weary *adj.* exhausted; tired. WEARY *v.* to exhaust or tire. WEARILY *adv.* WEARINESS *n.*

weasel *n.* a small, fierce, stoat-like animal.

weather *n.* the conditions of rain, sunshine, wind, etc., at a particular place and time. WEATHER *v.* 1 to wear by exposure to the weather. 2 to come successfully through some difficulty.

weathercock *n.* an indicator, often in the form of a cock, that shows which way the wind is blowing.

weave *v.* 1 to make fabric by interlacing threads, etc. 2 to operate a loom. 3 to wind in and out. WEAVER *n.*

web *n.* 1 anything that is woven. 2 the skin joining the toes of water-birds, bats, etc. 3 THE WEB *n.* an abbreviation for the WORLD WIDE WEB.

website *n.* a collection of information placed on a computer that is part of the world wide web, so that people using other computers can use it.

wed *v.* to marry.

wedding *n.* a marriage ceremony.

wedge *n.* a V-shaped piece of wood or metal used for splitting, forcing open or fastening. WEDGE *v.* to fix or fasten with a wedge. WEDGED *adj.*

Wednesday *n.* the fourth day of the week.

weed *n.* a wild plant growing where it is not wanted. WEED *v.* to remove weeds.

week *n.* a period of seven days.

weekly *adj.* happening once a week. WEEKLY *n.* a newspaper or magazine published once a week.

weep *v.* to cry; to shed tears. WEEPING *adj.*

weft *n.* the threads crossing a fabric from edge to edge.

weigh *v.* 1 to find out how heavy something is by using scales. 2 to have a certain heaviness.

weight *n.* 1 the heaviness of something. 2 a piece of metal of known weight used in weighing articles. 3 importance; influence. WEIGHTY *adj.*

weir *n.* a barrier or dam across a river to control the flow of water.

weird *adj.* uncanny; very strange. WEIRDLY *adv.*

welcome *v.* to greet with pleasure. WELCOME *n.* a friendly greeting. WELCOME *adj.* 1 giving pleasure. 2 freely permitted.

weld *v.* 1 to join two pieces of metal together by heat and pressure or by fusing the joint. 2 to unite firmly. WELD *n.* a joint made by welding.

welfare *n.* happiness; health; prosperity; well-being.

well *n.* 1 a deep hole or shaft sunk into the earth to obtain water or oil. 2 a space in a building enclosing a staircase or lift. WELL (UP) *v.* to flow or gush out. WELL *adj.* 1 in good health. 2 in a good and satisfactory manner. WELL *adv.* in a thorough and satisfactory manner.

Welsh *n. pl.* the people of Wales. WELSH *n. sing.* the language of the Welsh. WELSH *adj.* having to do with Wales or its people.

welt *n.* a strip of leather sewn between the sole and the upper part of a shoe.

Wesleyan *n.* a member of the church founded by John Wesley. WESLEYAN *adj.* relating to John Wesley or the Wesleyan Church.

west *n.* the point on the horizon where the sun sets. WEST *adj.* towards the west. WESTWARD *adv.* towards the west.

western *adj.* in the west.

wet *adj.* 1 covered or saturated with water or other liquid. 2 rainy; showery. WET *v.* to make wet or to moisten. WETNESS *n.*

whale *n.* a large sea mammal often hunted for its oil, whalebone, etc.

whaler *n.* a ship or person that hunts whales. WHALING *n.* hunting whales.

wharf *n.* a quay or platform where ships are loaded or unloaded.

what *pron.* that which; whatever. WHAT *adj.* 1 which. 2 how much. 3 which amount, kind of, etc.

wheat *n.* a cereal plant; its grains.

wheel *n.* a circular frame or disc which revolves on an axle. WHEEL *v.* 1 to move (something) on wheels. 2 to turn round like a wheel.

wheelbarrow *n.* a container with one wheel and a pair of handles.

wheelwright *n.* a person who makes or repairs wheels.

whelk *n.* a small, sea shellfish of the snail family.

when *adv.* 1 at what time. 2 how long ago. 3 as soon as. WHEN *conj.* 1 at the time. 2 although.

where *adv.* 1 in or to what place. 2 in the place which.

whether *pron.* which of the two. WHETHER *conj.* if; which.

whey *n.* the watery part of sour milk.

which *pron.* who, of a number of persons; what one, of a number of things.

while *n.* a period of time. WHILE *conj.* at the time that. WHILE (AWAY) *v.* to pass time.

whim *n.* a sudden fancy or impulse.

whimper *v.* to whine; to make feeble crying sounds. WHIMPER *n.* a feeble crying sound.

whine *n.* 1 a complaining tone. 2 a continuous high-pitched sound. WHINE *v.* to make a whining sound.

whip *v.* 1 to lash with a whip. 2 to beat. 3 WHIP OUT or AWAY to take or move suddenly. WHIP *n.* 1 a cord or leather thong attached to a handle. 2 a member of a political party who summons members to vote.

whipping *n.* a beating or thrashing.

whirl *v.* to rotate quickly; to spin. WHIRL *n.* a spinning motion. WHIRLING *n.*

whirlpool *n.* a strong and rapid circular movement of water in a sea or a river.

whirlwind *n.* a violent and spinning wind or air current.

whisk *n.* 1 a quick sweeping movement. 2 an implement for beating eggs, cream, etc. WHISK *v.* 1 to sweep lightly. 2 to beat.

whisker *n.* a hair growing on the face.

whisky *n.* an alcoholic drink distilled from fermented malt, barley, rye, etc.

whisper *v.* 1 to speak very softly. 2 to make a soft murmuring sound. WHISPER *n.* 1 a softly-made sound. 2 a hint or a rumour. WHISPERING *adj.*

whist *n.* a card game for four players.

whistle *n.* 1 a shrill sound produced by blowing air through the lips. 2 an instrument for making a shrill sound. WHISTLE *v.* to produce a shrill sound by blowing air through the lips or an instrument. WHISTLING *n.*

white *adj.* 1 the colour of fresh snow. 2 pale. WHITE *n.* 1 the colour white. 2 the part of an egg surrounding the yoke. WHITEN *v.* WHITENESS *n.*

whitewash *n.* a mixture of lime and water used for whitening. WHITEWASH *v.* 1 to coat with a mixture of lime and water. 2 to cover up guilt or faults intentionally.

Whitsuntide *n.* the seventh Sunday after Easter, and the days following.

whittle *v.* to trim or slice off pieces with a knife.

who, whom *pron.* which or what person; the person which.

whole *adj.* 1 entire and complete. 2 in one piece; perfect. WHOLE *n.* the complete or total amount.

wholesale *n.* the buying and selling of goods in large quantities. WHOLESALE *adj.* in large quantities; extensive. WHOLESALER *n.*

wholesome *adj.* favourable to health; nourishing.

wholly *adv.* completely; entirely.

whose *pron.* concerning or belonging to whom.

why *adv.* for what reason; for what purpose.

wick *n.* a cotton thread in a lamp or candle which draws up the oil or molten wax to the flame.

wicked *adj.* 1 evil; sinful. 2 mischievous. WICKEDLY *adv.* WICKEDNESS *n.*

wicker *n.* anything made of woven willow twigs, reeds or cane.

wicket *n.* 1 the three upright stumps bowled at in cricket; the cricket pitch. 2 a small door or gate made in a larger one.

wide *adj.* broad; stretching far. WIDE *adv.* 1 to the full extent. 2 off the target. WIDENESS *n.* WIDELY *adv.*

widen *v.* to make or become wider or broader.

widespread *adj.* extensive; distributed over a large area.

widow *n.* a woman whose husband is dead and who remains unmarried.

widower *n.* a man whose wife is dead and who remains unmarried.

width *n.* the distance or measurement from side to side; the breadth.

wield *v.* 1 to hold and use (a weapon, etc.); to brandish. 2 to exercise (power and authority).

wife *n.* a married woman. *pl.* WIVES.

wig *n.* an artificial covering of hair for the head.

wild *adj.* 1 living freely and naturally; untamed. 2 not cultivated or inhabited. 3 savage. WILDNESS *n.*

wilderness *n.* a desert; an uncultivated or a desolate area.

wile *n.* a cunning trick or deception.

wilful *adj.* obstinate; intentional; deliberate. WILFULLY *adv.*

will *n.* 1 a person's power to make decisions. 2 determination; resolve. 3 desire; intention. 4 a document showing what a person wishes to be done with his/her property after death. WILL *v.* to direct or bequeath.

willing *adj.* ready and eager to help. WILLINGLY *adv.* WILLINGNESS *n.*

willow *n.* a tree with slender, flexible branches usually growing near water.

wilt *v.* to droop; to become limp.

wily *adj.* crafty; cunning.

win *v.* 1 to gain or earn. 2 to be victorious. 3 to gain affection. WIN *n.* a victory; a success.

wince *v.* to draw back from; to flinch. WINCE *n.* a sudden movement or expression of pain.

winch *n.* a machine for pulling or lifting loads by a rope wound round a drum. WINCH *v.* to move by means of a winch.

wind *n.* (pron. WIND) 1 a current of air; a breeze. 2 breath.

wind v. (pron. WYND) 1 to turn or twist. 2 to make into a coil or ball. 3 to tighten. WINDING adj.

windlass n. a roller turned by a winch and used for lifting and pulling.

windmill n. a mill operated by the action of the wind on sails or vanes.

window n. an opening in the wall of a building, usually filled with glass, to let in light and air.

windpipe n. the passage from the mouth which admits air to the lungs.

windward n. lying in the direction from which the wind blows. WINDWARD adj.

wine n. a drink made from the juice of grapes or other fruits.

wing n. 1 the part of a bird, bat or insect by which it flies. 2 the plane, or flat surface, which supports an aircraft in flight. 3 a side extension to a building. WING v. 1 to fly. 2 to wound in the wing.

wink v. 1 to close and open an eyelid quickly. 2 to flicker or flash. WINK n. 1 a quick closing and opening of an eyelid. 2 a flicker of light. WINKING n.

winner n. a person who wins.

winning adj. 1 victorious. 2 charming; attractive. WINNING n. the gaining of a prize or victory.

winter n. the cold season of the year between autumn and spring. WINTER v. to spend the winter.

wipe v. to clean or dry by rubbing with a cloth. WIPE n. the act of wiping.

wire n. 1 a metal thread. 2 a telegram. WIRE (UP) v. to fit electrical wiring. WIRED adj.

wiry adj. 1 like wire. 2 lean and strong.

wisdom n. possession of experience and knowledge, with the ability to use these in making good judgements and decisions.

wise adj. having experience, knowledge and good judgement. WISELY adv.

wish v. to long for; to desire. WISH n. a longing or desire. WISHFUL adj.

wistful adj. sadly longing for something; thoughtful. WISTFULLY adv.

wit n. 1 the power of understanding and intelligence. 2 the ability to say or to see something that is amusing. 3 a person who has this ability.

witch n. a woman supposed to have evil magical powers. WITCHCRAFT n.

with prep. 1 in company of. 2 because of. 3 having or possessing.

withdraw v. 1 to go back or away; to retreat. 2 to take back. WITHDRAWAL n.

wither v. to become dry and shrivelled. WITHERED adj.

withhold v. to keep back; to refuse to grant.

within prep. inside; not beyond. WITHIN adv. indoors; inwardly.

without prep. 1 outside or out of. 2 in the absence of. WITHOUT adv. out of doors; outwardly.

withstand v. to resist; to oppose.

witness n. 1 an observer of an incident. 2 a person who gives evidence in court. 3 evidence; testimony. WITNESS v. 1 to see (something) happen. 2 to give evidence.

wizard n. a magician; a conjurer.

wizened adj. dried up; wrinkled and shrivelled.

woad n. 1 a plant yielding a blue dye. 2 its blue dye.

wobble v. 1 to move unsteadily from side to side. 2 to quiver; to shake.

woe n. sorrow; grief.

wold n. (pron. WOALD), an area of open undulating country.

wolf n. 1 a fierce wild animal which hunts in packs and belongs to the dog family. 2 a greedy person. pl. WOLVES. WOLF v. to eat greedily.

woman n. an adult female human being. pl. WOMEN.

wonder n. 1 a feeling of surprise and admiration. 2 anything which causes surprise or amazement. WONDER v. to marvel at; to be filled with surprise. WONDERFUL adj. WONDERING adj.

wood n. 1 an area of land covered by growing trees. 2 timber. WOODED adj. WOODLAND n.

wooden adj. 1 made of wood. 2 stiff; dull.

woodpecker n. a bird that pecks the bark of trees in searching for insects.

woodworm n. larva of the common furniture beetle which is destructive to wood.

wool n. 1 the soft wavy hair of sheep and some other animals. 2 thread or cloth made from this hair. WOOLLEN adj. WOOLLY adj.

word *n.* 1 any sound or combination of sounds forming a single part of speech. 2 news; information. 3 a speech or conversation. 4 a promise. WORD *v.* to express in words.

word processing *n.* using a computer program to edit text and prepare it for publication. WORD PROCESSOR *n.*

work *n.* 1 action which needs bodily or mental activity. 2 a person's employment. 3 something produced by effort. WORK *v.* 1 to be involved in action needing bodily or mental activity. 2 to be employed. 3 to produce by effort. WORKER *n.* WORKING *adj.*

works *n. pl.* 1 a factory, mill, etc. 2 the moving parts of machinery.

world *n.* 1 the Earth and all it contains. 2 the universe and all creation. 3 any planet or star. 4 an area of activity or interest.

World Wide Web *n.* the information held on computers around the world that are connected to the internet.

worm *n.* 1 a long, soft, limbless, creeping animal, without a backbone, such as the earthworm. 2 the thread of a screw.

worn *adj.* 1 showing signs of damage from use. 2 WORN OUT tired and weary.

worry *n.* anxiety; trouble. WORRY *v.* 1 to cause anxiety or trouble to. 2 to shake or pull about with the teeth, as a dog does. WORRIED *adj.*

worse *adj.* more bad; more ill. WORSE *adv.* more badly.

worship *n.* 1 reverence; honour and respect. 2 admiration. WORSHIP *v.* to revere, honour and respect.

worst *adj.* most bad. WORST *adv.* most badly.

worsted *n.* a fine woollen yarn or cloth.

worth *n.* 1 the value or cost of something. 2 the importance or merit. WORTH *adj.* 1 equal in value to. 2 deserving of. WORTHY *adj.*

wound *n.* (pron. WOOND), an injury caused by a blow or cut to the body. WOUND *v.* to injure or hurt. WOUNDED *adj.*

wrangle *v.* to argue angrily. WRANGLE *n.* a noisy quarrel.

wrap *v.* to fold up or put a covering round (something). WRAP *n.* a shawl or similar covering. WRAPPER *n.* WRAPPING *n.*

wrath *n.* violent anger; rage.

wreath *n.* flowers and leaves woven together into a ring.

wreck *n.* 1 the broken remains of something destroyed. 2 the destruction of something. 3 a person ruined in health or ruined by calamity. WRECK *v.* to ruin or destroy. WRECKAGE *n.*

wren *n.* a very small bird.

wrench *v.* to twist or pull violently. WRENCH *n.* 1 a violent burst or pull. 2 a tool for gripping and turning nuts and bolts.

wrestle *v.* 1 to struggle with an opponent and try to throw him to the ground. 2 to struggle with a problem or some difficulty. WRESTLING *n.*

wretched *adj.* 1 sad; miserable. 2 of poor quality.

wriggle *v.* to twist and squirm. WRIGGLE *n.* twisting and squirming movements.

wring *v.* to twist and squeeze.

wrinkle *n.* 1 a small fold or crease in the skin or in the surface of something. 2 a helpful hint or clue. WRINKLE *v.* to make small folds or creases.

wrist *n.* the joint between the hand and arm.

writ *n.* a legal order requiring a person to do or stop doing something.

write *v.* 1 to set down letters, words and sentences on paper or other material. 2 to be an author or composer. 3 to communicate by letter. WRITING *n.* WRITTEN *adj.*

writer *n.* 1 a person who writes. 2 an author.

wrong *adj.* 1 incorrect; unsuitable. 2 not according to rule or law. 3 not working properly. WRONG *v.* to be unfair or unjust to. WRONG *n.* an injustice; unfairness.

wry *adj.* twisted out of shape; turned to one side.

X

Xmas *n. abbrev.* Christmas.

X-ray *n.* 1 a ray of short waves which can penetrate solid things. 2 a photograph taken by X-rays. X-RAY *v.* to photograph by X-rays.

xylophone *n.* (pron. ZYLO-phone) a musical percussion instrument made up of a number of plates which vibrate to give different notes when struck with a small hammer.

Y

yacht *n.* (pron. YOT) a sailing-boat built for racing or cruising. YACHT *v.* to race or cruise a yacht. YACHTING *n.*

yak *n*. a long-haired, humped ox of central Asia.

yam *n*. a tropical climbing plant and its edible root.

yank *v*. to give a sudden, sharp pull or jerk to. YANK *n*. a sudden, sharp pull or jerk.

Yank, Yankee *n*. a citizen of the United States of America.

yard *n*. 1 an imperial measure of length, 36 inches or 3 feet (0.9144 metres). 2 a wooden spar supporting a sail. 3 an enclosed, unroofed space near a building.

yarn *n*. 1 a thread which has been spun and prepared for knitting or weaving. 2 a tale or story. YARN *v*. to tell a story.

yashmak *n*. a veil covering the lower part of the face, often worn by Muslim women in public.

yawl *n*. a type of small fishing-boat or sailing-boat.

yawn *v*. 1 to gape; to be wide open. 2 to open the mouth wide and take a deep breath when tired or bored. YAWN *n*. the act of yawning. YAWNING *adj*.

year *n*. 1 the time taken by the Earth to travel once round the sun. 12 months or 365 days. 2 a unit of time, 12 months.

yearling *n*. an animal which is one year old, esp. a colt. YEARLING *adj*. a year old.

yearly *adj*. happening once a year; lasting a year.

yearn (for) *v*. to long for or to desire something. YEARNING *n*.

yeast *n*. a microscopic plant which causes fermentation, used in making beer, wine and bread.

yell *v*. to shout or cry out loudly. YELL *n*. a loud shout or cry.

yellow *n*. a bright golden or lemon colour. YELLOW *adj*. of a bright golden or lemon colour.

yelp *n*. a sharp, sudden cry or bark. YELP *v*. to utter a sharp cry or bark.

yeoman *n*. 1 a man owning a small farm or estate. 2 one of the Yeoman of the Guard; a warder of the Tower of London.

yes *adv*. word which expresses agreement or consent.

yesterday *n*. the day before today.

yet *adv*. 1 up to the present time. 2 still; further. YET *conj*. however; nevertheless.

yew *n*. a dark-leaved evergreen tree and its wood.

yield *v*. 1 to give in; to surrender. 2 to produce (a crop) or give (a profit). YIELD *n*. the crop; the profit. YIELDING *adj*.

yoga *n*. a Hindu method of meditation and self-control.

yoghurt *n*. a semi-solid food made from fermented milk.

yoke *n*. 1 a curved wooden beam placed across the shoulders of oxen when working together. 2 a frame supported on a person's shoulders and carrying a pail at each end. YOKE *v*. to couple, or link, together.

yolk *n*. (pron. YOKE) the yellow part of an egg.

you *pron*. the person or persons spoken to.

young *adj*. 1 not old. 2 not far advanced in life, growth or development.

youth *n*. 1 being young. 2 the early part of life. 3 a young man. YOUTHFUL. *adj*.

yule *n*. the festival at Christmas.

Z

zeal *n*. great enthusiasm; eagerness. ZEALOUS *adj*.

zebra *n*. a wild, horse-like African animal with a striped body.

zero *n*. 1 the figure or symbol 0; nothing; nought; nil. 2 the starting-point of reckoning on a scale of measurement.

zest *n*. 1 great enthusiasm. 2 enjoyment.

zigzag *n*. a series of sharp alternate turns like those in the Z. ZIGZAG *v*. to make Z-like turns. ZIGZAG *adj*.

zip *n*. a zip-fastener; a zipper; a sliding fastener with interlocking toothed strips, for clothes and bags, etc.

zodiac *n*. the area of the sky containing the twelve constellations in astrology.

zone *n*. 1 a region or area with particular features or purposes. 2 one of the five belts into which the Earth is divided according to climate.

zoo *n*. a place where wild animals are kept and exhibited.

zoology *n*. the scientific study of animals. ZOOLOGICAL *adj*. ZOOLOGIST *n*.

Zulu *n*. a member or the language of one of the South African Bantu peoples.

Appendices

PARTS OF SPEECH

noun	the name of a person, place or thing, whether real or abstract: e.g. book, nurse, star, greed, truth, army, team, London, Elizabeth
pronoun	used in place of a noun: e.g. I, me, he, him, she, her, it, we, us, you, they, them; who, whom, whose, which, what, that; myself, himself, herself, itself, ourselves, yourself, yourselves, themselves
adjective	qualifies a noun; that is, it tells more about a noun: e.g. easy, green, horrible
verb	shows the action of a sentence or a clause; tells of being, doing or having: e.g. (to) accept, burn, come, worship, yawn
adverb	modifies a verb; that is, it tells more about the verb; tells how, when or where something is done: e.g. eagerly, fast, well; daily, never, soon; anywhere, here, nowhere An adverb can sometimes modify an adjective: e.g. It is a **very** cold day.
conjunction	joins words, phrases and clauses together: e.g. and, as, but, till, unless, if, either ... or, neither ... nor
preposition	names a special relationship between one word and another, where one thing is in relationship to another: e.g. after, around, beside, between, by, from, in, off, over, through, to, under, up, with
interjection	an exclamation: e.g. ah, bah, coo, hurrah, oh, phew, shush, tut, wow

CAPITAL LETTERS

Capital letters are used:

1   to begin sentences:
    e.g. The house is on the right-hand side of the road.

2   to begin the names of people and places.
    Notice the capital letters in an address:

    Ms Joan Brown   Mr J. Smith
    79 North Road   25 Bridge Street
    GLASGOW   LONDON
    G2 2YS   E7 7AD

3   to begin the names of relations:
    e.g. Aunt Christine, Uncle Clive
    and titles:
    e.g. Admiral Lord Nelson

4   for the pronoun I:
    e.g. Last week I was nine.

5   to begin the names of days, special days and months:
    e.g. Come and see me on Tuesday.
        Christmas Day is in December.

6   when speech marks (inverted commas) are used for the first time:
    e.g. We said, "Let's go to the cricket match tomorrow."

7   at the beginning of lines of poetry:
    e.g. The Pobble who has no toes
        Had once as many as we;
        When they said 'Some day you may lose them all'
        He replied: 'Fish fiddle-de-dee!'

8   for the important words in titles of books, stories, poems etc.:
    e.g. A Tale of Two Cities
        Jack and the Beanstalk
        The Pobble who has no Toes

COMMON ABBREVIATIONS

A1	first-class
AA	Automobile Association; Alcoholics Anonymous
A A A	Amateur Athletic Association
ABC	The alphabet
A D	(*L.* anno Domini) in the year of our Lord
a.m.	(*L.* ante meridiem) before midday
anon.	anonymous or unknown
appro.	approval
approx.	approximately
Apr.	April
Assoc.	Association
Asst.	Assistant
Aug.	August
BA	Bachelor of Arts
BBC	British Broadcasting Corporation
BC	before Christ
BMA	British Medical Association
Bros	Brothers
B.Sc.	Bachelor of Science
BST	British Summer Time
C	Celsius; century
Capt.	Captain
CBE	Commander of (the Order of) the British Empire
C.E., C. of E.	Church of England
ch., chap.	chapter
CID	Criminal Investigation Department
cm	centimetre(s)
cm^3	cubic centimetre(s)
Co.	Company; County
c/o	care of
Col.	Colonel
co-op	co-operative society
Dec.	December
Dept.	Department
dia.	diameter
DJ	disc jockey; dinner jacket
do.	ditto; the same
doz.	dozen

Dr	doctor; debtor
E	East
ed.	editor
EEC	European Economic Community (Common Market)
e.g.	(*L*. exempli gratia) for example
ETA	estimated time of arrival
etc.	(*L*. et cetera) and the rest; and so on
EU	European Union
exam	examination
f	(*Ital*. forte) loud
FA	Football Association
FBI	Federal Bureau of Investigation, USA
Feb.	February
ff	(*Ital*. fortissimo) very loud
Fri.	Friday
g	gram(s)
gal.	gallon
GB	Great Britain
GCSE	General Certificate of Secondary Education
GI	enlisted soldier, USA
GMT	Greenwich Mean Time
Govt	Government
GP	general practitioner (doctor)
HMS	Her/His Majesty's Ship
Hon.	Honorary; Honourable
HP, h.p.	hire purchase
HQ	headquarters
HRH	Her/His Royal Highness
i.e.	(*L*. id est) that is
IMF	International Monetary Fund
incl.	inclusive
IOU	'I owe you'
IQ	intelligence quotient
IRA	Irish Republican Army
ital.	italic
ITV	Independent Television
Jan.	January
Jnr., jr., jun.	junior
Jul.	July
Jun.	June

kg	kilogram(s)
km	kilometre(s)
kW	kilowatt(s)
l	litre(s)
lat.	latitude
lb.	pound (weight)
lbw	leg before wicket
Lieut., Lt.	Lieutenant
log	logarithm
long.	longitude
m	metre(s)
MA	Master of Arts
Mar.	March
maths	mathematics
max.	maximum
MBE	Member of (the Order of) the British Empire
MEP	Member of the European Parliament
Messrs	Sirs
min.	minute(s); minimum
misc.	miscellaneous
ml	millilitre(s)
mm	millimetre(s)
Mon.	Monday
MP	Member of Parliament
m.p.h.	miles per hour
Mr	Mister; Master
Mrs	Mistress
MSP	Member of the Scottish Parliament
MS(S)	manuscript(s)
N	north
NATO, Nato	North Atlantic Treaty Organisation
NB	(*L.* nota bene) note well
NE	north-east
NHS	National Health Service
NI	Northern Ireland
No(s).	number(s)
Nov.	November
NSPCC	National Society for the Prevention of Cruelty to Children
NW	north-west
NY	New York

NZ	New Zealand
OBE	Officer of (the Order of) the British Empire
Oct.	October
OHMS	On Her/His Majesty's Service
o.n.o.	or near offer
OS	Ordnance Survey
oz.	ounce
p	(*Ital.* piano) quiet
p.a.	(*L.* per annum) yearly
para.	paragraph
PAYE	Pay As You Earn (income tax)
P.C., p.c.	police constable; personal computer
PE	physical education
per cent	(*L.* per centum) in every hundred
PM	Prime Minister
p.m.	(*L.* post meridiem) after midday
PO	Post Office; postal order
pop.	population
POW	prisoner of war
pp	(*Ital.* pianissimo) very quiet
pp.	pages
PR	proportional representation; public relations
pro	professional
Prof.	Professor
PS	(*L.* post scriptum) postscript
PTO	please turn over
R.	(*L.* Rex) King; (*L.* Regina) Queen
RAC	Royal Automobile Club
RAF	Royal Air Force
RC	Roman Catholic
Rd.	road
ref.	reference
Revd	Reverend
RIP	(*L.* requiescat in pace) May (he or she or they) rest in peace
r.p.m.	revolutions per minute
RSPCA	Royal Society for the Prevention of Cruelty to Animals
RSVP	(*Fr.* répondez s'il vous plaît) Please reply
S	south
Sat.	Saturday
SE	south-east

Senr., sen.	senior
Sept.	September
Sgt.	Sergeant
Soc.	Society
SOS	Save Our Souls (Morse Code)
sq.	square
SRN	State Registered Nurse
SSE	south-south-east
SSW	south-south-west
St.	saint; street
sub	subscription
Sun.	Sunday
SW	south-west
tel.	telephone
Thurs.	Thursday
TUC	Trades Union Congress
Tues.	Tuesday
TV	television
UFO	unidentified flying object
UHF	ultra-high frequency
UN	United Nations
UNESCO, Unesco	United Nations Educational, Scientific and Cultural Organisation
UNICEF	United Nations International Children's Emergency Fund
Univ.	University
US, USA	United States, United States of America
USSR	Union of Soviet Socialist Republics
V	volt(s); Roman numeral (5)
v.	(L. versus) against
VAT	value-added tax
VIP	very important person
W	watt(s); west
w.c.	water closet (toilet)
WHO	World Health Organization
WNW	west-north-west
www	World Wide Web
Xmas	Christmas
YHA	Youth Hostels Association
YMCA	Young Men's Christian Association
yr.	year
YWCA	Young Women's Christian Association

CARDINAL AND ORDINAL NUMBERS

1	one	1st	first
2	two	2nd	second
3	three	3rd	third
4	four	4th	fourth
5	five	5th	fifth
6	six	6th	sixth
7	seven	7th	seventh
8	eight	8th	eighth
9	nine	9th	ninth
10	ten	10th	tenth
11	eleven	11th	eleventh
12	twelve	12th	twelfth
13	thirteen	13th	thirteenth
14	fourteen	14th	fourteenth
15	fifteen	15th	fifteenth
16	sixteen	16th	sixteenth
17	seventeen	17th	seventeenth
18	eighteen	18th	eighteenth
19	nineteen	19th	nineteenth
20	twenty	20th	twentieth
21	twenty-one	21st	twenty-first
22	twenty-two	22nd	twenty-second
23	twenty-three	23rd	twenty-third
24	twenty-four	24th	twenty-fourth
25	twenty-five	25th	twenty-fifth
26	twenty-six	26th	twenty-sixth
27	twenty-seven	27th	twenty-seventh
28	twenty-eight	28th	twenty-eighth
29	twenty-nine	29th	twenty-ninth
30	thirty	30th	thirtieth
40	forty	40th	fortieth
50	fifty	50th	fiftieth
60	sixty	60th	sixtieth
70	seventy	70th	seventieth
80	eighty	80th	eightieth
90	ninety	90th	ninetieth
100	(one) hundred	100th	(one) hundredth

MEASURES (SI UNITS)

Length				
	10	millimetres (mm)	=	1 centimetre (cm)
	1000	millimetres	=	1 metre (m)
	100	centimetres	=	1 metre
	1000	metres	=	1 kilometre (km)

Mass and Weight				
	10	milligrams (mg)	=	1 centigram (cg)
	1000	milligrams	=	1 gram (g)
	100	centigrams	=	1 gram
	1000	grams	=	1 kilogram (kg)

Capacity				
	10	millilitres (ml)	=	1 centilitre (cl)
	1000	millilitres	=	1 litre (l)
	100	centilitres	=	1 litre
	1000	litres	=	1 kilolitre (kl)

Area				
	100	square millimetres (mm^2)	=	1 square centimetre (cm^2)
	10 000	square centimetres	=	1 square metre (m^2)
	10 000	square metres	=	1 hectare (ha)
	100	hectares	=	1 square kilometre (km^2)

Volume				
	1000	cubic millimetres (mm^3)	=	1 cubic centimetre (cm^3)
	1 000 000	cubic centimetres	=	1 cubic metre (m^3)

TIME

60	seconds (s)	=	1 minute (min)
60	minutes	=	1 hour (h)
24	hours	=	1 day
7	days	=	1 week
2	weeks	=	1 fortnight
365	days	}	
52	weeks and 1 day	=	1 year
12	months		
366	days	=	1 leap year
100	years	=	1 century
1000	years	=	1 millennium

THE CALENDAR

January	31 days
February	28 days (+ 1 day in a leap year)
March	31 days
April	30 days
May	31 days
June	30 days
July	31 days
August	31 days
September	30 days
October	31 days
November	30 days
December	31 days

Here is a very old rhyme which may help you remember the number of days in each month:

Thirty days have September,
April, June and November.
All the rest have thirty-one
excepting February alone,
which has twenty-eight days each year
and twenty-nine in each leap year.

DAYS OF THE WEEK

Sunday
Monday
Tuesday
Wednesday
Thursday
Friday
Saturday

ROMAN NUMERALS

I	1		XXX	30
II	2		XL	40
III	3		L	50
IV	4		LX	60
V	5		LXX	70
VI	6		LXXX	80
VII	7		XC	90
VIII	8		C	100
IX	9		CC	200
X	10		CCC	300
XI	11		CD	400
XII	12		D	500
XIII	13		DC	600
XIV	14		DCC	700
XV	15		DCCC	800
XVI	16		CM	900
XVII	17		M	1000
XVIII	18		MM	2000
XIX	19			
XX	20			
XXI	21 etc.			

COMMON PREFIXES

al-	(= all)	altogether, always
anti-	(= against)	anticlockwise, anti-war
co-	(= together)	co-operate, co-ordinate
de-	(changes a word to its opposite)	debug, decode
dis-	(changes a word to its opposite)	disagree, dishonest
ex-	(= former)	ex-husband, ex-teacher
il-	(= not; used before l)	illegal, illogical
im-	(= not; used before b, m and p)	immature, imperfect
in-	(= not)	incomplete, inhuman
inter-	(= between)	international, internet
ir-	(= not; used before r)	irrational, irrelevant
mal-	(= wrongly)	maltreated, malnourished
mis-	(= wrongly)	mislead, misunderstood
non-	(= not)	non-fiction, nonsense
pro-	(= supporting, approving)	pro-Europe, pro-democracy
pre-	(= before)	prewarned, pre-packaged
re-	(= again)	rewrite, re-tie
sub-	(= under)	submarine, subway
un-	(= not)	unimportant, undo

COMMON SUFFIXES

-able/-ible	(= can be, worth being)	washable, forcible
-en	(= to make)	darken, lighten
-ful	(= full)	mouthful, beautiful
-hood	(= being)	childhood, parenthood
-less	(= without)	homeless, penniless
-like	(= like)	childlike, cat-like
-proof	(= resistant)	waterproof, fireproof
-ship	(forms a noun)	hardship, relationship
-worthy	(= worthy of)	trustworthy, roadworthy

HIGH-FREQUENCY WORDS

about
after
again
an
another
as
back
ball
be
because
bed
been
boy
brother
but
by
call(ed)
came
can't
could
did
do
don't
dig
door
down
first
from
girl
good
got
had
half
has
have
help
her
here

him
his
home
house
how
if
jump
just
last
laugh
little
live(d)
love
made
make
man
many
may
more
much
must
name
new
next
night
not
now
off
old
once
one
or
our
out
over
people
push
pull

put
ran
saw
school
seen
should
sister
so
some
take
than
that
their
them
then
there
these
three
time
too
took
tree
two
us
very
want
water
way
were
what
when
where
who
will
with
would
your

MEDIUM-FREQUENCY WORDS

above	goes	sometimes
across	gone	sound
almost	great	started
along	happy	still
also	head	stopped
always	heard	such
animals	high	suddenly
any	I'm	sure
around	important	swimming
asked	inside	think
baby	jumped	those
balloon	knew	thought
before	know	through
began	lady	today
being	leave	together
below	light	told
better	might	tries
between	money	turn(ed)
birthday	morning	under
both	mother	until
brought	near	upon
change	never	used
children	number	walk(ed)(ing)
clothes	often	watch
coming	only	while
didn't	opened	white
different	other	whole
does	outside	why
during	own	window
earth	paper	without
every	place	woke(n)
eyes	right	word
father	round	work
follow(ing)	second	world
found	show	write
friends	small	year
garden	something	young